D0867266

The Jack Sprat Cookbook

The Jack

Sprat Cookbook

OR GOOD EATING ON A LOW-CHOLESTEROL,
LOW-SATURATED-FAT DIET

Jack Sprat could eat no fat,
His wife could eat no lean;
And so between them both, you see,
They licked the platter clean.

POLLY ZANE

Drawings by John Zane

HARPER & ROW, PUBLISHERS
New York, Evanston, San Francisco, London

THE JACK SPRAT COOKBOOK. Copyright © 1973 by Olive C. Zane. Drawings copyright © 1973 by John Zane. All rights reserved. Printed in the
United States of America. No part of this book may be used or reproduced
in any manner whatsoever without written permission except in the case
of brief quotations embodied in critical articles and reviews. For information
address Harper & Row, Publishers, Inc., 10 East 53rd Street, New York,
N.Y. 10022. Published simultaneously in Canada by Fitzhenry & Whiteside
Limited, Toronto.

STANDARD BOOK NUMBER: 06-014801-2

LIBRARY OF CONGRESS CATALOG CARD NUMBER: 72-79701

Designed by Patricia Dunbar

To
my husband Jack Zane
and daughters,
Gretchen, Lauren, and Katy

Contents

Foreword

The *Jack Sprat Cookbook* goes a long way toward making meals for most patients with cholesterol problems not only palatable but interesting and even exciting. Mrs. Zane, faced with the practical problem of providing her husband with a diet low in saturated fat and cholesterol, has managed to use her considerable imagination to adapt recipes and cooking techniques to meet this goal. Throughout, she has followed the fat-controlled, low-cholesterol recommendations of the American Heart Association.

Too often, when faced with cholesterol problems, we resign ourselves to dull, repetitious meals. Mrs. Zane's innovative approach and sprightly description of her methods provides new hope for the low-cholesterol cook.

The introductory material by Dr. Daniel Steinberg provides a simplified account of the scientific basis for this book. For the more serious lay student of diet and its relationship to heart disease, Appendix I, also by Dr. Steinberg, is very useful. He is one of the leaders in research responsible for our current understanding of this field, and his presentation is therefore both accurate and knowledgeable.

This is a welcome addition to our armamentarium aimed at reducing the terrible toll from cardiovascular disease.

CAMPBELL MOSES, M.D.
Medical Director
American Heart Association

Acknowledgments

During the long hard task of producing this cookbook, I have been helped so generously by so many people that I am thankful for this opportunity at last to express my feelings of gratitude and appreciation.

First and foremost I must thank my family. I am deeply grateful to my husband, Jack, whose generous help, encouragement, and professional skill have made this book the particular thing that it is. His untiring efforts as editor, artist, and professional taster were essential to its final publication. I wish to thank him especially for producing the lively drawings that give this book so much added appeal. I am also profoundly appreciative of the contributions made by my three daughters, Gretchen, Lauren, and Katy, all of whom were active participants—cooking, testing, typing, filing—and who offered day-to-day encouragement when it was most needed.

Beyond the family effort, I am under special obligation to Dr. Daniel Steinberg, Professor of Medicine and Head of the Division of Metabolic Disease, U.C.S.D. School of Medicine: first for his early enthusiasm and support, which gave me the confidence to go on; next for his continuing generosity in finding time to advise and counsel me on technical matters; and finally, for his notable contribution to the book itself, a contribution that adds immeasurably to its worth. I am also grateful to Dr. Campbell Moses, Medical Director of the American Heart Association, who took time to review the material and offered many helpful comments, and who eventually wrote the foreword. I wish to thank Ruth Reznikoff, consulting dietitian for the San Diego County Chapter of the American Heart Association, who was the first to examine my recipes; she has offered help and encouragement ever since, and her excellent professional advice has been invaluable. Thanks also to Dr. Joseph Stokes, Professor of Medicine and Chairman of the Department of Community Medicine, U.C.S.D., School of Medicine, for his early suggestions and encouragement; to Dr. Roger Revelle, Director of the Center for Population Studies, Harvard University, for taking time to direct the book to several helpful people; to Dr. Frederick J. Stare, Professor of Nutrition and Chairman of the Department of Nutrition, Harvard University School of Public Health, for his professional effort in evaluating the material and his excellent and constructive criticism; and to my good friend Herbie Miles, whose idea this all was, and who would have been coauthor but for a stronger inclination to paint pictures. A cordial acknowledgment also to Theodore Geisel, Birgit Holtsmark, Robert Poteete, Neil Morgan, the Dutch Boy Bakery of La Jolla, California, for helpful hands along the way. I am further indebted to many friends who offered recipes for adaptation, kitchen equipment for photographs, and other services; to other cookbook authors, far too numerous to name here, whose recipes have sometimes provided a point of departure for some of mine; and to many institutions, particularly to the American Heart Association and the National Heart and Lung Institute, for an untold amount of information and material.

POLLY ZANE

La Jolla, California
May 15, 1972

Introduction

WHY I WROTE THIS BOOK

Recently, an old friend I hadn't seen in ages spent a few days with me while her husband attended meetings in San Diego.

After a nostalgic session of do-you-remember-when and what-ever-happened-to-whom, we talked our way around to the present. My friend asked what I was doing nowadays.

"Writing a cookbook," I said.

She looked stunned. "Good heavens! Why? There must be hundreds of them on the market already."

"Probably more than that," I said, "but none of them's like mine. I know because I've been trying to find one like it and it just doesn't exist. That's why I'm writing it myself."

It all began, I told her, about three years ago when my husband had a mild heart attack. Later, when I picked him up at the hospital, his doctor handed me an innocent-looking booklet and told me it would help me in preparing meals.

"Thanks," I said, feeling about as grateful as *he* might if I had just handed *him* a copy of the Girl Scouts' first-aid pamphlet. After all, I'd probably been cooking as long as he'd been doctoring.

"There's more to that booklet than you think," he said, reading my mind. "I have an idea you'll find it very handy when you make the changeover. You see, you're going to have to make a rather fundamental shift in *what* you cook and *how* you cook it."

For the first time, I actually read the title. *Planning Fat-Controlled Meals*, it said.

With a sinking feeling, I asked, "What does that mean?"

He told me. I didn't enjoy it, but he told me. He covered fats in our diets and fats in our blood—lipids, he called them—and he described a number of diseases of the heart and circulatory system which result in large part from meals that are not fat-controlled, polyunsaturated, and low in cholesterol. I didn't really understand most of what he said.

But I understood well enough when he got to the foods we shouldn't have but once in a long while. He began with dairy foods. Butter, whole milk, cream, and most cheeses were out. Next to go were lobster, crab, shrimp—in fact, *all* shellfish. Then marbled steaks, and lamb, *and* pork, *and* bacon, *and* spareribs—any meat at all that was high in fat unless, by chance, you found a lean cut. Even chicken, if it wasn't carefully skinned and trimmed. The list seemed endless. Creamed foods, casseroles, ice creams, and *fried* foods. Commercial biscuits and most bakery goods. For some perverse reason, the ban never seemed to include such items as spinach and rutabaga.

The final blow was having to cut way down on eggs. We could have eggs so seldom—two or three a week—that I felt I might as well forget them. Later on, as you will see, I devised a way around this obstacle.

But that was still in the future.

At the moment, I could have cried. Here, suddenly, and with no warning to brace myself, I was being told to forget not only most of the foods my family enjoyed but also a large number of my cooking methods. And not next month or next week but right away. Starting NOW.

So that's how it began. Overnight, I had to become a healthful cook or, more accurately, a cooker of healthful meals. To gain learning time, I fed my family tuna salad and banana bread—made with a whopping full cup of oil—every day for two solid weeks.

Meanwhile, I ransacked bookstores and libraries, wrote away for pamphlets and reports, and talked the doctor blue in the face trying to find out how I could follow the new rules in a way that made tasty meals instead of something a laboratory technician might feed to his guinea pigs.

I found a lot of information on low-cholesterol, low-saturated-fat diets; the recipes varied in reliability but seldom in dullness. And while my husband had a strong motivation to stay with the diet, unappetizing though it might have been, he wasn't the only one concerned. The food I cooked had to be eaten by *everybody* in the family.

Available information simply did not supply enjoyable meals. There had to be a better way.

There was—the hard way, the trial-and-error way. I wasn't looking for gourmet specials—just ways to turn the medically acceptable foods into plain but enjoyable home cooking.

As I gained experience, I grew more confident. Sooner than I would have imagined, I was doing a little experimenting, then a little more. All the while I kept careful notes on the ingredients, the cooking techniques, and the results—that is, how well each dish went over with the family, which was largely a matter of how well it went down.

At the same time, more and more friends grew interested in what I was up to. Even casual acquaintances would ask about the project. Then one day a friend called to say her doctor had put her husband on a low-cholesterol diet. Could I help? Shortly after that, a woman I'd met at a party asked me how to make sense of the same little booklet I'd struggled through. She'd had one of those chilling talks with the heart specialist about *her* husband.

It wasn't long until I felt as if I were running a kitchen clinic.

Gradually, I realized that there must be thousands of women all over the country who were suddenly facing the same dilemma that I had faced and that more and more of my friends were facing.

Although it took a while for the idea to jell, suddenly one day I thought that all these people and all my recipes should somehow be brought together. They needed each other.

That's how this book came about.

Here are my best recipes to date—the two-birds-with-one-stone recipes that both satisfy the doctor and gratify my family. And that's really the case. This collection has been checked by medical scientists concerned with blood lipids and each dish has survived the critical review of a tough team of food tasters: my family and friends.

I was gratified to learn from both the doctors and the critics that these are dishes to live by.

So don't despair if you are unexpectedly thrown on a polyunsaturated, low-cholesterol diet. This book will start you on the road to discovering that life at the dinner table can still be pleasant—and healthful.

Here's how!

WHAT THESE RECIPES OFFER YOU

Until a few years ago, I thought a cookbook was a cookbook—something that told you how to prepare food so people could enjoy it. Then came the coronary problem mentioned earlier, and I discovered a whole new class of cookbooks—the ones that solved everything from diabetes to being overweight. Everything, that is, but how to enjoy the food after it was cooked.

The trouble was, there was no overlap between the cookbooks that told you how to make food taste good and those that told you how to get or stay healthy. There weren't any that told you how to do both.

That's what I've tried to do here.

The recipes developed for this collection produce dishes which are both medically acceptable *and* a pleasure to eat.

When I say medically acceptable I mean that uppermost in my mind at all times has been keeping the ingredients within a tightly controlled low-cholesterol, low-saturated-fat budget. In order to secure this tight control, the following principles have been applied to every recipe and are rigidly held to:

1. No foods exceptionally high in cholesterol content are used, for example: egg yolks, organ meats, shellfish.
2. No butter, cream, or other dairy products high in saturated fats are used.
3. Oils are used in place of all other fats or shortenings almost exclusively. Where margarine is called for, it is seldom a major ingredient (there is one exception), and it may be replaced by oils without affecting the recipe in any way. This is especially true of the new butter-flavored oils.
4. Calorie content is generally below that of similar recipes in standard cookbooks for the following reasons:

   a. The substitutes I use for whole milk, whipped cream, sour cream, high-fat cheeses, and other dairy products are lower in calories than the ingredients they are replacing.
   b. All fat and skin are trimmed from meat before cooking, and high-fat meats are not used at all.
   c. Deep-frying is used to prepare one dish only.
   d. Every possible effort is made to use the minimum amount of oil

necessary to do the job and still retain a high standard of taste appeal. (Some cakes and other baked products may seem to be exceptions as the oil used is about equal to the amount of butter being replaced. This is because oil cakes tend to be tough and heavy if the proportion of oil and sugar to flour is too low.)

e. Recipes are simple to prepare, with preparation time cut to a minimum.

If your meals are consistently based on these recipes, you will derive certain advantages. First of all, you won't have to ponder such weighty questions as how many milligrams of cholesterol you have had in two slices of cake when one whole egg was used in the baking; or how many grams of saturated fat in three muffins when twelve were made using 4 ounces of partially hydrogenated margarine! My feeling has been—why get involved in higher mathematics when you don't have to? If you use none of the ingredients high in saturated fats and cholesterol, you're free to have that fried egg three times a week or a shrimp or lobster salad once in a while for lunch.

The one thing you must keep in mind is this: If any restrictions are placed upon you or your family—for example, limits on total fat, total calories, or total carbohydrates—such restrictions are your responsibility. Select your recipes accordingly. *This book is not intended as a diet manual or a book of meal plans for heart patients. Rather, it is a collection of recipes to choose from at random. It is intended for anyone, including the heart patient, who wishes to keep his blood cholesterol at a safe low level.* It should be used as a source of ideas for all meals and occasions, and especially when weekly cholesterol and saturated-fat limits have been reached and there are still 3 or 4 days to go and many meals to plan for; or, better still, it should easily keep you from ever reaching those limits.

Beyond that, this cookbook offers an expanded list of dishes— special standbys usually excluded from low-cholesterol diets. You'll find many old favorites revamped in healthy trappings which take them off the banned list and restore them to your table. Such dishes as creamy dips and cream soups are included. There are biscuits and muffins of all varieties. Chocolate cakes and puddings, cheese pies and spoon bread, Yorkshire pudding and popovers—all are here. There are even such festive gourmet touches as sesame chicken, moussaka, and walnut-crusted sea bass. Even veal sauerbraten. And many, many more!

While this book is based on new ingredients and some new techniques of preparation, in general the new dishes have chemical contents, appearance, and flavor very similar to those for which they are substituted. In order to retain some of the glamour of good eating, I have retained old and familiar names for some of the dishes based on these new ingredients. I felt it proper to do this so that the reader can quickly identify the recipe and its uses. I hope that those who feel that cream must be a dairy product, and that hollandaise must be made with egg yolks, will bear with me by allowing the minor liberties I have taken in this regard. Like poetic license, this might be considered to be a cook's license, and in a good cause.

DIET AND HEART DISEASE

by Daniel Steinberg, M.D., Ph.D.

In this highly organized society of ours there are fewer and fewer areas in which a man has total and unquestioned freedom to choose for himself. Diet is one such area. Every man is the master of his own menu. But even here he is bombarded from all sides by advice and exhortation. Often the prescriptions are dramatically opposed. What are we to believe? Well, I think we need to follow the lead of that scientist without portfolio, the man from Missouri, who says, "Show me!" As a physician and scientist, I believe that an excellent case has been made for a connection between diet and heart disease and I'll try to state it simply—to "show you."* The simple proposition is that people with high cholesterol levels in their blood are more likely to have a heart attack and to have it earlier; and that diet has a marked effect on cholesterol levels in the blood.

The Nature of Heart Attacks

Before we can really tell the story we have to lay the groundwork by talking about the disease process involved.

The particular form of heart disease we are dealing with is that

* For those interested, Appendix I includes a more detailed discussion of the basis for our present views on the subject in the form of answers to questions frequently asked by my patients.

which leads to the common "heart attack." I use the term "common" advisedly since over 600,000 people in the United States alone died of heart attacks last year! A heart attack results from the interruption of blood flow through one of the narrow blood vessels feeding the heart itself—the so-called coronary blood vessels. (Other terms for a heart attack include: "a coronary"; "infarction"; and "myocardial infarction.") These blood vessels undergo a progressive degeneration during life which eventually leads to scarring and even deposition of calcium—hence, the familiar designation "hardening of the arteries" or, more formally, atherosclerosis. This is accompanied by narrowing of the channel, like rusting in a pipe, and eventually the flow of blood just can't be maintained at a high enough rate. Up to that point the individual may not have been at all aware that anything was wrong and even the doctor, unless he carried out highly specialized tests, may not have known how serious things were getting. Then the narrowing gets to the point where blood just can't be pushed past the narrow places at a good enough rate and the patient may have chest pain—angina. Finally, because of progressive narrowing and sometimes complete obstruction caused by a sudden blood clot, blood supply falls below a critical point and we have a full-blown heart attack.

The underlying disease, then, is a disease of blood vessels—atherosclerosis, which we'll abbreviate AS. What do we know about AS, and what are the connections between that disease process and the diet?

The Nature of the Evidence

Studies in experimental animals. First, we can produce AS in animals simply by changing their diet. Take a perfectly healthy rabbit and slip some cholesterol into his food (it only needs to be an amount equal to 1 percent of the total diet) and in 4 to 6 months his blood vessels will show extensive AS. Chemical analysis of the damaged areas shows that they are loaded with *cholesterol!* Let him go on eating cholesterol —the rest of the diet doesn't need to be changed—and at the end of the year there will be scarring and calcium deposits very similar to what we see in human AS. On this cholesterol supplement over the year the cholesterol level in the rabbit's blood is sky-high. And the extent of the damage to blood vessels depends roughly on just how high the cholesterol level in the blood goes. Another way to produce AS in a rabbit is to add a large amount of saturated fat to his diet—

without adding cholesterol. That change alone is enough also to raise the cholesterol level in the blood and bring on AS. So right off the bat we come face to face with the two key diet constituents that we are most concerned about: cholesterol and saturated fats. To make the following discussion a little easier to relate to diets as we see them at table, let me say that in general animal fats are of the saturated type (e.g., butter, cream, beef fat, lard) and they are solid at room temperature. Vegetable fats (coconut oil is an exception) are generally of the polyunsaturated type, and they are liquid at room temperature (oils). Again for orientation let me point out that cholesterol is found only in foods of animal origin—notably in eggs, dairy products, and fatty meats—and in shellfish. Plants can't make cholesterol so vegetable products contain *none*.

Now, getting back to our experiments, you would be right to ask whether studies on rabbits allow us to say anything about *human* disease. The rabbit is normally a strict vegetarian and the experimenter gives him foods he ordinarily doesn't have to cope with. But experiments similar to these have now been done in many different animal species, including dogs, pigs, chickens, and monkeys. The diet changes necessary to produce the damage vary from species to species and sometimes the diets are pretty drastic. Keep in mind, however, that the experimenters are trying to telescope the whole process into a relatively short time period, six months to a year in most cases. We, on the other hand, have 50 to 70 years over which to damage our own arteries to the point of having a heart attack. The fact that changes in diet can consistently produce the disease in experimental animals cannot be ignored. The changes in diet used in such experiments (increasing the amounts of cholesterol and/or saturated fat) will also increase blood cholesterol concentration in people! We'll have more to say later about what cholesterol and saturated fats are, but first let's complete the case against them in relation to heart attacks.

Clinical experience. A second "show me" point comes from our clinical experience with certain families in which heart attacks occur with a frighteningly high frequency and at a painfully early age. I have seen one family in which a daughter died of a heart attack at age 18 and a son at age 23! Fortunately, it is not common to encounter such extreme examples, but they do occur and they must command our attention. The key point is that the outstanding thing that characterizes such families is that they have very high blood cholesterol levels. The 18-year-old girl had a cholesterol level over 400 and so did the boy; both parents had high levels and the father went on to a heart attack at age 45. Now it could be reasonably argued that the members of such a family may have an underlying abnormality that favors the early development of blood vessel damage and that the high cholesterol level is not really the *cause*. Granted. Also, you may legitimately argue that we may not be justified in applying findings in these extreme situations to people with only moderately elevated cholesterol levels. Also granted. So we must take a look at the more usual range of people in our population and see if we find similar although probably less dramatic connections between cholesterol levels and heart attacks.

Large population studies. The National Heart Institute set out to answer this question about 15 years ago. A special clinic was established in the "typical" town of Framingham, Massachusetts, and the cooperation of about 5,000 residents was enlisted. They had their blood cholesterol levels measured every year and were examined carefully for signs of heart disease. After 12 years the results were crystal clear: Those men with cholesterol levels over 260 had a heart attack rate 3 times that of men with cholesterol levels below 200. Furthermore, the heart attack rate for those with intermediate values of blood cholesterol was roughly related to just how high their cholesterol level was. In other words, we are not talking about something that touches only people with extremely high values. The results of this study, and many similar studies around the world, say that the apparent risk of having a heart attack creeps up as the cholesterol level creeps up. Note that we still can't say that the high cholesterol level *caused* the heart attacks. Nor do we want to leave the impression that the cholesterol level is the only factor we need to deal with. For example, cigarette smoking is extremely important and so is high blood pressure. (In Appendix I we discuss a number of additional factors that contribute to the risk of a heart attack.)

Prevention trials. The ultimate "show me" test is this: If by changing diet (or using drugs) we can correct a person's high blood cholesterol level, do we reduce the chances of his having a heart attack? The answer is a slightly qualified "Yes." The first carefully controlled demonstration of this proposition was made by a Norwegian cardiologist, Dr. Paul Leren. He studied a group of more than 400 men, all of whom had survived a first heart attack. Half of the men were put on a low-cholesterol, low-saturated-fat diet (using vegetable oils liberally) while the other half continued with their usual diet. The first group brought their blood cholesterol levels down very dramatically within a few weeks and kept them low over the 5 years of the study. Result: The men on the special diet had a lower heart attack rate than the men following their usual diet. Also, the number of men on the special diet who developed angina (chest pain due to AS) during the 5 years was well below that in the men following their regular diet. A second important study like this was carried out by Dr. Seymour Dayton and his colleagues at the Wadsworth Veterans Administration Hospital in Los Angeles. Here the men studied had *not* had a previous heart attack. Again, half were switched to a low-cholesterol, low-saturated-fat diet and half continued to plow into the eggs, cream, butter, beef, and pork as was their wont. Again, the heart attack rate was lowered in the special diet group. Let me mention just one more example—a study being done in Finland in which the diet kitchen at a mental hospital was converted to a low-cholesterol, low-saturated-fat pattern. A second mental hospital was identified for comparison of heart disease rates. Over an 8-year period, during which the blood cholesterol levels showed the expected difference, the patients at the hospital using the experimental diet had significantly fewer heart attacks. To be absolutely certain that the change in diet was the basis for the difference, the diet kitchen at the first hospital reverted to the usual Finnish pattern (which is quite high in cholesterol and saturated fats) and the second hospital adopted the low-cholesterol, low-saturated-fat diet. The second part of that study is still in progress at this moment but preliminary results suggest that the heart attack rate is falling among the patients now on the special diet and rising among the patients now back on their usual diet.

To Diet or Not to Diet

If you have been advised to change your diet, your doctor has based his recommendations on the kinds of evidence we have just discussed. It is a fairly compelling case. But the case is not without some holes and we have to recognize that. Statisticians are and should be very hard-nosed types—real "men from Missouri." They tell us that the studies to date *suggest* (some might go so far as to say *strongly suggest*) that diets lowering blood cholesterol levels are protective but they will tell you that they do not *prove* the case. The number of patients studied has been limited; there are ambiguities in some of the results; harmful effects of the diet over long periods need to be more carefully studied; etc., etc. These are not trivial points. I agree that more data are needed. I hope that more studies will be done and done soon.

Meanwhile, what do we do? For the individual who has a clearly abnormal cholesterol level* my answer is equally clear: He should try to bring it down by changing his diet. I say this because even though there are still some gaps in the chain of evidence, the case is sufficiently strong to warrant action where the risk is high. The medical profession, with very few exceptions, is committed on this point. For the individual who has a normal or nearly normal cholesterol level the decision is more difficult. The medical profession brings in a split vote on this one. Some contend that the strength of the evidence is such that we should *all*, every man, woman, and child, turn off the cholesterol and saturated fat. This school—and it includes the prestigious American Heart Association—takes the position that we can't afford to delay action while more research is being done (although they fully agree that more research needs to be done in order to clinch matters). The other school takes the position that we simply do not have a sound scientific basis for recommending dietary changes except where a definite abnormality exists. They point out that the long-term consequences of radical changes in diet are not yet known. They insist we need concrete evidence that there is something to be gained before we start tampering with something as basic as a man's diet. So the individual with a normal or marginally elevated cholesterol level is left to make a seat-of-the-pants judgment in consultation with his own doctor.

This Book

Once it has been decided that a low-cholesterol, low-saturated-fat diet is in order, the cook is faced with a tough problem. If anything worthwhile is to be accomplished, fairly extensive changes need to be

* As discussed in Appendix I, the risk of a heart attack also has been linked to the level of a second fatty substance in the blood—triglyceride. Generally a diet designed to lower cholesterol levels will also lower triglyceride levels, but additional factors come into play. In particular, a reducing diet may be the most valuable way to lower triglyceride levels.

made. *Tokenism will not work.* Cutting back from three-egg omelets to two-egg omelets or switching from butter to polyunsaturated margarine while leaving the rest of the diet "as is" will get you no-where. Careful research studies have repeatedly shown that certain minimum goals must be reached in terms of the *overall* makeup of the diet. The intake of cholesterol has to be cut to a target figure below 300 milligrams daily. Since *one* egg yolk alone contains that much cholesterol you can see that egg yolk has to become a virtual "no-no." The intake of saturated fat must be reduced drastically from what we Americans are accustomed to. That means limiting sharply the use of dairy products and other fats of animal origin. Fortunately polyunsaturated fats can be nicely substituted so we don't have to cope with a Spartan fat-free diet. How can you tell whether you have changed your diet enough to matter? Well, the only real test is whether your cholesterol level comes down satisfactorily. That's the yardstick you and your doctor must go by. But we have a large body of experience that lets us predict what will and won't work. If the cholesterol intake is kept below 300 milligrams daily and the amount of saturated fat relative to polyunsaturated fat is held down, the diet will work beautifully well in most cases. The measure we use to gauge the proper intake of fats is the ratio of polyunsaturated to saturated fat in the diet. Take the weight of polyunsaturated fat (P) and divide by the weight of saturated fat (S) in the daily diet and you get the polyunsaturated-saturated (P/S) ratio. If that's above 1.5, things are going fine.

We've taken a look at how things will go if you take Polly Zane's book into the kitchen and use her recipes as the cornerstone for your meal planning. A typical example of one week's worth of menus (see next section) was selected (2400 calories daily) and we calculated what it meant in terms of cholesterol intake and P/S ratio. It comes off beautifully on both counts: 1) cholesterol about 200 milligrams daily; 2) P/S ratio > 3! Now those figures are all one could ask for on a diet of this kind, and if you stick fairly close to Polly Zane's recipes and suggestions you'll be fine. The makeup of her recipes is so good, in fact, that you can wander from the straight and narrow a couple of times a week and still not be off limits.

Dietary habits are deeply ingrained in us. We strongly resist even minor changes and the prospect of major changes is terrifying. What Polly Zane has done is to show us that the necessary changes in diet composition can be made without giving up a lot of favorite, classical dishes. By making judicious substitutions and slightly modifying preparation she can produce familiar "friends" that in their unchanged form would be on the forbidden list. Not only that: she has also created many new and delicious dishes using only foods on the OK list. In short, she shows that by doing magic things in the kitchen all the needed adjustments in diet composition can be made while maintaining and improving the fun of the table. Her introduction has explained how it came about, and the recipe chapters will show how she does it. Let me only add that I have had the pleasure of her low-cholesterol, polyunsaturated-fat table on several occasions, and from pâté to chocolate cake the cuisine has been delightful—good and good for you.

SAMPLE WEEKLY MENU

CALORIES: approximately 2400 a day
P/S RATIO: over 3
CHOLESTEROL: less than 200 milligrams daily

Sunday

Breakfast   Half Cantaloupe
Feathery Buttermilk Pancakes*

Lunch   Baked Beans with Veal*
Hoop Cheese, Spinach, and Bacon Salad*
Old-Time Molasses Gingerbread*

Dinner   Hot Tuna Puffs*
Consommé
Chicken Breasts in Brandied Mushroom Sauce*
Cantonese Vegetables*
Bulghur Pilaf*
Bean-Sprout Salad*
Orange Chiffon Layer Cake*

* Starred dishes can be found in the recipe chapters; consult the index for pages.

Monday

Breakfast Frittata*
Oatmeal Muffins*
Fresh Raspberries

Lunch Portuguese Poached Chicken Breasts*
Banana Nut Bread*
Tossed Green Salad with Eggplant*
Apple Pie with Streusel Topping*

Dinner Borscht Poppy-seed Dip*
with Garden Chips*
Cheese Puffs*
Deviled Fish*
Rice and Spinach Pilaf*
Celeriac Salad*
Black Poppy-Seed Cake*

Tuesday

Breakfast Fresh Orange Juice
Stanley's Steamed Eggs*
with Imitation Bacon Bits (p. 430)
Pinwheel Cinnamon Rolls*

Lunch Corn Chowder*
Turkey Hash*
Pumpkin Nut Bread*
Lemon Sponge*

Dinner Chile con Queso*
Homemade Tortilla Chips*
Whipped Zucchini Soup*
Gourmet Meat Loaf*
Cabbage Chop Suey*
Dutch Hutspot Potatoes*
Caesar Salad*
Blackberry Sherbet

Wednesday

Breakfast Cantaloupe-Date Frost*
           Eggless Roman-Meal Muffins*

Lunch   Potage Esau*
           Crusty Cheese Soufflé*
           Sliced Tomatoes
           Chocolate Brownies*

Dinner   Jack Sprat Bacon-Stuffed Mushrooms*
           Cream of Corn Soup*
           Barbecued Brandywine Veal Cubes*
           Braised Celery*
           Greek Salad with Dry Cottage Cheese*
           Scotch Currant Scones*
           Green Apple Cake*

Thursday

Breakfast Papaya Slices
           Creamed Chipped Beef*
             on English Muffin

Lunch   Gazpacho*
           Working Man's Bean Sandwich*
           Banana Grapefruit Salad*
           Hermits*

Dinner   Marinated Tuna Chunks*
           Mushroom Pâté*
           Sole Bonne Femme*
           Paprika-Honey Onions*
           Saffron Rice*
           Cucumber Lime Salad*
           Banana Cream Pie*

Friday

Breakfast Sliced Peaches
Dutch Applesauce Omelet*
Pineapple Honey Muffins*

Lunch Cream of Tomato Soup*
Eggs Stuffed with Salmon and Capers*
Three-Bean Salad*
Lemon Snaps*

Dinner Poor Man's Caviar*
Vichyssoise*
Sea Bass Stuffed and Baked Sandwich Style*
Eggplant Creole*
Potato Cheese Puff*
Cauliflower-Bean Vinaigrette*
Popovers*
Rum Chiffon Pie*

Saturday

Breakfast Half Grapefruit
Lox and Bagels*
Mushrooms in Sherry-Flavored Sauce*

Lunch Tuna Soufflé*
Apple Raisin Salad*
Soft Molasses Drops*

Dinner Smoked Chicken Walnut Pâté*
Seviche*
French Onion Soup*
Chicken Curry Supreme*
Green Beans with Sherry and Orégano*
Fresh Mushroom Salad*
Blueberry Bake*

IMPORTANT NOTES ON THE RECIPES

1. Throughout these recipes you will find repeated use of the single word *oil*. This always means *polyunsaturated oil*—a term I feel is too long for comfortable reading if it appears frequently. When oil is called for, you should use one of these: corn, cottonseed, safflower, sesame, soybean, or sunflower.

2. When margarine is called for it always refers to the soft "special" margarines mentioned on page 421 in "Stocking the Larder."

3. The indication of servings given for most recipes refers to average-sized servings. It does not necessarily mean that the recipe will serve that number of people; many people eat more than one serving.

4. Buttermilk always means *cultured* buttermilk, which is made from skim milk; it does *not* mean *churned* buttermilk, which is made from whole milk.

5. Sugar, unless otherwise stated, means white granulated.

6. Baking powder always means double-acting baking powder.

7. Many recipes call for fortifying skim milk with dry skim milk. The dry milk should be thoroughly dissolved in the liquid before adding milk to other ingredients. This is for the purpose of adding body and nourishment, but it is not absolutely necessary. Omit it if you like. For more about this, see page 417 in "Stocking the Larder."

8. The "whipped cottage cheese" found in so many recipes can be cottage cheese commercially whipped. If unavailable, or if you prefer, prepare your own at home. It is a very simple procedure with instructions given on page 287.

9. Parmesan cheese as a flavoring has been replaced in most recipes by grated Swiss Sap Sago, sometimes in combination with bread crumbs and oil. Information on the cheese can be found in "Stocking the Larder," page 419, and a recipe for preparing Cheese Crumbs on page 304. A small amount of grated Parmesan cheese, however, has a relatively small amount of saturated fat and is reasonably harmless if not used too often. Therefore, if you cannot become accustomed to the slightly different flavor of Sap Sago, and if your fat budget is not too limited, replace the Sap Sago with Parmesan, at the rate of about 1 teaspoon per serving.

10. Plain low-fat yogurt has been used in many recipes to replace sour cream. There are other substitutes; see page 288 for sour-cream substitutes.

11. Butter-flavored products are increasingly available in the market: oils, salt, maple syrup, etc. Although not specifically mentioned in all recipes, if you enjoy the flavor, use them to increase butter flavor in your cooking. Be sure the oil is an acceptable one, however.

12. When the phrase, "grease the pan" occurs, it means "rub the pan with margarine."

13. When cooking with oil, keep the following in mind:

a. Oil goes much farther when heated.

b. When frying, wait until the oil is hot before adding other ingredients, or heat pan before adding oil.

c. Oil is particularly hard to clean off pans which have been baked for long periods of time. If possible, line pans with aluminum foil. Otherwise rub pans with margarine. When baking cakes, cookies, etc., rub pans with margarine and dust heavily with flour.

14. Be careful when cooking with low-fat ingredients such as egg whites, liquid skim milk, and dry skim milk as they tend to burn and stick to the pan. As a general rule it helps to use low heat, double boilers, asbestos pads, wire whisks, and straight-edged wooden spoons for stirring.

15. New products for use in fat-controlled cooking are constantly being marketed. An excellent way to keep abreast of these items is to ask your local chapter of the American Heart Association for their most recent publication listing such products. These pamphlets are extremely informative and helpful.

16. For those on a low-sodium diet, care should be taken to adjust recipes to particular diet requirements by lowering salt content as well as using less of salty ingredients such as bouillon, consommé, and soy sauce.

17. Certain things were important in helping me decide what recipes to include in this book. The principal goal was to keep the person on the low-saturated-fat, low-cholesterol diet both happy and healthy. To do this I felt I should restore to the menu, through adaptation, the things that had been declared off limits—that is, to replace unacceptable ingredients with acceptable ones in all the old-time favorites.

I also wanted to include a number of recipes suggesting alternatives to high meat meals, alternatives that were nourishing as well as attractive and appealing. Some low-calorie recipes were also needed, as weight is an important factor in heart disease.

Finally I wanted to share some of my own favorite recipes—newly adapted to polyunsaturated fats—simply because I thought they were so good.

18. The selection of ingredients for these recipes was based on the latest available figures from the United States Department of Agriculture, Research Division. From time to time these figures change. The reader should be aware of this and be alert to changes either through the news media or through correspondence with the Department of Agriculture. The American Heart Association is another excellent source.

KITCHEN EQUIPMENT

While it is possible to prepare most of these recipes with the equipment you probably have at hand, some processes will be simplified if you own the few items listed here. Nonstick pans (Teflon) are particularly helpful to the cook who is trying to reduce fats in the diet. The mixer and blender can help you to speed preparation time and give good texture to many dishes. Also, heavy saucepans or a double boiler will help to prevent scorching when cooking with low-fat milk.

1 large heavy butcher's knife
1 sharp paring knife
1 large Teflon frying pan with spatula
1 small Teflon frying pan
Teflon baking pans with racks to fit
Small heavy saucepan
Double boiler
Electric mixer (optional but helpful)
Electric blender (optional but extremely helpful)

Appetizers

BLACK BEAN DIP

MAKES ABOUT 2 CUPS

1 can (10½ ounces)
   condensed black bean
   soup, undiluted
¼ to ½ cup buttermilk
½ teaspoon garlic salt
1 tablespoon mayonnaise

3 or 4 drops of Tabasco
½ teaspoon ground orégano
1 tablespoon lemon juice
¼ to ½ cup poppy
   seeds (optional)

Combine all ingredients and chill. Serve with Melba toast rounds flavored with garlic, or with Homemade Tortilla Chips (p. 40).

BORSCHT POPPY-SEED DIP

The Russian soup transforms itself very well into a dip.

MAKES ABOUT 2½ CUPS

1 jar (4½ ounces) baby-food
   strained beets
1 tablespoon packaged French
   dressing mix
1 tablespoon water
1 tablespoon oil

1 teaspoon lemon juice
1 can (8¾ ounces) red
   kidney beans, well drained
½ cup poppy seeds
Salt and pepper
Vinegar (optional)

Pour beets into an electric blender. Dissolve French dressing mix in the tablespoon of water. Add to beets along with oil, lemon juice, and well-drained kidney beans. Purée in the blender. Add poppy seeds. Season with a little salt and pepper, or vinegar if desired. Serve with Melba toast rounds or saltines.

CAPER-DILL DIP

MAKES 2½ TO 3 CUPS

1½ cups dry-curd cottage
   cheese (see note below)
¾ cup buttermilk
3 tablespoons mayonnaise

½ teaspoon salt
2 teaspoons dried dillweed
1 jar (3½ ounces)
   capers (Reserve juice.)

Combine all ingredients. Thin to desired consistency with caper juice. Chill. Serve with saltines, Melba toast rounds, or rye flatbread; or use carrot, celery, and cucumber sticks.

NOTE: For low-fat or regular cottage cheese reduce buttermilk to ½ cup and omit salt.

HIGH-PROTEIN BLUE-CHEESE DIP

MAKES 2½ CUPS

8 ounces hoop cheese or
   dry-curd cottage cheese
4 tablespoons mayonnaise
Buttermilk (about ½ cup)
1½ teaspoons packaged
   salad seasoning

1 package (½ ounce)
   blue-cheese dip mix
½ cup minced chives

Mix hoop cheese, mayonnaise, and buttermilk in an electric blender or with a fork, alternating the cheese and liquid. Use enough buttermilk to give a good consistency. Add seasoning and blue-cheese mix and give another whirl. Stir in the chives and chill for 1 hour.

Serve with thin slices of cucumber, or with your favorite thin rye crispbread.

SPINACH-AND-SAP-SAGO DIP

MAKES ABOUT 2 CUPS

1 package (10 ounces) frozen
spinach
½ cup Whipped Cottage
Cheese (p. 287)
½ cup plain low-fat yogurt
2 tablespoons mayonnaise
1 tablespoon lemon juice

2 tablespoons grated fresh
onion, or 1 teaspoon dried
onion flakes
1 teaspoon grated Sap Sago
cheese
Salt and pepper
Buttermilk

Cook spinach according to package directions; be careful to avoid overcooking; spinach should be emerald green. Drain very thoroughly. Combine with other ingredients, season to taste, and thin with a little buttermilk if needed.

Serve with crisp carrot, celery, or cucumber sticks, or with Homemade Tortilla Chips (p. 40).

Variations

I. Serve the dip as a spread with Norwegian flatbread or Finnish rye crispbread.
II. Fill celery or mushroom caps with the dip, and serve chilled.
III. Stuff halved and seeded red peppers with the dip; chill. Cut into ¼-inch slices.
IV. Stuff small mushroom caps with the dip; bake in a 475°F. oven for 4 or 5 minutes; serve as hot hors-d'oeuvres.
V. Stuff large brown mushroom caps with the dip; bake. Serve as an accompaniment to any roast or broiled meat at dinner.

CUCUMBER-TARRAGON DIP

Tarragon has an unusual and distinctive flavor that will enhance the mildness of cucumber if it is not allowed to dominate. Start with just a pinch. You can add more if you want, but do so only sparingly.

MAKES ABOUT 2 CUPS

1 cucumber, chopped fine
1½ cups dry-curd cottage
  cheese
2 tablespoons mayonnaise
1 tablespoon lemon juice
¼ teaspoon black pepper

½ teaspoon garlic salt
½ teaspoon Worcestershire
  sauce
¼ teaspoon onion juice
Pinch of dried tarragon

Whirl cucumber in an electric blender until mushy. Add cottage cheese gradually, then remaining ingredients. Add more tarragon if you like. Chill thoroughly.

SEAFOAM DIP

MAKES AT LEAST 3 CUPS

1½ cups chopped green
  onions
1 cup buttermilk
2 cups dry-curd cottage
  cheese

1½ tablespoons Italian salad
  dressing mix
2 tablespoons mayonnaise
1 tablespoon lemon juice
Salt and pepper

Combine onions and buttermilk in an electric blender and purée. Add cottage cheese gradually along with other ingredients until the mixture has a creamy consistency. Season to taste. Thin with more buttermilk if desired. Chill.

"SLOPPY JOE" DIP OR SPREAD

"Sloppy Joe" mixes are much like chili mixes so one can be substituted for the other. The important thing is to check the label and find one that contains no fat. Many of them do not.

MAKES ABOUT 1½ CUPS

1 cup dry-curd or low-fat
   cottage cheese
¼ to ½ cup buttermilk

2 tablespoons packaged dry
   "Sloppy Joe" mix
2 tablespoons chopped chives

Combine all ingredients in an electric blender, adding as much of the buttermilk as necessary for desired consistency.

PEARLY ONION DIP

This is a relatively salty and highly seasoned dip. For weaker palates and a blander taste, substitute skim milk or buttermilk for the onion juice.

MAKES ABOUT 1½ CUPS

½ cup pickled cocktail onions
¼ cup juice from onions
1 cup Whipped Cottage
   Cheese (p. 287)

2 tablespoons chopped
   pimiento (optional)

Mix in an electric blender, and chill.

RED-PEPPER RELISH

A good relish can zip up a lot of things, and this one is the basis for a delicious dip (below). From my mother-in-law, Ruth Zane.

MAKES ABOUT 6 CUPS

12 large red peppers
1 tablespoon salt

3 cups sugar
½ cup vinegar

Stem and seed peppers and put them through a food grinder. Strain off the liquid. Add salt, sugar, and vinegar to the ground peppers. Let simmer until the mixture reaches the consistency of jam, about 1 hour.

RED-PEPPER RELISH DIP

MAKES ABOUT 2 CUPS

½ cup Red-Pepper Relish
   (above)
½ cup chopped green onions
½ cup buttermilk

½ cup low-fat cottage cheese
1 tablespoon mayonnaise
Lemon juice
Salt and pepper

Whirl relish, onions, buttermilk, cheese, and mayonnaise in an electric blender. Add more buttermilk or cheese to reach desired consistency. Season with lemon juice and salt and pepper to taste.

ONION-OLIVE SPREAD

For an occasional taste of olive, here is a spread that can easily be made into a dip.

MAKES ABOUT 2½ CUPS

1 package (⅜ ounce) onion
   dip mix
1 cup plain low-fat yogurt
1 cup low-fat cottage cheese

3 tablespoons French dressing
1 can (3½ ounces) sliced or
   chopped ripe olives, well
   drained (Save the juice.)

Combine all ingredients and chill. Adjust the consistency with a little of the olive juice if necessary.

HORSERADISH-BACON SPREAD

MAKES ABOUT 2 CUPS

1 cup dry-curd cottage cheese
¼ to ½ cup buttermilk
2 tablespoons mayonnaise
¼ teaspoon salt
1 package (⅝ ounce) horseradish and bacon dip, or 2
   tablespoons imitation bacon
   bits (p. 430) plus 2 teaspoons prepared horseradish
   sauce

2 tablespoons toasted sesame
   seeds

Blend first five ingredients together in a blender. Add sesame seeds and chill.

KIPPERED HERRING SPREAD

MAKES ABOUT 1 CUP

1 can (3½ to 4 ounces)
  kippered herring, drained
4 ounces hoop cheese
1 tablespoon mayonnaise
2 teaspoons each of lemon and
  onion juice

¼ teaspoon Worcestershire
  sauce
Salt and pepper
Liquid skim milk

Mash herring and hoop cheese. Combine with mayonnaise and flavorings. Add salt and pepper to taste, and as much skim milk as necessary for right consistency.

TAHINI APPETIZER

This unusual and exotic appetizer never fails to cause comment. Tahini is a thin oily paste made from ground sesame seeds; usually it can be found in specialty food stores. Traditionally, in Middle Eastern countries, it is served with bread and a salad. A little olive oil should be used for the authentic Middle Eastern flavor.

MAKES ABOUT 2 CUPS

¼ cup chopped parsley
2 tablespoons lemon juice
2 tablespoons olive oil
½ cup *tahini*
1 small garlic clove, minced
  (optional)

1 can (8¾ ounces) garbanzos
  (chick-peas), drained
  (Reserve juice.)
Salt and pepper

This can be made in a blender. If you prefer a thicker spread, prepare it by hand.

Combine parsley, lemon juice, olive oil, sesame paste, and minced garlic. Add garbanzos gradually, using their juice as necessary to liquefy for the desired consistency. Season with salt and pepper.

To blend by hand, mash garbanzos well with a fork. Combine with remaining ingredients.

Serve as a spread or dip with crackers, Armenian bread, or a hard-crusted bread.

POOR MAN'S CAVIAR

This dish is often served in countries where eggplant flourishes. The custom is to cook the eggplant over hot coals until the skin is charred and blistered, which gives the flesh a distinctive flavor. To simplify the procedure, cook the eggplant in the oven.

MAKES ABOUT 2 CUPS

1 large eggplant
2 tablespoons oil
1 small onion, chopped fine
1 garlic clove, minced
¼ cup fine-chopped green
   pepper

1½ tablespoons lemon juice
1 teaspoon salt
Coarse-ground pepper

Slice eggplant into halves. Oil flat surfaces, and place them flat side down on a baking pan. Broil on the middle shelf for 20 to 25 minutes, or until quite soft. Discard skin and mash pulp well with a fork. Sauté onion and garlic in remaining oil until brown. Combine with eggplant along with remaining ingredients. Chill for 2 or 3 hours.

Serve with dark coarse bread, crackers, or some kind of chips.

MOCK CAMEMBERT, ROQUEFORT, OR BLUE CHEESE

All three of these cheeses are strong enough in flavor to withstand diluting, so the spread has a strong resemblance to the taste of the original cheese. This recipe calls for 1 ounce of one of the three cheeses (not of all three) combined with 4 to 6 ounces of hoop cheese, sometimes called baker's, farmer's, or pot cheese.

MAKES ABOUT 1 CUP

1 ounce Camembert, Roquefort, or blue cheese
4 to 6 ounces hoop cheese
1 to 2 tablespoons oil

Buttermilk, sherry, dry white wine, or liquid skim milk
Salt

Mash cheeses and oil with a fork until smooth. Add liquid to reach desired consistency. Season with salt to taste.

GARDEN CHIPS FOR DIPS

Many fresh vegetables can substitute quite successfully for the high-calorie oversalted corn and potato chips. Here are just a few possibilities.

Select young fresh vegetables, wash carefully, and chill for maximum crispness.

Endive leaves
Inner leaves of romaine
Cauliflowerets
Strips of red and green peppers
Inner leaves from red cabbage
Slices of fresh mushrooms
Radishes and celery
Eggplant strips

Zucchini strips or rounds
Summer squash cut into thin strips
Jicima (a Mexican root vegetable) cut into thin slices
Turnips cut into thin slices
Cherry tomatoes

CHILLED ZUCCHINI SLIVERS

A very successful appetizer; tasty enough to keep nibbling but practically calorieless. From a good friend, Virginia Baron.

Select fresh young zucchini. Wash and remove ends. Cut into paper-thin slices and spread out flat on a serving plate. Sprinkle with your favorite seasoning salt or a combination of seasonings. Chill for 1 or 2 hours.

FRUIT AND PICKLE KEBABS

Appetizers needn't be loaded with calories. Try a few of these for the weight watchers. Serve with or without a dip.

Sweet Pickle Kebabs

Marinate halved sweet gherkins, canned small button mushrooms, and tiny whole pickled beets in French dressing. Thread on food picks or small skewers and chill.

Dill Pickle Kebabs

Cut dill pickles and smoked salmon into ½-inch pieces, and celery hearts into ½-inch cubes. Marinate all the pieces in pickle juice; chill. Thread on food picks or small skewers.

Fruit Kebabs

Select two or three of the following to thread on cocktail picks. Marinate in white wine and chill.

Fresh strawberries
Fresh pineapple, cubed
Fresh pears, cubed

Dried prunes or apricots, soaked in wine until plump and halved

MARINATED ARTICHOKE HEARTS

Quite a delicacy and not served often enough! Try to find large cans of artichoke hearts packed in water. They are occasionally on sale and then you can stock up for unexpected times and guests.

Cut artichoke hearts into quarters. Sprinkle them with a good wine vinegar, oil, coarse-ground pepper, salt, and paprika. Chill for at least 1 hour. Arrange in a bowl of contrasting color, and provide colored food picks for serving. Allow 4 to 6 pieces for a serving.

STUFFED CELERY

Select tender crisp celery. Discard tough outer ribs and remove most of the leaves. Fill with one of the following mixtures and refrigerate until well chilled.

1. Low-fat cottage cheese
   Blue cheese salad or dip
     mix (1 tablespoon per
     cup of cheese)

2. Low-fat cottage cheese
   Celery salt
   Chopped pimiento

3. Low-fat cottage cheese
     mixed with imitation
     bacon or sausage bits
     (p. 430)

4. Low-fat cottage cheese
   Worcestershire sauce
   Chopped chives

5. Chile con Queso (p. 38)

6. Chopped mushrooms
   Mayonnaise (1 tablespoon
     per cup of mushrooms)
   Salt and pepper

STUFFED CHERRY TOMATOES

Remove stems from cherry tomatoes. Cut out inner pulp. Stuff with leftover tuna salad or any other flavorful salad or dip. Chill.

ROASTED CHESTNUTS

Speaking of old-time favorites, this is truly a classic. Few people know that chestnuts are available in markets and even fewer have any idea how to cook them. You have to keep your eyes open to find them, for the season is short, about three months beginning in the late fall. Most chestnuts come from Italy; toward the end of the season they are apt to be dry and moldy, so pick them out individually, squeezing them with your fingers and selecting large firm ones. Avoid those that are dry and brittle and have air pockets inside.

To PREPARE: Hold a chestnut firmly with the left hand; with a strong kitchen knife slit the chestnut down the flat side so that steam can escape while cooking (otherwise they will explode). Now cook them in a heavy iron frying pan on top of the stove, in a baking pan in the oven, or in a popcorn popper.

I. ON TOP OF THE STOVE: Place the chestnuts, flat side down, in a heavy skillet. No fat is needed. Cook over medium heat until just slightly charred, 5 to 10 minutes. Turn and cook on the other side; be careful to watch so they do not burn. When both sides look roasted (just barely charred), lower the heat, cover, and steam for a few minutes. Crack one open with your fingers to check for doneness. The meat should be soft.

II. IN THE OVEN: Place chestnuts in a flat baking pan and bake in a 400°F. oven for 20 to 25 minutes, turning once. The chestnuts will not be charred but you will be spared having to clean a skillet which chars a bit along with the chestnuts in the top-of-the-stove method.

III. The third possibility is to cook them in a popcorn popper over an open fire, or even on top of the stove. A sprinkle of salt adds to this zestful cold-weather snack.

LEMON PEPPER MUSHROOMS

MAKES 4 SERVINGS

8 very large brown mushrooms
1 tablespoon chopped chives
2 tablespoons lemon juice
1 tablespoon mayonnaise

1 tablespoon oil
1½ teaspoons lemon
  pepper
1 teaspoon salt

Select large firm mushrooms and wipe with a damp cloth. Chop about half of the stems into very fine bits and combine with remaining ingredients. Stuff mushroom caps with the mixture and bake in a 450°F. oven for 7 minutes.

Serve immediately, as an appetizer, or serve 2 large mushrooms as a garnish to any entrée.

ELEGANT HOT MUSHROOMS

Gooey but good—low in calories and high in the things that nourish you. Serve as canapés or for dinner as an accompaniment to the entrée, or even for lunch with a green salad and homemade bread.

Clean firm brown mushrooms; use small ones for hors-d'oeuvres, large for other occasions. Separate stems from caps, reserving stems for another time. Fill mushroom caps with Whipped Cottage Cheese (p. 287). If cavity is extra large, only half fill. Season with celery salt and pepper. Sprinkle Cheese Crumbs (p. 304) on top and bake in a 450°F. oven for about 7 minutes. Serve immediately.

CHILLED SUMMER MUSHROOMS

Stuff mushroom caps with cottage cheese. Sprinkle liberally with celery salt and chill.

JACK SPRAT BACON-STUFFED MUSHROOMS

Walnuts, sherry, and bacon bits give these mushrooms an elegance Jack Sprat never dreamed of—poor man!

MAKES 4 SERVINGS

8 extra-large brown mush-
  rooms
½ cup ground walnuts
1 tablespoon minced parsley
1 tablespoon minced chives
2 tablespoons imitation bacon
  bits (p. 430)

⅛ teaspoon pepper
¼ teaspoon salt
2 tablespoons sherry
1 tablespoon oil

Separate mushroom stems from caps. Chop the stems very fine and mix with remaining ingredients. Add more sherry if too dry to stick together. Fill mushroom caps with the mixture. Broil in a hot broiler for 5 to 8 minutes, or bake in a 450°F. oven for 10 to 12 minutes.

Bread crumbs can be substituted for the walnuts, buttermilk for the sherry.

EGGS STUFFED WITH TUNA AND DILL

MAKES 12 SERVINGS

12 hard-boiled eggs
1 can (6½ ounces) water-
  packed tuna, drained
5 to 6 tablespoons mayonnaise
1 teaspoon minced fresh dill

4 tablespoons chopped
  pimientos
6 tablespoons minced celery
Salt, pepper, paprika

Peel eggs and cut into halves. Discard the yolks. Mash tuna and mayonnaise with a fork until you have an almost smooth paste. Add other ingredients with seasoning to taste. Fill eggs, covering the whole surface. Chill and serve.

EGGS STUFFED WITH SALMON AND CAPERS

MAKES 12 SERVINGS

12 hard-boiled eggs
1 can (6½ ounces) pink
  salmon, drained
5 to 6 tablespoons mayonnaise
2 tablespoons chopped capers

2 tablespoons chopped parsley
1 tablespoon lemon juice
1 or 2 drops of Tabasco
Salt and pepper

Follow the same procedure as for Eggs Stuffed with Tuna and Dill.

CHILE CON QUESO (a Mexican fondue)

By using almost fat-free cheese, this excellent hot dip can be eaten with utter abandon. The Mexican hot sauce, called chile salsa, *may be difficult to find but can be replaced with any tomato-based hot sauce mixed with canned green chili peppers. Just chop the peppers and add to the hot sauce.*

MAKES ABOUT 2 CUPS

1 onion, chopped fine
2 tablespoons oil
½ cup *chile salsa*
½ cup stewed tomatoes or
  tomato purée

½ pound processed vegetable-
  oil cheese (p. 419)

Sauté the onion in the oil until well browned. Place over hot water in the top part of a double boiler. Add other ingredients and heat gradually, stirring from time to time.

Serve warm with one of the following: thin rye-bread wafers, Norwegian flatbread, Homemade Tortilla Chips (p. 40), or crisp celery sticks.

CHEESE PUFFS

Who would ever believe that hoop cheese—an unsalted, pressed, dry-curd cottage cheese with no fat content (p. 418)—could be so delectable? Make canapés or open-faced sandwiches with this mixture.

MAKES ABOUT 1 CUP

4 ounces hoop cheese or
   dry-curd cottage cheese
1 tablespoon mayonnaise
2 tablespoons liquid skim milk

1 teaspoon fine-grated
   Sap Sago cheese
⅛ teaspoon salt

Combine all ingredients either in an electric blender or with a fork.

For canapés, spread ¼ inch thick on crackers or small rounds of bread toasted on one side.

For sandwiches, spread on English muffins or your favorite bread, also toasted on one side.

Broil very slowly on the lowest rack in an oven broiler until cheese puffs up, approximately 20 minutes. This takes longer than you might expect because of the low percentage of fat in the cheese.

CHEESE CORN PUFFS

Tasty hot tidbits for the cocktail hour, or to serve as an accompaniment to soup or salad.

MAKES ABOUT 5 DOZEN TINY PUFFS

1½ cups water
½ cup yellow cornmeal
1 tablespoon sugar
¼ teaspoon salt
2 tablespoons butter-flavored
   oil

2 tablespoons grated
   Sap Sago cheese
2 large egg whites,
   beaten stiff

Bring the water to a rolling boil in a heavy saucepan. Pour cornmeal all at once into the water and stir vigorously with a wire whisk until well mixed. Continue to cook and stir over medium heat until thickened, 1 or 2 minutes. Remove from heat and beat in the sugar, salt, oil, and cheese. Cool.

Fold the stiff egg whites into the cooled mush. Drop by teaspoon onto a greased and floured baking sheet. Bake in a preheated 400°F. oven for 25 to 30 minutes, until golden brown. Serve at once.

HOMEMADE TORTILLAS AND TORTILLA CHIPS

If you are unable to buy tortillas in local markets, you can make your own at home. They have a delicious fresh flavor, even though they may be a little heavier than commercial ones. You should use corn masa, a finely ground cornmeal, as the regular cornmeal is too coarse. However, if this special grain is also unavailable, you can use part wheat flour with the cornmeal or make them completely from wheat flour. All three recipes are given below.

TORTILLAS DE MAÍZ I

MAKES 12 TORTILLAS

1¼ cups water
2 cups *masa* flour

Oil
Salt

Combine water and *masa* flour and knead until well mixed. Form into 12 balls and flatten between 2 pieces of wax paper, making the tortillas as thin as possible for handling. They should be about 6 inches in diameter. Using a pastry brush, lightly brush both sides with oil.

To shape corn chips, cut oiled rolled-out tortillas into ½- to 1-inch strips approximately 1½ inches long. Sprinkle lightly with salt. Bake in a heavy skillet on top of the stove, or on a baking sheet in a 350°F. oven for 15 to 20 minutes, until lightly browned.

TORTILLAS DE MAÍZ II

MAKES 12 TORTILLAS

¾ cup cornmeal
1¼ cups all-purpose flour

1 teaspoon salt
½ to 1 cup water

Combine cornmeal, flour, and salt and follow the same procedure as in Tortillas de Maíz I.

TORTILLAS DE HARINA

MAKES 12 TORTILLAS

2 cups all-purpose flour
1 teaspoon salt
1 teaspoon baking powder

1 tablespoon oil
½ to 1 cup hot water

Sift flour, salt, and baking powder together. (Some people prefer not to use the baking powder.) Add oil and just enough water to hold dough together. Proceed as in Tortillas de Maíz I.

TORTILLA CHIPS FROM PACKAGED TORTILLAS

With almost no trouble at all you can make your own corn or wheat chips. They will have less oil and salt than those you buy and you will also be sure the oil is the right kind. I prefer the wheat chips as they are flakier but many prefer the flavor of corn.

With a pastry brush lightly brush both sides of each tortilla with oil. Stack up, and slice into strips 1 by 2 inches, or cut from the center into wedge shapes. Place a sheet of aluminum foil on a large baking sheet. Lay tortilla pieces on foil and sprinkle lightly with salt. Bake in a 400°F. oven for about 10 minutes. They should be light tan in color. Cool. Store in an airtight container.

NUTS AND BOLTS PARTY MIX

MAKES 6 CUPS

2 tablespoons oil
1 tablespoon Worcestershire
  sauce
2 cups pretzel sticks

2 cups Cheerios
2 cups Corn or Wheat Chex
½ cup Spanish peanuts
1 teaspoon garlic salt

Heat oil and Worcestershire sauce in a large shallow baking pan. Add pretzels, Cheerios, Corn or Wheat Chex, and peanuts. Sprinkle with garlic salt and stir until well coated with seasoned oil. Bake in a 325°F. oven for 30 minutes, mixing and stirring from time to time. Cool. Store in an airtight container.

SMOKED SALMON CANAPÉS

This is a "prepare-your-own" snack, using sliced salmon that has been smoked and packed in oil.

Drain sliced salmon and blot with paper towels to remove most of the oil. Cut into 1-inch pieces, place in a bowl, and chill. Put the bowl of salmon and a cocktail fork for serving on a tray; add a small dish of lime quarters, a pepper mill, and a basket of saltines.

The same thing can be done with pickled herring, but use lemons instead of limes.

MARINATED TUNA CHUNKS

Serve this substantial hors-d'oeuvre when the cocktail hour is going to be an extended one.

MAKES 10 TO 12 APPETIZERS

1 can (13 ounces) water-
  packed tuna
2 tablespoons oil
1 tablespoon wine vinegar
  with garlic

1 tablespoon capers with
  1 tablespoon juice
Freshly ground pepper,
  garlic salt, paprika

Drain tuna and separate into bite-sized chunks. Marinate in oil, vinegar, capers, and seasonings; chill. Serve with food picks, accompanied with saltines and 1-inch slices of dill pickle.

HOT TUNA PUFFS

Tempting morsel for canapés or sandwiches. Mashed potato flakes can be used in place of already cooked mashed potatoes. Try these with different kinds of English muffins: sourdough, cornmeal, whole-wheat, Roman Meal.

MAKES 32 CANAPÉS OR 8 OPEN-FACED SANDWICHES

1 cup (7 ounces) water-packed tuna, well drained
¼ cup mayonnaise
½ cup low-fat or dry-curd cottage cheese
2 tablespoons each of minced chives, celery, and parsley
1 tablespoon lemon juice
¼ teaspoon each of salt, pepper, and paprika
½ to 1 cup mashed potatoes
2 egg whites
½ teaspoon baking powder
4 English muffins, split and toasted
Margarine

Combine tuna, mayonnaise, cottage cheese, and seasonings. Mix well. Add mashed potatoes, using just enough potatoes to absorb the moisture. Beat egg whites until stiff, adding baking powder at the last minute. Fold eggs into the tuna. Spread muffins with a little margarine, then spread generously with tuna mixture. Broil in a 450°F. broiler until bubbly, puffed up, and golden brown on top, 10 to 15 minutes.

Cut each muffin into quarters when serving as canapés.

SEVICHE

Icy cold tidbits of fresh fish "cooked" in lime or lemon juice and seasoned with a little French dressing or mayonnaise. This dish is very popular in South America, Mexico, and South Pacific islands, and in fact almost everywhere nowadays. Serve as an hors-d'oeuvre or first course in hot summer weather.

MAKES 4 TO 6 SERVINGS

1 pound firm fresh white fish, cut into small pieces

1 cup lime or lemon juice

Marinate fish in lime juice for at least 3 to 4 hours, keeping well refrigerated. Drain and add one of the following combinations.

I.

2 tablespoons mayonnaise
1 cup diced cucumber

Salt, pepper, and paprika

II.

1 tablespoon olive oil
1 tablespoon regular oil
1 tablespoon minced onion
1 tablespoon chopped green chili pepper

¼ cup chopped tomato
Pinch of cayenne
Salt and pepper

III.

2 tablespoons French dressing
¼ cup chopped green pepper
2 tablespoons chopped green onion

1 tablespoon chopped parsley

Chill fish and dressing thoroughly and serve in very small bowls with cocktail forks.

MUSHROOM PÂTÉ

2 tablespoons butter-flavored oil
1 small onion, chopped fine
¾ pound fresh brown mushrooms, sliced
2 teaspoons unflavored gelatin
⅓ cup cold water
1 tablespoon beef bouillon granules

2 tablespoons brandy
1½ tablespoons lemon juice
1 tablespoon mayonnaise
1 teaspoon salt
½ teaspoon pepper
4 drops of Tabasco
1 to 2 tablespoons poppy seeds

Heat oil in a skillet and sauté onion until golden. Add mushrooms and continue cooking for a few more minutes, stirring briskly. Remove from heat.

Soften the gelatin in the cold water in a small saucepan. Add the bouillon granules and bring just to a boil to dissolve both. Remove from heat. Purée the onions and mushrooms in an electric blender along with all other ingredients, including the gelatin-bouillon mixture. Pour into a greased mold and chill for several hours or overnight.

Serve with saltines, matzo crackers, or sesame Melba rounds.

SMOKED CHICKEN WALNUT PÂTÉ

1 double chicken breast
Liquid barbecue smoke sauce
1 teaspoon oil
¾ cup walnut meats
2 tablespoons mayonnaise
2 tablespoons oil
2 tablespoons Marsala or sherry

2 tablespoons minced onion
2 teaspoons Worcestershire sauce
4 or 5 drops of Tabasco
Salt and pepper

Remove skin and fat from chicken breast. Wash and pat dry with a paper towel. Rub flesh with liquid smoke sauce and 1 teaspoon oil. Wrap in aluminum foil and bake in a 400°F. oven for 20 to 25 minutes, or until meat is cooked and white throughout. Cool. Remove meat from bones.

Put chicken and walnuts separately through a food grinder. Reserve 2 tablespoons ground nuts for sprinkling on top. Combine remaining nuts and chicken with all other ingredients. Mix well and season to taste. Add additional smoke sauce if desired. Place mixture in a mold and chill.

When ready to serve remove pâté from mold and dust with reserved ground nuts. Serve with wheat saltines or Norwegian flatbread.

MELON AND DRIED BEEF

Prosciutto (dry-cured raw Italian ham) is the customary wrapping for melon in this chilled hors-d'oeuvre. Here paper-thin slices of dried beef are substituted for the ham.

Squeeze lime juice over cubes of chilled honeydew, cantaloupe, or Crenshaw melon. Wrap each cube in a small piece of dried beef. Secure with food picks. Chill.

DRIED BEEF ROLLS

Buy thin slices of smoked dried beef (usually packaged in 4-ounce containers). Spread each slice with one of the fillings suggested for Stuffed Celery (p. 34). Roll tightly and chill. Slice into 1-inch pieces and secure with food picks.

Soups

FRENCH ONION SOUP

We can always be thankful to the French for the inspiration that created this soup. A delicious and hearty lunch, summer or winter.

MAKES 8 SERVINGS

1 tablespoon oil
2 tablespoons margarine
8 cups thin slices of yellow
   onions (about 2 pounds
   onions)
Salt and pepper

3 tablespoons flour
8 cups beef stock
8 slices of French bread,
   toasted
8 teaspoons grated Parmesan
   cheese

This soup requires only 15 minutes to prepare, but for a better flavor start 2 or 3 hours before.

Heat oil and margarine in a heavy 4-quart saucepan. Sauté the onions until golden brown. Season with salt and pepper to taste. Sprinkle in flour and stir for a few minutes. Add the stock and simmer as long as time allows.

Serve each bowl of soup topped with a slice of toast on which you have sprinkled 1 teaspoon of the cheese.

SPLIT-PEA SOUP

MAKES 8 SERVINGS

2 cups dried split peas
2½ quarts cold water or ham
   stock (see note below)
3 tablespoons chicken
   bouillon granules
½ cup imitation bacon
   bits (p. 430)

1 teaspoon sugar
1 cup chopped onion
½ cup each of minced
   celery and carrot
1 garlic clove, minced
Salt and pepper

Combine all ingredients and cook for 2½ to 3 hours, until peas are soft and mushy. Put through a strainer if desired. Season with salt and pepper to taste. Serve with homemade croutons.

NOTE: Ham stock can be made by simmering a ham hock in 3 quarts water for 1 to 2 hours; chill the stock and remove hardened fat. Omit bouillon granules and bacon bits if using ham stock.

BLACK BEAN SOUP

MAKES 8 SERVINGS

2 cups dried black beans
2½ quarts water
2 tablespoons chicken
   bouillon granules
¼ cup imitation bacon
   bits (p. 430)
Pinch of dry mustard

1 onion, minced
2 celery ribs, minced
1 tablespoon butter-
   flavored oil
2 tablespoons lemon juice
¼ cup dry sherry

Combine all ingredients except oil, lemon juice, and sherry. Cook for 2½ to 3 hours, until beans are soft and mushy. Put through a sieve if desired. Add oil, lemon juice, and sherry just before serving. Serve with lemon slices.

POTAGE ESAU

Lentils are one of the oldest of leguminous food plants, going back to prehistoric times in the countries of Central Asia. Presumably lentil soup is the "mess of potage" for which Esau sold his birthright. Although this recipe is not a duplicate of the biblical dish, it is delicious as well as nutritious; it makes a superb luncheon when accompanied by hard rolls or toasted whole-grain breads. Preparation time is about 10 minutes, cooking time about 2 hours, with no overnight soaking necessary.

MAKES 12 SERVINGS

1 garlic clove, minced
1 large yellow onion, chopped
1 tablespoon oil
2 cups dried lentils
2½ quarts water
½ cup dry red wine
3 tablespoons beef bouillon granules
¼ cup imitation bacon bits (p. 430)

2 celery ribs with leaves, chopped
2 cups shredded red cabbage
Pinch each of ground thyme and cloves
2 bay leaves
1 tablespoon flour
Salt and pepper

Sauté garlic and onion in oil until limp. Add all other ingredients except flour, salt, and pepper. Simmer slowly for 2 hours.

Stir flour into 1 cup water and add to soup. Cook and stir over low heat until thickened. Season with salt and pepper to taste.

Variations: Replace cabbage with other vegetables such as chopped carrots, tomatoes, etc.

CORN CHOWDER

This robust chowder is designed for hearty appetites on cold winter days. Preparation time is not much more than 5 minutes. If you can find it, use canned corn containing a small amount of green pepper and pimiento. Otherwise add peppers as recipe describes.

MAKES 8 SERVINGS

2 tablespoons oil
1 medium-sized onion, chopped
2 tablespoons imitation bacon bits (p. 430)
2 celery ribs, chopped
½ green pepper, chopped (optional)
1 cup water
2 cups cubed uncooked potatoes

2 tablespoons flour
1 teaspoon sugar
1 cup dry skim milk
2½ cups liquid skim milk
2 cups whole-kernel corn
2 tablespoons chopped pimiento (optional)
Pepper

Heat oil in a heavy saucepan. Sauté onion, bacon bits, celery, and green pepper until limp. Add water and potatoes. Cover and simmer slowly until potatoes are soft. If necessary add a little more water to keep potatoes from sticking. Do not add too much as milk is added later. Dissolve flour, sugar, and dry milk in the liquid milk. Stir into potatoes as soon as they are soft. Add corn and pimiento and heat slowly but do not boil. As soon as chowder is hot, season with a little pepper and serve in large bowls.

NEW ENGLAND FISH CHOWDER

Out of his 82 years of accumulated New England know-how, my cousin Stanley Lawton has this to say about fish chowder:

"The flavor of fish chowder depends on the quality of the fish and this presents a large immediate problem. There is very little fresh ocean fish sold in the interior, 90 to 95 percent of our country. Even near the coast there is a lot of weary, hence tasteless or semispoiled fish

in the markets, which doesn't show nearly as much in fried as in boiled fish. So for country-wide usage you have to include fish under refrigeration and frozen fish.

"Also fish should be firm and of a low-fat variety. It's a cinch in New England where haddock is number 1, but cod, pollock, cusk, turbot, maybe hake, sole, and halibut are usable. Cod is a bit soft, but very good when fresh. Lemon sole is very expensive but extremely good however it is cooked. Small bay flounder and sole are too thin.

"In the markets there are also native bluefish, mackerel, shad, salmon—high-fat types. The first three would darken the chowder unless the fat were removed. Shad is too bony, and salmon makes wonderful cream soup, but not chowder. . . ."

The following recipe is an adapted version of his own recipe.

MAKES 4 OR 5 SERVINGS

1½ pounds white-fleshed fish (sole, halibut, cod, etc.)
2 tablespoons oil
2 small onions, chopped
2 cups diced potatoes
Salt and pepper
2 cups liquid skim milk
1 cup dry skim milk
1 tablespoon imitation bacon bits (p. 430)
2 tablespoons chopped parsley
½ cup plain low-fat yogurt (optional)
2 tablespoons flour

Wash fish fillets. Heat oil in the bottom of a soup kettle. Sauté onions until limp. Add potatoes and just enough water to cover. Season with salt and pepper. Wrap fish fillets in aluminum foil. Puncture 2 or 3 holes on the under side, and lay foil packages on top of potatoes and onions, sealed edge upwards. Cover kettle and simmer until vegetables are tender and fish is cooked through, 20 to 25 minutes.

Take fish from the kettle. Remove any tough cartilage and bones. Remove a small amount of potatoes, about ½ cup, and mash them. Return them to the kettle. Flake fish and return to kettle. Mix liquid and dry milk until dry milk is dissolved. Add to soup with bacon bits and parsley. Stir well. Simmer until flavors are blended. Use an asbestos pad under the kettle to prevent burning. Combine yogurt and flour and blend to a smooth paste. Add to chowder just before serving.

FINNAN HADDIE CHOWDER

Follow the recipe for New England Fish Chowder (p. 52) but substitute for the white fish one third smoked finnan haddie. Omit the bacon bits.

For a more delicate flavor, as part of the liquid use only the fish stock from a small amount of finnan haddie and save the fish itself for another purpose.

TUNA OR SALMON BISQUE

MAKES ABOUT 6 SERVINGS

2 tablespoons oil
1 tablespoon butter flavoring
1 tablespoon chicken
  bouillon granules
3 tablespoons flour
2½ cups liquid skim milk
½ cup dry skim milk
1 can (7 ounces) water-
  packed tuna, drained

¼ cup chopped chives
1 can (4 ounces) mushroom
  pieces, drained
1 teaspoon each of
  Worcestershire sauce and
  onion juice
Salt and pepper
2 to 3 tablespoons dry sherry
Chopped parsley

Combine in a heavy saucepan the oil, butter flavoring, bouillon granules, and flour. Blend well. Add liquid and dry skim milk gradually, stirring over low heat until dry milk is dissolved and the mixture thickened and smooth. Add tuna, chives, mushroom pieces, Worcestershire sauce, and onion juice. Continue to stir over low heat until bisque is quite hot. Season with salt and pepper to taste. Remove from heat and add sherry.

Serve in individual bowls sprinkled with chopped parsley.

CREAM OF ASPARAGUS SOUP

MAKES 4 SERVINGS

1 pound fresh asparagus,
   or 1 can (16 ounces)
   asparagus spears
1 cup chicken stock
½ small onion, chopped
2 tablespoons butter-flavored
   oil

2 tablespoons flour
1 to 2 cups liquid skim
   milk
½ cup dry skim milk
Salt and pepper

Clean asparagus and cut off tough ends. In a covered saucepan simmer asparagus in chicken stock along with the onion until asparagus is very tender, about 15 minutes. Reserve cooking liquid and chop asparagus, or purée in a blender if you prefer. Make a creamy sauce by blending oil and flour over low heat and adding liquid and dry milk gradually, stirring until dry milk is dissolved and sauce is thickened and smooth. Add asparagus and reserved cooking liquid to sauce, and season with salt and pepper to taste.

If using canned asparagus, add the asparagus and liquid to the thickened sauce; asparagus can be puréed or not as preferred.

For a very thick soup, use the smaller amount of liquid milk.

CREAM OF CELERY SOUP

Substitute 2 cups chopped celery and leaves for the asparagus in Cream of Asparagus Soup.

CREAM OF CAULIFLOWER SOUP

Even if you're crazy about cauliflower don't make more of this soup than you can eat at one meal. Cauliflower is good only when freshly cooked.

MAKES 4 SERVINGS

1 very small head of
  cauliflower
2 cups water
2 cups dry skim milk
1 tablespoon oil

1 tablespoon flour
2 tablespoons chopped
  green onions
Salt and pepper

Discard stem from cauliflower and break the head into flowerets. Parboil flowerets and green leaves in boiling salted water for about 10 minutes, until still slightly firm. Drain. While cauliflower is cooking, whirl remaining ingredients, including the 2 cups water, in an electric blender. Add cauliflower and continue to blend at low speed; stop before the vegetable is completely puréed to keep some texture. Season to taste. Return soup to pot and heat slowly, stirring with a whisk to keep from sticking. Thin with a little skim milk if necessary.

Serve with toasted rye bread for a delicious lunch.

CREAM OF CORN SOUP

MAKES 6 SERVINGS

2 cups water
1 cup dry skim milk
2 tablespoons chopped green
  onions or chives
2 tablespoons flour

1 tablespoon oil
1 can (12 ounces) whole-
  kernel corn (about 2 cups)
Salt and pepper

Combine 1 cup of the water, the dry milk, green onions, flour, and oil in an electric blender and mix thoroughly. Add corn and blend until corn has been chopped fine. Pour soup into a heavy saucepan. Add remaining water and heat slowly, stirring well. When soup comes to a boil, simmer for 1 to 2 minutes only. Prolonged cooking will produce a mushy texture. Season with salt and pepper to taste.

FRESH MUSHROOM SOUP ✳ ✳ ✳ ✳

Heady with fresh mushrooms, this is a luscious creamy soup with a great deal of nourishment. For a whipped effect, use an electric blender. If you don't have a blender, mince the mushrooms, and combine everything in a heavy saucepan.

MAKES 4 SERVINGS

Pinch of tarragon

½ pound fresh brown
  mushrooms
1–2 tablespoons oil
2 cups water *or wet skim milk*
2 cups dry skim milk

1 teaspoon onion flakes
1 tablespoon parsley flakes
1 tablespoon flour
2 teaspoons sherry
Salt and pepper

Cut mushrooms, caps and stems, into thick slices. Heat oil in a heavy saucepan and sauté the mushrooms for just a few minutes. Remove while still crisp. Combine all other ingredients in an electric blender. Whirl for a few seconds, until thick and foamy. Add mushrooms and blend again at lowest speed for 4 or 5 seconds, or until mushrooms are chopped into fine pieces but not pulverized. Pour mixture back into the saucepan and heat slowly, stirring all the while with a wire whisk to keep from burning. Use an asbestos pad if soup is to be left on the stove. Season to taste.

PUMPKIN SOUP

MAKES ABOUT 4 SERVINGS

1 tablespoon oil
1 onion, minced
2 cups liquid skim milk
⅓ cup dry skim milk
1 cup canned stewed tomatoes
1 cup pumpkin purée

2 teaspoons imitation
  bacon bits (p. 430)
2 teaspoons chicken
  bouillon granules
Salt and pepper
1 tablespoon sherry

Sauté onion in oil until brown and crisp. Add all other ingredients except sherry and seasonings and slowly bring to a boil. Stir well to blend ingredients. Add more skim milk to thin if necessary. Season to taste. Add sherry just before serving.

CREAM OF TOMATO SOUP

MAKES 6 SERVINGS

2 cups fresh or canned
   tomatoes, chopped fine
½ small onion, chopped fine
1 teaspoon celery powder
2 teaspoons sugar

¾ cup dry skim milk
2 tablespoons flour
2½ cups water
1 tablespoon oil
Salt and pepper

Simmer tomatoes, onion, and seasonings in a saucepan for about 15 minutes, until vegetables are tender. Put through a strainer, if you wish, and return to saucepan. Dissolve dry milk and flour in the 2½ cups water and add to the tomatoes, along with the oil and a little salt and pepper. Stir and heat slowly.

Serve as soon as hot, garnished with chopped parsley, chives, or croutons.

WHIPPED ZUCCHINI SOUP

MAKES 6 SERVINGS

1 pound small fresh zucchini
2 cups dry skim milk
1 tablespoon oil

1 tablespoon flour
1 tablespoon onion flakes
Salt and pepper

Wash and quarter the zucchini, discarding ends. Parboil in boiling salted water to cover for 5 minutes. Drain zucchini, reserving 2 cups of the cooking water. Mix remaining ingredients with the reserved cooking water in an electric blender. Add zucchini, and whirl at high speed to produce a whipped consistency. Pour mixture into a heavy saucepan and heat slowly to desired temperature. Taste and correct seasoning. Stir with a whisk to keep from sticking.

Serve immediately with cracked-wheat croutons or toast.

Variations

Many additional whipped soups may be made by substituting other fresh, frozen, or canned vegetables:

Summer or yellow squash are particularly adaptable.

Fresh or frozen peas and lima beans make excellent soups.

Canned, fresh, or frozen carrots are colorful and delicately flavored, as are broccoli and watercress. The latter, of course, shouldn't be cooked. General rules to follow:

1. Use approximately 2 cups each cooked vegetables, liquids, and dry milk.

2. Never cook vegetables long enough for them to lose their bright color.

3. Increase eye appeal and flavor by adding a very small amount of such things as chopped parsley, watercress, paprika, dill weed, sesame seeds, sherry, and Worcestershire sauce.

BLENDER BORSCHT

MAKES 4 SERVINGS

1 can (16 ounces) beets with liquid

1 can (10½ ounces) condensed consommé, undiluted

1 tablespoon each of minced onion and lemon juice

Plain low-fat yogurt

Purée beets, consommé, onion, and lemon juice in an electric blender. Chill thoroughly. Serve with a tablespoon of yogurt in each bowl.

CHILLED CUCUMBER SOUP

MAKES 4 SERVINGS

1 pound cucumbers, peeled
and seeded
1 cup chicken bouillon
2 cups dry skim milk

2 cups buttermilk
1 tablespoon minced green
onion
Salt and pepper

Chop cucumbers and simmer gently, covered, in the chicken bouillon until tender, 10 to 15 minutes. Purée the cucumbers either in an electric blender or by forcing them through a sieve. Cool puréed cucumbers along with liquid they were cooked in. Dissolve dry milk in buttermilk. Mix with remaining ingredients including cucumbers. Season with salt and pepper to taste. Chill thoroughly.

VICHYSSOISE

MAKES 8 SERVINGS

3 cups peeled cubed potatoes
3 cups chopped white parts of
leeks or green onions
1½ quarts chicken stock or
bouillon made from granules
1 cup dry skim milk

1 cup water
½ cup Whipped Cottage
Cheese (p. 287)
Salt and pepper
Chopped chives

Simmer the vegetables in the stock until soft and mushy. Purée vegetables and stock in an electric blender or force through a sieve. Dissolve the dry milk in the water and mix well with the cottage cheese; stir this creamy mixture into the vegetables. Season with salt and pepper to taste. Chill overnight if possible.

Serve in very cold soup bowls with a sprinkling of chives on top.

LEEK AND POTATO SOUP

Follow recipe for Vichyssoise (preceding recipe), increasing chicken stock to 2 quarts and omitting whipped cheese. Heat, but do not let it boil. Serve hot, garnished with minced chives or a sprinkle of paprika.

GAZPACHO

A famous chilled vegetable soup from Spain. Everything can be chopped by hand but using a blender is much easier.

MAKES 10 TO 12 SERVINGS

3 pounds tomatoes	4 tablespoons lemon juice
2 medium-sized cucumbers	⅓ cup oil
1 green pepper	2 or 3 drops of Tabasco
2 garlic cloves	Salt and pepper
½ cup chopped onions or green onions	10 to 12 tablespoons plain low-fat yogurt (optional)
2 cups tomato juice	

Prepare the vegetables: Peel and quarter the tomatoes; peel and chop only one of the cucumbers; quarter the pepper and remove seeds. Rub a large serving bowl with one of the garlic cloves. Crush the other and put it in an electric blender. Add the tomato and pepper quarters and the chopped cucumber and onions, and blend. Use the tomato and lemon juices to liquefy. Pour into the serving bowl. Peel the reserved cucumber and mince; add to soup to give texture. Stir in the oil and seasonings to taste. Chill thoroughly.

Top each serving with 1 tablespoon yogurt if desired. If the weather turns cold, serve the soup hot after simmering for a few minutes.

Fish

BARBECUED CATFISH WITH
SOY-GARLIC BASTE

Catfish farming is an industry of the moment; in combination with conventional fishing methods, it produces an abundance of comparatively inexpensive, tender, mild-flavored fish. Catfish usually appear on the market skinned but not filleted. However, the bones are neither small nor difficult to handle. The skeleton consists mostly of a sturdy backbone and this is easily separated from the meat after cooking.

MAKES 4 SERVINGS

1½ pounds fresh catfish
2 tablespoons oil
2 tablespoons soy sauce

¼ teaspoon garlic salt
¼ teaspoon pepper

Marinate catfish in oil, soy sauce, and seasonings. Barbecue on both sides until fish flakes when tested with a fork.

DEVILED FISH

MAKES 4 SERVINGS

1 pound fish fillets
2 tablespoons each of minced onion and green pepper
2 tablespoons butter-flavored oil
3 tablespoons flour
2 teaspoons prepared mustard

½ teaspoon each of dry mustard and paprika
1½ cups liquid skim milk
⅓ cup dry skim milk
3 tablespoons dry sherry
Salt and pepper

Select firm, lean, white-fleshed fresh fish. Poach the fish in water in a flat skillet with a tight-fitting lid just until flaky. Keep warm.

Meanwhile, simmer onion and green pepper in the butter-flavored oil in a small saucepan. As soon as vegetables are limp, stir in the flour and mustards and paprika. Add liquid and dry skim milk gradually, stirring until dry milk is dissolved and sauce is thick and smooth. Add sherry, and season with salt and pepper to taste. Pour the sauce over the fish. Serve with hot fluffy rice.

FRIED FISH PASQUARO

This delicate method of preparing fish comes from the interior of Mexico.

MAKES 4 SERVINGS

3 egg whites
2 tablespoons oil
3 tablespoons flour
1 to 1½ pounds thick fish fillets

Oil for cooking
Salt and pepper
Lemon wedges

Beat egg whites until frothy, add the oil, and blend in the flour to make a batter. Wash fillets and pat dry with paper towels. Heat more oil in a heavy skillet. When quite hot, dip fish fillets into batter until well coated on both sides. Sauté in oil until lightly browned; fish should flake when tested with a fork. Season with a little salt and pepper. Serve with lemon wedges.

WHOLE FISH BAKED IN FOIL

Onion, lemon juice, and spices enhance the flavor of fish baked in aluminum foil. Good for a hurried day.

Select any size, any amount of whole fish. Brush with oil, and place on a piece of aluminum foil large enough to wrap around the fish. Place onion slices over fish and season with lemon juice, salt, pepper, and paprika. Or add a favorite spice of your own. Wrap foil tightly around fish. Place the packet on a baking sheet, and bake in a 350°F. oven for approximately 20 minutes for 1-inch thickness; 30 minutes for 2-inch thickness; 35 minutes for 3-inch thickness.

TERIYAKI HALIBUT

Sliced pineapple and a sweet-sour sauce give halibut a new flavor.

MAKES 6 SERVINGS

½ cup soy sauce
1 tablespoon brown sugar
2 tablespoons oil
1 teaspoon flour

½ cup dry white wine
½ teaspoon dry mustard
2 pounds halibut fillets
6 slices of canned pineapple

Combine soy sauce, brown sugar, oil, flour, white wine, and mustard in a small saucepan; simmer for a few minutes to make a marinade. Marinate fillets and pineapple slices in this mixture for 30 minutes.

Fish   67

Place fish and pineapple on an oiled broiling pan, pour the marinade over, and broil 5 to 6 inches from the source of heat for about 5 minutes on each side. Test for doneness; fish should flake when tested with a fork. Remove to a warm platter and spoon the sauce over the halibut and pineapple.

ROCKFISH EN PAPILLOTE

A fancy name for a simple but excellent fish dish. Red snapper or rock cod are sometimes called rockfish. Use any lean white fish. Use the plastic bags expressly made for oven cooking.

MAKES 4 SERVINGS

1 pound fillets of rock cod or other lean white-fleshed fish	¼ teaspoon each of pepper and paprika
2 tablespoons butter-flavored oil	1 cup chopped onion
	1 cup chopped celery
½ teaspoon salt	2 tablespoons lemon juice

Wash fish and dry with paper towels. Rub with 1 tablespoon oil and season with half of the salt, pepper, and paprika. Place onion and celery in a plastic oven bag. Add lemon juice and remaining oil and seasonings. Hold bag tightly closed and shake vigorously to mix the ingredients. Lay fish fillets on top of vegetables inside the bag. Close bag tightly, securing with the tie, and turn over once or twice so that fish becomes coated with lemon juice and seasonings. Place bag in a baking dish with fish uppermost, vegetables underneath. Puncture upper surface of bag with a fork in 5 or 6 places. Bake in a 375°F. oven for 20 to 25 minutes. Serve immediately.

SEA BASS STUFFED AND
BAKED SANDWICH STYLE

Sesame seeds give a crunchy texture to this stuffing. You may prefer to use bread or cracker crumbs or part sesame seeds and part crumbs. Almost any lean white-fleshed fish can be used in place of sea bass. If fillets are thick, as sea bass fillets often are, halve each fillet horizontally to make 2 thin fillets.

MAKES 6 SERVINGS

1½ pounds fillets of sea bass
2 tablespoons oil
1 small onion, chopped
½ cup chopped celery
½ cup sesame seeds or bread
   crumbs

1 tablespoon lemon juice
1 tablespoon soy sauce
Flour

Cut fillets into pieces 3 to 4 inches long. Slice horizontally into halves if they are thicker than ½ inch to get thin fillets and twice as many. Try to keep them in pairs so the "sandwiches" will fit as slices of bread do. Heat 1 tablespoon oil in a small skillet. Add onion, celery, and sesame seeds and sauté until vegetables are limp. If bread crumbs are used, add them after sautéing vegetables. Add lemon juice and half of soy sauce.

To make sandwiches, arrange half of fillets on the bottom of a greased ovenproof baking dish. Spread each piece with 1 rounded tablespoon of onion-celery stuffing. Top with second fillet. Brush top fillets with oil, sprinkle with flour, and shake remaining soy sauce over all. Cover baking dish. Bake in a 350°F. oven for 15 minutes. Uncover and bake for another 15 minutes, basting with juices from the pan.

Serve "sandwiches" directly from baking dish with sauce spooned over them.

WALNUT-CRUSTED SEA BASS

Unusual flavor and feathery light. Serve without lemon the better to appreciate the walnut flavor.

MAKES 4 SERVINGS

2 large fillets of sea bass
   (1 to 1½ pounds)
2 egg whites

1 tablespoon water
1 cup fine-ground walnuts
2 tablespoons oil

The fillets can be sautéed or oven-fried. The coating is crustier when sautéed but a little more flavor is retained with oven cooking. Wipe the fillets with a damp cloth or rinse and pat dry with paper towels. Beat egg whites with water until frothy.

To sauté: Dip fillets into egg whites, then into nuts. Repeat. Sauté in oil over medium heat until golden brown.

To oven-fry: Coat fish with oil, then proceed with double coating of egg whites and ground nuts. Bake in a 425°F. oven for 15 to 20 minutes. Remove from oven, dribble a little oil over the top, and broil for 3 to 5 minutes.

POACHED TUTUAVA OR SEA BASS MORNAY

Tutuava and sea bass are members of the same fish family. Both are firm, lean, and mild-flavored.

MAKES 4 SERVINGS

2 tablespoons minced onion
2 tablespoons minced celery
2 tablespoons butter-flavored
   oil
1½ pounds fillets of tutuava
   or sea bass
¼ cup dry white wine
Salt and pepper

3 tablespoons flour
1 teaspoon grated Sap Sago
   cheese
1 teaspoon chicken bouillon
   granules
1¼ cups buttermilk
1 tablespoon chopped fresh
   parsley

Sauté onion and celery in oil for a minute or two. Place fish on vegetables, pour on wine, and season lightly with salt and pepper. Cover fish with a piece of aluminum foil, puncturing the foil in 2 or 3 places. Cover the sauté pan and poach the fish very gently for 10 to 12 minutes, or until fish flakes when tested with a fork. Drain juices from the fish into a small saucepan. Set fish and vegetables aside for a minute, covering the sauté pan to keep them warm.

Stir flour, cheese, and bouillon granules into the fish juices. Add buttermilk to the fish juices and heat gradually, stirring with a wire whisk, until sauce is thick and bubbling. Pour sauce over the fish, sprinkle with parsley, and heat for a minute or two.

SOLE BONNE FEMME

Any other lean white fish may be substituted for the sole.

MAKES 4 SERVINGS

¼ to ½ pound fresh
  mushrooms, sliced
2 green onions, chopped
2 tablespoons butter-flavored
  oil
¼ teaspoon each of salt and
  pepper
1¼ pounds sole fillets

½ cup dry white wine
2 tablespoons lemon juice
½ cup dry skim milk
3 tablespoons flour
½ cup water
2 drops of yellow food
  coloring

Sauté mushrooms and green onions in oil until limp. Season lightly with salt and pepper. Lay fish fillets over the vegetables. Pour on wine and lemon juice. Cover fish with aluminum foil and puncture with 5 or 6 holes. Cover sauté pan with a tight-fitting lid and simmer gently for 5 to 7 minutes, or until fish flakes. Set the pan aside for a minute with the cover on.

Combine dry milk, flour, and ½ cup water in a small saucepan. Stir until milk and flour are dissolved. Pour juices from the fish into the saucepan and add food coloring. Simmer for a minute or two, stirring briskly with a wire whisk, until thick and smooth. Pour sauce over fish and serve.

SOLE DUGLÈRE

This recipe is similar to Sole Bonne Femme (p. 71) except that toma-
toes are substituted for the mushrooms and a little less wine is used
because of the liquid from the tomatoes.

MAKES 4 SERVINGS

1½ cups chopped fresh
   tomatoes
2 green onions, chopped
1 tablespoon oil
¼ teaspoon each of
   salt and pepper
1¼ pounds sole fillets
¼ cup dry white wine

½ lemon, sliced thin
Pinch of dried tarragon
3 tablespoons flour
¼ cup dry skim milk
¼ cup water
Yellow food coloring
   (optional)

Sauté tomatoes and onions in oil for a minute or two. Season lightly with salt and pepper. Lay fish fillets over the vegetables; add wine, lemon slices, and tarragon. Cover fillets with aluminum foil, puncturing the foil with 5 or 6 holes. Cover sauté pan with a tight-fitting lid. Simmer very gently for 8 to 10 minutes, or until fish flakes. Do not overcook as fish will cook a little more when the sauce is added.

When done, set fish aside and measure the juices. Pour 1¼ cups into a small saucepan. Discard the rest, or set aside to thin sauce later if desired. Dissolve flour and dry milk in the ¼ cup water and add to fish juices in the saucepan. Heat over low heat, stirring constantly with a wire whisk, until sauce is blended and thick. Adjust seasonings and add a little yellow food coloring if desired. Pour sauce over fish, heat for a few seconds, and serve.

SOLE FLORENTINE

Chopped green onions, spinach, and fish seem to be made for each other. Almost as good the next day if you're lucky enough to have some left over.

MAKES 8 SERVINGS

3 packages (10 ounces each) frozen chopped spinach
2½ cups plain low-fat yogurt
4 tablespoons flour
⅔ cup minced green onions

Juice of 1 lemon
1½ teaspoons salt
2 pounds sole fillets
2 tablespoons margarine
Paprika

Cook spinach according to package directions; be sure not to overcook. Drain very thoroughly through a large strainer; use a heavy spoon to press out the last drops of water.

Combine yogurt, flour, onions, lemon juice, and salt. Stir half of this mixture thoroughly into the spinach. Spread the spinach mixture over the bottom of an oiled shallow casserole dish. Arrange fish on top of spinach, cover with remaining yogurt mixture, and dot with margarine. Dust with paprika. Bake in a 375°F. oven for 15 to 20 minutes, or until fish flakes when tested with a fork.

Serve with large crusty French rolls, broiled tomatoes, and a tossed salad.

This same recipe can be made with tutuava or sea bass or other mild-flavored white-fleshed fish. Cook tutuava or sea bass a little longer than sole as the fillets are thicker.

SOLE OR SALMON FLORENTINE IN SCALLOP SHELLS

When the dinner calls for a special dish, serve sole or salmon and spinach in scallop shells, topped with a hot sauce. Use hot poached fish, hot cooked spinach, and Velouté Sauce (p. 292) or Mock Hollandaise Sauce (pp. 297–98).

Spread hot drained spinach on the bottom of individual scallop shells. Place a piece of hot fish on top and cover with sauce. Heat in a 450°F. oven for just long enough to make the sauce bubbly, a few minutes only. Garnish with a slice of lemon and a sprinkling of chopped parsley.

SOLE VÉRONIQUE

MAKES 4 SERVINGS

Oil
1 tablespoon chopped chives
  or green onions
8 sole fillets (about 1½
  pounds)
Salt and pepper
½ cup white wine

1 can (8 ounces) seedless
  grapes with juice
1 lemon
2 tablespoons margarine
2 tablespoons flour
1 tablespoon dry skim milk

Oil a sauté pan and sprinkle the bottom with chives. Wash fillets and pat dry with paper towels. Season with salt and pepper, and roll up each one into a loop. Place on top of the chives. Add wine and ½ cup juice from the grapes. Squeeze the lemon over the fillets, and cover. Simmer very, very gently for 10 to 15 minutes, until fish is tender and flakes when tested with a fork. Remove fish to a heated platter. Lift the grapes with a slotted spoon and arrange over the fish. Keep warm.

Melt margarine in a saucepan and blend in the flour; add cooking liquid from the fish and the dry milk. Heat slowly, stirring with a wire whisk to dissolve milk solids. Pour sauce over the warm fillets.

SKILLET SOLE

Good and quick. Fillets of halibut, sea bass, or any other fish can be prepared this way.

MAKES 2 SERVINGS

½ cup chopped onion
½ cup chopped green pepper
1 tablespoon oil
1 can (3 ounces) sliced
  button mushrooms
1 medium-sized tomato,
  chopped fine

½ pound sole fillets
Salt and pepper
1 teaspoon grated Sap
  Sago cheese
2 teaspoons sesame seeds

Sauté onion and pepper in the oil for just a few minutes. Add mushrooms and tomato. Stir and cook for another 2 to 3 minutes. Lay fish fillets on top of vegetables and sprinkle with salt and pepper and the mixed cheese and sesame seeds. Cover tightly, lower heat, and simmer gently for 5 to 10 minutes. Serve with sauce spooned over the fillets.

Variation: Omit the tomato and sprinkle a generous amount of soy sauce over vegetables and fillets.

CELESTIAL SOLE (rolled sole fillets baked in a variety of sauces)

Heavenly meals can be prepared in almost no time at all by using simple sauces and dips left over from earlier occasions. For added interest and a more complete casserole, garnish the fish with a few raw mushrooms or sliced or halved small tomatoes. All these recipes make 4 servings.

Fish   75

Sole with Mustard-Hollandaise Sauce

Margarine	½ cup Mustard-Hollandaise
1 pound sole fillets	Sauce (p. 298)
Vegetables	Liquid skim milk

Rub a medium-sized ovenproof baking dish with a little margarine. Wash the fillets and pat dry with paper towels. Roll up and arrange in the baking dish along with any vegetables you are including. Spread the sauce over the fillets, diluting with a little skim milk if too thick. Bake in a 375°F. oven for 20 to 25 minutes, or until fish flakes when tested with a fork.

Sole with Seafoam Dip

Follow same procedure as in Sole with Mustard-Hollandaise Sauce, using leftover Seafoam Dip (p. 26).

Sole with Cucumber-Tarragon Dip

Follow same procedure as in Sole with Mustard-Hollandaise Sauce, using leftover Cucumber-Tarragon Dip (p. 26).

Sole with Caper-Dill Dip

Follow same procedure as in Sole with Mustard-Hollandaise Sauce, using leftover Caper-Dill Dip (p. 24).

Sole with Foamy Buttermilk Sauce

1 tablespoon oil	1 cup sliced canned
3 tablespoons flour	mushrooms
2 tablespoons sauterne	1 tablespoon chopped
1 cup buttermilk	parsley

Make a sauce with oil, flour, sauterne, and buttermilk. Beat with a rotary egg beater until foamy. Arrange mushrooms around the rolled sole fillets, pour sauce over, and sprinkle with parsley. Bake as in Sole with Mustard-Hollandaise Sauce.

FIVE-MINUTE TUNA CHOW MEIN

MAKES 4 SERVINGS

1 can (7 ounces) water-packed
white-meat tuna
2 tablespoons cornstarch
1 tablespoon molasses
2 tablespoons soy sauce
1½ cups beef bouillon
1 medium-sized onion,
chopped

1 cup diagonally sliced celery
1 green pepper, quartered
and sliced
1 tablespoon oil
1 can (16 ounces) chop
suey vegetables or bean
sprouts, washed and drained

Drain tuna and break into chunks. Dissolve cornstarch and
molasses in soy sauce and bouillon. Set aside. Sauté onion, celery, and
green pepper in oil for 3 or 4 minutes. Add tuna and chop suey vegetables. Pour liquid mixture over tuna and vegetables. Cover and simmer
for 3 or 4 minutes, until hot.

Serve over hot fluffy rice or vermicelli.

TUNA AND RICE WITH PIMIENTOS

MAKES 6 SERVINGS

3 tablespoons oil
3 tablespoons flour
1½ cups liquid skim milk
½ cup dry skim milk
1 can (4 ounces) sliced
button mushrooms
Salt and pepper
1⅓ cups uncooked Minute
Rice
1½ tablespoons grated Sap
Sago cheese

½ teaspoon dried orégano
1 can (16 ounces) tomatoes
1 cup water
1 small onion, sliced thin
2 cans (6½ ounces each)
water-packed tuna, drained
⅓ cup chopped pimientos
¼ cup sesame seeds
¼ cup bread crumbs
1 teaspoon butter-flavored oil

Make a white sauce with first four ingredients. Add mushrooms and season lightly with salt and pepper. Set aside.

Oil a 1½- to 2-quart shallow baking dish. Spread the rice on the bottom. Sprinkle with Sap Sago and orégano. Combine ½ cup of liquid from the can of tomatoes with the cup of water and stir into the rice. Slice tomatoes and lay on top of rice. Add onion slices, tuna, and pimientos. Pour the sauce over all. Combine sesame seeds, bread crumbs, and butter-flavored oil. (If you like, use ½ cup sesame seeds instead of the bread crumbs, and omit the oil.) Sprinkle seeds on top. Bake in a 350°F. oven for 25 to 30 minutes.

TUNA AND RICE WITH WINE

Dry white wine and curry give an exotic touch to this quick top-of-the-stove tuna recipe. From Jim Clarke, La Jolla, California.

MAKES 4 SERVINGS

1 garlic clove, split
2 tablespoons oil
½ small onion, minced
½ celery rib, chopped fine
1 can (13 ounces) water-packed tuna, drained and flaked
½ cup dry white wine
½ teaspoon curry powder
½ teaspoon paprika
Few drops of lemon juice
½ teaspoon each of dried marjoram and thyme
Salt and pepper
2 cups cooked rice
1 heaping tablespoon plain low-fat yogurt, at room temperature

Sauté garlic in oil until brown. Add onion and celery and sauté for 10 minutes. Remove and discard garlic. Add flaked tuna, then the wine. Stir and cook for 5 minutes. Add curry powder, paprika, lemon juice, marjoram, and thyme. Season with salt and pepper to taste. Add rice, cover, and simmer gently until rice is heated. Stir in yogurt and serve.

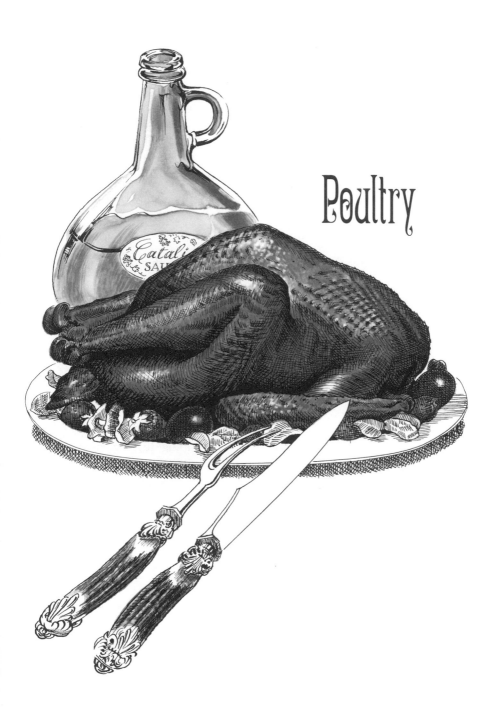

Poultry

PREPARING CHICKEN FOR COOKING

Whenever you feel like throwing together a chicken dinner, remember that the birds you buy should be both young and small, regardless of whether you buy them whole or cut into parts. It's easy enough to spot a small chicken, and for practical purposes you can come close enough on age by checking the coloring. Young birds tend to be whiter; old birds tend to be yellower—and tougher.

You've probably found that a sectioned chicken is easier to cook than a whole one, that a half breast is less awkward in the frying pan than a whole one. The hitch, as far as the breast is concerned, is that the butcher seldom cuts it in two and you are left with the problem of doing it yourself. If you find this a chore, and a frequent one at that now that you are probably concentrating rather heavily on white meat, I have a useful technique to pass on to you.

To start with, buy a large heavy butcher's knife if you don't already have one. It is an invaluable tool and well worth the cost. Pull the skin off the whole breast of the chicken and trim away any fat you see. Wash the chicken, dry it with paper towels, and lay it flat on a large bread board—flesh side up, bone side down. Now break the breast bone by pressing heavily on the flesh with both hands. This flattens the breast and makes it easier to cut. Next, turn it over and with your knife cut the flesh along the white tendon from the center outward. Now rotate the breast so that the cut side is away from you. Grab it firmly with the left hand, insert the knife vertically at the outer uncut edge with the right hand, and proceed to cut downwards, adding pressure on the knife with the left hand now that you have the breast pinned down with the knife. In this fashion you can cut through the bones quite easily without splintering them, and you will sever the breast in two. In case you're left-handed reverse the hand motions or you may remove a few fingers along with the breast.

Here's another point about chicken breasts. After you have skinned, trimmed, and split them, you have a small piece of chicken that has to cook with no insulating layer of skin. If you are not careful you may cook out the juices and end up with a dry unpalatable piece of meat. To avoid this, coat the washed and dried pieces thoroughly with oil and afterwards with flour, crumbs, or whatever you wish. Chicken breasts that have been coated with oil and dipped into bread crumbs will cook in a 350°F. oven in 35 to 40 minutes, depending on the size of the chicken breast. The meat should be white throughout and very juicy in this time.

Before leaving the subject of chicken breasts it might be best to mention the standard terminology. Each chicken has one whole, or double, breast. Half a breast, or one side only, is called a single chicken breast and usually weighs 3 to 4 ounces. When skinned and deboned it is called a *suprême*—that is in French culinary language, but the term is not used very often in this book.

ARMENIAN CINNAMON CHICKEN AND RICE

Dusting chicken with cinnamon gives a Near Eastern flavor, especially when combined with currant-studded rice. Prepare the rice first.

MAKES 4 SERVINGS

Rice with Currants

1 tablespoon oil
1 cup uncooked white rice
1 small onion, sliced
1 can (10½ ounces)
  condensed consommé plus
  water to equal 2 cups

½ cup dried currants

Heat oil in a skillet. Brown rice and onion. Transfer both to a flat ovenproof baking dish and add consommé and water and the currants; stir to mix.

Cinnamon Chicken

1 frying chicken (3 pounds), cut into pieces	¼ teaspoon pepper
½ cup flour	1 teaspoon ground cinnamon
½ teaspoon salt	1 to 2 tablespoons oil

Remove visible fat from chicken and at least half of the loose skin. Shake chicken in a bag with flour, salt, pepper, and cinnamon. Heat oil in a skillet and brown chicken pieces. Place chicken on top of rice. Cover, and bake in a 350°F. oven for 1 hour. Uncover and bake for another 30 minutes.

CRISPY BAKED CHICKEN

This recipe sounds incredibly simple but the finished chicken is crisp outside and tender inside and tastes delicious. I asked my friend Joanne Crosby for the recipe.

Cut frying chickens into serving pieces. Wash and dry chicken pieces. Remove fat and skin edges. Dip the top sides into oil. Arrange the pieces flat in a baking dish. Dust generously with garlic and onion powder, a good poultry seasoning, and some paprika. Cover tightly with lid or aluminum foil. Bake in a 325°F. oven for 2 to 2½ hours. Uncover for the last 30 to 45 minutes. Baste once or twice, while uncovered, with the juices in the pan.

CHICKEN BAKED IN A CRUST

The juices of the chicken are retained in the crust. This makes a good company dish.

MAKES 6 SERVINGS

4 tablespoons soy sauce
6 single chicken breasts with skin removed, or 1 frying chicken (3 pounds), cut into serving pieces

1 tablespoon water
2 tablespoons oil
3 egg whites, whipped with a fork
¾ cup fine cracker crumbs

Put soy sauce in a flat dish and roll chicken in it until well covered. Stir water and oil into egg whites, and mix with cracker crumbs. Mixture should have the consistency of unbaked bread dough. Add water or crumbs to adjust if necessary. Pat mixture onto fleshy side of chicken. Arrange pieces on a baking sheet. Bake in a 250°F. oven, uncovered, for 2 hours.

Serve with Cantonese Vegetables (p. 257) and a rice dish.

CHICKEN BAKED WITH LIME

MAKES 6 SERVINGS

2 frying chickens (2½ pounds each), cut into serving pieces
4 tablespoons oil
1½ cups cornflake crumbs

Garlic salt
Lemon pepper
Unsweetened lime juice (fresh or bottled)

Cut off all fat and at least half of the skin from chicken pieces; remove all of the skin if your diet requires it. Put the oil in large flat baking pan and roll chicken pieces in it. Dip chicken into cornflake crumbs and return to pan, skin side up. Season with garlic salt and lemon pepper. Shake lime juice liberally over the chicken. Bake in a 400°F. oven for about 45 minutes. Lower heat to 350°F. and continue baking for another 30 minutes. If necessary, add more lime juice and a little water to the pan to keep chicken moist.

ORANGE CURRY CHICKEN

MAKES 6 SERVINGS

2 frying chickens (about 2½ pounds each), cut into serving pieces
2 tablespoons oil
1 can (6 ounces) frozen orange-juice concentrate
¼ cup water

1½ teaspoons curry powder
Garlic salt
Pepper
½ cup bread crumbs
1 tablespoon butter-flavored oil

Remove half of the skin and all of the fat from chickens. If desired, remove all skin. Mix 2 tablespoons oil, orange-juice concentrate, ¼ cup water, and curry powder in a large flat baking pan. Roll chicken pieces in the marinade until completely covered. Arrange the pieces flat in the pan, skin side up. Sprinkle with garlic salt and pepper. Mix bread crumbs and the tablespoon of butter-flavored oil and sprinkle over the chicken. Bake in a 400°F. oven for about 45 minutes. Lower heat to 350°F. and continue baking for another 30 minutes. Baste with pan juices several times, checking to see that the chicken is not getting too brown.

Serve garnished with fresh orange slices, and accompany with white rice cooked with a few currants.

BAKED CHICKEN WITH WALNUT SOY SAUCE

MAKES 4 SERVINGS

1 frying chicken (3 pounds), quartered, or 4 single chicken breasts
½ cup flour

1 tablespoon paprika
4 tablespoons oil
½ cup bread crumbs
Walnut Soy Sauce (p. 86)

Wash chicken and pat dry with paper towels. Combine flour and paprika and thoroughly coat chicken. Brush with 2 tablespoons of the oil and then roll in bread crumbs. Place on a rack in a baking pan and bake in a 350°F. oven for 1 hour. Dribble additional oil on chicken if it becomes dry. Make the sauce.

Serve chicken on a platter, pour sauce over all, and surround with hot steamed rice.

Walnut Soy Sauce

3 ounces sliced walnuts	1 cup buttermilk
1 tablespoon oil	½ cup plain low-fat yogurt
3 tablespoons flour	1 tablespoon soy sauce

Brown walnuts in the oil. Stir in flour, and gradually add the buttermilk, yogurt, and soy sauce, stirring until hot and thickened. Adjust seasonings.

GREEN-BEAN STUFFING FOR CHICKENS AND CORNISH HENS

A nice change from the usual bread stuffing, and with many fewer calories.

MAKES ENOUGH FOR 2 FRYERS (3 POUNDS EACH) OR 4 ROCK CORNISH GAME HENS

1 large Bermuda onion, chopped	¼ cup sliced almonds or sunflower seeds
1 tablespoon oil	Salt and pepper
1 can (16 ounces) French-style green beans with seasoning	

Sauté chopped onion in oil. Combine with other ingredients, adding seasoning to taste. Remove all visible fat from birds and fill cavities.

CHICKEN BREASTS IN ALUMINUM FOIL

One of the fastest and most successful ways to cook chicken breasts is to bake them in aluminum foil. There are no dirty pots and pans to worry about, preparation time is very brief, and time in the oven can be adjusted to your schedule. There are many ways to use these succulent chicken breasts. They are delicious perfectly plain with salt and pepper. Hot chicken sandwiches made with warm sourdough bread can't be beaten. Or the meat can easily be peeled off the bones and served with a sauce that can be prepared in a few minutes. Good sauces to use are Curry Sauce (p. 294) made with buttermilk. Béchamel Sauce (p. 291), or Cheese Sauce (p. 293).

After removing the fat and skin from either single or double chicken breasts, wash them and pat dry with paper towels. Rub or brush oil on all surfaces and wrap individually in squares of foil. Be sure to seal completely. Place the foil packets in an ungreased pan with sealed side upward so the juices will not run out into the pan. If time permits, cook in a 300°F. oven for 45 minutes to 1 hour. If time does not permit, bake in a 450°F. to 500°F. oven for 15 to 20 minutes. Do not overcook! The meat should have just turned white while still remaining very juicy. Remember to do your seasoning after cooking as salt draws out the juices!

handwritten margin note:
per ch. half:
S & P
½ lemon juice
¼ t dry
tarragon
omit oil

CHICKEN CURRY SUPRÊMES

MAKES 4 SERVINGS

2 large double chicken breasts	1 teaspoon paprika
3 to 4 tablespoons flour	1 teaspoon curry powder
3 tablespoons oil	Salt and pepper
2 cups buttermilk	

Remove skin and fat from chicken breasts and cut them into halves. Follow aluminum foil method of cooking (above) or oven-poach in a plastic bag, preparing chicken in the same manner beforehand.

Prepare sauce while chicken is cooking. Blend flour and oil over low heat. Cook and stir for 2 to 3 minutes. Add ½ cup buttermilk, stirring with a wire whisk until smooth. Blend in paprika and curry powder. Season with salt and pepper to taste. Add remaining buttermilk gradually; stir until smooth.

Remove chicken from oven and debone if desired. Serve the breasts over hot steaming rice with sauce poured generously over all.

CHICKEN SUPRÊMES WRAPPED IN SMOKED BEEF

This is an adaptation of a delicious recipe given to me by Eunice Tyler. I have eliminated bacon, sour cream, and mushroom soup, but it still makes a good dish.

MAKES 6 SERVINGS

6 single chicken breasts (suprêmes), skinned and boned
4 ounces smoked beef slices
Oil
2 cups sliced fresh mushrooms, or 1 large can (8 ounces) button mushrooms

1 tablespoon margarine
1 tablespoon oil
4 tablespoons flour
1 cup liquid skim milk
¼ cup dry skim milk
1 cup plain low-fat yogurt
1 teaspoon Worcestershire sauce

Wrap uncooked chicken breasts in thin slices of smoked beef. Place in an oiled heatproof glass dish. Shred any extra beef over the chicken.

Sauté mushrooms in margarine and oil. Blend in 2 tablespoons of the flour and gradually add the mixed liquid and dry milk to make a smooth creamy sauce. Stir remaining 2 tablespoons flour into the yogurt and add to sauce along with the Worcestershire. Pour the sauce over the chicken. Bake in a 300°F. oven for 2½ hours. Keep covered for the first hour.

88 **Poultry**

CHICKEN BREASTS WITH MUSHROOMS AND LEMON RIND

MAKES 4 SERVINGS

2 double chicken beasts	¾ cup plain low-fat yogurt
2 cups sliced mushrooms	¼ cup white wine
2 tablespoons oil	2 teaspoons grated lemon rind
3 tablespoons flour	1 teaspoon salt
½ cup chicken bouillon	½ teaspoon pepper

Cut chicken breasts into halves, remove skin, and debone if desired. Place chicken in a greased baking dish. Add mushrooms. Make a creamy sauce with oil, flour, bouillon, yogurt, wine, lemon rind, salt, and pepper as described in Chicken Curry Suprêmes (p. 87). Pour over chicken and mushrooms. Bake, covered, in a 350°F. oven for 45 minutes to 1 hour.

CHICKEN CACCIATORE

MAKES 6 SERVINGS

3 double chicken breasts (1½ to 2 pounds)	¼ cup chopped fresh parsley, or 1 tablespoon dried parsley flakes
Flour	
3 to 4 tablespoons oil	Pinch each of dried orégano and basil
1 large onion, chopped	
1 green pepper, chopped	½ cup dry red wine
1 garlic clove, minced	2 cups sliced mushrooms
1 can (16 ounces) peeled plum tomatoes	

Remove skin from chicken breasts and halve them. Sprinkle with flour and sauté in 2 tablespoons of the oil. Set chicken aside. Add remaining oil to the pan. Sauté onion, green pepper, and garlic. Add remaining ingredients except mushrooms, and stir until blended. Return chicken breasts to the pan, spoon sauce over them, cover, and simmer slowly for 20 minutes.

Add mushrooms, stir into the sauce, and simmer for another 10 minutes. Serve over hot spaghetti.

CHICKEN BREASTS WITH SESAME CRUST

Sesame seeds give this chicken a crunchy and unusual crust.

MAKES 4 SERVINGS

2 double chicken breasts
Oil
Salt and pepper

½ cup sesame seeds
1 teaspoon grated lemon rind

Cut chicken breasts into halves and remove the skin. Wash the pieces and pat dry with paper towels. Dip chicken into oil, sprinkle with salt and pepper, and roll in a mixture of the sesame seeds and lemon rind until well coated. Place on a baking sheet. Broil at the middle level of an oven broiler, using low heat, for 20 to 25 minutes, or until lightly browned. For greater crustiness dribble on additional oil. Turn oven to bake, 350°F., and continue cooking for another 10 to 15 minutes, or until done.

TAHITIAN CHICKEN

MAKES 6 SERVINGS

3 large double chicken breasts
1 cup soy sauce
1 cup dark brown sugar

1 teaspoon dry mustard
2 tablespoons oil
1 tablespoon onion juice

Split the chicken breasts, and remove the skin. Mix all ingredients of the marinade in a flat baking pan. Marinate chicken for 1 hour, turning once or twice. When ready to cook, pour off marinade and reserve for basting.

Spread out chicken breasts bone side up in the pan. Broil on the middle rack of the broiler under medium-high heat for 10 minutes. Turn chicken over, baste, and continue to broil until top side is a deep reddish brown; baste a second time after 5 minutes. In 15 to 20 minutes cut into one breast and test for doneness; do not overcook. Meat should be firm and white but not dry. Remove from oven when done and transfer chicken to a platter. Scrape up juices in the pan, adding a little extra marinade if desired. Pour juices over chicken.

Serve with rice pilaf, sautéed pineapple rings, broiled tomatoes, and a tossed green salad.

CHICKEN BREASTS WITH LEMON CAPER SAUCE

MAKES 4 SERVINGS

4 single chicken breasts	2 tablespoons white wine
2 to 4 tablespoons oil	½ cup chicken bouillon
Cornflake crumbs	2 teaspoons flour
2 tablespoons lemon juice	Capers

Remove skin from chicken breasts, then wash and pat dry with paper towels. Brush with a little of the oil and dip into cornflake crumbs. Heat 1½ tablespoons oil in a skillet and sauté the chicken until golden on both sides, adding more oil if necessary. Add lemon juice, wine, and bouillon. Cover, reduce heat to as low as possible, and simmer for approximately 15 to 20 minutes. Remove chicken to a hot platter. Stir flour into the mixture remaining in the pan and simmer until thickened. Add capers to taste, and pour the sauce over the chicken.

PORTUGUESE POACHED CHICKEN BREASTS

The Portuguese have something very special here. Only 10 minutes of preparation time, 20 minutes to cook, and a superb lunch is ready.

MAKES 2 SERVINGS

1 large double chicken breast

1 small yellow onion, sliced thin

1½ teaspoons oil

1 can (16 ounces) stewed tomatoes

Pinch each of dried thyme and rosemary

Pinch each of garlic salt and pepper

1 teaspoon grated Sap Sago cheese

1 tablespoon toasted sesame seeds

Split the chicken breast and remove skin and fat. Debone if you wish. Sauté onion in oil in a medium-sized heavy saucepan or a skillet with a lid. Add tomatoes, herbs, garlic salt, and pepper, and stir to blend. Submerge chicken breasts in tomatoes, reduce heat to as low as possible, and simmer very, very gently for 15 to 20 minutes. Keep covered unless there is too much juice for your taste; in that case, uncover for last part of the cooking time to evaporate some.

Serve in shallow bowls with knife, fork, and spoon. Sprinkle with a mixture of the grated cheese and sesame seeds.

CHINESE STIR-FRIED CHICKEN

Chinese stir-frying requires but a few minutes of cooking time, but the ingredients must be prepared in advance so there are no delays at the last moment. In this recipe three things must be readied: the chicken, the vegetables, and the sauce. The vermicelli must be cooked during the last few minutes. It may then be left to drain for a short while without cooling off too much. The end result is a delicate and colorful dish!

2 double chicken breasts
3 tablespoons white wine
3 tablespoons soy sauce
1 teaspoon sugar
1 medium-sized onion
1 red pepper
2 tablespoons cornstarch
1 teaspoon chicken bouillon
 granules
1 cup water
2 tablespoons oil
½ teaspoon salt
8 ounces vermicelli
2 cups shredded cabbage

Remove the skin and bones from the uncooked chicken. Cut meat into 1-inch cubes. Marinate the chicken cubes in the white wine, soy sauce, and sugar for at least 15 minutes, longer if possible.

Cut onion and pepper into ½-inch pieces. Dissolve cornstarch and bouillon granules in the cup of water. Set aside. Heat 1 tablespoon of the oil in a large skillet or frying pan. When quite hot, sauté the onion and red pepper for 2 or 3 minutes, stirring all the time. Transfer to a plate. The vegetables should be about half cooked and still quite crisp.

Heat a pot of water to the boiling point while vegetables are cooking. Add the salt. When ready to fry chicken, add the vermicelli to the water and boil for about 5 minutes, until tender but still firm. Drain.

Drain off marinade from the chicken and add to cornstarch mixture. Set aside for a moment. Heat the second tablespoon of oil in the skillet. When hot, add the chicken cubes and sauté quickly, stirring constantly. This should take only 3 to 5 minutes. Chicken should be opaque on the outside but not quite cooked throughout. Add sautéed onion and pepper and the shredded cabbage to the chicken. Stir and sauté for a minute or two. Pour on the cornstarch-bouillon mixture. Cover and steam for a few seconds.

Serve with vermicelli and additional soy sauce.

CHICKEN MANDARIN

MAKES 4 SERVINGS

2 large double chicken breasts
2 tablespoons soy sauce
2 tablespoons honey
2 tablespoons white wine
¼ teaspoon dry mustard
¼ teaspoon garlic salt
¼ teaspoon pepper
2 tablespoons oil

1 onion, quartered and sliced
1 green pepper, chopped
8 ounces vermicelli
1 cup chicken bouillon
2 tablespoons cornstarch
1 can (8 ounces) mandarin
oranges, drained

Separate uncooked chicken meat from skin and bones. Cut into bite-sized pieces. Marinate in soy sauce, honey, wine, mustard, garlic salt, and pepper for at least 30 minutes.

Heat 1 tablespoon of the oil in a large heavy skillet. When quite hot, sauté the onion and green pepper for 2 or 3 minutes, stirring all the while. Transfer to a plate while still crisp and about half cooked.

Start the water for the vermicelli. Just before cooking the chicken, put the vermicelli in boiling salted water. It takes about 5 minutes to cook and can drain for 2 or 3 minutes without cooling too much.

Drain chicken, saving the marinade. Combine marinade, chicken bouillon, and cornstarch. Stir until cornstarch is dissolved. Set sauce aside.

Heat remaining oil in a skillet. Fry chicken cubes very quickly for 3 to 5 minutes, turning so that all sides are cooked. When almost done, add the sautéed vegetables, drained mandarin oranges, and marinade-bouillon mixture. Cover and steam for a minute or two.

Serve with vermicelli and additional soy sauce.

CHICKEN BREASTS AND PRUNES IN WINE SAUCE

MAKES 4 SERVINGS

2 large double chicken breasts
1 large yellow onion, sliced thin
¾ cup pitted prunes, chopped into small pieces
½ cup canned tomato sauce
½ cup chicken bouillon
1 tablespoon dry cooking sherry
1 tablespoon oil
½ teaspoon salt
¼ teaspoon pepper

Split chicken breasts into halves, remove skin, and debone. Place in a greased shallow casserole that can come to the table. Add onion slices and prunes. Combine remaining ingredients and pour over chicken. Bake, covered, in a 400°F. oven for 20 to 25 minutes. Test for doneness; chicken breasts should be firm when pressed with a finger. Serve from the baking dish.

STEAMED CHICKEN—WHOLE OR PARTS ＊＊＊＊

For recipes that require precooked chicken follow this method to achieve the greatest tenderness and flavor.

Pour ½ to 1 cup water into a heavy saucepan; add any extra bones such as the neck or wing ends. Add ¼ cup dry wine or 1 tablespoon white vinegar for every 2 pounds of chicken. Bring the liquid to a very low simmer. The water should not show any bubbles. To get used to judging the right temperature use a thermometer at first. The water should not be over 185°F. If your burner cannot be reduced enough to reach this low temperature, move the saucepan until it is partly off the burner. Place the chicken or chicken parts on a rack over the bones; cover the pan. Simmer from 30 minutes to 2½ hours, depending on the size and amount of chicken. To eliminate any vinegar odor remove the lid for the last few minutes of cooking.

If you plan to use the broth for a sauce or casserole, pour it into a receptacle and chill. Remove the fat when hardened. If time is too short for this method, remove the broth with a bulb baster.

CHICKEN BREASTS IN BRANDIED MUSHROOM SAUCE

MAKES 6 SERVINGS

3 double chicken breasts, split into halves
1 tablespoon margarine
1 tablespoon oil
1 small onion, chopped fine
16 whole mushrooms
¼ cup dry skim milk
2 tablespoons cornstarch
1 cup liquid skim milk

Juice of 1 lemon
1 teaspoon chicken bouillon granules
⅛ teaspoon crumbled dillweed
⅛ teaspoon dry mustard
1 teaspoon parsley flakes
2 tablespoons brandy

Steam chicken breasts (p. 95). Remove skin and bones. Set aside.

Heat margarine and oil in a large heavy skillet. Sauté onion until golden. Add mushrooms and cook for a few minutes more. Dissolve dry milk and cornstarch in liquid milk. Blend into mushrooms and onion. Add remaining ingredients and stir gently until well mixed and thickened. Submerge the chicken breasts in the sauce and continue to simmer gently until chicken is hot.

Serve over white rice, with fresh green asparagus.

CHICKEN, RICE, AND MUSHROOM PILAU

MAKES 6 SERVINGS

3 double chicken breasts, halved
1 green pepper, chopped
2 medium-sized yellow onions, chopped
2 tablespoons oil
1¼ cups uncooked white rice

2 cups sliced mushrooms
1 can (16 ounces) stewed tomatoes
2 tablespoons chopped parsley
¼ teaspoon garlic powder
1 teaspoon salt
½ teaspoon pepper

Steam chicken breasts (p. 95). Separate the meat from the fat and bones, and save the broth. This can be done a day ahead.

Sauté pepper and onions in oil until lightly browned. Add rice and continue to cook for 5 minutes, stirring frequently. Add mushrooms, tomatoes, parsley, garlic powder, salt, and pepper. Simmer gently for 15 minutes.

Place chicken breasts on the bottom of a large ovenproof dish and cover with vegetable-rice mixture. (If you have been using a heavy skillet that can be transferred to the oven, just slip the chicken breasts under the vegetables.) Add reserved chicken broth just to cover ingredients. If there is not enough liquid, prepare extra broth with bouillon granules. Bake in a 350°F. oven for 40 to 50 minutes; add more broth if necessary to keep rice from drying out.

CHICKEN CHOW MEIN CASSEROLE

Preparation time is minimal for this casserole, which is cooked on top of the stove. Start with leftover chicken if you have it. Otherwise steam, poach, or foil-bake 2 double chicken breasts to have about 3 cups cubed cooked chicken.

MAKES 6 SERVINGS

¾ cup uncooked rice
1 tablespoon oil
3 cups chicken broth
1 package (10 ounces) frozen green peas
3 cups ½-inch cubes of cooked chicken
½ cup chopped green onions

1 can (5 ounces) water chestnuts, sliced
3 tablespoons chopped pimiento, or ½ cup chopped fresh red pepper
3 tablespoons soy sauce
½ teaspoon pepper

Sauté rice in oil until grains are opaque. Add 1½ cups chicken broth, cover, and simmer very slowly for 25 minutes. Add remaining ingredients in this order: 1 cup broth (reserve ½ cup for later if needed), peas, chicken cubes, green onions, water chestnuts, pimiento or pepper, soy sauce, and black pepper. Stir gently with a fork, cover, and simmer for 3 or 4 minutes, until vegetables are tender but still crisp. Add remaining ½ cup broth if necessary for moisture.

Serve with Mandarin Salad (p. 273).

CHICKEN CHOP SUEY

MAKES 4 SERVINGS

2 cups cubes or strips of cooked chicken
1 tablespoon oil
½ cup chopped celery
½ cup chopped green onions
1 can (5 ounces) water chestnuts, sliced
1 package (7 ounces) frozen Chinese pea pods, thawed

2 cups bean sprouts
1½ cups consommé or chicken bouillon
1½ tablespoons cornstarch
1 tablespoon brown sugar
2 tablespoons soy sauce

Prepare chicken. Heat oil in a frying pan and quickly sauté the celery, green onions, water chestnuts, and pea pods for 3 or 4 minutes. Add the chicken pieces. Stir and cook for another minute or two. Add the bean sprouts. Combine consommé, cornstarch, and brown sugar and pour over the chicken and vegetables. Season with soy sauce. Cover and steam for a minute or two. Serve over hot rice.

EAST INDIAN APPLE CURRY

The incorporation of apples, onions, and stewed tomatoes in the sauce makes an unusual curry which is extremely adaptable for serving to large groups of people. This recipe originally called for corned beef, which augmented the red coloring of the tomatoes. Dried chipped beef can be used in place of the turkey for this effect. Or brown gravy maker and red food coloring can be added for color. This is an excellent way to use up any leftover dark meat of a turkey.

3 tablespoons oil
3 large onions, chopped
4 garlic cloves, minced
4 cups ½-inch pieces or shreds of cooked turkey or chicken
3 large cooking apples, chopped

3 cans (16 ounces each) stewed tomatoes
4 teaspoons curry powder, or less according to your taste
Raisins, any amount

Heat oil in a large heavy pot. Sauté onions and garlic until lightly browned. Add turkey pieces and cook for a minute or two longer. Mix in remaining ingredients and simmer gently for 15 to 20 minutes.

Serve over brown rice or bulghur (cracked wheat). Pass the chutney, homemade (p. 304) or otherwise.

TURKEY OR CHICKEN HASH

MAKES 4 SERVINGS

1 small onion, chopped
¼ cup chopped celery
2 tablespoons oil
1 tablespoon chicken bouillon granules
1½ tablespoons flour
1 cup liquid skim milk

1½ cups cubed boiled potatoes
1½ cups diced cooked turkey or chicken
1 tablespoon chopped parsley
Salt and pepper

Sauté onion and celery in oil until limp. Dissolve bouillon granules and flour in skim milk. Combine with potatoes, turkey, parsley, and salt and pepper to taste. Add to onion and celery and cook over low heat until some of the moisture has been absorbed. Turn hash over with a spatula to brown well on both sides.

JAVANESE TURKEY

MAKES 4 SERVINGS

¼ cup chopped green pepper
2 tablespoons oil
2 tablespoons flour
1 teaspoon curry powder
1 can (10½ ounces) condensed onion soup, fat removed

½ cup water
2 cups diced cooked turkey
1 can (4 ounces) sliced mushrooms
¼ cup chopped walnuts

Sauté green pepper in oil. Mix in flour and curry powder. Add onion soup and water. Stir and simmer slowly until thickened. Add turkey, mushrooms, and walnuts. Simmer over low heat for 5 to 10 minutes.

Serve over steamed rice, with chutney and condiments if desired.

CREAMED TURKEY CURRY

Very good for a crowd. The original from which this evolved came from a friend, Marj Bradner of La Jolla, California.

MAKES 8 SERVINGS

3 tablespoons oil
3 tablespoons margarine
2 large onions, chopped
6 tablespoons flour
3 tablespoons curry powder
2½ cups liquid skim milk

½ cup dry skim milk
1 can (13 ounces) evaporated skim milk
5 cups ½-inch cubes of leftover turkey
Salt and pepper

Heat the oil and margarine in a very large heavy saucepan or skillet. Cook the onions until yellow. Stir in flour and curry powder. Make a white sauce by gradually adding the liquid, dry, and evaporated skim milks to the onions. Spoon in the turkey and season with salt and pepper to taste. Simmer for a few minutes until everything is hot.

Serve with fluffy white rice and any condiments you like: raisins, chopped chives, soybeans, chutney, etc.

TURKEY CURRY IN PINEAPPLE SHELLS

To be really festive for a small group, buy 1 fresh pineapple for every 2 people, cut it lengthwise into halves, and scoop out the pulp to within ½ inch of the rind. Cut the pulp into small pieces. Add some of the pineapple pieces to the above curry mixture and fill pineapple shells. Serve 1 half shell to each person.

TURKEY DIVAN WITH CRUSTY TOPPING

An old favorite for the day after the holiday feast. Substitute tuna, salmon, or chicken for an equally tasty dish.

MAKES 4 SERVINGS

1 package (10 ounces) frozen broccoli	1 teaspoon salt
4 large turkey slices (white meat)	½ teaspoon pepper
	1 can (4 ounces) mushroom pieces, drained
1 tablespoon oil	½ cup Cheese Crumbs (p. 304)
2 tablespoons flour	
1 tablespoon mayonnaise	4 thin slices of processed vegetable-oil cheese (p. 419)
1½ cups buttermilk	
2 tablespoons dry sherry	

Cook broccoli according to package instructions. Arrange in an oiled baking dish. Top with turkey slices. Heat oil in a small saucepan. Add flour and cook for a minute or two, stirring. Blend in mayonnaise. Add buttermilk, sherry, salt, and pepper. Stir with a wire whisk and simmer until sauce is thickened and smooth. Add mushrooms. Pour sauce over turkey and broccoli. Spread out evenly. Sprinkle casserole with crumbs and lay cheese slices over the crumbs. Bake in a 425°F. oven for 15 to 20 minutes, until hot and bubbly.

TURKEY TETRAZZINI

MAKES 5 OR 6 SERVINGS

4 ounces spaghetti
¼ to ½ pound fresh
   mushrooms, sliced
3 tablespoons oil
1 tablespoon margarine
3 tablespoons flour
2 cups buttermilk
¼ cup dry sherry

1 teaspoon salt
½ teaspoon pepper
2½ cups cubed cooked
   turkey
½ cup chopped pimientos
½ cup bread crumbs
1 tablespoon grated Sap
   Sago cheese

Cook spaghetti according to directions. Drain and set aside.

Sauté mushrooms briskly in 2 tablespoons of the oil and the margarine for 2 or 3 minutes only. They should be crisp and firm. Stir in the flour, mixing well. Add buttermilk gradually, stirring until thickened. Remove from heat. Add sherry, salt, pepper, turkey cubes, and pimientos. Mix well with spaghetti and pour all into a large oiled casserole. Combine bread crumbs, remaining tablespoon of oil, and Sap Sago cheese and sprinkle over turkey-spaghetti mixture. Bake in a 350°F. oven until hot and bubbly, 35 to 40 minutes.

Veal

VEAL STEAK WITH PEPPERS

MAKES 4 SERVINGS

1¼ pounds lean veal
Flour
Salt and pepper
1 garlic clove, minced
1 medium-sized onion,
　sliced
2 tablespoons oil
½ cup chili sauce

1 can (10½ ounces)
　condensed onion soup,
　fat removed
1 large green pepper, cut into
　strips
1 large red pepper, cut into
　strips

Cut meat into serving pieces about ⅓ inch thick. Rub in a little flour, salt, and pepper. Sauté the garlic and onion in 1 tablespoon of the oil until wilted. Set aside. Add second tablespoon of oil to the skillet. Brown the pieces of meat on both sides. Return the garlic and onion to the pan. Pour in chili sauce and onion soup. Cover and simmer for 1¼ hours, or until tender. Add pepper strips to meat for the last 15 minutes of cooking.

Serve with thin spaghetti or mashed potatoes.

SICILIAN VEAL CHOPS WITH ZUCCHINI

Of all squashes, zucchini, whose popularity is no longer confined to the southern European countries, seems to have the freshest and most delicate of flavors. Like other fresh vegetables it should be cooked for only a very few moments, never until it is mushy and has lost its color.

MAKES 6 SERVINGS

6 lean veal chops
2 tablespoons oil
Flour
1 large onion, sliced
1 cup sliced mushrooms
2 cups canned stewed
  tomatoes
½ cup Marsala wine
1 tablespoon beef bouillon
  granules

½ teaspoon pepper
1 teaspoon garlic salt
½ teaspoon dried marjoram
¼ teaspoon grated Sap Sago
  cheese
5 or 6 medium-sized zucchini,
  cut into thin slices

Trim all fat from veal chops. Heat oil in a heavy skillet. Dredge chops with flour and brown on both sides. Set aside. Brown onion and mushrooms in the same skillet. Add all other ingredients except zucchini. Cover, and simmer over the lowest possible heat for 30 to 40 minutes. Add the zucchini for the last 5 to 7 minutes of cooking.

Serve with whipped potatoes or rice pilaf.

VEAL SCALOPPINE MARSALA

MAKES 4 SERVINGS

1½ pounds veal, cut into
  thin scallops
½ cup seasoned flour
½ teaspoon grated Sap Sago
  cheese
2 tablespoons butter-flavored
  oil

1 teaspoon lemon juice
½ cup chicken bouillon
½ cup Marsala or sherry
  wine
¼ teaspoon dried orégano
¼ teaspoon garlic salt

Pound the veal scallops on both sides with a mallet. Dredge with the seasoned flour mixed with the cheese. Heat the oil and sauté the scallops until light brown. Mix lemon juice, bouillon, wine, orégano, and garlic salt. Add to meat, cover, and simmer very slowly for 30 minutes.

Serve with whipped or oven-roasted potatoes and fresh zucchini.

VEAL STEAK SMOTHERED IN ONIONS

MAKES 6 SERVINGS

2 pounds veal steak	Flour
2 red onions	¼ cup water
2 tablespoons oil	¼ cup red wine
Garlic salt and pepper	

Cut veal into serving pieces ¼ inch thick; cut onions into thin half slices. Sauté onions in 1 tablespoon of the oil and set aside. Rub some garlic salt and pepper into the veal steaks. Dredge with flour. Add another tablespoon of oil to the skillet and brown veal on both sides. Return onions to pan. Add the water and wine and reduce heat until the liquid is barely simmering. Cover and cook for 1 hour, or until tender.

Serve with whipped potatoes and parsleyed carrots.

VEAL STEAK MADEIRA

MAKES 4 SERVINGS

1 pound veal	1 tablespoon tomato paste
Flour (about 3 tablespoons)	½ cup chicken bouillon
2 tablespoons oil	½ cup Madeira wine
¼ teaspoon garlic salt	1 tablespoon dried parsley
¼ teaspoon pepper	flakes
¼ pound mushrooms, sliced	½ cup plain low-fat yogurt
2 small onions, sliced thin	(see note on next page)
¼ teaspoon dried marjoram	

Cut veal into slices ¼ inch thick. Dust veal slices with about 4 teaspoons of flour. Sauté them in 1 tablespoon of the oil. Season with garlic salt and pepper. Remove to a platter. Add another tablespoon of oil to the pan and sauté the mushrooms and onions. Stir in 1 tablespoon flour and then add the marjoram, tomato paste, bouillon, Madeira, and parsley flakes. Simmer uncovered for a few minutes. Return veal to the pan, cover, and cook very slowly for 30 to 40 minutes, or until tender. Transfer slices to a warm platter. Mix 2 teaspoons flour into the yogurt and add to the mixture in the pan, stirring until blended into a sauce. Pour sauce over veal.

Serve with a rice pilaf.

NOTE: Buttermilk can be used to replace the yogurt. If you use buttermilk, add 2 teaspoons lemon juice and stir in 4 teaspoons flour.

VEAL WITH SESAME-SEED SAUCE

MAKES 4 SERVINGS

1 pound veal
Flour (about 3 tablespoons)
2 tablespoons oil
1 onion, sliced
Juice and grated rind
    of ½ lemon
2 tablespoons sesame seeds
2 tablespoons sherry
½ cup beef bouillon
¼ teaspoon each of garlic
    salt, pepper, and paprika
¾ cup plain low-fat yogurt
    (see note below)
Macaroni, small elbows or
    shells, cooked

Cut veal into slices ¼ inch thick. Dredge slices with about 1 tablespoon of the flour and sauté in 1½ tablespoons of the oil until brown on both sides. Set aside. Add remaining oil and brown the onion. Stir in lemon juice and grated rind, sesame seeds, sherry, bouillon, and seasonings. Return veal to skillet and cover tightly. Simmer over lowest possible heat for 45 minutes, or until veal is tender. Transfer veal to a hot platter. Stir 2 tablespoons flour into the yogurt and add to the mixture in the pan. Blend well into a sauce and pour over the meat. Surround with hot cooked macaroni.

NOTE: Buttermilk can be used to replace the yogurt. Add the juice and grated rind of 1 lemon and stir in 3 tablespoons flour.

BARBECUED BRANDYWINE VEAL CUBES

MAKES 6 TO 8 SERVINGS

1½ to 2 pounds lean veal,
    cut into 2- to 3-inch cubes
¼ cup brandy
½ cup sherry
½ teaspoon dried tarragon
2 medium-sized onions, sliced
    thin

Fresh mushrooms
Fresh tomato quarters
¼ cup oil
Salt and pepper
4 medium-sized new
    potatoes, baked

Marinate the veal cubes in brandy, sherry, tarragon, and sliced onions for at least 2 hours, longer if possible. Be sure all the meat is immersed in marinade, and turn over from time to time.

Drain the marinade into another bowl 15 to 20 minutes before barbecuing. Toss into the marinade the mushrooms, tomato quarters, or any other vegetables you may want to use. Marinate them until ready to cook. Pour the oil over the meat cubes. Mix with a fork to be sure all sides are coated. Season with salt and pepper. Brush potato halves with oil. Alternate potatoes, veal cubes, and marinated vegetables on long skewers. Barbecue until meat is a delicate pink, unless you prefer it well done.

Meanwhile sauté the onions from the marinade in a little oil until delicately browned. Serve with meat along with an appropriate sauce.

If you use part of a roast for your veal cubes (p. 425), marinate the rest of the roast in the leftover marinade to give a delicate flavor to the finished roast. An easy method is to pour the marinade into a plastic bag with the veal, seal tightly, and refrigerate for 24 hours.

VEAL STROGANOFF CASSEROLE

A meal in one dish with beets and tiny little new potatoes.

MAKES 4 SERVINGS

1 tablespoon oil
1 tablespoon margarine
1 pound lean veal, cut into
1½-inch cubes
2 or 3 spring onions, chopped
1 can (16 ounces) tiny new
potatoes, drained

1 can (16 ounces) tiny whole
beets, drained
3 tablespoons flour
2 teaspoons curry powder
¼ teaspoon ground ginger
2 cups plain low-fat yogurt

Heat oil and margarine in a large skillet over medium heat and sauté the veal and onions until lightly browned. Arrange veal and onions in a large shallow casserole. Brown potatoes in the same skillet and add to casserole along with the beets. Blend the flour, curry powder, and ginger into the yogurt and pour over the meat and vegetables. Bake in a 325°F. oven for 1 hour.

Serve with dark bread and a tossed green salad.

VEAL CANTONESE

Molasses, ginger, and soy sauce combine to make an unusual sauce for this colorful dish. Lean beef or chicken can be substituted for the veal.

MAKES 4 SERVINGS

1 pound lean veal
2 teaspoons molasses
2 tablespoons white wine
4 tablespoons soy sauce
¼ teaspoon ground ginger
¼ teaspoon pepper
¾ cup chicken bouillon
½ cup pineapple juice
2 tablespoons cornstarch

1 tablespoon oil
1 medium-sized onion,
chopped
1 package (7 ounces) frozen
Chinese pea pods, thawed
1 cup canned pineapple
chunks with juice
¼ cup chopped pimiento

Slice veal across the grain into thin diagonal strips. Combine molasses, white wine, 2 tablespoons of the soy sauce, the ginger, and pepper, and marinate the veal strips in this mixture for at least 15 minutes.

Combine bouillon, pineapple juice, cornstarch, and remaining 2 tablespoons of soy sauce; stir until cornstarch is dissolved. Drain marinade from meat and combine the two liquid mixtures.

Heat the oil in a large skillet or frying pan. Sauté meat quickly on one side, turn, add onion, and continue to sauté for another 2 or 3 minutes. Add pea pods, pineapple chunks and juice, pimiento, and liquid mixture. Cover and steam for 2 to 4 minutes.

Serve over hot rice.

VEAL PAPRIKA I

For the hardy souls who like lots of paprika.

MAKES 6 TO 9 SERVINGS

4 tablespoons oil	½ garlic clove, minced
2 pounds veal, cut into 2-inch cubes	2 tablespoons paprika
	1 teaspoon salt
4 cups sliced onions (4 medium-sized onions)	½ teaspoon pepper
	2 cups bouillon
1 green pepper, seeded and chopped fine	2 tablespoons cornstarch
	3 tablespoons water

Heat 2 tablespoons of the oil in a heavy skillet and sauté the cubes of veal. Transfer them to a plate. Add remaining oil and brown the onions, green pepper, and garlic. Return meat to skillet. Add paprika, salt, pepper, and bouillon. Cover and simmer slowly for 2 hours.

Blend cornstarch with the water and stir into the meat. Cover and cook for 10 more minutes, until thickened. Adjust seasonings to taste, adding more paprika if desired.

Serve over riced potatoes or small shell macaroni.

VEAL PAPRIKA II

For those who like a milder dish, with yogurt and 2 teaspoons paprika.

MAKES 4 TO 6 SERVINGS

1½ pounds veal, cut into 2-inch cubes

½ cup plus 1½ tablespoons flour

1 teaspoon salt

½ teaspoon pepper

2 teaspoons paprika

3 tablespoons oil

1 large onion, quartered and sliced

¼ pound mushrooms, sliced

1 cup beef consommé or bouillon

¼ teaspoon garlic powder

1 cup yogurt

Dredge veal cubes with a mixture of ½ cup flour, the salt, pepper, and paprika. Sauté in 2 tablespoons of the oil until brown. Remove to a platter. Add remaining oil to skillet and brown onion and mushrooms. Return meat to pan and add the consommé and garlic powder. Cover, and simmer for 30 minutes, or until veal is tender. Remove meat and onions to a warm platter. Mix yogurt with 1½ tablespoons flour and add to skillet; mix well to make a sauce. Taste, and adjust seasonings. Pour sauce over meat.

Serve surrounded by potatoes, rice, or thin spaghetti.

SAUTÉED VEAL HASH

Leftovers from your weekly roast, of course! (See p. 425 for buying veal roasts.)

MAKES 6 SERVINGS

2 cups cooked veal
1 medium-sized yellow onion
1 large new potato, boiled
in the skin
½ green pepper
½ cup leftover gravy, stock,
or liquid skim milk

1 tablespoon parsley
flakes
2 teaspoons vinegar
Salt, pepper, garlic powder
2 tablespoons oil

Chop very fine or grind the veal, onion, unpeeled potato, and green pepper. Moisten the mixture with the gravy, and add the parsley and vinegar, and seasonings to taste. Turn this mixture into a hot skillet to which you have added the oil. Cover and cook over low heat for 10 minutes to partially cook the ingredients. Remove lid and sauté on both sides until nicely browned.

Serve the hash with tomato catsup.

SAUERBRATEN VEAL PATTIES

MAKES 4 SERVINGS

3 slices of bread
1 pound lean veal, ground
1 medium-sized onion, chopped fine
2 egg whites
1 teaspoon salt
1 tablespoon oil
1 tablespoon margarine

½ cup wine vinegar with garlic
1½ cups water
5 whole cloves
3 bay leaves
6 ginger snaps, crushed
8 ounces thin spaghetti

Mix first five ingredients and shape into four patties. Heat oil and margarine in a skillet and brown patties on both sides. Add vinegar, water, cloves, bay leaves, and ginger snaps. Simmer, covered, for 1 hour. Cook spaghetti according to directions; drain.

Serve spaghetti topped with meat patties and pour sauce over all.

SAUTÉED VEAL PATTIES WITH LEMON AND CAPERS

MAKES 8 SERVINGS

2 pounds lean veal, ground
2 tablespoons oil
Salt and pepper
3 cups sliced mushrooms
2 tablespoons flour
1 can (10½ ounces) condensed consommé

½ cup white wine
1 large lemon, halved lengthwise and sliced very thin
2 tablespoons capers (or more if you wish)

Shape the meat into eight patties. Brown them in 1 tablespoon of the oil until well done, seasoning with a little salt and pepper. Set aside and drain off all fat from the pan. Put remaining oil in the pan and sauté mushrooms for 2 or 3 minutes. Stir in the flour. Add the consommé and stir over low heat until thickened. Add wine, lemon slices, and capers. Return veal patties to skillet, baste with sauce, cover, and simmer gently for 10 minutes.

Serve with French-style green beans and whipped potatoes.

Beef, Lamb, Pork

HOW TO MAKE FAT-FREE GRAVIES

There are several ways to make fat-free gravies from meat drippings; of course, some are more efficient than others as far as removing the fat is concerned. The following methods apply both to cooking in the oven and on top of the stove.

Method 1. Here's the most effective way to make a gravy that is completely free of saturated fat. Start enough ahead of time so that the pan juices can be refrigerated until the fat hardens on top of the liquid. This solid fat can be easily skimmed off and discarded. This method is not very practical, however, when you want a rare roast or when cooking things quickly on top of the stove. In such cases, you can substitute Horseradish Cream Sauce (p. 299) for the gravy, or use method 2 or 3.

For stews and pot roasts, which can be prepared as much as a day ahead of time, or when cooking an oven roast, turkey, or large roasting chicken for an extended period of time, it is an ideal method. Here's how it works. For the last hour or so of cooking time, transfer the meat or fowl to a heatproof serving platter and return to oven. Put the original pan over low heat and quickly loosen the drippings with a little water; put the liquid in the freezer. When the fat has hardened, discard it. It is then easy to make a gravy with the defatted juices, beginning with a little oil and flour as if making a white sauce. Use 2 tablespoons each of oil and flour to 1 cup of the defatted juices to make a fairly thick gravy. The amount of oil can be halved if calories have to be watched. A small amount of bouillon granules or liquid concentrated gravy color and flavoring can be added.

Method 2. Transfer meat to another pan or plate when the cooking is finished. Pour off and throw away the liquid fat. Add water to the drippings and simmer on top of the stove, scraping the crusted meat drippings loose with a spatula. When done, tilt the pan and with a bulb baster extract the juices below the surface fat; use the defatted juices to make your gravy. If you transfer the juices to a small, fairly tall container, it will be even easier to avoid the fat.

Method 3. After the meat has cooked, transfer it from the pan it has cooked in to a platter or another pan and keep warm as desired. Pour off and discard all liquid in the pan. Then, with very hot water from your sink, quickly wash out remaining fat, leaving only the crusty meat drippings that stick to the pan. By now a considerable part of the fat will be gone. Once again, add more water, and with a spatula scrape together what remains in the pan. Add flour to thicken a little, or even oil and flour to reconstitute a complete gravy.

BARBECUED FLANK STEAK WITH SESAME-SEED STUFFING

MAKES 4 SERVINGS

1 to 1½ pounds flank steak	⅓ cup sesame seeds
1 medium-sized onion, chopped fine	2 teaspoons oil
	Salt and pepper
2 cups chopped celery with leaves	Soy sauce

Cut all fat from flank steak. If you want to have a larger but thinner steak, pound with a mallet.

Sauté onion, celery, and sesame seeds in the oil until vegetables are limp. Season. Use 6-inch metal skewers to secure sides of flank steak; fold the steak over, in envelope fashion, and pin sides together near edges. Fill cavity with as much of the stuffing as possible and fasten the open end with a final pin. Brush with soy sauce. Barbecue as you would any other meat. Turn to cook on both sides, and cook to the degree of doneness you prefer.

Cut slices across the grain to serve.

BEEF STROGANOFF WITH MUSHROOMS

This is very different from the Veal Stroganoff Casserole but it is equally tempting. Men are particularly enthusiastic.

MAKES 6 SERVINGS

1 tablespoon margarine
1 tablespoon oil
1½ to 2 pounds lean round steak, cut into thin strips
1 onion, sliced
2 small tomatoes, chopped
1 large can (8 ounces) mushrooms and juice

½ cup water
2½ tablespoons plain low-fat yogurt
2½ tablespoons flour
2 teaspoons curry powder

Heat margarine and oil in a heavy skillet and brown the beef strips. Add the onion and tomatoes and cook for a few minutes longer. Mix the mushrooms and juice, water, yogurt, flour, and curry powder until well blended and pour over meat. Simmer, covered, for 2 to 3 hours, until meat is tender.

Very good with wild rice.

CHINESE BEEF

MAKES 4 SERVINGS

3 or 4 green onions, chopped
1 large green pepper, sliced
1 large tomato, sliced
2 cups bean sprouts or shredded cabbage
3 tablespoons soy sauce
1 cup beef bouillon

1 tablespoon brown sugar
¼ teaspoon pepper
1 tablespoon cornstarch
1 pound lean beef
1 tablespoon oil
1 small piece of ginger root, minced

Prepare vegetables. Blend soy sauce, bouillon, sugar, pepper, and cornstarch. Set aside. Cut beef into thin strips, slicing across the grain.

Beef, Lamb, Pork   119

Heat oil in a heavy skillet; add meat and ginger root. Brown meat on both sides, about 3 minutes. Add onions and green pepper; cook and stir for another minute or two. Add tomato; cook for 1 minute. Add bean sprouts. Pour liquid mixture over all, cover, and simmer for 2 or 3 minutes.

Serve over hot steamed rice.

JAPANESE SUKIYAKI

MAKES 4 SERVINGS

1 pound lean round steak	1 tablespoon sugar
1 small bunch of green onions, chopped	⅓ cup water
2 cups diagonal slices of celery	1 tablespoon beef bouillon granules
½ pound mushrooms, sliced	2 tablespoons oil
1 tablespoon cornstarch	½ pound fresh spinach,
⅓ cup soy sauce	cleaned, with stems removed

Slice meat into diagonal strips, ¼ inch thick at the most, cutting across the grain. Dry with paper towels. Prepare vegetables. Combine cornstarch, soy sauce, sugar, water, and bouillon granules. Stir until dry ingredients are dissolved.

Heat oil in a large heavy frying pan. Sear meat strips on both sides, taking 1 or 2 minutes only. Push to one side. Add onions, celery, and mushrooms. Sauté quickly for 4 or 5 minutes, stirring briskly. Add the liquid mixture and stir to mix all ingredients. Place spinach on top, cover, and steam for 1 or 2 minutes to barely soften the spinach.

Serve over hot fluffy steamed rice with additional soy sauce.

HUNGARIAN GOULASH

Good fresh Hungarian paprika is the secret of a good goulash. This dish can also be made with veal.

MAKES 6 TO 8 SERVINGS

2 large onions, sliced thin
1 large green pepper, chopped
3 tablespoons butter-flavored oil
2 pounds lean beef, cubed
Flour
2 tablespoons paprika
½ teaspoon caraway seeds
1 teaspoon poppy seeds
Garlic salt and pepper
2 to 3 cups beef bouillon
4 ounces tomato paste
2 heaping tablespoons plain low-fat yogurt

Sauté onions and green pepper in oil until soft. Dredge the beef cubes with flour and add to onions and pepper; continue to cook until beef cubes are brown. Add seasonings, bouillon, and tomato paste. There should be just enough liquid to cover the meat. Simmer, covered, for 2 to 3 hours. Take off the heat and stir in the yogurt.

Serve with fresh green peas. If preferred, omit yogurt and add boiled small potatoes to the pot 15 minutes before serving.

CARBONNADES À LA FLAMANDE (BELGIAN BEEF STEW)

Braised beef and onions simmered in dark beer is a combination that is hard to surpass. Serve with parsley potatoes or some form of pasta.

MAKES 4 SERVINGS

1½ pounds lean beef, round or rump, all fat removed
Dijon-type mustard
Flour, salt, and pepper
2 to 3 tablespoons oil
2 or 3 large onions, sliced
1 tablespoon beef bouillon granules
1 tablespoon brown sugar
1 to 2 teaspoons wine vinegar
1 can (12 ounces) dark beer
1 tablespoon cornstarch (optional)

Spread both sides of beef with mustard. Cut beef into 1½- to 2-inch cubes and dredge with flour seasoned with salt and pepper. Heat 2 tablespoons oil in a skillet and sauté the beef cubes. When brown, set them aside. Add 1 tablespoon oil to skillet if needed and sauté the onion slices until limp. Drain off any excess oil. Return meat to the skillet. Combine bouillon granules, sugar, wine vinegar, and beer. Pour over the meat and onions. Simmer, covered, for 1½ to 2 hours, or until meat is tender. Strain off liquid and remove fat (p. 117). Thicken liquid if desired with the cornstarch mixed with 2 tablespoons cold water. Pour sauce over meat and onions.

SIRLOIN TIPS

MAKES 10 SERVINGS

6½- to 7-pound lean beef roast	2 cups chopped celery
4 to 5 tablespoons oil	2 cups sliced mushrooms
Flour	1 green pepper, chopped
4 to 5 cups water	2 onions, chopped
1 small onion, sliced	2 tomatoes, chopped
Salt and pepper	½ cup red wine

Remove all visible fat from meat. Heat 2 tablespoons of the oil in a large heavy pot. Sprinkle the roast with a little flour and brown in the oil on all sides; lower heat. Add the water and onion and a little salt and pepper. Cover and simmer on top of the stove or in a 325°F. oven for 2 to 3 hours.

When done, transfer roast to a platter, cool, and separate meat from bones. Strain the cooking liquid, chill, and discard hardened fat. Cut or shred meat into small pieces and return to original pot. Sauté vegetables in remaining oil and add to meat along with the wine and 1½ cups of the defatted cooking liquid. Simmer until vegetables are well done, adding more of the liquid from the roast as needed. The sauce should have a rich red-brown color.

Serve with rice; use remaining cooking liquid from the roast as liquid for cooking the rice.

BOEUF EN MIROTON

This ancient French dish has been described as "a sort of stew from leftover boiled beef." Actually it doesn't taste much like a stew at all.

Real beef stock from cooking meat adds much more flavor than canned bouillon or granules, so start out by braising a lean roast or thick slices of round steak with all visible fat removed. Use a reasonable quantity of water, 4 to 6 cups, and include an onion, celery, and other seasonings. When meat has finished cooking, remove only the fat and larger pieces of vegetable from the stock; do not strain. Use this stock to make the *miroton*, and cook rice in any beef stock that remains.

MAKES 8 SERVINGS

2 pounds cooked lean beef
4 large yellow onions
3½ tablespoons oil
1½ tablespoons flour
6 cups beef stock
1 tablespoon white vinegar
Salt and pepper

1 cup grated "part skim" milk cheese (see note below)
2 tablespoons Parmesan cheese
1½ cups uncooked long-grain rice

Slice the beef. Slice onions very thin and sauté in 1½ tablespoons of the oil until soft. Stir flour into onions, add 3 cups of the stock and the vinegar, and season with salt and pepper. Taste. You may want to add 1 more teaspoon of vinegar as vinegar gives this dish its unique flavor. Place beef slices in a greased shallow casserole. Pour the onion sauce over beef, and sprinkle on the cheeses. Bake in a 350°F. oven for about 30 minutes, until hot and bubbly.

Prepare rice as for a pilaf. Sauté in remaining 2 tablespoons oil, then cook slowly in the beef stock that remains. Add water to make 4 to 4½ cups liquid. Serve beef and sauce over the rice.

NOTE: Use 2 cups shredded processed vegetable-oil yellow cheese (p. 419), if you can find it, as a substitute for both cheeses.

HOW TO COOK GROUND BEEF

The best way to have fat-free ground beef is this: Carefully select a slice of round steak and have it specially ground for you by your butcher; ask him to trim off all the fat before grinding. Even a conscientious butcher, though, will leave a vestige of fat and, if he's careless, a great deal more than that. So it's helpful to know a technique for getting rid of the still remaining saturated fat.

As your meat will then be comparatively lean, always add a little oil to the skillet to keep the meat from sticking. When the oil is hot, add the ground round and cook as you usually do, stirring and breaking up the meat with a fork or spatula, until it is well done. Drain off all the liquid and add ¼ to ½ cup of water. Cover, and simmer over low heat for 3 to 4 minutes. Remove from the heat and drain again. Return the skillet to the stove and with only one side of the pan resting on a cool burner, leave the pan in a tilted position for another 3 to 4 minutes, pushing the meat with your spatula to the high side of the pan. Shortly, any remaining juice and fat will have drained to the lower side of the skillet and can be removed with a large spoon. Your meat should now be reasonably lean. If you wish to use the meat juices instead of throwing them away, use either Method 2 or 3 (p. 117) for making gravy.

BEEF-MACARONI CASSEROLE
WITH A GREEK FLAVOR

MAKES 8 SERVINGS

2 pounds lean beef, ground
2 medium-sized onions, chopped
3 tablespoons oil
1 teaspoon salt
½ teaspoon pepper
½ teaspoon ground cinnamon
½ teaspoon dried orégano

3 cans (8 ounces each) tomato sauce
½ pound macaroni
½ cup Cheese Crumbs (p. 304)
4 egg whites
2 cups liquid skim milk
½ cup dry skim milk

Brown meat and onions in 2 tablespoons of the oil. Add salt, pepper, cinnamon, orégano, and tomato sauce. Simmer for 30 minutes, stirring occasionally.

Cook macaroni according to directions (p. 146). Arrange half of the macaroni in a greased baking dish and cover with half of the meat mixture. Sprinkle with half of cheese crumbs. Repeat. Whip egg whites lightly in a small bowl. Mix in liquid and dry milk and remaining tablespoon of oil. Pour this over macaroni-meat mixture, separating with a fork so that custard will penetrate to the bottom. Cover; bake in a 400°F. oven for 30 minutes. Lower heat to 350°F. and bake for another 30 to 40 minutes, until custard is set.

If any of the casserole is left over, use it to make Jiffy Eggplant Casserole (below).

JIFFY EGGPLANT CASSEROLE

This casserole calls for leftovers from the preceding recipe, Beef-Macaroni Casserole with a Greek Flavor. It could be used equally well with any meat and pasta leftovers you feel like dressing up for another meal. The addition of eggplant produces a dish with a new accent.

Use eggplant slices ½ inch thick. Oil the slices, season with salt and pepper, and place on a baking sheet. Broil on both sides until slightly browned. Place on the bottom of a greased casserole dish. Cover with any amount of leftover beef-macaroni casserole and sprinkle with ample amounts of cheese crumbs. Bake in a 350°F. oven for 25 to 30 minutes, until bubbly and hot.

MOUSSAKA À LA GRECQUE

A Balkan meat pie with a delicious flavor! It is somewhat elaborate to prepare, but worth every second of the time. Serve with steamed rice or bulghur (cracked wheat), a green salad, and hard-crusted bread. Or just serve with salad and bread. The preparation is divided into four parts: eggplant, meat sauce, custard, and crumb and cheese mixture. All are put together at the end and baked to a golden brown. Originally from my friend Mary Stroll.

MAKES 8 SERVINGS

Eggplant

2 large eggplants   1 to 2 tablespoons oil
Salt

Peel eggplants and cut crosswise into slices ½ inch thick. Salt both sides lightly and set aside for 30 minutes while preparing meat and custard sauce. When eggplant has "sweated," wipe the water from it with paper towels, brush both sides with oil, and broil in the oven until lightly browned on both sides. Set aside.

Meat Sauce

If you have leftover spaghetti sauce made with meat, you'll save considerable time. To 3 or 4 cups of the sauce, add ½ cup red wine, ½ cup chopped parsley, and ¼ teaspoon ground cinnamon. Simmer until almost all liquid has been absorbed. If you're starting from scratch, make the following sauce.

1 to 2 tablespoons oil	1 can (8 ounces) tomato
2 large onions, chopped fine	sauce
1½ pounds lean beef round,	½ cup chopped parsley
ground	¼ teaspoon ground cinnamon
½ cup red wine	Salt and pepper

Heat oil in a skillet and sauté onions until golden. Set aside. Brown meat in the same skillet, crumbling with a fork. Remove fat (p. 124). Combine sautéed onions and meat, the wine, tomato sauce, parsley, cinnamon, and salt and pepper to taste. Simmer over low heat, stirring often, until almost all liquid has been absorbed.

Custard

3 tablespoons oil	⅛ teaspoon grated nutmeg
4 tablespoons flour	Salt and pepper
3 cups liquid skim milk	1 cup low-fat cottage cheese
2 drops of yellow food coloring	6 egg whites, beaten until frothy

Heat oil in a small saucepan. Blend in the flour. Gradually add skim milk, stirring with a wire whisk, and cook slowly until the sauce is thick and smooth. Remove from the heat and add yellow food coloring and nutmeg. Season with salt and pepper to taste. Stir in the cottage cheese and egg whites.

Crumb and Cheese Mixture

1 tablespoon grated Sap Sago cheese	½ cup fine bread crumbs

Mix together in a small bowl.

To ASSEMBLE THE DISH: Oil a rectangular 2-quart baking pan and sprinkle with some of the crumb mixture. Make alternate layers of eggplant slices and meat sauce, sprinkling each layer with some of the crumb mixture. Pour custard over the top, separating the ingredients a little with a fork so that custard runs through. Bake in a 375°F. oven for 1 hour, until golden brown. Turn oven to lower heat if *moussaka* becomes too dark.

Cool for 10 minutes. Cut into squares and serve.

SPEEDY GROUND BEEF CASSEROLE

Try this one when you're really pressed for time.

MAKES 4 SERVINGS

½ cup uncooked white rice
2 large onions, peeled and
sliced
1 tablespoon oil
1 pound lean beef round,
ground

Salt and pepper
1 can (16 ounces) green
beans with juice
1 teaspoon beef bouillon
granules

Spread rice on the bottom of a greased casserole dish. Cook onions in the oil until tender, and spoon over rice. Brown the meat, seasoning with salt and pepper. Remove fat (p. 124) and add meat to casserole. Drain beans and measure liquid. Add enough water to make 1 cup and stir in the bouillon granules. Place beans over meat and pour liquid over all. Bake, covered, in a 350°F. oven for 30 to 40 minutes.

STUFFED AUBERGINE

Aubergine is the name for eggplant in England and France; it's fun to upstage your friends occasionally with a different name for an old favorite. Eggplant is one of the oldest known vegetables; it is believed to have originated in southern Asia. There are hundreds of recipes for this vegetable; this is one of the simplest.

MAKES 2 SERVINGS

1 medium-sized eggplant
1 tablespoon oil
1 small onion, chopped
½ pound lean beef round,
ground
1 cup cooked rice
1 can (6 ounces) tomato sauce

½ teaspoon garlic powder
½ teaspoon ground cinnamon
¼ teaspoon grated Sap
Sago cheese
Salt and pepper
¼ cup Cheese Crumbs
(p. 304)

Cut eggplant lengthwise into halves and cut the flat surfaces with a crisscross pattern ½ inch deep. Heat about half of the oil and in it place the eggplant, cut side down. Sauté very slowly until soft but not mushy, for 10 to 15 minutes. Remove to a platter. Brown the onion and ground beef in the same pan, adding a little oil as needed, until meat is cooked through. Drain off fat.

Remove pulp of eggplant to within ½ inch of the skin. Mash the pulp and add to meat mixture. Add remaining ingredients except cheese crumbs and season to taste. Simmer for a few minutes. When mixture is well blended and sauce somewhat reduced, fill eggplant cavities; sprinkle with cheese crumbs. Place in a shallow baking dish and bake in a 350°F. oven for 30 to 40 minutes.

SPINACH MEAT LOAF

MAKES 4 TO 6 SERVINGS

1 package (10 ounces) frozen chopped spinach	2 egg whites
¼ cup dried minced onion	½ cup toasted bread or cracker crumbs
¼ cup liquid skim milk	¼ teaspoon garlic powder
1½ pounds lean beef, ground	1 teaspoon salt
1 medium-sized tomato, chopped	½ teaspoon pepper
	1 cup beef bouillon

Let the spinach thaw partially. Soak dried minced onion in skim milk. Cook spinach according to package directions. Combine onion, spinach, beef, tomato, egg whites, crumbs, and seasoning; mix well. Form into an oval shape and place in an oiled baking pan. Pour ¼ cup bouillon over top. Bake in a 350°F. oven for 1 hour. Add remaining ¾ cup bouillon as moisture evaporates.

Serve with Whipped Potatoes (p. 234) or Spanish Rice with Chile-tepín (p. 242) or Bulghur Pilaf (p. 244).

GOURMET MEAT LOAF

Elegant enough for guests, and very simple to prepare. The original version came from Gourmet *magazine.*

MAKES 10 SERVINGS

3 pounds lean beef round, ground
2 tablespoons minced onion
1 tablespoon minced parsley
1 garlic clove, minced
½ cup dry bread crumbs or wheat germ

3 egg whites, lightly beaten
3 tablespoons oil
8 to 10 medium-sized or small onions, parboiled and peeled
1 cup tomato purée
2 cups red wine
16 large mushrooms

Mix the first seven ingredients well. Shape into an oblong loaf 2 inches high and place in a large shallow casserole dish. Surround with the onions. Blend the tomato purée and wine and pour about half over the loaf. Bake, uncovered, in a 350°F. oven for 1½ hours. Add the mushrooms for the last 30 minutes of cooking. Baste often, adding additional sauce as needed. There should be a generous amount of sauce to serve with the meat and vegetables.

Serve in the casserole dish with baked small new potatoes and a tossed green salad.

LEMON-RIND MEAT LOAF BAKED IN BROWN PAPER

An old family recipe that has been popular for many generations.

MAKES 6 SERVINGS

2 pounds very lean beef round, ground
½ cup bread crumbs
Grated rind of 1 large lemon
½ cup chopped fresh parsley
1 teaspoon salt

1 teaspoon pepper
2 egg whites
2 tablespoons oil
Juice of 1 large lemon
¼ cup water

Mix all the ingredients except lemon juice and water. Mold into an oblong shape.

Cut a brown paper bag down the sides to make a flat sheet. Then cut out a rectangle large enough to wrap around the meat loaf, allowing for an inch overlap at the fold and a little to tuck under both ends. Oil the paper lavishly. Wrap it around the meat loaf with the oiled side against the meat. Place the package in a greased baking pan with the sealed edge on the bottom and the ends tucked underneath. Pour lemon juice plus ¼ cup water over the top of wrapped meat loaf. Bake in a 350° F. oven for 1 hour. Baste frequently; add water or more lemon juice if pan becomes dry.

Remove from paper when done and serve on a platter. Add a little water to the pan and scrape up juices. Use a bulb baster to extract juices (thereby avoiding the fat) and pour them over meat loaf.

Serve with Spanish Rice with Chiletepín (p. 242) or Simple Rice Pilaf (p. 238).

PEPPERS FILLED WITH MEAT AND RICE

Almost anything can go into a stuffed pepper. Here is a basic recipe for a meat and rice stuffing for 4 peppers. You can experiment and add whatever other ingredients you like. Instead of beef, you can use veal, chicken, or fish.

MAKES 4 SERVINGS

4 large peppers
2 tablespoons plus 1 teaspoon oil
2 medium-sized onions, chopped
2 cups cooked beef, ground or chopped
½ cup beef bouillon
¼ teaspoon garlic powder

½ teaspoon each of salt and pepper
2 cups cooked rice, macaroni, or potatoes
¼ cup bread crumbs
1 teaspoon grated Sap Sago cheese
½ cup water

Cut off tops of peppers and remove seeds. Parboil peppers for 5 minutes. Heat 2 tablespoons oil in a skillet and brown onions. Add beef, bouillon, and seasonings. Simmer, covered, for 5 minutes, until meat is soft and moist. Mix in the rice or other starch. Fill peppers. Mix crumbs, 1 teaspoon oil, and cheese. Sprinkle crumb mixture over tops of peppers. Place peppers in a flat baking dish and pour ½ cup water around them. Bake in a 350°F. oven until well heated, about 20 minutes.

BEEF-STUFFED CABBAGE LEAVES

A particularly good recipe for this familiar dish. Start well enough ahead of time so as to be able to refrigerate the meat juices and discard the fat (see p. 124).

MAKES 6 SERVINGS

1 large head of cabbage	2 egg whites
1 cup boiling water	1 teaspoon salt
½ cup uncooked white rice	1 teaspoon pepper
1½ pounds lean beef round, ground	1 small onion, chopped fine
1 tablespoon oil	1 to 2 tablespoons grated lemon rind
Salt	Tomato-Yogurt Sauce
¼ cup water	(p .133)

Cut out the thick cabbage core. Place the head, stem end down, in a large saucepan of boiling water so that water covers about half of the head. Simmer for 2 or 3 minutes, until leaves are partially softened. Remove the cabbage head and gently pull off the leaves. Set them aside to cool.

Pour the cup of boiling water over the rice and set aside for 15 minutes.

Brown the meat in the oil, crumbling it with a spatula. Season with salt. When meat is cooked through, add ¼ cup water, cover, and simmer for 2 or 3 minutes. Drain off the liquid and place it in the freezer. Remove fat when hardened; save the meat juices.

In a large bowl combine drained rice, meat and juices, egg whites, 1 teaspoon salt, the pepper, onion, and lemon rind. Place a heaping tablespoon of the mixture in the center of each cabbage leaf; use more in the larger leaves. Fold ends toward the center and roll up. Arrange in a greased ovenproof baking dish so that rolls fit snugly together. Chop up any leftover cabbage and spread over the stuffed leaves. Pour the sauce over all and bake in a 350°F. oven for about 1 hour.

These can also be cooked in a large heavy skillet with a lid on top of the stove; simmer for about 45 minutes.

Tomato-Yogurt Sauce

1 tablespoon flour
1 cup plain low-fat yogurt or
  buttermilk (see note below)
1 can (16 ounces) stewed
  tomatoes

2 tablespoons lemon juice
2 teaspoons grated Sap
  Sago cheese

Blend flour with yogurt. Combine with other ingredients.

NOTE: If you are using buttermilk, increase flour to 1½ tablespoons and lemon juice to 3 tablespoons.

SWEET-SOUR MEATBALLS

MAKES 8 SERVINGS

2 pounds lean beef, ground
1 cup bread crumbs
¼ cup chopped pimientos
¼ cup chopped onion
6 tablespoons water
½ teaspoon each of salt
  and pepper

Pinch each of grated nutmeg
  and dried thyme
4 large onions
3 tablespoons oil
¼ cup brown sugar
½ teaspoon dry mustard
¼ cup vinegar

Combine meat, crumbs, pimientos, chopped onion, 4 tablespoons water, and the seasonings. Shape into 2-inch balls. Cut the 4 large onions into ¼-inch slices and sauté in 2 tablespoons of the oil until golden. Remove to a platter. Add remaining 1 tablespoon oil to the skillet and sauté the meatballs on all sides until brown. Return onion slices to the pan. Stir brown sugar, mustard, vinegar, and 2 tablespoons water together and pour over meat and onions. Simmer, covered, for about 30 minutes.

Serve meatballs over steamed white rice or a platter of shell macaroni. Accompany with a dish of sautéed and steamed Chinese pea pods and bean sprouts, seasoned with soy sauce.

TACOS, HOME STYLE

This favorite simple supper doesn't taste like Mexico, but no one complains. We usually buy wheat tortillas, often labeled flour tortillas, but those made with cornmeal are just as good. Prepare 1 flour or 2 cornmeal tortillas per person (flour tortillas are larger), but don't be surprised if you get a reorder.

MAKES 4 SERVINGS

4 flour tortillas
3 to 4 tablespoons oil
2 medium-sized onions, chopped
1 pound lean beef round, ground
¼ teaspoon ground cuminseed
Garlic salt and pepper

1 small can (8 ounces) Mexican hot sauce, red chili sauce, or taco and enchilada sauce
1 large tomato, chopped
¼ head of iceberg lettuce, shredded
Grated Parmesan or Sap Sago cheese (see note below)

Heat 1 tablespoon of the oil in a skillet and sauté onions until golden. Transfer to a medium-sized saucepan. Brown beef in the same pan. Stir and break up with a spatula until crumbly and well done. Drain off excess fat. Season with the cuminseed, and garlic salt and pepper to taste. Add to onions. Clean the skillet. Mix the hot sauce

134   Beef, Lamb, Pork

with an equal amount of water. Pour about a quarter of the sauce into the meat-onion mixture and pour the remainder into a small saucepan. Cover both saucepans and keep warm on back of the stove.

Add 2 to 3 tablespoons oil to the skillet and heat to a moderate temperature. Slip in the tortillas, gently folding them over so the edges meet. Cook on each side until golden and fairly crispy, using forks to turn them over.

Place a tortilla on each plate, gently spread open, and fill amply with part of the meat mixture, a heaping spoonful of chopped tomato, and a handful of shredded lettuce. Fold over again. Serve the hot sauce and grated cheese at the table. A tossed romaine salad and some Refritos (p. 143) go well with this.

NOTE: If you use grated Parmesan cheese, limit it to 1 teaspoon per person.

LAMB SHISH KEBAB

The marinade seems especially suited to the flavor of lamb, so no vegetables have been included. However, zucchini might be a good addition; cut it into 1-inch lengths and marinate it along with the lamb. For fewer servings, lamb shoulder will do well.

MAKES 8 SERVINGS

1 leg of lamb, 5 to 6 pounds	1 teaspoon dried orégano
½ pound onions, sliced	1 teaspoon salt
⅓ cup dry sherry	½ teaspoon pepper
2 tablespoons oil	

Remove all fat and bones from the lamb and cut the meat into 1-inch cubes; or ask your butcher to do it. Combine the other ingredients to make a marinade and let the lamb cubes marinate for 6 hours or more.

Thread cubes on skewers and barbecue or broil.

Serve over rice pilaf. You can sauté some of the onions from the marinade and add to the rice.

BARBECUED PORK TENDERLOIN CHARCUTIÈRE

Lean pork chops can be selected instead of the tenderloin, but there is no substitute for the charcoal flavor imparted by an open fire. While the fire is being built up, start the sauce.

MAKES 4 SERVINGS

1 to 1½ pounds pork tenderloin, or 4 loin pork chops
  ¾ inch thick
2 large yellow onions
2 tablespoons oil
2 tablespoons flour
1½ teaspoons prepared
  mustard
¼ teaspoon prepared
  horseradish
1 can (10½ ounces)
  condensed consommé,
  undiluted
½ cup dry white wine
Coarse-ground black pepper

Trim all fat from pork. Barbecue until completely cooked throughout. Meanwhile make the sauce. Peel the onions, halve, and slice very thin. Sauté slices in the oil until golden. With the heat at a low temperature, stir in the flour, mustard, and horseradish. Add the consommé, wine, and pepper to taste; stir until thickened. Transfer, if desired, to a small saucepan and simmer over low heat for 30 minutes. Adjust seasonings before serving with the pork.

HAM BALI

An inexpensive and delicious company dish. This will solve the problem of how to use up leftover ham.

MAKES 4 SERVINGS

2 cups lean cooked ham,
  cut into thin strips
2 tablespoons oil
1 cup diced celery
1 large onion, chopped
1 teaspoon curry powder
1 can (9 ounces) pineapple
  tidbits

1 package (10 ounces) frozen
  French-style green beans
1 tablespoon cornstarch
½ cup orange juice
1 can (5 ounces) water
  chestnuts, sliced

Remove all visible fat from ham before cutting into strips. Repeat after slicing. To further remove fat, heat 1 tablespoon of the oil in a skillet and sauté the ham strips for a few minutes. Add ½ cup water, cover, and simmer slowly for 3 to 5 minutes. Remove from heat and drain off all fat and liquid. Transfer ham to a separate platter.

Heat remaining tablespoon of oil in the skillet and sauté the celery and onion lightly. Blend in the curry powder. Drain syrup from pineapple and add enough water to make 1 cup. Add this liquid to the celery and onion along with green beans. Cover, and cook gently for 10 minutes. Combine cornstarch and orange juice. Stir into vegetables and continue to simmer for 1 or 2 minutes, stirring constantly as mixture thickens. Add pineapple, water chestnuts, and ham strips. Simmer for another few minutes until well heated.

Serve over steamed rice.

SKILLET HAM WITH VEGETABLES, BROWN SUGAR, AND ORANGE RICE

Here is another way to use leftover ham. Vegetables and rice keep the amount of ham per portion fairly low.

MAKES 4 SERVINGS

2 cups diced cooked lean ham
2 tablespoons oil
1 red pepper, seeded and chopped
1 large onion, chopped
2 tablespoons brown sugar
½ teaspoon salt
⅛ teaspoon dry mustard
½ cup orange juice
1 tablespoon grated orange rind
2 cups cooked rice

Remove all fat from the ham as in Ham Bali (p. 137). Use 1 tablespoon of the oil for this. Set ham aside. Sauté pepper and onion in remaining oil until tender. Add all other ingredients, cover, and simmer for 10 minutes, until hot.

Dried Bean Dishes,
Pasta Dishes

BEAN TOMATO BAKE

2 cans (16 ounces each) red
  kidney beans
1 large onion, chopped
½ garlic clove, minced
1 cup chopped celery
1 can (16 ounces) tomatoes,
  drained

2 tablespoons oil
2 tablespoons imitation bacon
  bits (p. 430)
2 tablespoons packaged chili
  seasoning mix (no fat added)

Combine all ingredients and bake in a 350°F. oven for 2 hours.
Remove cover after first hour to let a crust form on top.

CHILI BEANS WITH OLIVES

Mostly a matter of opening up cans, but the results are quite satisfying.

MAKES 6 TO 8 SERVINGS

1 large onion, chopped
1 tablespoon oil
1 can (16 ounces) light red kidney beans
1 can (16 ounces) dark red kidney beans
1 can (4 ounces) chopped ripe olives

1 can (6 ounces) tomato sauce
¾ cup water
3 tablespoons packaged chili seasoning mix (no fat added)
1 teaspoon grated Sap Sago cheese

Sauté onion in oil until limp. Add all other ingredients, mix well, and simmer until bubbly and hot. Add extra chili powder to taste.

A small can of whole-kernel corn can be added for variety.

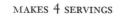

EASY CHILI BEANS

MAKES 4 SERVINGS

1 can (16 ounces) red kidney beans

2 cups Italian Spaghetti Sauce (p. 301)

Simmer together for 30 minutes.

EASY CHILI SIZE

Make meat cakes with ground beef round; sauté them and remove fat (p. 124). Heat Easy Chili Beans. Split and toast hamburger buns. Place meat cakes on split buns. Pour sauce and beans over all.

BEAN AND APPLE-BUTTER BAKE

MAKES 6 SERVINGS

2 cans (16 ounces each) pinto
   beans with juice
½ cup apple butter, or 1
   chopped apple, 2 tablespoons brown sugar, and ½
   teaspoon ground cinnamon

1 large onion, chopped
2 tablespoons imitation bacon
   bits (p. 430)
2 tablespoons oil

Combine all ingredients in a greased ovenproof baking dish. Bake in a 325°F. oven for 2 to 3 hours, uncovering for the last hour to allow a crusty topping to form.

FRIJOLES OR REFRITOS

A Mexican meal is incomplete without a few fried beans. They are generally fried and often refried in bacon fat, which of course is off limits for us. However, the flavor is well simulated by using imitation bacon bits.

MAKES 4 SERVINGS

1½ tablespoons oil
1 medium-sized onion,
   chopped fine
1 tablespoon imitation bacon
   bits (p. 430)

1 can (15 ounces) pinto or
   light red kidney beans
   with juice

Heat oil in a medium-sized nonstick pan. Fry onion and bacon bits in the oil until onion is slightly browned. Drain the beans and set aside half of the juice. Mash the beans with a fork or potato masher and add to the onion. Fry the bean cake slowly on one side until crusty and brown. Turn over with a spatula and brown slowly on the other side, adding a little of the bean juice to keep moist. When crusty on both sides, pour remaining juice around the outside edges, cover with a lid, and let steam for a few minutes to add additional moisture. The heat may be turned off at this point.

TOSTADAS

In Mexico fried beans are a common accompaniment to other dishes, but they can be made into the primary attraction in a superbly satisfying inexpensive meal. For this occasion I have included a very small amount of avocado and Parmesan cheese. However, some may prefer Sap Sago to Parmesan and may wish to eliminate the avocado because it is high in calories.

MAKES 2 SERVINGS

1 recipe Frijoles (p. 143)
3 or 4 slices, ⅛ inch, processed vegetable-oil cheese (p. 419)
2 flour tortillas
2 tablespoons oil

¼ avocado, sliced very thin
Shredded lettuce
Diced tomato
2 teaspoons grated Parmesan or Sap Sago cheese

Cook *frijoles* according to instructions. When crusty on both sides, place cheese slices on top and cover. Keep warm. Sauté the tortillas in the oil until lightly browned on both sides. Do not fold. One may be kept warm in the oven while the second is being cooked. When ready, spread beans over tortillas, being careful to keep the cheese on top. Add avocado slices. Sprinkle with shredded lettuce, diced tomato, and grated cheese.

Serve with beer or dry red wine.

BAKED SOYBEANS WITH SHERRY

This dish is rich in protein.

MAKES 6 SERVINGS

1 cup dried soybeans
3 to 4 cups water
1 teaspoon salt
1 small onion, chopped
¼ cup sherry
2 tablespoons catsup

1 tablespoon molasses
1 tablespoon brown sugar
2 tablespoons oil
¼ to ½ cup shredded dried beef

Cover beans with the water and soak for 2 hours. Add more water if necessary to keep well covered. Freeze overnight in the same container with the soaking water.

Place beans and water in a *large* saucepan (they tend to boil over). Add salt, bring slowly to a boil, and simmer for 2 to 3 hours, until soft. Add more water as necessary. Add all other ingredients. Bake in an ovenproof beanpot for 6 to 8 hours, or longer. Remove the cover for the last hour or two to form a crust on the top.

These can be baked overnight instead, to be ready for breakfast in the morning. Longer cooking doesn't hurt.

BAKED BEANS WITH VEAL

You won't believe it until you've tried it, but these beans make for pretty happy eating. Smoky sauce substitutes for the flavor of salt pork.

MAKES 6 SERVINGS

1 cup dried navy beans	½ teaspoon smoky sauce
1 teaspoon salt	4 tablespoons oil
3 tablespoons catsup	1 large yellow onion, sliced
2 tablespoons molasses	½ pound veal, cut into
1 tablespoon dark brown sugar	½-inch cubes
2 teaspoons dry mustard	

Soak beans in water overnight. The next morning simmer beans in the soaking water with the salt for 2 to 2½ hours, adding more water as necessary. Place beans with water in a deep casserole. Stir in all other ingredients; cover. Bake in a 300°F. oven for 6 hours. Uncover for the last 1½ hours to let a crust form on the top.

CHILI CON CARNE

Nothing more satisfying than a bowl of hot homemade chili! Some people go so far as to have it for breakfast if there happens to be any left over.

1 large or 2 small onions, chopped	1 tablespoon chili powder
1 garlic clove, minced	1 teaspoon ground cuminseed
2 tablespoons oil	1 teaspoon dried orégano
1 pound veal or lean beef, cut into 1-inch pieces	1 tablespoon flour
1 teaspoon salt	1 can (16 ounces) tomatoes
	1 can (16 ounces) red kidney beans (optional)

Brown onions and garlic in the oil until golden. Set aside. Brown meat in the same pan, adding an extra tablespoon of oil if necessary. Combine salt, chili powder, cuminseed, orégano, and flour in a small bowl, and stir the mixture into the meat. Return onions to the pan; add tomatoes and beans. Simmer gently for 2 to 3 hours. Taste after 1 hour and add more chili powder if desired.

How to Cook Pasta

For 2 cups pasta use 2 cups water. If you are cooking long thin pasta like spaghetti, break it into lengths so it can be measured. Bring the water to a brisk boil and add the pasta gradually so as to keep the water at a constant boil. Add salt. When all the pasta has been added, lower the heat to medium and cook, covered, until the water has been absorbed and the pasta is tender, which should happen at about the same time. If necessary, add a little extra water. (If all the water is absorbed, the vitamins are retained and not thrown out with the excess water.) The pasta will not be sticky and does not need to be washed. Do not overcook. Pasta should be firm, not mushy. If it has to wait for a while, add 1 to 2 teaspoons oil to keep the pieces from sticking together.

ITALIAN SPAGHETTI

Cook spaghetti by above method and pour Italian Spaghetti Sauce (p. 301) over the top. Sprinkle with grated Sap Sago cheese or a small amount of grated Parmesan cheese.

VERMICELLI ROMANOFF WITH POPPY SEEDS

MAKES 4 TO 6 SERVINGS

6 ounces vermicelli
1 tablespoon flour
¾ cup plain low-fat yogurt
¾ cup whipped or low-fat cottage cheese
¼ cup chopped chives
¼ teaspoon pepper

¼ teaspoon garlic salt
1 tablespoon dry white wine
1 tablespoon poppy seeds
1 teaspoon Worcestershire sauce
¼ cup Cheese Crumbs (p. 304)

Cook vermicelli until just *al dente*, drain, and keep hot. Blend flour with yogurt and add to vermicelli with all other ingredients except cheese crumbs. Mix gently with a fork. Place in a greased 2-quart baking dish and sprinkle with cheese crumbs. Bake in a 350°F. oven for 40 minutes.

MACARONI AND CHEESE

MAKES 8 SERVINGS

4 cups cooked macaroni
2 cups dry-curd or rinsed cottage cheese
¼ cup chopped pimiento
2 cups Sap Sago Sauce (p. 293)

½ package (10-ounce size) frozen peas, cooked and drained
½ cup Sesame Crumbs (p. 304)

Combine drained cooked macaroni with other ingredients except crumbs and pour into a greased casserole. Sprinkle on crumbs. Bake in a 350°F. oven for 40 to 50 minutes, until bubbly and hot.

Dried Bean Dishes, Pasta Dishes   147

MACARONI AND TUNA CASSEROLE

MAKES 8 SERVINGS

4 cups cooked macaroni
1 can (7 ounces) water-
   packed tuna, drained
1 onion, chopped
1 green pepper, chopped
2 tablespoons oil

Salt and pepper
3 tablespoons flour
2 cups liquid skim milk
½ cup dry skim milk
2 tablespoons sherry

Drain macaroni. Break up tuna with a fork. Sauté onion and pepper in oil until limp; season with salt and pepper to taste. Stir in flour and blend well. Add liquid and dry skim milk gradually, and continue to cook over low heat, stirring until dry milk is dissolved and the sauce is thickened. Add sherry, tuna, and macaroni and pour into a greased baking dish. Bake in a 350°F. oven for 25 to 35 minutes.

MACARONI WITH MUSHROOMS AND TOMATOES

MAKES 8 SERVINGS

4 cups cooked macaroni
2 cans (16 ounces each)
   stewed tomatoes
½ pound fresh mushrooms,
   sliced
2 tablespoons oil
1 tablespoon grated Sap Sago
   cheese

1 teaspoon each of
   Worcestershire sauce
   and prepared mustard
2 tablespoons chopped chives
1 cup Cheese Crumbs
   (p. 304)

Drain cooked macaroni and place in a greased casserole with the tomatoes. Sauté mushrooms in oil for a few minutes. Add to macaroni, along with cheese, seasonings, chives, and ½ cup of the cheese crumbs. Mix ingredients together and top with remaining cheese crumbs. Bake in a 350°F. oven for 40 to 45 minutes, or until moisture has been absorbed and crust is golden brown.

EASY LASAGNE

Be sure to buy lasagne noodles without egg yolks. If unavailable, use large shell macaroni or wide noodles made without egg yolks.

MAKES 6 SERVINGS

4 ounces lasagne noodles
3 cups Italian Spaghetti Sauce (p. 301), made with meat
2 cups dry-curd or rinsed cottage cheese

2 tablespoons grated Parmesan cheese, or 1 tablespoon grated Sap Sago cheese, or both mixed

Cook noodles until *al dente*. Make alternate layers of sauce, noodles, and cheeses in a shallow 1½-quart baking dish. Bake in a 350°F. oven for about 20 minutes.

CANNELLONI

An Italian dish made of tubular pasta squares stuffed with meat and spinach, topped with tomato sauce. As with most Italian dishes, garlic and olive oil are essential flavors, but only a little of both is used in this recipe. It is possible to make your own pasta but simpler to buy manicotti or rigatoni pasta tubes. Allow 2 large manicotti per person, more of the smaller rigatoni for a serving. This is a very good company dish as it can be prepared a day or two in advance.

MAKES 6 SERVINGS

First make the filling.

1 package (10 ounces) frozen leaf spinach
1 garlic clove, minced
1 medium-sized onion, chopped
1 tablespoon olive oil

1 tablespoon regular oil
1 pound lean beef round, ground
½ teaspoon dried orégano
1 teaspoon salt
½ teaspoon pepper

Dried Bean Dishes, Pasta Dishes 149

Let spinach thaw for 30 minutes or more. Cook according to directions; be sure not to overcook, for that spoils color and flavor. Chop into large pieces.

Sauté garlic and onion in oils for a few minutes. Add ground beef. Brown the meat, breaking it up with a fork. Drain off fat. Add seasonings and spinach. Set aside.

Now make the sauce.

1 garlic clove, minced	1 can (6 ounces) tomato paste
1 large onion, chopped	1 can (6 ounces) tomato sauce
1 tablespoon olive oil	½ cup red wine
1 tablespoon regular oil	1 teaspoon dried basil
½ cup chopped fresh parsley, or 2 tablespoons dried	1 teaspoon salt
2 cans (16 ounces each) peeled plum tomatoes	½ teaspoon pepper

Sauté garlic and onion in oils until limp. Add all other ingredients. Simmer uncovered, stirring all the time, for 20 to 30 minutes, or until thickened.

Grease a shallow baking dish and pour a little of the hot sauce on the bottom before adding the stuffed pasta. Now you can proceed in either of the following ways.

12 manicotti, or about 24 rigatoni	½ cup beef bouillon (for method 1)
1 cup dry-curd or low-fat cottage cheese (optional)	

I. Fill *uncooked* manicotti or rigatoni with meat and spinach filling. Place the pasta in the prepared baking dish with extra filling tucked among them. Spread cottage cheese over manicotti. Add bouillon to remaining sauce, and pour hot sauce over manicotti to cover them completely. Spread aluminum foil over the baking dish and seal edges. Bake in a 350°F. oven for 40 minutes. Uncover, and bake for another 5 to 10 minutes, until slightly crusty on top. These manicotti will double in size when cooked.

II. Parboil manicotti or rigatoni until soft but not limp; drain. Fill pasta with meat and spinach filling. Place pasta in the prepared baking dish, side by side, filling spaces with extra filling. Spread with cottage cheese. Pour the hot sauce over to cover pasta. Bake in a 350°F. oven for 20 minutes, or until bubbly.

Serve following cold melon slices, with crusty bread, and a tossed green salad.

GNOCCHI

MAKES 6 SERVINGS

This classical Italian dish can be made with various cereals: farina, polenta, cream of rice, cream of wheat, cornmeal, etc. Recipe I is an excellent substitute for potatoes or rice. Recipe II is hardy enough for a luncheon main course.

I.

3 cups skim milk
1 teaspoon salt
¼ teaspoon pepper
¾ cup farina, etc.
4–6 drops yellow food coloring, depending on color of cereal used

2 tablespoons butter-flavored oil
½ cup Cheese Crumbs (p. 304)
Paprika

Scald milk. Add salt and pepper. Pour farina in gradually, stirring with a wooden spoon or wire whisk all the while until well blended and free of lumps. Add coloring. Continue to cook and stir for another minute or two or until cereal is quite thickened. Remove from heat and spread out about ¼-inch thick onto a greased baking sheet. Refrigerate for at least 1 hour or until firm.

Remove from refrigerator and cut into small circles with a biscuit cutter or into 1½-inch squares. Spread out uniformly in a greased baking dish so that one just overlaps the next. Dribble the oil over the farina, dust with paprika, and sprinkle over the crumbs. Bake in a 400°F. oven for 15 or 20 minutes, until crisp and delicately browned. They may be broiled for a minute or two before serving.

II.

3 cups skim milk	4 to 6 drops yellow food
1 teaspoon salt	coloring
¼ teaspoon pepper	1 tablespoon oil
¾ cup farina, etc.	3 lightly beaten egg whites

Scald milk and add salt, pepper, and farina as in I. Cook until thickened. Add food coloring. Remove from heat and beat in the oil and egg whites. Spread out onto pan and chill as in I.

Cut into small circles or squares and transfer to shallow baking dish, overlapping them by about ¼ inch. Pour the following sauce over them. Bake as in I. The sauce should be bubbly and golden. A little additional paprika may be dusted over the sauce.

Cheese Sauce

1 cup rinsed cottage cheese	⅓ cup skim milk
2 tablespoons butter-flavored oil	¼ teaspoon each salt and paprika
2 tablespoons finely grated Sap Sago cheese	

Combine all ingredients in blender and whip until smooth.

Breakfast and Luncheon Specialties

BREAKFAST FRUIT AND CEREAL COMBINATIONS

Hot cooked cereals and cold packaged cereals can be combined in many ways with different kinds of fruits, nuts, and seeds to create interesting and nourishing breakfasts. For some possibilities, select one from each of the groups below and combine for an early-morning energy-producing start to the day. Many more possibilities exist, of course.

I. Hot Cooked Cereals

Rolled or steel-cut oats
Oatmeal
Whole grains—millet, bulghur, buckwheat, rye
Cracked wheat
Cornmeal, farina, or hominy grits
Cream of Wheat or Rice
Roman Meal
Wheat germ

II. Cold Packaged Cereals

Rice Krispies, Puffed Rice
Whole bran flakes, 40% Bran Flakes
Wheat, Corn, or Rice Chex
Cornflakes
Shredded wheat, Puffed Wheat
Toasted wheat germ

III. Fruits, Nuts, Seeds

Dried fruits: apricots, dates, figs, prunes, raisins
Fresh fruits: apples, apricots, bananas, all berries, cherries, guavas, melons, papayas, peaches, pears, pineapple, plums, etc.
Canned fruits: same as above
Stewed fruits: same as above
Nuts: walnuts especially, also almonds, peanuts, pecans
Seeds: poppy, pumpkin, sesame, squash, sunflower

IV. Sweeteners

Sugar: white, dark and light brown, raw
Honey: orange, clover, plum, etc.
Maple syrup
Applesauce and apple butter
Jams and preserves
Cinnamon-sugar
Sweetened yogurts
Noncaloric sweeteners

V. Liquids and Proteins

Jack Sprat Cream (p. 290)
Liquid skim milk with added dry skim milk
Low-fat milk
Yogurts: plain and with fruit, thinned with skim milk or fruit juice
Cottage cheese: plain low-fat or dry-curd cheese, or rinsed cheese, combined with yogurt or liquid skim milk
Fruit juices or nectars: alone or in combination with yogurt or cottage cheese
Granulated yeast: added to hot cereals
Soybeans: added to dry cereals

BANANA MILK SHAKE

MAKES 2 SERVINGS

2 bananas
½ to 1 cup liquid skim milk, orange juice, apricot or peach nectar

2 or 3 ice cubes
1 tablespoon honey (optional)

Combine all ingredients in an electric blender, using the smaller amount of liquid for a thicker milk shake.

PEACH AND WALNUT MILK SHAKE

MAKES 2 SERVINGS

1 cup canned peaches, drained, or 2 fresh peaches, peeled and pitted

⅔ cup liquid skim milk
¼ cup dry skim milk
¼ cup walnut meats

Combine all ingredients in an electric blender. Chill.

CRUSHED PINEAPPLE MILK SHAKE

Substitute pineapple for peaches in Peach and Walnut Milk Shake.

CANTALOUPE-DATE FROST

MAKES 3 TO 4 SERVINGS

2 cups cubed cantaloupe
½ cup pitted dates
½ cup liquid skim milk

½ cup dry skim milk
2 or 3 ice cubes

Combine all ingredients in an electric blender and whip until smooth.

Breakfast and Luncheon Specialties   157

PLUM FROST

MAKES 2 TO 3 SERVINGS

1 cup buttermilk	2 or 3 ice cubes
1 cup puréed plums	½ cup dry skim milk
2 tablespoons sugar	

Combine all ingredients in an electric blender and whip until smooth.

If you don't have fresh plums, a very good substitute is junior food plums with tapioca.

BROILED BREAKFAST GEMS

Cottage cheese on toast topped with cinnamon and sugar can offer a good way to start the day. Select a substantial variety of bread—whole-wheat, soya, millet, cornmeal, etc. Spread bread slices liberally with low-fat cottage cheese. Sprinkle with toasted wheat germ with honey and mixed cinnamon and sugar. Broil for just a few minutes; the cheese should be heated and beginning to puff up. If you prefer, toast bread on one side before spreading it with cheese so that it will be crusty on the bottom.

On hot summer days toast the bread in a toaster and spread with ice-cold cottage cheese.

BREAKFAST OR LUNCHEON KIPPERS

Broiled Kippers and Scrambled Eggs

Brush smoked canned kipper or herring with a little oil. Sprinkle with lemon juice. Broil until piping hot. Serve with Scrambled Eggs (p. 166).

Broiled Kippers and Sliced Tomatoes on Toast

Brush kipper and tomatoes with oil and sprinkle with lemon juice. Broil until hot and bubbly. Serve on toast lightly spread with margarine.

BUCKWHEAT BUTTERMILK CAKES

MAKES ABOUT TWELVE 3-INCH PANCAKES

¼ cup all-purpose flour
¾ cup buckwheat flour
½ teaspoon baking powder
1 teaspoon sugar

½ teaspoon baking soda
1 cup buttermilk
1 tablespoon oil

Combine and sift dry ingredients. Mix buttermilk and oil. Pour liquid into dry ingredients and stir thoroughly. Drop large spoonfuls of the batter onto a heavy griddle over medium heat. Bake until bubbles appear and outer edges are dry. Turn, and bake on the other side.

BUCKWHEAT PANCAKES FROM PREPARED MIX

When buckwheat flour is not available, a mix may be used if it contains no harmful or unidentified shortening. Buckwheat mix usually does not.

MAKES ABOUT TWELVE 3-INCH PANCAKES

1 cup buckwheat pancake mix
1 cup liquid skim milk
¼ cup dry skim milk

1 tablespoon oil
2 egg whites, lightly beaten

Beat pancake mix, liquid and dry skim milks, and oil to a smooth batter. Fold in egg whites. Bake on a heavy griddle in the usual fashion.

Breakfast and Luncheon Specialties   159

FEATHERY BUTTERMILK PANCAKES

MAKES FIFTEEN 3-INCH PANCAKES

1 cup all-purpose flour	1 cup buttermilk
½ teaspoon each of baking soda and salt	2 tablespoons butter-flavored oil
1 teaspoon sugar	2 drops of yellow food coloring
2 egg whites	

Sift dry ingredients together. Whip egg whites in a separate bowl until foamy. Add buttermilk, oil, and food coloring. Add liquids to dry ingredients and beat until smooth. Drop small spoonfuls of the batter onto a greased griddle and bake until browned.

Fluffy Apple Pancakes

Fold 1 cup minced apple into buttermilk pancake batter.

Pineapple Pancakes

Fold ½ cup well-drained crushed pineapple into buttermilk pancake batter.

BUTTERMILK PANCAKES FROM PREPARED MIX

Buttermilk pancake mix usually contains no shortening. However, check ingredients on the package before using. These pancakes are light and thin and can be made in a few seconds.

MAKES ABOUT FIFTEEN 3-INCH PANCAKES

1 cup buttermilk pancake mix	2 tablespoons oil
1 cup liquid skim milk	½ cup dry-curd cottage cheese

Combine everything in a bowl and stir vigorously. Drop small spoonfuls of the batter onto a greased hot griddle and bake until golden brown. Allow space between the small cakes for easy turning.

UP AND AT 'EM PANCAKES

A high-protein pancake that will keep you going far into the day.

MAKES ABOUT TWELVE 3-INCH PANCAKES

2 egg whites
¾ to 1 cup liquid skim milk
1 tablespoon oil
1 cup all-purpose flour
¼ cup toasted wheat germ

1½ teaspoons baking powder
¼ teaspoon salt
½ cup dry-curd or low-fat
   cottage cheese

Whip egg whites with a fork; add ¾ cup milk and the oil; stir. Mix together flour, wheat germ, baking powder, and salt, and add to liquid ingredients. Beat until well blended. Stir in the cottage cheese. Thin the batter with remaining milk if you want a thinner mix. Bake on a greased hot griddle.

ROLLED OAT PANCAKES

These pancakes are too delicate and fluffy for stacking.

MAKES TWELVE 4-INCH PANCAKES

1½ cups rolled oats
1½ cups buttermilk
½ cup all-purpose flour
1 tablespoon sugar

1 teaspoon baking soda
1 teaspoon salt
2 tablespoons oil
2 egg whites, lightly beaten

Stir the oats into the buttermilk. Mix the dry ingredients together and add to the oat mixture. Add oil and egg whites and stir until smooth. Thin the batter with a little skim milk if you like a thinner mix. Rub a heavy griddle with oil and heat until a drop of water bounces and sputters. Drop spoonfuls of batter onto the griddle and bake on one side until puffed and full of bubbles. Lift with a spatula; if brown, turn, and bake on the other side.

WHEAT GERM PANCAKES

MAKES ABOUT TEN 4-INCH PANCAKES

1 cup all-purpose flour
2½ teaspoons baking powder
½ teaspoon salt
1 tablespoon sugar
½ cup toasted wheat germ
   with honey

1¼ cups liquid skim milk
2 tablespoons oil
½ cup low-fat cottage cheese

Sift together flour, baking powder, salt, and sugar. Add wheat germ. Combine milk and oil. Add liquid mixture to dry ingredients and stir enough to moisten dry ingredients. Stir in cottage cheese. Drop batter by spoonfuls onto a nonstick pan brushed with a very little oil. Bake over medium heat until lightly browned on both sides.

FLUTED CHEESE PANCAKES

Cottage cheese drifts to the edge, giving a fluted appearance to these very delicate pancakes.

MAKES ABOUT TWENTY 3-INCH PANCAKES

1 cup all-purpose flour
½ teaspoon salt
1 teaspoon baking powder
1 tablespoon sugar

2 egg whites
¾ cup liquid skim milk
2 tablespoons oil
1 cup low-fat cottage cheese

Sift the dry ingredients together into a bowl. Whip egg whites with a fork. Combine with skim milk and oil. Stir briskly into the dry ingredients until just blended. Add more skim milk to make a thinner batter if desired. Fold in the cottage cheese. Bake on a hot griddle lightly greased with margarine or butter-flavored oil.

CRISP CORNMEAL GRIDDLE CAKES

MAKES ABOUT TWELVE 3-INCH PANCAKES

½ cup white cornmeal
½ cup all-purpose flour
½ teaspoon baking soda
¼ teaspoon salt

1 teaspoon sugar
1¼ cups buttermilk
2 tablespoons oil

Sift the dry ingredients together. Add buttermilk and oil and stir with a few quick strokes until mixed. Cook on a greased hot griddle until golden on both sides. Serve with maple syrup or honey.

FRENCH PANCAKES

MAKES ABOUT TWELVE 5-INCH PANCAKES

1 cup sifted all-purpose flour
1 tablespoon sugar
¼ teaspoon salt
1 teaspoon baking powder
¾ cup liquid skim milk

2 tablespoons oil
2 egg whites, lightly beaten
2 drops of yellow food
coloring

Sift together flour, sugar, salt, and baking powder. Combine skim milk, oil, egg whites, and food coloring. Pour liquids into dry ingredients and beat until smooth. Pour about 3 tablespoons of the batter into a moderately hot greased 5- or 7-inch skillet. Tip the pan slightly to spread the batter over the bottom. Brown on both sides.

Spread jelly, preserves, honey, apple butter, etc., over the pancakes. Roll up, sprinkle with confectioners' sugar, and serve.

FRENCH CRÊPES

These are thinner than French pancakes, and are more suitable for desserts than for breakfast.

Follow recipe for French Pancakes but increase milk to 1 or 1¼ cups, depending on how thin you want crêpes to be. Baking powder can be omitted.

When done, fold crêpes into quarters and place in Orange Sauce (p. 349), to which you have added 1 ounce each of Curaçao and kirsch. Simmer for a few minutes, and serve.

CHEESE BLINTZES

Fill French Pancakes (p. 163) or Crêpes (p. 164) with a rounded tablespoon of cottage cheese, ricotta cheese, or yogurt. Cheese can be flavored with a little sugar and vanilla. Roll up or fold ends toward the center. Arrange pancakes in a baking dish and heat in a 400°F. oven for about 10 minutes. If cheese is at room temperature, this step can be omitted.

Serve blintzes sprinkled with cinnamon and sugar, confectioners' sugar, or a small amount of preserves.

HEAVENLY WAFFLES

These buttermilk waffles are crisp and delicately flavored. The batter is rich and foamy and looks like eggnog.

MAKES TWELVE 4-INCH WAFFLES

2 cups all-purpose flour
2 teaspoons baking powder
1 teaspoon baking soda
½ teaspoon salt
1 tablespoon sugar

6 tablespoons oil
2 cups buttermilk
4 drops of yellow food coloring
4 egg whites, beaten stiff

Sift the dry ingredients together. Combine oil, buttermilk, and food coloring. Add all at once to dry ingredients and mix with a few quick strokes. Fold in the egg whites. Brush waffle iron with oil. Pour on just enough batter to make a thin layer. Bake until golden brown and crisp.

EGGS

No need to give up eggs! At least not altogether. Such things as fried eggs, poached eggs, coddled eggs, or any other form in which the yolk looks at you directly will have to be forgotten.* But all sorts and varieties of scrambled eggs and omelets can be prepared with a little culinary skill. What is important is that you practice a little to develop just the right technique and exact formula to suit your family.

The basic ingredient, of course, is the white of the egg. Three egg whites seem to make a reasonable single serving; you can use more if the eggs are small. To this, add 1 or 2 drops of yellow food coloring and 1 teaspoon of oil if you wish, to replace the fat in the yolks. But the oil isn't at all necessary, and remember that you need a teaspoon of oil to cook with, so let your calorie budget be your guide. Next, you need about 1 teaspoon of water or liquid skim milk to facilitate beating the eggs. And last, you may add a filler to give body to the egg whites; I say "may" because, again, it isn't necessary. Without the filler an extremely light and fluffy omelet can be produced, which is quite delicious. For more substance, however, add 1 to 3 teaspoons of any of the following, mixed with a little water. (Do not add water directly to egg whites when using a filler.)

For 1 serving of 3 egg whites add:
   1 to 3 teaspoons dry skim milk mixed with 1 to 3 teaspoons water
   1 tablespoon cottage cheese mixed with 1 teaspoon water
   1 to 3 teaspoons Cream of Wheat or Cream of Rice mixed with 1 to 3 tablespoons water
   1 to 3 teaspoons potato flakes, or mashed potato mix, or potato cake mix, mixed with 1 to 3 tablespoons water

* For recommended number of whole eggs or egg yolks per week see page 460.

SCRAMBLED EGGS

Don't be afraid to try these eggs. Keep the whole thing a secret the first time you serve them to the family. No one will suspect that you are about to produce a miracle.

MAKES 2 SERVINGS

6 egg whites
1 to 2 tablespoons water
1 to 2 tablespoons filler
 (p. 165)
2 teaspoons oil or margarine
 (optional)

3 drops of yellow food
 coloring
Salt and pepper

Beat egg whites, water combined with filler, oil, and food coloring until foamy. Heat the oil or margarine in a nonstick pan. Add the egg mixture, reduce heat, and cook slowly, stirring with a spatula or large spoon constantly. Season with salt and pepper to taste.

PLAIN OR FLUFFY OMELET

Another miracle! Use a nonstick pan and don't forget the food coloring. For a Fluffy Omelet, leave out the filler.

MAKES 2 SERVINGS

5 or 6 egg whites
1 tablespoon water
2 drops of yellow food
 coloring

2 teaspoons butter-flavored oil,
 or 1 teaspoon regular oil and
 1 teaspoon margarine
1 tablespoon filler (p. 165)

Whip egg whites, water, filler, and food coloring with a fork until foamy. Heat oil in a nonstick pan until quite hot. Add eggs. Reduce heat almost immediately and cook slowly, lifting the edges of the omelet and tipping the pan to let the uncooked part run underneath. When the omelet is cooked, fold ends toward the middle and serve.

Bacon and Eggs

Make Scrambled Eggs or Plain Omelet (above); add 1 tablespoon imitation bacon bits (p. 430) for every 2 servings.

Sausage and Eggs

Make Scrambled Eggs or Plain Omelet (p. 166); add 1 tablespoon imitation sausage bits (p. 430) for every 2 servings.

STANLEY'S STEAMED EGGS

This is not a true recipe but it is an excellent method of cooking scrambled eggs and omelets. Although originally intended as a means of solidifying the gelatinous upper surface of a fried egg, when cooked sunny side up, the technique applies equally well to beaten eggs. Not only do they become solid throughout, which is not too easy when cooking just egg whites, but the effect produced is much like a soufflé. After a very few moments of steaming, the eggs become all puffed up.

To prepare steamed eggs you must include a little moisture when beating them. Add 1 teaspoon of water to the whites if you have not included any other liquid. Omit the additional water if any other liquid is included; for instance, remember that both cottage cheese and yogurt contain some moisture. Next, find a very tight-fitting lid for your frying pan. When ready, pour the eggs into the hot greased pan and scramble them briefly (for scrambled eggs), or lift up sides and tilt pan to let uncooked part run underneath (for omelets). As soon as eggs are partially set, reduce heat to very low and cover pan with the tight-fitting lid. Within 2 or 3 minutes the upper surfaces will be well solidified and the omelet or scrambled eggs will be greatly puffed up. Serve immediately.

EGGS CHINESE STYLE

MAKES 2 SERVINGS

2 teaspoons oil
½ cup chopped onion
½ cup chopped green pepper
4 egg whites
2 teaspoons water

2 drops of yellow food
   coloring
1 teaspoon soy sauce
Pepper

Heat oil in a nonstick pan and sauté onion and green pepper until soft and golden. Whip egg whites, water, food coloring, and soy sauce with a fork; add to onion and pepper and season with pepper to taste. Continue to cook, stirring, until eggs are done. Add more soy sauce if desired. Celery, mushrooms, bean sprouts, or tomatoes can also be used.

DENVER EGGS

Follow recipe for Eggs Chinese Style, but increase oil to 1 tablespoon and sauté 1 cup sliced dried beef with the onion and pepper. Or use 1 or 2 tablespoons imitation bacon bits (p. 430) in place of the beef.
   These eggs can be used to make Denver sandwiches.

OMELET VARIATIONS

Once you've gotten over the hurdle of eating yolkless omelets, the sky's the limit! It is difficult to detect a difference between these and the omelets you used to eat.

CHEESE OMELET

Plain Omelet
  (p. 166)
2 tablespoons minced chives
4 thin slices of processed vege-
    table-oil cheese (p. 419), or
    ⅓ cup cottage cheese com-
    bined with 1 tablespoon
    grated Parmesan

Follow instructions for Plain Omelet, sprinkling on the chives and laying cheese slices on omelet to melt as it cooks.

French Omelet

Replace yellow cheese in Cheese Omelet with 1 heaping tablespoon of cottage cheese and 2 to 3 teaspoons of your favorite jelly or preserves.

Omelette aux Fines Herbes

Use the same proportions as in Cheese Omelet, but replace the cheese with 1 tablespoon each of minced fresh parsley and chives. Add a pinch of thyme, basil, or marjoram for extra flavoring if you wish.

Mushroom Omelet

Replace the cheese in Cheese Omelet with lightly sautéed canned or fresh mushrooms.

Spanish Omelet

Replace the cheese in Cheese Omelet with 2 to 3 tablespoons of Creole Sauce (p. 297).

Omelet with Kippered Herring

Use 1 can (3¼ ounces) smoked kippered herring. Sauté the fish in 1 teaspoon oil. Use instead of cheese in Cheese Omelet, or lay herring on top of the cheese.

Dutch Applesauce Omelet

Replace the cheese in Cheese Omelet with 2 or 3 tablespoons of warm applesauce. Fold over the omelet and sprinkle with ground cinnamon and sugar mixed.

Omelet with Creamed Chipped Beef

Heat leftover creamed chipped beef and use to replace the cheese in Cheese Omelet.

FRITTATA

This Italian omelet combines freshly cooked vegetables, eggs, and a few bread crumbs. Crisply fried, it is excellent fare for breakfast, lunch, or as a hot hors-d'oeuvre. Zucchini and artichoke hearts are particularly suited to the frittata.

MAKES 2 SERVINGS

1 cup puréed cooked zucchini, artichoke hearts, or other vegetable
½ cup bread crumbs
2 tablespoons oil
2 tablespoons flour
¼ teaspoon each of salt and pepper
3 egg whites
2 tablespoons butter-flavored oil

Combine puréed vegetable, bread crumbs, oil, flour, salt, and pepper. Mix well. Beat egg whites until soft peaks form. Fold into the vegetable mixture. Heat the butter-flavored oil in a large skillet. Drop batter by tablespoon onto hot surface. (Small cakes can be formed ahead of time and lightly dusted with flour on each side for a heavier crust.) Fry on both sides until brown and firmly set. Serve immediately.

SPINACH OMELET

MAKES 2 SERVINGS

6 egg whites
½ cup frozen chopped
   spinach, thawed and drained

1 tablespoon mayonnaise
2 drops of yellow food coloring
Salt and pepper

Whip egg whites until frothy. Mix in other ingredients with seasoning to taste. Cook on a hot nonstick pan that has been rubbed lightly with a little oil or margarine.

These may be cooked as small omelets only 2 or 3 inches in diameter.

Spinach "Panlet"

A crossbreed—pancake and omelet.

To Spinach Omelet add 4 tablespoons toasted bread crumbs, a pinch of curry powder (optional), and a few drops of lemon juice. Cook as an omelet. Serve with honey or chutney.

Spinach French Pancakes

To Spinach Omelet add 6 tablespoons flour and enough milk or buttermilk to thin. Mix thoroughly. Make 2 large French pancakes: Pour half of the batter onto the greased hot griddle and tilt pan to spread out the batter. Flip over when almost dry and cook for a few seconds on the other side. Serve rolled, with a filling of whipped cottage cheese. Sprinkle with a little sugar or ground cinnamon and sugar combined.

Spinach Soufflé

Follow recipe for Tuna Soufflé (p. 184), substituting 1 cup thawed and well-drained frozen chopped spinach for the tuna.

Breakfast and Luncheon Specialties   171

FRENCH TOAST

MAKES 2 SERVINGS

2 egg whites	Pinch of salt
1 teaspoon oil	2 slices of bread
1 tablespoon liquid skim milk	1 teaspoon margarine
1 drop of yellow food coloring	

Whip egg whites with a fork until fluffy; add oil, skim milk, food coloring, and salt. Soak bread in this mixture until all moisture is absorbed, turning so that both sides of bread are equally moistened. Heat half of the margarine in a nonstick pan and brown bread slices on one side. Add remaining margarine to the pan when lifting the toast to turn. Brown on the other side.

Serve with ground cinnamon and sugar mixed, or maple syrup, or honey, or powdered sugar.

MUSHROOMS IN SHERRY-FLAVORED SAUCE

This dish is a happy solution for breakfast, lunch, brunch, supper, or what-have-you. You may prefer this over rice, or on toast, or in a casserole with spaghetti and a crusty topping. If you're a mushroom lover, they'll all taste good.

MAKES 4 SERVINGS

1 pound fresh mushrooms	¼ cup dry skim milk
2 tablespoons oil	1 to 2 tablespoons sherry
2 tablespoons flour	Salt and pepper
1 cup liquid skim milk	

Slice mushrooms or, if they are very small, simply separate stems from caps. Sauté in the oil for 3 to 5 minutes, until just tender. Blend in flour and add liquid and dry skim milk, gradually, to form a smooth sauce. Season with sherry and salt and pepper to taste.

Serve over steamed white rice, toast, muffins, spaghetti, bulghur (cracked wheat), etc. Parsley, paprika, Parmesan cheese, or other flavorings or condiments can be added.

SHERRIED TURKEY OVER ENGLISH MUFFINS

MAKES 4 SERVINGS

1 tablespoon oil
1 tablespoon margarine
1 cup sliced mushrooms
1 small red or green pepper, chopped fine
3 tablespoons flour
1½ cups buttermilk

1 heaping tablespoon Whipped Cottage Cheese (p. 287)
2 to 3 tablespoons sherry
1½ cups diced cooked turkey
Salt and pepper
4 English muffins, toasted

Heat oil and margarine in a skillet and sauté the mushrooms and pepper for 3 or 4 minutes. Add flour and stir until blended. Combine buttermilk, cottage cheese, and sherry and stir into mushrooms and pepper to make a smooth cream sauce. Add turkey, season with salt and pepper to taste, and continue to stir and simmer until well heated.

Serve over toasted English muffins for Sunday morning brunch.

Veal, chicken, tuna, salmon, or other fish can be substituted for the turkey.

CREAMED CHIPPED BEEF I (WITH MUSHROOMS)

Creamed chipped beef is an old favorite and a good way to satisfy a ravenous early morning or noontime appetite. Here are two dressed-up ways to serve it, but you may prefer no garnishes at all.

MAKES 4 SERVINGS

2 packages (3 ounces each) dried or chipped beef
2 cups sliced mushrooms
2 tablespoons oil
3 tablespoons flour
2 cups liquid skim milk

½ cup dry skim milk
1 teaspoon sherry
¼ teaspoon paprika
Salt and pepper
4 English muffins
Margarine

Tear apart the dried beef and soak in cold water for 10 minutes. Drain and press out water. Sauté mushrooms in the oil. Mix in flour and add liquid and dry skim milk gradually, stirring to make a smooth creamy sauce. Add beef, sherry, paprika, and salt and pepper to taste (probably very little salt will be needed). Heat slowly.

Break English muffins apart, spread lightly with margarine, and broil until golden. Serve the chipped beef over the muffins.

CREAMED CHIPPED BEEF II (WITH SMALL WHITE ONIONS)

Follow the first recipe, but instead of the mushrooms, use 12 very small boiled onions, cooked fresh or frozen, or canned, plus 2 tablespoons capers. Add more sherry to taste.

ONION CAKE

A friend brought this to a beach picnic. She said it took just a few minutes to whip up, so of course I asked for the recipe. Here it is, with some adjusting for the low-cholesterol club. Actually it takes more than just a few minutes to make but it's well worth it. In addition to serving at picnics, you can use it at cocktail parties, or as an accompaniment to roasts or barbecued chicken and steak. From a friend, Paula Rotenberg.

MAKES 12 TO 14 SERVINGS

1 package (13 to 14 ounces) hot-roll mix (see note below)
4 large yellow onions, peeled and sliced thin
4 tablespoons oil
¼ cup flour
1 cup plain low-fat yogurt
2 cups low-fat cottage cheese
2 tablespoons lemon juice
½ teaspoon salt
½ teaspoon seasoned pepper or caraway seeds
4 egg whites, lightly beaten
2 tablespoons grated Parmesan cheese

174   Breakfast and Luncheon Specialties

Prepare mix according to directions. Let the dough rise.

Sauté onion slices in oil until limp and soft. Cool slightly. Stir flour into yogurt until well blended. Combine yogurt and cottage cheese with remaining ingredients. Stir into onions.

Punch down dough when it has doubled. Let it rise for 10 more minutes and then roll out on floured board into a rectangle 11 by 15 inches for a pan 9 by 13 inches. Line the greased pan with this dough, turning up 1 inch at the edge on all sides. Pour in onion filling. Bake in a 350°F. oven for 55 minutes, or until browned.

NOTE: The packaged hot-roll mix called for in this recipe may contain a small amount of saturated fat. For strict diets you can make your own dough; use the recipe for Dinner Rolls (p. 211), or for Baking Powder Biscuits (p. 198).

ONION QUICHE

MAKES TWO 9-INCH TARTS, ABOUT 12 SERVINGS

Pastry for two 1-crust 9-inch
  pies (p. 330)
4 large yellow onions
3 tablespoons oil
Pepper
3 tablespoons flour
4 cups cottage cheese

2 tablespoons lemon juice
2 teaspoons celery salt
3 drops of yellow food
  coloring
¼ cup grated Parmesan cheese
6 egg whites, lightly beaten

Make the pastry, and use it to line two 9-inch pie pans. Chill while making the filling.

Slice onions very thin, then sauté them in oil. Season with a little pepper. Set aside. Blend flour into cottage cheese. Add lemon juice, celery salt, food coloring, and Parmesan. Mix well. Fold onions and egg whites into the cheese mixture. Divide the mixture between the pastry-lined pie pans. Bake in a preheated 350°F. oven for 1 hour, or until center is firm to the touch.

Serve warm or cold, either as a separate course before the entrée or in small wedges as a substantial appetizer with cocktails.

Breakfast and Luncheon Specialties   175

QUICHE LORRAINE

Pastry for 1-crust 9-inch pie
  (p. 330)
1 large onion, chopped
4 tablespoons imitation bacon
  bits (p. 430)
½ cup dried beef, blanched
1 tablespoon oil
2 cups low-fat cottage cheese
¼ cup liquid skim milk or
  buttermilk

1 tablespoon flour
1 tablespoon each of grated
  Sap Sago cheese and lemon
  juice
4 drops of yellow food coloring
¼ teaspoon each of salt and
  pepper
4 egg whites, beaten stiff

Line a 9-inch pie plate with pastry and set aside in a cool place. Sauté onion, bacon bits, and dried beef in oil until onion is limp. Stir in remaining ingredients except for egg whites and blend well. Fold in the egg whites. Pour mixture into the pastry-lined pan. Bake in a 350°F. oven for 30 to 40 minutes, or until a knife inserted in the center comes out clean and top is golden brown.

CHEESE AND BACON CRUMB PUDDING

A fast substitute for Quiche Lorraine. Good for practically all occasions.

MAKES 6 SERVINGS

1 pound cottage cheese
1 tablespoon butter-flavored
  oil
2 large egg whites
1 tablespoon grated Sap Sago
  cheese

1 tablespoon imitation bacon
  bits (p. 430)
⅛ teaspoon each of salt and
  pepper
⅓ cup Cheese Crumbs
  (p. 304)

Place cheese in a colander and run water through it to rinse out cream. Whip together all ingredients except cheese crumbs, beating until smooth. A blender is best for this but a rotary beater can be used. Pour into a greased 7- or 8-inch pie tin. Top with crumbs. Bake in a preheated 400°F. oven for 30 to 35 minutes, or until a knife inserted in the center comes out clean. Serve while still warm.

GREEN-BEAN-AND-COTTAGE-CHEESE CASSEROLE

This variation of the filling for onion quiche can make a hearty supper for a lazy cook. Also very popular with the kids. Whip up a batch the next time you're off to a party and want to remain popular while gone. Any other vegetable can be substituted for the beans.

MAKES 8 SERVINGS

2 cans (16 ounces each) green beans
4 large Spanish onions, quartered and sliced thin
3 tablespoons oil
Salt and pepper
3 tablespoons flour
4 cups Whipped Cottage Cheese (p. 287)

1 teaspoon celery salt
3 tablespoons grated Parmesan cheese
2 tablespoons lemon juice
1 tablespoon imitation bacon bits (p. 430)
6 egg whites, lightly beaten

Drain all liquid from beans, using a colander or strainer to remove the last drops. Arrange the beans in the bottom of an oiled baking dish. Sauté onions in oil until limp and golden, seasoning lightly with salt and pepper. Stir flour into cottage cheese. Add celery salt, Parmesan, lemon juice, and bacon bits. (Or omit bacon bits if you prefer.) Fold onions and egg whites into cheese mixture. Spread evenly over the beans. Bake in a 350°F. oven for 1 hour.

WELSH RABBIT

MAKES 3 TO 4 SERVINGS

1 tablespoon butter-flavored oil

1 small onion, chopped

1 can (10½ ounces) condensed tomato soup

1½ cups cottage cheese, rinsed and drained

3 tablespoons grated Sap Sago cheese

1 teaspoon Worcestershire sauce

½ teaspoon dry mustard

¼ cup beer

Salt and pepper

2 egg whites, beaten until foamy

Heat oil in the top part of a double boiler, and sauté the onion in it over direct heat until crisp. If this does not work well with your double boiler, use a small sauté pan and transfer when sautéed to the double boiler. Add remaining ingredients except egg whites, and place the double boiler top over hot water. Heat until cheese curd has broken and all ingredients are well blended. Stir often but keep covered part of the time. Add egg whites and cook for another few minutes.

Serve over crackers, toast, or English muffins (whole-wheat or Roman-Meal muffins are particularly good). For variety place hot cooked asparagus, kippered herring, or shredded blanched chipped beef on toast before covering with the cheese mixture.

SWISS FONDUE

The green Sap Sago cheese from Switzerland gives the flavor basis to this fondue.

MAKES ABOUT 8 SERVINGS

1 garlic clove
1½ cups dry white wine
1 pound dry-curd or rinsed
   cottage cheese
¼ cup grated Sap Sago cheese
¼ cup butter-flavored oil
Salt

2 tablespoons cornstarch
2 to 3 tablespoons kirsch
Pepper
Minced chives (optional)
1 loaf of crusty Italian or
   French bread

Rub a heavy saucepan with the garlic. Add the wine and heat slowly until just simmering. Add the cheeses, oil, and ½ teaspoon salt. Continue to simmer, stirring constantly, until cheese curd has broken. If this does not occur within 5 to 10 minutes beat with a rotary beater or pour into a blender and purée. Dissolve the cornstarch in the kirsch and stir into the fondue. Continue to cook for another minute or two until thick and creamy. Season with salt, pepper, and a few minced chives if desired.

Serve in a chafing dish, keeping it warm over a low flame. Cut bread into 1-inch pieces. Provide each guest with a long-handled heatproof fork with which to spear the bread and dip it into the fondue.

BLUE CHEESE FONDUE

MAKES ABOUT 8 SERVINGS

½ cup liquid skim milk
½ cup white wine
2 tablespoons cornstarch
½ cup mayonnaise
1 pound cottage cheese, rinsed
¼ teaspoon dry mustard
1 teaspoon Worcestershire sauce

2 tablespoons blue cheese dip or salad dressing mix
2 or 3 drops of yellow food coloring
Salt and pepper
1 loaf of French or Italian bread

Stir skim milk, wine, and cornstarch together in a heavy saucepan. Cornstarch should be completely dissolved. Add remaining ingredients except bread, and heat slowly. Simmer, stirring constantly, until cheese curd has broken. Adjust seasonings, adding more blue cheese mix if desired.

Serve hot with cubes of crusty bread in the same manner as with Swiss Fondue.

FLUFFY FONDUE CASSEROLES (CHEESE PUDDINGS)

These crusty puddings take only a few minutes to prepare. Added benefits include a very high protein content and almost no saturated fat. They'll probably become a standby in your household as they are in ours. After you've tried these, experiment with a few variations of your own. Different kinds of bread will lend different flavors. Replace the chives with a few sliced water chestnuts, sautéed mushrooms, sunflower seeds, or diced walnuts.

FONDUE WITH YELLOW CHEESE

MAKES 4 SERVINGS

4 slices of bread
Margarine
1½ cups cubed processed
   vegetable-oil cheese (p. 419)
¼ cup dry skim milk
¼ teaspoon dry mustard
¼ teaspoon paprika

1¼ cups liquid skim milk
¼ teaspoon Worcestershire
   sauce
¼ teaspoon salt
⅛ teaspoon black pepper
1 tablespoon minced chives
4 large egg whites, beaten stiff

Grease a 1½-quart ovenproof baking dish 3 to 4 inches deep. Spread the bread slices sparingly with margarine, and cut them into cubes. Arrange alternate layers of the cubes of bread and cheese in the baking dish. Mix together the dry milk, mustard, and paprika, and add to the liquid milk along with Worcestershire sauce, salt, pepper, and chives. Stir until dry milk and salt are dissolved. Fold in beaten egg whites. Pour this mixture over the bread and cheese. Bake in a 350°F. oven for 45 minutes to 1 hour, or until a knife inserted in the center comes out clean.

Serve with a green salad, sliced tomatoes, or fresh fruits.

FONDUE WITH COTTAGE CHEESE

MAKES 4 SERVINGS

4 slices of bread, lightly
   toasted
Margarine
1½ cups dry-curd or low-fat
   cottage cheese
¼ cup dry skim milk
¼ teaspoon dry mustard
¼ teaspoon paprika
1¼ cups liquid skim milk
2 tablespoons oil

¼ teaspoon Worcestershire
   sauce
½ teaspoon salt
¼ teaspoon black pepper
1 heaping tablespoon minced
   chives
1 tablespoon sherry
2 drops of yellow food
   coloring
4 large egg whites, beaten stiff

Follow the same procedure as for Fondue with Yellow Cheese. Add the oil to the liquid milk if using dry-curd cottage cheese. Omit oil when using low-fat cottage cheese.

CRUSTY CHEESE SOUFFLÉ

Light and fluffy on the inside, slightly crusty on the top.

MAKES 6 SERVINGS

⅓ cup oil
⅓ cup flour
1 cup liquid skim milk
1 cup dry-curd cottage cheese
¼ teaspoon each of paprika and dry mustard
½ teaspoon each of prepared mustard and Worcestershire sauce

Few grains of cayenne pepper
1 teaspoon salt
1 teaspoon butter flavoring
¼ teaspoon yellow food coloring
1 cup egg whites (about 8), at room temperature
½ teaspoon cream of tartar

Preheat oven to 325°F. Mix oil and flour in a heavy saucepan and stir and cook for a minute or two. Add skim milk, cottage cheese, all seasonings, and coloring. Continue to cook, stirring with a heavy wooden spoon, until cheese curd has broken and sauce is smooth and thick. Set aside to cool.

Beat egg whites until foamy, add cream of tartar, and beat until soft peaks form and egg whites are almost stiff. Fold cheese sauce gently into the egg whites. Pour into an ungreased 2-quart soufflé dish and bake in the preheated oven for 1½ hours. Serve immediately.

CARROT PUFF

A quick and effective dish, good for lunch with rolls and a chicken salad. Ingredients should be at room temperature.

MAKES 6 SERVINGS

¼ cup dry skim milk
1½ cups liquid skim milk
1 tablespoon oil
3 drops of yellow food
  coloring
2 tablespoons brown sugar
2 teaspoons lemon juice

½ teaspoon salt
½ teaspoon pepper
1½ cups canned julienne
  carrots
½ cup toasted bread crumbs
4 egg whites, beaten until
  frothy

Dissolve the dry milk in the liquid. Add oil, coloring, brown sugar, lemon juice, salt, and pepper. Mix with the milk. Stir in the carrots and bread crumbs, and fold in the beaten egg whites. Pour pudding into an ungreased baking dish and set the dish in a pan of hot water. Bake in a 350°F. oven for 1 hour or more, until firm.

POTATO CHEESE PUFF

MAKES 4 SERVINGS

1 cup dried mashed-potato
  flakes
⅓ cup dry skim milk
1 cup boiling water
¼ teaspoon salt
⅓ cup buttermilk
2 tablespoons butter-flavored
  oil

1 tablespoon grated Sap Sago
  cheese
1 to 2 tablespoons minced
  chives
2 egg whites, beaten stiff
2 tablespoons sesame seeds
  (optional)

Dissolve potato flakes and dry milk in the boiling water. Add remaining ingredients except egg whites and sesame seeds, and mix well. Fold in the egg whites. Pour into a greased casserole and sprinkle with sesame seeds. Bake in a 425°F. oven for 20 to 30 minutes, or until puffed and golden.

TUNA OR SALMON SOUFFLÉ

A true tour de force! Only the cook will know there are no egg yolks or butter in this soufflé. Start at least an hour before mealtime. Ingredients should be at room temperature.

MAKES 4 SERVINGS

1 tablespoon mayonnaise
2 tablespoons oil
3 tablespoons flour
1 cup liquid skim milk
6 egg whites
3 drops of yellow food
   coloring

Salt, pepper, and paprika
1 cup canned water-packed
   tuna or salmon
¼ cup chopped green onions
1 tablespoon lemon juice

Make a creamy sauce in a heavy saucepan over low heat: blend mayonnaise, oil, and flour into a smooth paste and add milk gradually; stir until thickened.

In a small bowl whip two of the egg whites lightly with a fork. Add them along with the food coloring to the sauce. Cook for 1 minute, stirring with a wire whisk. Season with salt, pepper, and paprika to taste. Drain the tuna well and mash with a fork until quite smooth. Add to the sauce along with green onions and lemon juice. Cool slightly.

Beat remaining 4 egg whites with an electric mixer until stiff. Fold into the sauce and tuna mixture. Pour into an ungreased 4-cup soufflé dish or casserole. Bake in a preheated 325°F. oven for 40 to 45 minutes.

TUNA AND MASHED-POTATO SOUFFLÉ

Follow recipe for Hot Tuna Puffs (p. 43), increasing mashed potatoes to 2 cups and egg whites to 4. Pour into a greased 6-cup soufflé dish and bake in a 350°F. oven for about 30 minutes.

HOT SALMON MOUSSE

This cousin to the soufflé is simple to prepare and makes an excellent lunch or supper. Any cooked fish can be used in place of salmon. Serve with Tartar Sauce (p. 300) or Béchamel Sauce (p. 291), if desired.

Salmon Mousse with Rice or Bulghur

MAKES 6 SERVINGS

2 cups flaked cooked salmon, tuna, or other fish
½ cup plain low-fat yogurt
2 tablespoons flour
1 tablespoon grated onion or chopped chives

¼ teaspoon each of salt, pepper, and paprika
5 large egg whites, beaten stiff
1 cup cooked rice or bulghur (cracked wheat)

Prepare fish. Blend yogurt and flour. Mix with fish, onion, and seasonings. Fold egg whites and rice or wheat into fish mixture. Fill oiled custard cups two thirds full. Place cups on a rack in a pan with hot water 1 inch deep. Bake in a 350°F. oven for 25 to 30 minutes.

Salmon Mousse with Mushrooms

This makes a much lighter mousse.

Follow the same procedure, but substitute for the rice 1 can (5 ounces) mushrooms, minced.

Other good ideas for breakfast and luncheon dishes might include many of the bean and pasta dishes, as, for instance, Gnocchi made with cottage cheese, Baked Soy or Chili Beans, Frijoles or Tostadas Macaroni Vermicelli Romanoff with Poppy Seeds, with Cheese or with Mushrooms and Tomatoes.

Breads
and
Coffee Cakes

BOSTON BROWN BREAD

½ cup cornmeal
½ cup sifted all-purpose flour
1 cup sifted whole-wheat flour
2 tablespoons sugar
1½ teaspoons baking soda

¾ teaspoon salt
½ cup dark molasses
1⅓ cups buttermilk
¾ cup raisins

Preheat oven to 350°F. Grease and flour a loaf pan 8 by 4 inches. Sift dry ingredients together. Combine molasses and buttermilk. Add liquids to dry ingredients and beat to a smooth batter. Stir in the raisins. Pour into the prepared pan. Bake in the preheated oven for 1 hour, or until bread has just begun to leave sides of pan. Remove from pan immediately and serve piping hot.

Boston brown bread can also be steamed. Pour batter into a greased and floured 2-quart steamer (a 2-pound coffee can will do) and steam for 3 to 3½ hours.

BANANA NUT BREAD

Saturated with the flavor of bananas, this moist and tender cakelike bread contains surprisingly little sugar and oil.

MAKES 1 LOAF

2 cups all-purpose flour
½ cup sugar
2 teaspoons baking powder
1 teaspoon baking soda
½ teaspoon salt
3 medium-sized bananas,
  mashed (about 1 cup)

¼ cup buttermilk
¼ cup oil
4 egg whites, beaten stiff
½ cup chopped walnuts

Preheat oven to 350°F. Grease and flour a loaf pan 8 by 4 inches. Sift together flour, sugar, baking powder, baking soda, and salt. Combine bananas, buttermilk, and oil. Add to dry ingredients and beat until well blended. Fold in the egg whites and walnuts. Pour into the prepared pan. Bake in the preheated oven for about 1 hour. Test with a straw for doneness.

BLACK WALNUT BREAD

MAKES 1 LARGE OR 2 SMALL LOAVES

1 egg white
2 tablespoons oil
1 cup light-brown sugar
3 cups all-purpose flour

1 teaspoon salt
3½ teaspoons baking powder
1½ cups liquid skim milk
1½ cups ground black walnuts

Preheat oven to 350°F. Line 1 large or 2 small pans with wax paper and brush the paper with oil. Whip egg white until stiff. Mix in oil and brown sugar. Sift flour, salt, and baking powder together. Add dry ingredients to egg mixture alternately with skim milk until well blended. Stir in ground walnuts. Turn dough into the prepared pans. Let rise in a warm place for 30 minutes. Bake in the preheated oven for approximately 1 hour.

ORANGE DATE BREAD

A fine-grained and delicately flavored bread made with no eggs at all.

MAKES 1 LOAF

2¼ cups all-purpose flour
2 teaspoons baking powder
½ teaspoon baking soda
½ teaspoon salt
½ cup sugar
2 tablespoons oil

½ cup liquid skim milk
½ cup orange juice
1 cup chopped dates
1 tablespoon grated orange rind

Preheat oven to 350°F. Grease and flour a loaf pan 9 by 5 by 3 inches. Sift dry ingredients together. Combine oil, skim milk, and orange juice in a separate bowl. Add to dry ingredients and mix well. Fold in the chopped dates and orange rind. Pour into the prepared pan. Bake in the preheated oven for 40 to 45 minutes, or until a knife inserted at the center comes out clean and the top is slightly browned.

PUMPKIN NUT BREAD

MAKES 1 LOAF

1 cup sifted all-purpose flour
1 teaspoon baking powder
1 teaspoon baking soda
1 teaspoon salt
¾ cup sugar
1 teaspoon ground allspice

1 cup Roman Meal
2 egg whites, lightly beaten
1 cup pumpkin purée
½ cup orange juice
¼ cup oil
½ to 1 cup raisins

Preheat oven to 350°F. Grease and flour a loaf pan 9 by 5 by 3 inches. Sift together all dry ingredients. Add Roman Meal. Combine egg whites, pumpkin purée, orange juice, and oil in a separate bowl. Add liquids all at once to dry ingredients and beat into a smooth batter. Fold in the raisins and pour into the prepared pan. Bake in the preheated oven for 55 to 60 minutes.

QUICK CINNAMON SWIRL COFFEE CAKE

For added interest I have substituted Roman Meal for some of the flour. If you prefer, use all white flour.

MAKES 6 TO 8 SERVINGS

1 cup sifted all-purpose flour	½ cup Roman Meal
2 teaspoons baking powder	2 tablespoons oil
½ teaspoon baking soda	⅔ cup buttermilk
½ teaspoon salt	½ cup raisins
½ cup sugar	Topping (below)

Preheat oven to 375°F. Grease a baking pan 6 by 10 inches. Sift dry ingredients together, including sugar. Add Roman Meal. Combine oil and buttermilk and add all at once to dry ingredients. Mix well. Fold in the raisins. Pour into the prepared pan. Sprinkle with topping. Using a fork, swirl the topping into the batter in a circular motion to make an interesting pattern. Do not mix in. Bake in the preheated oven for 30 to 35 minutes.

Topping

⅓ cup chopped walnuts	2 tablespoons oil
⅓ cup brown sugar	2 teaspoons ground
2 tablespoons flour	cinnamon

Mix together.

CRAZY LAZY RAISIN CAKE

A simple but delicious all-in-one coffee cake. Better for dessert than breakfast, but especially good for picnics. Thanks go to Inga Malcolmson of La Jolla, California, for giving me the recipe many years ago.

MAKES 8 OR MORE SERVINGS

2 cups sifted all-purpose flour
1 cup granulated sugar
1 cup light brown sugar
1 teaspoon baking powder
¼ teaspoon salt
⅔ cup oil
½ cup walnut meats

1 teaspoon ground cinnamon
¼ teaspoon ground cloves
1 teaspoon baking soda
1 cup buttermilk
2 egg whites, lightly beaten
½ cup raisins

Preheat oven to 400°F. Grease and flour a 10-inch-square pan. In a large bowl mix together with your hands the flour, white and brown sugars, baking powder, and salt. Add oil and blend in with 2 knives. Transfer ⅔ cup of the mixture to a small bowl and stir in walnut meats, cinnamon, and cloves. Save to use for topping.

Return to cake. Stir baking soda into buttermilk and add to batter along with egg whites. Stir quickly, scraping the bottom of the bowl with a rubber scraper. Batter will be lumpy but do not worry about it. Pour into the prepared pan. Dot top with raisins, poking them slightly into the batter with your finger. Sprinkle the reserved walnut topping over all. Bake in the preheated oven for 25 to 30 minutes.

NORWEGIAN COFFEE CAKE WITH STREUSEL FILLING

A fine crumbly coffee cake with a new flavor in the streusel filling.

MAKES 8 OR MORE SERVINGS

1½ cups sifted cake flour
2 teaspoons baking powder
½ teaspoon salt
¾ cup sugar
¼ cup oil

⅔ cup liquid skim milk
2 drops of yellow food
coloring
2 egg whites, beaten stiff
Streusel Filling (below)

Preheat oven to 375°F. Grease and flour a 9-inch-square pan. Sift flour, baking powder, salt, and sugar into a large bowl. Mix oil, skim milk, and food coloring and add all at once to flour. Stir vigorously until well mixed. Fold beaten egg whites into batter. Spread half of the batter in the prepared pan and cover with half of the streusel mixture. Add the rest of the batter and top with remaining streusel. Bake in the preheated oven for 25 to 35 minutes. Serve warm.

Streusel Filling

2 tablespoons oil
⅔ cup light brown sugar
2 tablespoons flour

1½ teaspoons ground
cardamom
½ cup chopped walnuts

Mix ingredients together until crumbly.

HUNGARIAN COFFEE CAKE

The brittle brown sugar topping adds appeal to a delicious coffee cake.

MAKES 8 OR MORE SERVINGS

3 tablespoons oil
1 cup light brown sugar
1 cup plain low-fat yogurt
4 egg whites
1⅝ cups sifted cake flour

2 teaspoons baking powder
½ teaspoon baking soda
¼ teaspoon salt
½ cup dried currants
Topping (below)

Preheat oven to 350°F. Grease a baking pan 8 by 10 inches. Mix the oil and brown sugar in a mixing bowl. Add yogurt and egg whites and beat until light and fluffy. Sift dry ingredients together and add to the sugar mixture, one third at a time. Beat until smooth. Stir in currants. Pour batter into the prepared pan, and spread on topping. Bake in the preheated oven for 25 to 30 minutes.

Topping

This topping becomes extremely brittle when baked and will crumble, as hard candy will, when cut. For a less brittle topping select one of the streusel mixtures (see Index).

2 egg whites
¼ teaspoon salt
1 cup brown sugar

1 teaspoon ground cinnamon
⅛ teaspoon ground cloves
½ cup walnuts (optional)

Beat egg whites with salt until stiff. Add sugar and spices and beat until smooth. Fold in nuts.

SOUTHERN-STYLE BUTTERMILK CORN BREAD

Buttermilk and a large proportion of cornmeal make this bread both moist and crunchy. Serve piping hot with unsalted margarine and your favorite honey.

MAKES 12 LARGE MUFFINS OR ONE 9-INCH-SQUARE PAN OF BREAD

1½ cups cornmeal (see note below)	1 teaspoon salt
½ cup all-purpose flour	2 egg whites
2 tablespoons sugar	1½ cups buttermilk
1 tablespoon baking powder	¼ cup oil
½ teaspoon baking soda	1 drop of yellow food coloring

Preheat oven to 425°F. Grease and flour a 9-inch-square pan or 12 muffin cups. Sift dry ingredients together into a large bowl. Beat egg whites with a rotary beater until stiff. Combine with buttermilk and oil. Add food coloring. Pour liquid ingredients into dry and stir quickly to make a smooth batter. Do not overmix. Pour into the prepared pan or muffin cups. Bake muffins for 10 to 15 minutes, corn bread for 20 to 25 minutes.

NOTE: Southerners traditionally use white cornmeal, Northerners yellow; the flavor is much the same; the difference is mostly in color.

BROWN-SUGAR CORN BREAD ＊ ＊ ＊

MAKES 10 MEDIUM-SIZED MUFFINS OR ONE 8-INCH-SQUARE PAN OF BREAD

¾ cup all-purpose flour	½ teaspoon salt
¾ cup cornmeal	1 cup liquid skim milk
¼ cup toasted wheat germ	¼ cup oil
2 tablespoons brown sugar	2 egg whites, beaten stiff
1 tablespoon baking powder	

Preheat oven to 425°F. Grease and flour an 8-inch-square pan or 10 muffin cups. Sift and mix together all dry ingredients. Stir in the milk and oil and fold in the egg whites. Pour into the prepared pan or muffin cups. Bake corn bread for 20 to 25 minutes, muffins for 20 minutes.

SPOON BREAD

This soft-textured Southern bread is an interesting replacement for rice or potatoes. It is so soft, it is served with a spoon.

MAKES 4 TO 6 SERVINGS

3 cups liquid skim milk
¾ cup cornmeal (white or yellow) (see note below)
3 tablespoons oil

1 teaspoon salt
1½ teaspoons baking powder
4 egg whites, beaten stiff

Preheat oven to 350°F. Grease a 1-quart casserole. Heat 2 cups of the milk in the top part of a double boiler. Mix cornmeal with remaining cold milk and stir into the hot milk. Cook slowly for 15 minutes, stirring frequently. Cool. Add oil, salt, and baking powder. Beat until well blended. Fold in egg whites and pour into the prepared casserole. Bake in the preheated oven for 35 to 40 minutes. Serve immediately.

NOTE: If using white cornmeal, add 4 or 5 drops of yellow food coloring to the milk.

YORKSHIRE PUDDING

Good news! Here's a way to keep this homey old favorite on the menu. It is an easy success if directions are followed carefully, especially if the batter is beaten well. Be sure ingredients are at room temperature, otherwise the egg whites will not puff up. Serve with a lean beef roast (rump, round, sirloin tip).

MAKES 6 SERVINGS

2½ tablespoons butter-
   flavored oil
1 cup flour
½ teaspoon salt

1 cup liquid skim milk
3 egg whites
2 drops of yellow food
   coloring

Let ingredients stand at room temperature for at least 1 hour before starting. Preheat oven to 400°F. Prepare an ovenproof glass baking dish approximately 10 inches square by heating it in the oven with 1 tablespoon of the oil.

Sift the flour and salt into a bowl and make a well in the center. Pour ½ cup of the skim milk into the well and stir until mixed. Beat the egg whites until fluffy. Combine them with the remaining ½ cup milk and 1½ tablespoons oil, and the food coloring. Pour this into the flour mixture. Beat the batter with the electric mixer at high speed for a few minutes, until large bubbles appear. Pour into the sizzling baking dish. Bake in the preheated oven for 20 minutes, then reduce temperature to 350°F. and bake for another 15 to 20 minutes.

Serve the pudding in the dish in which it was cooked; cut into squares to serve.

BAKING-POWDER BISCUITS

MAKES ABOUT 12 BISCUITS

2 cups sifted all-purpose
   flour
1 tablespoon baking powder

1 teaspoon salt
⅓ cup oil
⅔ cup liquid skim milk

Preheat oven to 475°F. Sift dry ingredients together. Combine oil and skim milk and pour all at once into dry ingredients. Stir with a fork until mixture clings together and forms a ball. Dump the dough onto a floured board or, better still, onto a sheet of wax paper, and knead very gently 6 to 8 times. Put dough on a large sheet of wax paper and pat out to ½-inch thickness. Cut with a floured 2-inch biscuit cutter. Place biscuits on an ungreased baking sheet, 1 inch apart for browned crusty sides, close together with sides touching for soft, higher biscuits. Bake in the preheated oven for 10 to 12 minutes.

Drop Biscuits

Increase milk to ¾ cup. Instead of kneading, rolling out, and cutting, drop by spoon onto an ungreased baking sheet.

FLUFFY BUTTERMILK BISCUITS

MAKES ABOUT 12 BISCUITS

1¾ cups sifted all-purpose flour	¼ cup oil
2 teaspoons baking powder	1 cup buttermilk
½ teaspoon baking soda	½ teaspoon butter flavoring (optional)
½ teaspoon salt	

Preheat oven to 450°F. Sift dry ingredients together. Combine oil, buttermilk, and flavoring without stirring, and add all at once to dry ingredients. Stir with a fork until mixture clings together and forms a ball. Knead on a lightly floured board 10 to 12 times with your finger tips. Pat out dough to ½- to 1-inch thickness depending on size desired. Biscuits double in size when baked. Cut with a floured 2-inch biscuit cutter; try not to twist them when cutting. Place on an ungreased baking sheet, close together for soft sides, 1 inch apart for crusty sides. Bake in a preheated oven for about 10 minutes.

GRIDDLE SCONES

These are similar to English muffins. The method of cooking them makes them especially suitable for the camper's open fire. However, they are equally good for a lazy Sunday morning breakfast at home. Serve with your favorite jam and some pot cheese.

MAKES ABOUT 12 SCONES

2 cups all-purpose flour
2 tablespoons sugar
2½ teaspoons baking powder
½ teaspoon baking soda
½ teaspoon salt

2 egg whites, beaten lightly
¼ cup oil
¾ cup buttermilk
Margarine

Sift the dry ingredients together. Combine egg whites, oil, and buttermilk. Stir liquids into dry ingredients just enough to mix. Pat out the dough on a floured board to ½-inch thickness. Cut rounds with a 3-inch cutter. Rub griddle with margarine and bring to medium heat. Cook scones for about 10 minutes on each side, adding a tiny dab of margarine to top side before turning. Break open the first scone to be sure it is fully cooked; if not, cook the others for a few minutes longer.

SCOTCH CURRANT SCONES

To recipe for Griddle Scones (above) add ½ cup dried currants. Divide dough into 2 sections and roll out into circles ½ inch thick. Cut each circle into 6 wedges and place wedges on a greased baking sheet. Brush tops with milk or lightly beaten egg white. Sprinkle lightly with sugar. Bake in a 425°F. oven for 12 to 15 minutes.

BASIC MUFFINS

MAKES 12 LARGE OR 24 SMALL MUFFINS

2 cups sifted all-purpose flour
3 tablespoons sugar
4 teaspoons baking powder
½ teaspoon salt
2 egg whites, lightly beaten

¼ cup oil
1 cup liquid skim milk
2 drops of yellow food
coloring

Preheat oven to 400°F. Grease and flour muffin cups. Sift dry ingredients together. Combine egg whites, oil, skim milk, and food coloring. Pour liquids into dry ingredients all at once and mix with a few quick strokes, just until dough sticks together. Pour batter into prepared muffin cups, filling two thirds full. Bake in the preheated oven for 20 to 25 minutes, or until golden brown. Be careful not to overcook.

BUTTERMILK MUFFINS

MAKES 12 LARGE OR 24 SMALL MUFFINS

2 cups sifted all-purpose flour
1½ teaspoons baking powder
½ teaspoon baking soda
½ teaspoon salt
2 tablespoons light brown
sugar

1 tablespoon granulated sugar
2 egg whites, lightly beaten
3 tablespoons oil
1¼ cups buttermilk
2 drops of yellow food
coloring

Follow the same procedure for mixing as in Basic Muffins, above.

Lemon Muffins

Add 1 tablespoon grated lemon rind and 1 tablespoon lemon juice to the batter. Glaze with a mixture of ½ cup confectioners' sugar, ¼ teaspoon grated lemon rind, and 1 teaspoon lemon juice.

Walnut Muffins

Add ¾ cup chopped walnuts to the batter.

Raisin Muffins

Add ¾ cup golden or dark raisins to the batter.

Date Muffins

Add 1 cup chopped dates to the batter.

Bacon Muffins

Add ¼ cup imitation bacon bits (p. 430) to the batter.

Apple Muffins

Add ½ cup chopped apple plus ½ teaspoon ground cinnamon or grated nutmeg to the batter.

BUTTERMILK BRAN MUFFINS

This recipe calls for whole-bran cereal; there are several brands available on the market. As these cereals have been slightly sweetened, use only ¼ cup sugar. For unsweetened bran flakes use ⅓ cup. Salt has been omitted as bran cereals also contain salt.

MAKES ABOUT 24 MUFFINS, 2-INCH SIZE

1 cup sifted all-purpose flour
1 teaspoon baking powder
1 teaspoon baking soda
¼ teaspoon ground allspice
¼ to ⅓ cup light brown
   sugar
¼ cup oil

⅓ cup dark molasses or
   corn syrup
1¼ cups buttermilk
3 cups whole-bran cereal
2 egg whites, lightly beaten
½ cup raisins

Preheat oven to 400°F. Grease and flour 24 muffin cups. Sift together flour, baking powder, baking soda, allspice, and brown sugar. Mix the oil, molasses, buttermilk, cereal, and egg whites together. Stir well and set aside for 5 minutes.

Pour the liquid-bran mixture into the dry ingredients. Stir with a few quick strokes or just until dry ingredients are dampened. Fold in the raisins. Fill the prepared muffin cups about two thirds full. Bake in the preheated oven for 15 to 20 minutes, or until muffins are just beginning to pull away from the sides of the pan. Serve piping hot.

For a crunchier muffin, do not soak cereal in the liquids for 5 minutes.

PUMPKIN BRAN MUFFINS

MAKES ABOUT 18 MUFFINS

1½ cups all-purpose flour
2 teaspoons baking powder
½ teaspoon baking soda
½ teaspoon each of salt
   and ground cinnamon
3 tablespoons sugar
1 cup whole-bran cereal

2 egg whites, lightly beaten
⅓ cup liquid skim milk
3 tablespoons oil
1 cup pumpkin purée
½ cup raisins
Sugar

Preheat oven to 400°F. Grease and flour 18 muffin cups. Sift together flour, baking powder, baking soda, salt, cinnamon, and sugar. Add cereal. Combine egg whites, skim milk, oil, and pumpkin purée in a separate bowl. Fold the liquids into the dry ingredients and mix well. Add raisins. Fill prepared muffin cups two thirds full. Sprinkle a small amount of raw or white granulated sugar on muffin tops. Bake in the preheated oven for 20 minutes, or until firm to the touch and brown on top.

BLUEBERRY MUFFINS WITH ORANGE-RIND TOPPING

The crunchy orange topping makes these muffins especially good. For a lemony flavor, substitute grated lemon rind.

MAKES 12 TO 14 LARGE MUFFINS

2¼ cups all-purpose flour
⅓ cup sugar
1 tablespoon baking powder
½ teaspoon salt
1 cup liquid skim milk
¼ cup dry skim milk
⅓ cup oil

2 egg whites, lightly beaten
1 cup fresh or well-drained canned blueberries, lightly floured
1 teaspoon fine-grated lemon rind
Topping (below)

Preheat oven to 425°F. Grease and flour 12 to 14 large muffin cups. Sift flour, sugar, baking powder, and salt into a large bowl. Add mixed liquid and dry milk, oil, and egg whites, and stir just until blended. Fold in blueberries and grated lemon rind. Fill prepared muffin cups two thirds full. Sprinkle with topping. Bake in the preheated oven for 20 to 25 minutes.

Topping

2 tablespoons sugar
2 teaspoons grated orange rind

¼ teaspoon ground cinnamon

Combine ingredients.

CARROT AND SUNFLOWER-SEED MUFFINS

Carrots supply color and flavor, sunflower seeds a crunchy texture.

MAKES 24 MEDIUM MUFFINS

1¼ cups grated carrot
¾ cup liquid skim milk
¼ cup oil
2 egg whites
2 cups all-purpose flour

¼ cup sugar
1 tablespoon baking powder
½ teaspoon salt
⅓ cup toasted and salted
    sunflower seeds

Preheat oven to 425°F. Grease and flour 12 muffin cups. Combine the first four ingredients in a small bowl and mix well. Sift the flour, sugar, baking powder, and salt. Pour carrot mixture into flour and stir vigorously for 1 or 2 minutes. Add sunflower seeds. Fill prepared muffin cups two thirds full. Bake in the preheated oven for 25 minutes. Test with a straw and be sure that muffins are pulling away from the sides of the pans slightly.

Serve with your favorite honey.

OATMEAL MUFFINS

MAKES 12 LARGE MUFFINS

1 cup rolled oats
1 cup buttermilk
¼ cup oil
⅓ cup brown sugar
2 egg whites, beaten until
    foamy

1 cup all-purpose flour
1 teaspoon baking powder
½ teaspoon baking soda
½ teaspoon salt

Soak oats in buttermilk for 1 hour. Preheat oven to 400°F. Grease and flour 12 muffin cups. Mix oil, brown sugar, and egg whites in a large bowl. Sift together the flour, baking powder, baking soda, and salt. Stir dry ingredients into sugar-oil mixture alternately with oats-buttermilk mixture. Spoon batter into the prepared muffin cups. Bake in the preheated oven for 25 to 30 minutes.

Variations: Add ½ cup of any of the following: nuts, raisins, chopped dates, dried currants, diced prunes, sunflower seeds.

PINEAPPLE HONEY MUFFINS

MAKES 12 LARGE MUFFINS

2 cups all-purpose flour	½ cup liquid skim milk
1 tablespoon baking powder	¼ cup pineapple juice
¾ teaspoon salt	3 tablespoons oil
⅓ cup honey	½ cup crushed pineapple,
2 egg whites, lightly beaten	drained

Preheat oven to 400°F. Grease and flour 12 muffin cups. Sift dry ingredients together. Add all other ingredients and stir until well blended. Fill prepared muffin cups two thirds full. Bake in the preheated oven for 25 to 30 minutes.

EGGLESS MUFFINS

A light muffin with a good texture.

MAKES ABOUT 12 LARGE MUFFINS

2 cups sifted all-purpose flour	¾ teaspoon baking soda
¼ cup sugar	1 cup buttermilk
½ teaspoon salt	3 tablespoons oil
2 teaspoons baking powder	½ teaspoon butter flavoring

Preheat oven to 400°F. Grease and flour 12 muffin cups. Sift dry ingredients together. Combine buttermilk, oil, and butter flavoring. Add liquids all at once to dry ingredients. Stir until well blended. Fill prepared muffin cups two thirds full. Bake in the preheated oven for 20 to 25 minutes, or until lightly browned on top and firm to the touch.

Eggless Whole-Wheat Muffins

Substitute 1 cup whole-wheat flour for 1 cup all-purpose flour. Add 2 tablespoons molasses to the liquid ingredients.

Eggless Roman-Meal Muffins

Substitute 1 cup Roman Meal for 1 cup all-purpose flour. Add 2 tablespoons honey to the liquid ingredients.

Eggless Date, Raisin, or Walnut Muffins

Add ½ cup chopped dates, raisins, or walnuts to any of the recipes for Eggless Muffins.

POPOVERS

This recipe comes from my aunt, Leah Overton. Even without egg yolks, these pop sky high, emerging from the oven light as a feather and golden brown. An extra tablespoon of oil can be used in place of the margarine; in that case add a drop or two of yellow food coloring. Butter-flavored oil works wonders here.

MAKES 12 VERY LARGE OR 18 MEDIUM-SIZED POPOVERS

6 egg whites
3 tablespoons oil
1 tablespoon melted margarine
2 cups liquid skim or low-fat milk
2 cups sifted all-purpose flour
½ teaspoon salt

Do not preheat oven! Grease popover pans or custard cups. Beat egg whites lightly with a fork and combine with oil, margarine, and milk. Place flour and salt in the bowl of an electric mixer and add liquids gradually, beating at low speed until well blended. Turn to high speed for a minute or two. Fill pans or custard cups half full and place them in a cold oven. Set oven at 400°F. and bake the popovers for 1 hour.

Breads and Coffee Cakes   207

CAMPER'S SOURDOUGH ROLLS

These rolls are just as good cooked at home on top of the stove as they are when cooked over the open fire. The only requirement is to start proceedings 3 days before you plan to bake to give the dough time to sour. On your next outdoor vacation, take the sourdough (called the starter) to camp with you, along with the extra flour and soda. You'll be all set for ravenous appetites your first night out. Some of the starter can be saved for making more rolls or sourdough pancakes.

MAKES 12 TO 15 LARGE ROLLS PLUS STARTER FOR ANOTHER BAKING

Starter

2 cups all-purpose flour   1 teaspoon salt
2 tablespoons sugar   2 cups warm water

Additional Ingredients for Rolls

½ cup flour, or more   Poppy or sesame seeds
1 teaspoon baking soda

Mix the 2 cups flour, sugar, salt, and warm water. Beat well until you have a smooth batter. Put batter in a large crock or bowl so that it has room to expand. Cover and set in a warm place without drafts (about 85°F.) for 2 days. This spongy mass is called the starter and it will become quite odorous by the end of 2 days. Don't let it bother you; eventually it will have a most fragrant bouquet.

On the third day, mix ½ cup flour and the baking soda with three quarters of the starter. Add enough more flour to make a dough and knead until smooth. Shape pieces of the dough into balls about the size of a lemon, then roll in poppy or sesame seeds until well coated on top. Place in the bottom of a greased Dutch oven with space in between for expansion. Let the rolls rise for 20 to 25 minutes, until doubled in size.

When the rolls have risen, place the Dutch oven over a moderate flame on a campfire or stove. Cover and cook for about 20 minutes.

Use the remainder of the starter for more rolls, bread, or pancakes. To keep it going, add more flour to it.

LEMON-PARSLEY SPREAD

The distinctive flavor and fine crunchy texture of this spread make it especially good with crusty sourdough rolls. Serve these rolls with any casserole and a green salad. One half roll serves one.

MAKES ENOUGH SPREAD FOR 8 LARGE ROLLS

8 tablespoons (1 cube) margarine, softened
2 tablespoons minced fresh parsley

1 tablespoon lemon juice
1½ tablespoons grated lemon rind

Mix margarine, parsley, lemon juice and rind. Pull sourdough rolls apart and spread with the mixture. Put halves together and wrap in aluminum foil. Heat in a 350° to 375°F. oven for 15 minutes.

This spread can be used in many other ways. It is especially good with potatoes and other vegetables; see Index for other uses.

OATMEAL BREAD

If you're an enthusiastic bread maker, you'll be even more so after trying this one. Perfect for lunch with a bowl of salad or soup. If you double the recipe it will make 3 small round loaves.

MAKES 1 LOAF

1½ cups water
1½ teaspoons salt
1½ cups rolled oats
¼ cup brown sugar
1 tablespoon oil
1½ cakes or packages of yeast

¼ cup lukewarm water
2½ cups all-purpose flour
½ cup dry skim milk
½ cup wheat germ or ground walnuts
Margarine

Bring the water and salt to a boil and stir in the rolled oats. Cool to lukewarm. Add brown sugar and oil to the oats. Crumble the yeast into the lukewarm water; stir until dissolved. Blend into oatmeal mix-

Breads and Coffee Cakes   209

ture. Mix flour, dry skim milk, and wheat germ or walnuts. Stir them into the oatmeal mixture with a spoon, then use your hands when the dough becomes too sticky and hard to handle with a spoon. Turn out the dough onto a floured board and knead until dough is elastic and does not stick to the board. Let it rise in a warm place until doubled; it may take 2 to 3 hours. You can use the oven with the pilot light on for heat, and set a pan of warm water on the rack below the bread.

Punch down the dough when doubled. Grease a bread pan 9 by 5 by 3 inches. Turn the dough into the pan and let it rise until doubled again, about 1 hour. Meanwhile preheat oven to 375°F. Bake the risen loaf in the preheated oven for 40 to 45 minutes, until light brown. You may brush the top with a little margarine. If the bread begins to get too brown, reduce heat to 350°F. Remove bread from the pan when done and place on a rack to cool.

CASSEROLE BATTER BREAD

Batter bread is too moist to knead, so it must be beaten vigorously instead. In this recipe the batter requires only one rising, so it is quick to prepare.

½ cup warm water	1½ teaspoons salt
1 package dry yeast	2 tablespoons sugar
¾ cup liquid skim milk	3 cups sifted all-purpose
2 tablespoons oil	flour

Pour warm water into a large mixing bowl. Sprinkle the yeast over the water and stir until dissolved. Scrape the bowl with a rubber scraper to mix well. Add skim milk, oil, salt, sugar, and 1½ cups of the flour. Beat for 3 or 4 minutes with an electric mixer at medium speed, or for 300 strokes by hand. Stir in remaining flour and beat with a wooden spoon until smooth. Cover dough with a clean cloth and let rise in a warm place (85°F.) for about 1 hour, or until doubled in bulk.

Preheat oven to 375°F. Grease an oval casserole or stainless-steel mixing bowl. Stir batter again vigorously for a minute or so. Turn batter into the prepared casserole and bake in the preheated oven for 50 minutes.

Remove from the casserole and cool for a few minutes before slicing.

DINNER ROLLS (CRESCENTS, CLOVER-LEAF ROLLS, PARKERHOUSE ROLLS, FANTANS)

The new Rapidmix method is used here and it proves very successful.

MAKES ABOUT 36 SMALL ROLLS

3 to 3½ cups sifted all-purpose flour
1 package dry yeast
1 cup liquid skim milk

2 tablespoons oil
2 tablespoons sugar
1 teaspoon salt

Sift together about one third of the flour and all of the yeast. Heat skim milk, oil, sugar, and salt over low heat until hot to the finger but no more. Stir to dissolve sugar and salt. Add liquids to the flour-yeast mixture and beat with an electric mixer at medium speed for 2 minutes, or 300 strokes by hand. Add another ½ to 1 cup of flour and beat for another minute with the electric mixer. Stir in enough more flour to make a soft dough. Turn out onto a floured board and knead until smooth and elastic, 8 to 10 minutes. Place in a greased bowl, turning dough over to grease all surfaces. Cover with wax paper and over that place a dry cloth. Place in a warm place (80° to 85°F.), free from drafts, and let rise until doubled, about 1 hour.

Punch dough down. Turn out onto a floured board again and shape into any desired form (instructions follow). Place rolls on greased baking sheets or in muffin cups and let rise again until doubled, 1 to 1½ hours. Preheat oven to 425°F. Bake for about 10 minutes, and serve piping hot.

Cloverleaf Rolls

Form dough into little balls about ½ inch in diameter. Brush with a little oil and place 3 balls together in a muffin cup for each cloverleaf.

Crescents

Crescent rolls are made from triangular shapes about 3 inches to a side. Roll out the dough to a scant ¼-inch thickness. Cut wedges from a 6-inch circle. Or roll dough into a rectangle 3 inches wide, cut into squares, and make triangles by slicing diagonally. Brush with butter-flavored oil or margarine. Roll up the triangles, starting with the wide end, and curve into crescents.

Parkerhouse Rolls

Cut rolled-out dough, ¼ inch thick, with a 3-inch biscuit cutter. Make a depression with a spoon just below the center. Brush with margarine or oil and fold over from the top envelope fashion, with the lower portion, with depression, larger than the upper portion.

Fantans

Roll out dough into a ⅛-inch-thick rectangle. Cut into 1-inch strips. Brush with margarine or butter-flavored oil. Pile 6 or 7 strips one on top of the other. Cut pieces about 1¼ inches long and place in greased muffin cups with cut sides up. They will open out in a fan shape as they bake.

BASIC SWEET DOUGH

Many delicious sweet breads and buns can be made from this one basic sweet dough. This also uses the Rapidmix method.

MAKES ABOUT 24 ROLLS OR 2 COFFEE CAKES

4½ to 5 cups sifted all-purpose flour	½ cup sugar
2 packages dry yeast	⅓ cup oil
½ cup liquid skim milk	1½ teaspoons salt
½ cup water	4 egg whites
	Oil

Sift 2 cups of the flour and the yeast together into a large bowl. Stir to mix well. Heat skim milk, water, sugar, oil, and salt over low heat until warm, stirring to dissolve sugar. Add liquids to flour-yeast mixture and beat until smooth, 2 to 3 minutes with an electric mixer, 300 strokes by hand. Mix in egg whites. Add 1 more cup of flour and beat for another minute. Add more flour, and continue to beat until the dough is too stiff to continue. Turn out onto a floured board and knead for 8 to 10 minutes, adding remaining flour as needed. Do not stint on the kneading time as it is necessary to develop the gluten. Form the dough into a ball and place in a greased bowl. Cover and let rise in a warm place (80° to 85°F.), until doubled in bulk, 1½ to 2 hours. (If the pilot light is left on in the oven for a while the temperature will be close to 85°F. Check with a thermometer; the correct temperature is important.)

Punch down the dough and let it rest for 10 minutes. Then shape it into rolls, wreaths, buns, etc. Place in greased pans, and brush tops with oil. Cover and let rise again until doubled, 30 to 45 minutes.

Bake in a preheated 350°F. oven for 20 to 25 minutes, depending on size. Remove from pans immediately.

PINWHEEL CINNAMON ROLLS

MAKES ABOUT 18 ROLLS

½ recipe Basic Sweet Dough (p. 212)	2½ teaspoons ground cinnamon
3 tablespoons oil	⅔ cup sugar

After the first rising, roll the dough into a rectangle 9 by 18 inches. Brush with 2 tablespoons of the oil. Mix cinnamon and sugar. Sprinkle ½ cup of this evenly over the dough. Roll up the dough lengthwise, pinching to seal edge. Cut roll into 1-inch slices. Place each slice in a greased muffin cup, or arrange them in a greased pan 9 by 13 inches, leaving a little space between the slices. Brush tops with remaining oil and sprinkle with remaining cinnamon and sugar. Let rise in a warm place (80° to 85°F.) until doubled; this will take 35 to 40 minutes.

Bake in a preheated 350°F. oven for 20 to 25 minutes. Remove from pans to cool.

Breads and Coffee Cakes   213

CARAMEL BUNS

Melt-in-the-mouth buns for a Sunday brunch.

Follow the recipe for Pinwheel Cinnamon Rolls (p. 213), but bake in a caramel mixture. Cut the roll of dough into 1-inch slices and let them rise until doubled.

⅓ cup oil   ½ cup walnut meats
½ cup brown sugar

Mix oil, sugar, and walnuts in a 7-inch skillet with heatproof handle. Heat enough to melt the sugar and mix all together. Put the risen slices of dough in the caramel and bake in a preheated 350°F. oven for 20 to 25 minutes.

When rolls are done, turn upside down immediately onto a large platter. Let them rest for a minute or two so that the caramel topping runs down over the rolls.

GLAZED ORANGE BUNS

½ recipe Basic Sweet Dough   ½ cup light brown sugar
  (p. 212)   1 teaspoon ground cinnamon
2 tablespoons oil   Orange Sauce (below)

After first rising, roll dough into an oblong 9 by 18 inches and brush with oil. Sprinkle with combined brown sugar and cinnamon. Roll up the dough, seal the edge, and cut into 1-inch slices. Grease a pan 9 by 13 inches. Spoon orange sauce into the bottom of the pan and lay sliced buns on top. Bake in a preheated 350°F. oven for 20 to 25 minutes.

Turn upside down onto a plate as soon as done so that the sauce runs down over the buns.

Orange Sauce for Buns

½ cup sugar
2 tablespoons grated orange
   rind

¼ cup orange juice
1 tablespoon lemon juice

Mix all together, then simmer for 2 or 3 minutes. Cool.

NORWEGIAN TEA RING

MAKES 8 TO 12 SERVINGS

Follow recipe for Pinwheel Cinnamon Rolls (p. 213), except sprinkle ⅔ cup of raisins (with the cinnamon and sugar) on the rolled-out dough. Roll up dough and place on a greased baking sheet with the sealed edge on the bottom. Bring ends together to form a wreath. Cut wreath at 1-inch intervals about two thirds of the way through to the bottom. Let rise in warm place until doubled, 35 to 40 minutes. Brush with oil. Bake in a preheated 350°F. oven for 20 to 25 minutes, or until golden brown. Spoon Sugar Glaze (below) over the tea ring while ring is still a little warm.

Sugar Glaze

½ cup sifted confectioners'
   sugar

½ tablespoon hot water
½ teaspoon vanilla extract

Beat until smooth.

Sandwiches

GOOD EARTH SANDWICH

Raw brown mushrooms and alfalfa sprouts combine in an unusual but delightful sandwich, full of texture and good smells. A contribution from my daughter Gretchen.

Use coarse-grained wheat bread. Spread both bread slices with mayonnaise. Lay vegetables on in layers; use thick slices of raw brown mushrooms, slices of tomato, and alfalfa or bean sprouts. Season with salt and pepper and close sandwich.

PUMPERNICKEL AND RED-ONION SANDWICHES

The story goes that Napoleon, when forced to stop at a wayside inn, was served dark coarse bread instead of the fine white bread he was used to. Incensed, he shouted, "C'est bon pour Nickel!," and refused to eat it. Nickel was the name of his horse! Ever since this type of dark coarse bread has been called Bon pour Nickel *or "Pumpernickel."*

Well, when you add sliced raw onions to pumpernickel you have something you too may feel should be given to Napoleon's horse. However, there are some hardy souls who will love these sandwiches, so give them a try.

Slice pumpernickel no thicker than ¼ inch. Spread both sides of the bread with mayonnaise, lay on thin slices of red onion, and sprinkle with salt and pepper. Wrap in wax paper. Chill for 5 or 6 hours! This is most important as the onions mellow a bit and lose some of their pungency. Chilling overnight is even better.

Serve to hungry guests, with beer, for a late snack. Or cut into small wedge shapes and serve as canapés.

WILTED CUCUMBER SANDWICH

A light and refreshing lunch when served with a large glass of cold milk (skim, of course!). Use thin-sliced bread to match the delicacy of the cucumbers.

Use Swedish rye, whole-grain, or enriched white bread. Pare cucumbers and slice very thin. Sprinkle with salt and refrigerate for 30 minutes. Remove from refrigerator and drain on paper towels. Spread one side of bread with margarine, the other side rather lavishly with mayonnaise. Cover with cucumber slices. Sprinkle with pepper and paprika.

PEANUT-BUTTER, BANANA, AND RAISIN SANDWICH

Dreamed up by my daughter Lauren.

Spread one side of whole-grain cracked-wheat bread with peanut butter, the other with mayonnaise. Lay on slices of banana and sprinkle with a few raisins. Put all together, grab a large glass of skim milk, go out, and relax in the sun and enjoy life.

WORKING MAN'S BEAN SANDWICH

Use kidney, pinto, garbanzo, or any other canned or cooked beans without sauce containing fat. Drain liquid from beans, but reserve it. Mash beans well with a fork and add chopped celery, minced chives, and imitation bacon bits (p. 430). Moisten with French dressing and a little bean liquid if desired. Season with salt and pepper. Spread one slice of bread with mayonnaise; add lettuce. Spread the other slice with bean filling. Close sandwich.

WATERCRESS TEA SANDWICHES

Cut crusts from very thin slices of white bread. Spread lightly with mayonnaise. Place an ample amount of watercress on one slice. Spread low-fat cottage cheese on another, or have plain watercress without cheese. Season. Close sandwich and wrap tightly in wax paper. Store in refrigerator until thoroughly chilled. Slice diagonally into thin strips to serve.

RED-PEPPER AND COTTAGE-CHEESE SANDWICH

Spread Red-Pepper Relish (p. 28) on one slice of 100 percent whole-wheat bread, mayonnaise and cottage cheese on the other. Top with lettuce leaves and close sandwich.

OPEN-FACED COTTAGE-CHEESE AND SUNFLOWER-SEED SANDWICH

A great early morning or late evening snack.

Toast raisin, millet, or soya bread lightly on both sides and spread with margarine. Add a thick layer of low-fat cottage cheese and top with toasted sunflower seeds. Eat as it is, or pop into the broiler for a quick browning.

GRILLED CHEESE SANDWICH

This all-time favorite is only possible if you have the right kind of cheese; otherwise it is off limits.

Use cornmeal, rye, or whole-wheat bread, and processed vegetable-oil cheese (p. 419). Spread one piece of bread with mayonnaise, the other with prepared mustard. Lay slices of cheese on bread and top with dill pickle. Close sandwich. Grill slowly on a nonstick pan with or without oil or margarine. Low-fat cheese will take longer to melt than ordinary cheese. To speed the process, cover sandwich with a tight-fitting lid for part of the time.

OPEN-FACED MELTED TUMA CHEESE SANDWICH

Tuma cheese (p. 419), one of many brands of pressed cottage cheese (now available on the West Coast), contains about 9 percent butterfat, approximately the same as Italian ricotta. Compared to Cheddar, with over 30 percent fat content, it is relatively safe for a once-in-a-while lunch. Substitute any suitable pressed cottage cheese that is available to you. Even hoop cheese, creamed with a little oil, will do.

Use a favorite bread—sourdough, cracked wheat, cornmeal, pumpernickel, whole wheat, etc. Toast bread on one side. Spread with mayonnaise and a very small amount of prepared mustard if you wish. Tuma is salty so don't overdo the seasoning. Lay on tomato slices to just cover the toast. Sprinkle with pepper and top with ¼-inch-thick slices of cheese. Broil on the lowest shelf in an oven broiler, very slowly, for 15 to 20 minutes, or until puffy and slightly browned. Cheese with a low fat content takes longer to melt.

SALMON-CUCUMBER SANDWICH

Mash canned pink salmon with a fork. Blend with mayonnaise, lemon juice, and chopped celery; season with salt and pepper. Spread this liberally on one slice of white bread, top with slices of wilted cucumber, then with another slice of bread.

SALMON BEACHCOMBER

MAKES 4 SANDWICHES

8 slices of rye bread
Margarine
Lettuce leaves
1 can (7¾ ounces) salmon
½ cup low-fat cottage cheese

⅓ cup chopped green onion
¼ cup minced celery
¼ cup chopped dill pickle
¼ cup mayonnaise

Spread bread lightly with margarine. Add lettuce. Drain and flake salmon. Combine with remaining ingredients, mixing well with a fork. Spread on top of lettuce leaves. Cover with the second slice of bread. Garnish with carrot sticks and cherry tomatoes.

OCEANBURGER

A hot fish sandwich, ideal for a cold winter day.

MAKES 4 SANDWICHES

4 hamburger buns
1 pound fish fillets, ½ inch
   thick
Bread crumbs
1 tablespoon oil

Salt and pepper
Tomato slices
¼ to ½ cup Sauce Louis
   (p. 282)

Split the buns and toast lightly. Divide fish fillets into 4 sections. Coat with a few bread crumbs and sauté in oil until flaky and cooked throughout. Season to taste. Place one fillet on bottom half of each bun, cover with a tomato slice, add 1 or 2 tablespoons of sauce, and top with other half of bun.

Serve with pickle slices and a knife and fork if the sandwich is very moist.

TUNA SALAD SANDWICHES

As popular as peanut butter and jelly! Here's our favorite simple version.

MAKES 4 LARGE SANDWICHES

1 can (13 ounces) water-
   packed tuna, well drained
⅓ cup mayonnaise
½ cup chopped celery
2 tablespoons chopped chives
2 tablespoons chopped dill
   pickle

1 tablespoon wine vinegar
1 tablespoon (or more)
   liquid skim milk
Very large, very thin slices of
   sourdough bread
Margarine
Lettuce leaves

Mash tuna with a fork. Mix with mayonnaise, celery, chives, and pickle. Stir in vinegar and milk; add more milk if necessary to give good consistency. Spread on slices of sourdough bread. Spread other side with margarine if desired. Top with lettuce leaves.

Wonderful for a picnic with a chilled bottle of dry white wine.

TUNA BOATS

Unanimous yes vote for this one! Quite a few ingredients, but it takes only a minute to assemble them.

MAKES 6 SERVINGS

6 large (7-inch) French or
    sourdough rolls
1 can (13 ounces) water-
    packed tuna, or 2 small cans
    (6 ounces each), drained
1 cup hoop or dry-curd cottage
    cheese

1 cup fine-chopped celery
½ cup fine-chopped chives
¼ cup chopped pimiento
1 can (4 ounces) button
    mushrooms
Dressing (below)
Bread crumbs

Split rolls into halves and scoop out inside dough, leaving a casing of ¼ to ½ inch. Discard inside dough. Break up tuna in a large bowl. Crumble hoop cheese and add to tuna along with celery, chives, pimiento, and mushrooms. Combine dressing ingredients, and mix well with tuna-cheese mixture. Fill rolls and sprinkle with a few bread crumbs. Wrap aluminum foil around the bottom of each roll to keep them from drying out. Bake in a 350°F. oven for 30 to 45 minutes, or until heated through.

Dressing

½ cup mayonnaise
½ cup plain low-fat yogurt
1 tablespoon wine vinegar
    with garlic

1 teaspoon salt
¼ teaspoon pepper
1 teaspoon dillweed

Variation: Omit bread crumbs and spoon 1 or 2 tablespoons of tomato sauce over each roll before baking.

TUNABURGERS

MAKES 4 SERVINGS

1 can (7 ounces) water-
packed tuna, drained and
flaked
½ cup bread crumbs, cornflake
crumbs, or cracker crumbs
½ cup chopped celery
2 tablespoons chopped green
onions, or 1 teaspoon onion
flakes soaked in 1 tablespoon
water

4 tablespoons mayonnaise
2½ tablespoons chili sauce
1½ teaspoons lemon juice
Oil
4 hamburger buns
Margarine
Lettuce
Tomato slices

Mix together tuna, bread crumbs, celery, and onions. Combine mayonnaise, chili sauce, and lemon juice. Stir into tuna mixture. Shape into 4 patties. Sauté in a lightly oiled skillet over medium heat for 4 or 5 minutes. Turn patties once; they should be browned on both sides.

Split and toast buns. Spread lightly with margarine. Place a patty on one side, cover with lettuce and tomato slices, and top with second half of bun.

Or make 8 smaller patties and serve on English muffin halves as open-faced sandwiches.

LOX AND BAGELS (a fair approximation)

As bagels usually contain more eggs than you need, substitute some other rolls; kaiser, French, sourdough, sesame-seed, or English muffins.

Rinse oil from a jar of smoked salmon and dry the fish between paper towels. Mix salt, pepper, and mayonnaise into hoop cheese to make a smooth spread. Pat this lavishly on both sides of rolls and lay slices of salmon in between.

OPEN-FACED COPENHAGEN SANDWICH

MAKES 4 SANDWICHES

4 very large slices of heavy
   dark rye or pumpernickel
   bread
Unsalted margarine
4 large green lettuce leaves
Marinated wilted cucumber
   slices
2 cans (3½ ounces each)
   kipper snacks (smoked fillets
   of herring)

1 can (16 ounces) asparagus
   stalks, drained
Thin slices of Bermuda onion
½ cup Thousand Island
   Dressing (p. 281) or
   mayonnaise
Thin slices of pimiento

Spread bread with margarine. Place a leaf of lettuce on each slice. Add a thin layer of marinated cucumber. Arrange smoked herring alternately with asparagus spears on the cucumber slices. Top with 2 or 3 onion rings and a spoonful of dressing or mayonnaise. Garnish with pimiento slices.

Serve with cold potato salad and additional wilted cucumbers sprinkled with French dressing.

CHICKEN SALAD BOATS

Capers and chives lend added interest to this hot chicken sandwich.

Split frankfurter rolls. Remove some of the inside dough. Spread one side lightly with margarine, the other with mayonnaise. Fill cavity with chicken salad. Sprinkle with capers, chives and imitation bacon bits (p. 430). Heat in oven until piping hot.

SPECIAL CLUB SANDWICH

MAKES 1 SANDWICH, FOR A HEFTY APPETITE

2 thin slices of Canadian
   bacon
3 slices of white bread
1½ tablespoons mayonnaise
2 slices of tomato

2 slices of cooked white meat
   of turkey or chicken
1 large lettuce leaf
Salt and pepper

Remove all fat from Canadian bacon. Sauté until crisp. Pat dry with a paper towel to remove any remaining fat. Keep warm. Toast bread slices and spread with mayonnaise. Place Canadian bacon and tomato on one slice of toast. Cover with second slice. Place turkey and lettuce on second slice. Season lightly. Top with third piece of toast. Cut sandwich diagonally into quarters.

Serve with a large glass of skim milk and a few pickle slices.

HOT CHICKEN, CANADIAN BACON, AND LETTUCE ON SOURDOUGH

Something special for a cold day!

Broil thin slices of Canadian bacon on a rack in an oven broiler. Toast large slices of sourdough bread on one side. Spread both pieces of bread with mayonnaise. Lay on chicken, lettuce, and Canadian bacon. Spread with prepared French-style mustard and season with salt and pepper. Serve warm.

HOT TURKEY AND ASPARAGUS OPEN-FACER

MAKES 4 SANDWICHES

1 package (10 ounces) frozen asparagus spears, or 1 can (15 ounces), drained
4 large slices of white meat of turkey, cut into halves
8 medium-sized slices of French bread

2 tablespoons margarine
1 cup Mustard-Hollandaise Sauce (p. 298)
¼ cup liquid skim milk

Place frozen asparagus in correct amount of boiling water. Lay turkey slices over them and cook together according to directions for asparagus, until the vegetable is done. Toast bread on both sides and spread lightly with margarine. Heat sauce and skim milk together.

To serve, place a half slice of turkey on each piece of toast; top with well-drained asparagus spears, and spoon sauce over all.

TURKEY OR CHICKEN PUFFS

MAKES 4 SANDWICHES OR 32 CANAPÉS

4 large slices of bread
1 cup minced cooked turkey or chicken
2 tablespoons chopped chives
⅓ cup mayonnaise
½ cup chopped celery

¼ cup chopped pimiento
1 teaspoon prepared horseradish
Salt and pepper
2 egg whites
¼ teaspoon salt

Toast bread in broiler. Keep warm. Mix turkey or chicken with chives, mayonnaise, celery, pimiento, and horseradish. Blend well and season with salt and pepper to taste. Beat egg whites and ¼ teaspoon salt until stiff. Fold into the other mixture. Spread on toasted bread. Broil under medium heat for 5 to 7 minutes, until nicely browned and puffed up.

Crackers or small rounds of toasted bread can be used for canapés.

ROAST VEAL ON RYE

Spread mayonnaise on one slice of rye bread and place layers of lettuce and tomatoes over it. Spread the other slice with Horseradish Cream Sauce (p. 299). Top with slices of cold roast veal and dill pickle. Season with salt and pepper, and close the sandwich.

Serve with a tall glass of cold skim milk or your favorite brand of beer.

GROUND VEAL AND PICKLE SANDWICH

Put leftover roast veal through the meat grinder. Combine it with mayonnaise, pickle relish, grated onion, and chopped celery. Season with salt and pepper. Place 1 heaping tablespoon of this mixture on one piece of oatmeal bread. Spread another piece of bread with mayonnaise and cover with lettuce and sliced tomatoes. Put all together and broil, on both sides if desired.

KAISER SPECIAL WITH SAUERKRAUT AND SMOKED BEEF

MAKES 4 SANDWICHES

4 kaiser rolls with poppy seeds	2 packages (4 ounces each) smoked sliced beef
2 tablespoons margarine	French-style mustard
1 can (16 ounces) sauerkraut	

Split rolls and spread with margarine. Place under the broiler and toast. Keep warm in aluminum foil. Heat the can of sauerkraut. Divide sliced beef into 4 portions and sauté in a nonstick pan or broil until crispy. To assemble, spread bottom half of roll with mustard, lay on beef slices, and cover with well-drained sauerkraut. Top with other half of roll.

Serve with a glass of cold beer, sliced radishes, and dill pickle spears.

Potatoes, Rice, and Other Cereals

QUICK-ROASTED NEW POTATOES

An easy way to simulate the crusty potatoes that traditionally surround the roast. Don't be limited to serving these with a roast; they go with everything!

MAKES 4 SERVINGS

4 small new potatoes, or 2 large baking potatoes	1 tablespoon oil Salt and pepper

Peel potatoes and halve or quarter them according to the size. Place oil in a small baking or heatproof glass dish so that potatoes can be spread out comfortably without too much extra room. Heat oil slowly. Roll potatoes in the oil or use a pastry brush to coat them. Season with salt and pepper to taste. Bake in a 450°F. to 500°F. oven for about 25 minutes, turning the potatoes and brushing them with the oil 2 or 3 times so that they become brown and crusty.

Variation: Do not peel potatoes. Simply cut them into halves, lay them flat side down on an oiled pan, and bake until under side is brown.

BARBECUED NEW POTATOES

Few people realize that new potatoes do not always have to be boiled. In fact they are infinitely better when baked, barbecued, roasted, or sautéed. *The skin is tender and flavorful and should always be eaten. When new potatoes are barbecued they are sweet and juicy and need no butter, just a little salt and pepper. When dinner is being prepared on the barbecue, try these for a delicious change.*

Prick small whole new potatoes with a fork. Bake in a 450°F. oven for 15 to 20 minutes while the barbecue fire is getting hot. Cut potatoes into halves and take them out to the barbecue for a last 10 minutes of cooking on the grill. The moisture is sealed in by the hot fire and the potatoes pick up barbecue flavor from smoke and meat juices.

LEMON-PARSLEY POTATOES

For a different flavor for stuffed or baked potatoes, use leftover Lemon-Parsley Spread (p. 209).

Bake your favorite kind of potato. Remove pulp and mash with enough fortified skim milk (half liquid skim milk and half dry skim milk) to make a smooth paste. Add 1 teaspoon Lemon-Parsley Spread for each small potato half. Season with salt and pepper to taste. Stuff the mixture into the potato shells. Return them to the oven and heat through.

WHIPPED POTATOES

These whipped potatoes have a marvelous earthy flavor because of using the cooking water in the recipe. Be sure to scrub the potatoes well; you don't want them to be too earthy!

MAKES 4 SERVINGS

4 medium-sized new or other clean-skinned potatoes (about 1 pound)
½ teaspoon salt

Dry skim milk
1½ tablespoons margarine
¼ teaspoon pepper

Scrub potatoes well and cut them into eighths. Place in a medium-sized saucepan with the salt and add water just to cover. Simmer until tender. Drain cooking liquid into a 16-ounce measuring cup (2 cups) and add dry skim milk equal to half of the amount of liquid, plus 2 more tablespoons. Stir until milk is dissolved.

Peel the drained potatoes and whip or mash while still hot; add 1 tablespoon of the margarine. Gradually stir in the prepared milk until the potatoes reach the right consistency. To keep warm while preparing remainder of dinner, add a little more of the liquid and place the saucepan of potatoes on an asbestos pad over low heat. Cover. Serve with tiny dabs of remaining margarine. Sprinkle with pepper.

For an elegant smooth texture, stir in a spoonful of plain low-fat yogurt just before serving.

OVEN-FRIED POTATOES

MAKES 4 SERVINGS

2 medium-sized baking potatoes (Idaho, new red, etc.)

1 to 2 tablespoons oil
Salt

Peel potatoes and cut into medium- to large-sized strips as you would for French fried potatoes. Pat dry with paper towels. Heat the oil (this thins it and less is needed). With a pastry brush, brush all sides of the potato strips with oil, but not too lavishly. Place a rack on a good-sized baking pan and lay potatoes crosswise on the rack. Bake in a 500°F. oven for 30 minutes. If potatoes brown too much, reduce heat. Broil for another 5 to 10 minutes, until puffed and golden. Since so little oil is used, there is no need to drain these. Sprinkle with salt.

DELMONICO POTATOES

Here is an unconventional version of Delmonico potatoes. If you use new potatoes, bake them rather than boil them and they'll cut up fairly well and have more flavor. Steam whole older potatoes to save flavor and vitamins.

MAKES 4 SERVINGS

¼ cup dry skim milk
1½ cups liquid skim milk
1 tablespoon oil
1 teaspoon mayonnaise
2 tablespoons flour
3 tablespoons minced chives
2 teaspoons lemon juice

½ teaspoon grated Sap Sago cheese, or more
3 drops of yellow food coloring
Salt and pepper
2½ to 3 cups diced cooked potatoes without skins

Dissolve the dry milk in the liquid. Place oil, mayonnaise, and flour in a heavy saucepan. Stir over low heat until hot and well blended. Gradually add the milk and continue to stir over heat until thickened and smooth. Add all other ingredients except potatoes, and mix well. Season to taste. Gently fold in the potatoes and keep over low heat until potatoes are hot.

Serve with a roast or any plainly cooked meat.

POTATOES AND ONIONS ESCALLOPED IN CONSOMMÉ

MAKES 4 SERVINGS

Oil
3 cups thin slices of potatoes
2 tablespoons flour
¼ teaspoon pepper
1 tablespoon margarine
1 large yellow onion, sliced thin

1 can (10½ ounces) condensed consommé, undiluted
¼ teaspoon prepared mustard

Oil a flat ovenproof baking dish not more than 2 inches deep. Spread half of the potatoes on the bottom. Sprinkle with 1 tablespoon flour and a little pepper. Dot with half of the margarine. Lay the onion slices on top. Repeat with remainder of potatoes, flour, pepper, and margarine. Pour on half of the consommé. Blend mustard with remaining consommé and add to casserole. Bake in a 350°F. oven for 1 hour, until potatoes are soft.

DUTCH HUTSPOT POTATOES

MAKES 4 SERVINGS

3 large new potatoes
1 large yellow onion
4 small carrots
½ cup dry skim milk
2 tablespoons butter-flavored
  oil

1 tablespoon sugar
Salt and pepper
⅓ cup Cheese Crumbs
  (p. 304)

Peel and dice vegetables. Place in a medium-sized saucepan with just enough water to cover ¾ to 1 cup and simmer, covered, until tender. Drain off cooking liquid into a bowl; add the dry milk and stir until dissolved. Set aside. Mash vegetables with oil, sugar, and salt and pepper to taste. Add the liquid and beat until smooth and fluffy. Pour into a greased casserole and sprinkle with cheese crumbs. Place in a hot oven just long enough to heat through.

KARTOFFEL LATKES (potato pancakes)

A traditional Jewish dish for Hanukkah. Serve with meat or, for a special treat, with applesauce or strawberry jam.

MAKES 4 SERVINGS

2 medium-large potatoes, peeled and grated
1 medium-sized onion, grated or minced
3 egg whites
2 drops of yellow food coloring

2 to 3 tablespoons flour
½ teaspoon baking powder
½ teaspoon salt
¼ teaspoon pepper
2 tablespoons oil

Drain moisture from potatoes and pat the shreds between paper towels. Combine potatoes and onion. Beat egg whites lightly with food coloring and add to potatoes. Sift flour with baking powder. Add salt and pepper and mix with potatoes. Bring oil to medium heat in a large skillet. Drop potato mixture by spoonfuls onto skillet and brown the pancakes on both sides. Serve immediately.

SIMPLE RICE PILAF

You can develop a different texture, color, and taste with very slight changes in the method of cooking rice. Here is the simplest version of a pilaf.

MAKES 4 SERVINGS

1 cup uncooked long-grain rice
1 tablespoon oil

2 cups bouillon or consommé

Sauté rice in oil until it reaches the color you wish. Drain off excess oil. Reduce the heat to as low as possible, add bouillon, cover, and steam for 20 minutes, or until all the liquid is absorbed. For fluffier rice, use 3 cups liquid.

SAFFRON RICE

Saffron is expensive. For a less expensive substitute, use an equal amount of turmeric to give the rice an equally beautiful yellow color. The flavor is not significant because the amount is so small.

MAKES 4 SERVINGS

1 small onion, chopped fine
1 tablespoon oil
1 cup uncooked long-grain white rice

⅛ teaspoon ground saffron or turmeric
2 cups chicken bouillon

Sauté onion in oil until translucent. Add rice and continue to cook, stirring with a spoon, until rice has turned milky. Add saffron and bouillon, cover tightly, and simmer for 18 to 20 minutes, or until liquid is absorbed.

RISOTTO MILANESE

MAKES 6 SERVINGS

2 tablespoons butter-flavored oil
1½ cups uncooked rice
3 or 4 green onions, chopped fine
¼ cup dry white wine

½ cup chopped mushrooms
Pinch of ground turmeric or saffron
4 cups chicken bouillon
1 tablespoon grated Parmesan cheese

Heat oil in a heavy saucepan. Add the rice and green onions and cook slowly, stirring with a wooden spoon, until rice is milky. Add the wine and continue cooking and stirring until wine is absorbed by the rice. Reduce heat and stir in remaining ingredients. Cover and simmer slowly for about 20 minutes.

The next three rice recipes are delightfully simple, and require no sautéing or preliminary cooking of any kind. Use 2 bouillon cubes plus 2 cups water instead of the consommé if you prefer.

MUSHROOM RICE

MAKES 4 SERVINGS

1 cup uncooked long-grain
   rice
1 can (3 ounces) sliced
   mushrooms, drained
½ cup chopped green onions

1 tablespoon oil
1 can (10½ ounces)
   consommé plus water to
   equal 2 cups

Place all ingredients in a greased ovenproof casserole. Cover. Bake in a 375°F. oven for 25 to 30 minutes.

GREEN RICE

MAKES 4 SERVINGS

1 cup uncooked long-grain rice
½ cup chopped green pepper
½ cup chopped green onions
½ cup chopped fresh parsley,
   or ¼ cup dried

1 tablespoon oil
1 can (10½ ounces)
   consommé plus water to
   equal 2 cups

Combine all ingredients in a greased ovenproof casserole. Cover. Bake in a 375°F. oven for 25 to 30 minutes. Check moisture after 20 minutes. If too dry, add another 1 to 2 tablespoons of water and stir gently.

LEMON RICE

MAKES 4 SERVINGS

1 cup uncooked long-grain
   rice
1 cup fine-chopped celery
2 tablespoons grated lemon
   rind
2 tablespoons lemon juice

1 tablespoon dried onion
   flakes
1 can (10½ ounces)
   consommé plus water to
   make 2 cups

Combine all ingredients in a greased ovenproof casserole. Cover. Bake in a 375°F. oven for 25 to 30 minutes.

RICE AND SPINACH PILAF

MAKES 4 SERVINGS

1 pound fresh spinach
1 large onion, chopped
2 tablespoons oil

1 cup uncooked rice
2 cups beef bouillon
1 tablespoon tomato paste

Wash and drain spinach and chop into large pieces. Sauté onion in oil until limp. Add rice and continue to sauté until rice is golden brown. Stir occasionally while sautéing. Add the beef bouillon and tomato paste. Mix well. Place as much spinach on top of rice as there is room for in the pan; cover, and simmer slowly. After the first 5 minutes, stir down spinach and rice and add more spinach if there is room. Simmer for another 15 minutes, or until rice is tender.

RICE AND YELLOW-SQUASH PILAF

An interesting dish to be served cold for a buffet meal. The olive oil is essential to the flavor.

MAKES 6 TO 8 SERVINGS

3 medium-sized yellow squash, sliced very thin
3 cups cooked long-grain white rice, cooled
3 green onions, sliced thin
½ cup toasted and salted sunflower seeds
½ cup garlic-flavored wine vinegar

2 teaspoons minced fresh dill or dillweed
½ teaspoon pepper
½ teaspoon salt
1 tablespoon olive oil
2 tablespoons regular oil

Stir together in a large bowl the squash slices, cooled rice, green onions, and sunflower seeds, being careful not to mash or crush the rice and squash. Blend the remaining ingredients in a smaller bowl and pour over the rice mixture. Toss gently with 2 forks until well mixed. Chill.

SPANISH RICE WITH CHILETEPÍN

This simple Spanish version of pilaf is a great favorite. It is not a fluffy rice; each grain is separate because of the initial browning. Be careful of using too many of the little Mexican peppers, however, until you know the tolerance of your taste buds. They are there to add flavor, not blisters! You can find the peppers in any market, usually labeled chiletepín, chili tepinis, *or "hot chilies." The fiery* chiletepín *has a bigger clout than its 1-inch size suggests, so I advise using only half of one as a start. Some of the other varieties of peppers are round and about ¼ inch in diameter. In this case use one or two for your first try.*

1 small onion, chopped
2 tablespoons oil
1 cup uncooked long-grain
   rice
½ *chiletepín*, including the
   seeds

1 can (10½ ounces) beef
   consommé plus water to
   make 2 cups

Use a skillet or a heavy saucepan with a tight-fitting lid. Sauté onion in the oil until golden. Add rice and *chiletepín* and continue to cook over medium heat. Stir constantly. The longer you cook, the browner the rice. When done, drain off the excess oil if you are watching calories.

Add liquid to rice, cover tightly, and simmer over the lowest possible heat for about 20 minutes, or until rice is soft and liquid absorbed. Should the liquid evaporate before rice is done, add a little water. If it evaporates without your noticing it so that rice sticks to the bottom of the saucepan, add 2 or 3 tablespoons water, remove pan from heat, and let it stand for a few minutes. The added moisture will help to loosen the part stuck on the bottom; it also makes the gummiest, yummiest part of the dish. Be sure to serve it.

TURKISH RICE

MAKES 6 SERVINGS

1 large onion, chopped
2 tablespoons oil
Pinch each of ground turmeric,
   cinnamon, and cloves
2 or 3 bay leaves
1 cup uncooked long-grain
   white rice

2 cups boiling stock or water
1 package (10 ounces)
   frozen peas
½ cup chopped walnuts

Potatoes, Rice, and Other Cereals 243

Sauté onion in oil until brown. Stir in spices, bay leaves, and rice; cook for another minute or two. Pour boiling stock or water over the rice, stir, and bring to a boil again. Add peas and walnuts. Cover and simmer for about 30 minutes. Check to be sure rice is not sticking. A few more tablespoons of liquid may be necessary.

WILD RICE COMBO

The rough-textured, brown-skinned wild rice was a great favorite of the American Indian and the early colonist. It is still a great favorite but is rarely eaten these days because of its high price. Combining it with other things makes it less expensive, but the distinctive texture and flavor can still dominate the dish.

MAKES 6 SERVINGS

1 large onion, quartered and sliced thin
1 tablespoon oil
2 large tomatoes, quartered and sliced
1½ cups cooked wild rice
1½ cups cooked Simple Rice Pilaf (p. 238)
1 tablespoon chopped parsley
1 tablespoon grated Parmesan cheese

Sauté onion slices in oil until lightly browned. Add tomatoes and simmer until soft, just a few minutes. With a fork gently stir in both kinds of rice, the parsley, and cheese. Cover and heat slowly until everything is quite hot.

BULGHUR PILAF

Bulghur (cracked wheat) is unfamiliar to many Americans, but to people of the Near East it is a commonplace food. There it is eaten in many ways: in salads and stuffings, as a cereal, and most frequently as a pilaf. The processed wheat kernels are cooked as rice is, but the resulting flavor and texture are infinitely more interesting. You may have some difficulty locating the raw product. Look for it in specialty food stores, where it is sold as cracked wheat, or try to find a handy Greek or Armenian food store. You may even find it in some of the large chain markets where there may be such varied spellings as "bulghur," "bulgur," and "bulghour."

MAKES 4 SERVINGS

1 medium-sized onion, chopped fine	1 cup bulghur (cracked wheat)
2 tablespoons oil	2 cups bouillon

Sauté onion in oil until golden. Add bulghur and continue to cook until lightly browned, stirring all the time. Add bouillon, cover, and simmer over lowest possible heat for about 20 minutes, or until all liquid has been absorbed. Serve immediately.

HOMINY PUDDING

MAKES 6 SERVINGS

4 cups water	1 teaspoon salt
1½ cups dry skim milk	½ teaspoon pepper
1 cup dry hominy grits	2½ tablespoons margarine

Bring water to a boil in a heavy saucepan. Remove from heat and stir in dry skim milk until thoroughly dissolved. Add hominy grits, salt, and pepper. Return saucepan to heat and simmer for 15 to 20 minutes, until thickened; do not let the pudding thicken to the consistency of cereal. Stir constantly. Remove again from the heat, and add 2 tablespoons of the margarine. Stir until melted. Beat with an electric beater at high speed for 5 minutes. Pour into a greased oven-proof casserole and dot the pudding with remaining margarine. Bake in a 350°F. oven for 1 hour.

A perfect accompaniment to any kind of barbecued, broiled, or roasted meat.

Other good accompaniments to main dishes are Vermicelli Romanoff with Poppy Seeds, Gnocchi, Spoon Bread or any other corn bread, Yorkshire Pudding. All these starchy dishes are listed in the Index.

Potatoes, Rice, and Other Cereals   245

Vegetables

GREEN BEANS WITH ONIONS AND ORÉGANO

MAKES 4 SERVINGS

1 pound fresh green beans	5 tablespoons sherry
1 tablespoon oil	¼ teaspoon crumbled dried
1 large onion, quartered and	orégano
sliced thin	Garlic salt
1 cup water	Pepper

Wash beans, snip off ends, and slice into small pieces. Heat oil in a heavy skillet and sauté onion until golden. Add beans to the skillet with the water, 4 tablespoons sherry, orégano, and garlic salt and pepper to taste. Cover, and simmer gently for 1 hour or so, until almost all liquid has evaporated and beans are very tender. Add remaining tablespoon of sherry for flavor just before serving.

BEETS WITH YOGURT

MAKES 4 SERVINGS

1 can (16 ounces) julienne
  beets
1 teaspoon flour

¼ teaspoon prepared
  horseradish
⅓ cup plain low-fat yogurt

Heat beets in a saucepan until very hot. Remove from heat and drain. Stir flour and horseradish into yogurt and pour over beets.

GLAZED JULIENNE CARROTS

MAKES 4 SERVINGS

1 can (16 ounces) julienne
  carrots
1 teaspoon oil
1 teaspoon margarine

1 tablespoon minced chives
1 tablespoon sauterne
1 teaspoon sugar

Drain liquid from carrots. Heat oil and margarine in a saucepan and add remaining ingredients, including carrots. Simmer until carrots are well heated and glazed.

CAULIFLOWER WITH LEMON-PARSLEY SAUCE

MAKES 8 SERVINGS

1 large cauliflower
¼ cup Lemon-Parsley Spread
  (p. 209)

2 tablespoons flour
1 cup buttermilk

Break cauliflower into flowerets and cook them in boiling salted water for 8 to 10 minutes, until tender but not mushy. Heat the spread in a small saucepan. Blend in the flour. Add buttermilk gradually. Simmer over low heat, stirring until thickened. Pour over hot cauliflower.

BRAISED CELERY

MAKES 4 SERVINGS

1 large or 2 small celery
stalks
2 teaspoons butter-flavored
oil
1 teaspoon beef bouillon
granules

2 tablespoons warm water
1 tablespoon sherry
Salt and pepper

Peel off tough outer ribs of the celery stalk; wash the celery well. If a large stalk is used, split it from top to bottom into 6 sections; if small stalks are used, split each into 4 sections. Sauté these in oil until lightly browned on all sides. Dissolve the bouillon granules in the warm water and add to celery along with sherry. Cover and simmer slowly until celery is tender, about 15 minutes. Season with salt and pepper. Add more liquid if necessary.

Leftover braised celery can be chilled and served as a salad.

BRAISED CUCUMBER

Follow the same procedure as for Braised Celery. For 4 servings use 2 medium-sized cucumbers; peel them and cut into strips. Simmer for about 5 minutes only.

BAKED EGGPLANT SLICES

Cut eggplant into slices ½ inch thick. Sprinkle lemon juice and onion salt over both sides of slices. Bake on a greased baking sheet in a 350° to 400°F. oven for 10 to 12 minutes, until eggplant is tender and a little brown. Turn if you wish. These can also be broiled and are especially good barbecued.

EGGPLANT CREOLE

A quick version of ratatouille *that makes a good accompaniment for any main dish.*

MAKES 6 TO 8 SERVINGS

2 large yellow onions,
    sliced thin
3 to 4 tablespoons oil
1 eggplant, peeled and cubed
½ teaspoon crumbled dried
    basil

Salt and pepper
2 cans (16 ounces each)
    stewed tomatoes

Sauté onions in oil until lightly browned. Add eggplant cubes and sauté for a few minutes, turning over gently with a fork all the while. Add basil and season with salt and pepper to taste. Pour the tomatoes into the eggplant and simmer for 5 to 10 minutes. Serve in bowls.

RATATOUILLE À LA SUE OXLEY

In this classic Provençal dish olive oil is essential to the flavor so a little is included in the recipe.

MAKES 6 TO 8 SERVINGS

2 garlic cloves, minced
2 Bermuda onions, sliced
    very thin
2 tablespoons olive oil
2 tablespoons regular
    vegetable oil
1 large eggplant, peeled
    and diced

2 medium-sized zucchini,
    sliced
3 green peppers, seeded and
    cut into strips
5 tomatoes, chopped
1 tablespoon minced parsley
2 tablespoons flour
Salt and pepper

Sauté garlic and onions in olive oil until transparent. Transfer to a large pot. Add vegetable oil to the skillet and sauté the eggplant and zucchini. Add the peppers, tomatoes, and parsley. Sprinkle with the flour and season with salt and pepper to taste. Cook for another few minutes. Transfer all to the large pot and simmer over low heat for 1 hour. Uncover and adjust seasonings. Cook uncovered for another 15 minutes, or until liquid has partially evaporated.

LAYERED MUSHROOM CASSEROLE

MAKES 8 SERVINGS

1 pound fresh brown mushrooms
½ cup freshly toasted bread crumbs
½ cup sesame seeds
¼ cup butter-flavored oil

½ cup dry white wine
½ teaspoon salt
¼ teaspoon pepper

Wipe mushrooms clean. Remove stems and slice both stems and caps. Combine all other ingredients and mix well with a fork. Arrange half of the mushrooms in an oiled baking dish; cover with half of the crumb mixture. Repeat. Bake in a 350°F. oven for 30 to 35 minutes, or until mushrooms are tender.

If you don't care about the layering effect, the mushrooms can be tossed with the crumb mixture before baking.

PAPRIKA-HONEY ONIONS

MAKES 8 SERVINGS

1 tablespoon oil
1 tablespoon margarine
¼ cup honey
2 tablespoons water

1 teaspoon paprika
¼ teaspoon salt
4 large yellow onions,
    peeled and halved

Combine oil, margarine, honey, water, paprika, and salt in a small saucepan and simmer until bubbly. Place onions, cut side up, in a shallow baking pan or cast-iron skillet. Pour the sauce over them and cover. Bake in a 350°F. oven for 1½ hours, or until tender. Baste 2 or 3 times during baking with the sauce in the pan.

FRENCH-STYLE PEAS OR BEANS

MAKES 4 SERVINGS

1 tablespoon butter-flavored
    oil
1 tablespoon water
1 package (10 ounces) frozen
    peas or green beans

Pinch of sugar
Salt and pepper
6 to 8 large wet lettuce
    leaves

Put oil and water in a saucepan. Add frozen vegetable, sugar, and seasonings to taste. Place lettuce leaves on top. Cook, covered, over low heat until tender. Check to see if more water is needed, and turn over the frozen block to speed thawing if necessary.

BROILED TOMATOES I (with cheese and chives)

Brush large ripe tomatoes with oil and season with salt and pepper. Sprinkle with a pinch each of chives and grated Sap Sago cheese. Broil under moderate heat for 10 to 15 minutes, or until tender when poked with a fork.

BROILED TOMATOES II (with brown sugar)

Follow instructions for Broiled Tomatoes I, substituting brown sugar for chives and cheese.

STIR-FRYING WITH CHINESE VEGETABLES

The term *stir-frying* describes a cooking method in which small pieces of meats, vegetables, or fruits are fried quickly in a very small amount of oil. Stirring is continuous. The primary aim, especially with vegetables, is to retain crispness. The most satisfactory pan for this purpose migrated here from China. This large round-bottomed pot is called a *wok*. However, skillets, frying pans, or large heavy saucepans do the job quite well.

Almost all vegetables can be cooked by this method, but some will need a few minutes of steaming, after frying, to make them tender. Obviously such vegetables as artichokes are not well adapted to stir-frying. Those vegetables considered typically Chinese and most suitable include: Chinese and regular cabbage, celery, onions of all varieties, red and green peppers, mushrooms, bamboo shoots, water chestnuts, bean sprouts, tomatoes, Chinese pea pods, cauliflower, pimientos. These vegetables can be fresh, frozen, or canned, but of course fresh are preferred.

Fruits are sometimes used in sweet dishes. For instance, pineapple, grapes, and mandarin oranges are very popular.

Sauces are simple; they can be made from any of the following: water, wine, bouillon or consommé, vinegar, fruit juices, etc. They are thickened with cornstarch rather than flour. The sauce almost always includes soy sauce and may, in addition, be seasoned with sugar, ginger, molasses, garlic, mustard, catsup, etc.

A little experimenting with this way of cooking will undoubtedly prove rewarding to you. As you become expert, try frying a few thin slices of meat along with the vegetables. A few recipes of this type may be found in this book indexed under "Chinese-style cooking."

CABBAGE CHOP SUEY

If you don't overcook the vegetables, this dish can be a good source of vitamin C.

MAKES 6 SERVINGS

3 cups shredded cabbage
1 cup chopped celery
1 cup chopped green pepper
1 can (5 ounces) sliced
    water chestnuts

3 or 4 green onions, chopped
1 tablespoon oil
Salt and pepper
Soy sauce

Prepare all the vegetables. Heat the oil in a large heavy skillet or saucepan. Drop in the vegetables, season with salt and pepper, and stir briskly. Lower heat, cover, and steam gently for 5 to 8 minutes. Stir again and add several tablespoons of soy sauce, according to your taste. Pour into a large bowl and serve immediately.

Very good with broiled veal chops or steaks.

RED PEPPER ORIENTAL MEDLEY

Contrasting colors in this vegetable medley are spectacular and the flavor is a delicate blend of sweet and sour. Serve as an accompaniment to any kind of meat, poultry, or fish that has been prepared simply.

MAKES 6 SERVINGS

2 red peppers
1 pound fresh spinach
¼ cup soy sauce
2 to 3 tablespoons dark
    corn syrup
½ cup water
1 tablespoon cornstarch

1 package (7 ounces) frozen
    Chinese pea pods
Salt
1 tablespoon oil
1 cup chopped green onions
3 cups bean sprouts

Remove seeds and ribs from peppers and cut them into 1-inch pieces. Remove stems from spinach and tear leaves into large pieces. Mix soy sauce, corn syrup, water, and cornstarch. Set aside. Simmer pea pods in salted water for 1 or 2 minutes; drain and set aside.

Heat the oil in a large skillet. Sauté green onions and red peppers for 3 or 4 minutes, until peppers are about half cooked. Add drained pea pods. Pour soy mixture over peppers and pea pods. Cover with bean sprouts and finally make a layer of the spinach. Cover and simmer for 3 to 4 minutes, stirring vegetables once or twice. Do not cook until vegetables are mushy! They should be very crisp.

CANTONESE VEGETABLES (mushrooms, peas, bean sprouts)

This light vegetable combination can accompany any kind of plain meat, fish, or poultry. Serve with rice, not potatoes.

MAKES 6 SERVINGS

1 tablespoon oil	3 tablespoons water
½ pound brown mushrooms, sliced	3 or 4 handfuls of bean sprouts
1 package (10 ounces) frozen peas	1 to 2 tablespoons soy sauce

Put oil in a large skillet or saucepan and bring to medium heat. Sauté the mushrooms for 3 to 4 minutes, stirring frequently. Reduce heat. Add peas and water, cover, and simmer until peas are almost tender. Place bean sprouts over peas. Shake on soy sauce according to taste. Cover again and steam for another 2 to 4 minutes. Stir everything together and toss into a large bowl for serving.

QUICK-FRY ZUCCHINI

MAKES 4 OR 5 SERVINGS

½ teaspoon dried onion flakes
1 tablespoon water
1 pound zucchini
1 tablespoon oil

1 tablespoon soy sauce
1 teaspoon each of salt
  and pepper

Soak onion flakes in water for a few minutes. Wash zucchini and slice into ½-inch pieces, discarding the ends. Sauté in the oil for 2 or 3 minutes. Add all other ingredients, cover, and simmer for 4 or 5 minutes, until just tender.

Salads
and
Salad Dressings

ALFALFA-SPROUT SALAD

Almost any variety of lettuce can be combined with alfalfa sprouts to produce an unusual salad.

MAKES 6 SERVINGS

1 package (4 ounces) fresh
    alfalfa sprouts
1 small head of Boston lettuce
1 small bunch of watercress,
    stems removed
½ cup French dressing

1 tablespoon imitation
    bacon bits (p. 430)
2 tablespoons chopped chives
1 tablespoon brown sugar
    (optional)

Clean and chill alfalfa sprouts, lettuce, and watercress. Combine all ingredients and toss.

BEAN-SPROUT SALAD

MAKES 4 SERVINGS

½ head of iceberg lettuce
1 red pepper
2 cups fresh bean sprouts

½ cup chopped green onions
1 tablespoon soy sauce
¼ cup French dressing

Chop lettuce into small pieces. Remove seeds and ribs from red pepper and cut into thin slices. Chill all ingredients. Toss vegetables with soy sauce and dressing.

MARINATED ASPARAGUS, ARTICHOKE, OR MUSHROOM SALAD

Marinate asparagus spears, artichoke hearts, or mushrooms, fresh, frozen, or canned, in French dressing. Serve on Boston or Bibb lettuce. Garnish with pimientos, chives, poppy seeds, or sunflower seeds.

GREEN BEAN SALAD

Good for picnics. If you can't find canned dilled beans, use plain green beans, fresh cooked or canned, and marinate them with dill seeds.

MAKES 6 TO 8 SERVINGS

1 can (16 ounces) dilled green beans, drained
1 can (16 ounces) French-style green beans, drained
1 cup chopped celery
½ head of iceberg lettuce, shredded

½ cup chopped dill pickle
½ cup buttermilk
⅓ cup mayonnaise
Salt and pepper
Paprika

Mix vegetables. Mix buttermilk and mayonnaise and toss with vegetables. Season to taste and sprinkle with paprika.

ITALIAN GARBANZO SALAD

MAKES 8 SERVINGS

1 can (16 ounces) garbanzo
   beans (chick-peas), drained
1 can (16 ounces) cut green
   beans, drained
½ cup chopped pimientos
¼ cup chopped green onions
½ cup thin-sliced radishes
¼ cup wine vinegar
¼ cup oil
½ teaspoon garlic salt
½ teaspoon pepper

Mix all ingredients and chill overnight. Serve on greens, with a dab of mayonnaise if desired.

THREE-BEAN SALAD

MAKES 8 SERVINGS

1 can (16 ounces) cut
   green beans
1 can (16 ounces) cut
   wax beans
1 can (16 ounces) red
   kidney beans
1 cup chopped celery
3 green onions, chopped
1 tablespoon pickle relish
¼ to ⅓ cup French dressing
Lettuce leaves

Drain liquid from beans. Combine beans, celery, onions, pickle relish, and French dressing. Chill for a few hours. Serve over lettuce leaves.

BROCCOLI-CARROT VINAIGRETTE

MAKES 4 SERVINGS

¼ cup French dressing
1 package (10 ounces) frozen broccoli, cooked and drained
1 can (8 ounces) julienne carrots, drained

Green lettuce leaves
1 tablespoon chopped chives

Pour French dressing over drained broccoli and carrots. Chill thoroughly. Serve on lettuce leaves and garnish with chives.

CAULIFLOWER-BEAN VINAIGRETTE

MAKES 4 SERVINGS

¼ cup French dressing
1 package (10 ounces) frozen cauliflower, cooked and drained

1 can (8 ounces) whole green beans, drained
Green lettuce leaves
Chopped pimiento

Pour French dressing over drained cauliflower and green beans. Chill thoroughly. Serve over lettuce leaves and garnish with pimiento.

CELERIAC SALAD

The large rough-skinned celeriac or celery knob used for this salad is the root of a different plant from the celery used chiefly for the stalks. These roots are native to Western European countries, and the salad made from them is very common in continental cuisine. Look for the roots in the produce section of your market among the other root vegetables.

2 or 3 celery knobs	½ teaspoon dill seeds
2 tablespoons oil	Salt and pepper
2 tablespoons vinegar	Bibb lettuce
Pinch of dry mustard	Paprika (optional)
2 tablespoons minced onion	

Pare the celery knobs and slice into long thin strips ¼ to ⅛ inch wide. Drop into boiling water and cook for 10 minutes, or until just tender. They should still be a little crisp. (Squeeze lemon juice over them if you do not drop them into water immediately, for they will discolor in the air.) Drain, and combine with other ingredients (except lettuce and paprika) and seasoning to taste. Chill.

Serve on a bed of Bibb lettuce or watercress. Dust with paprika if desired.

TOSSED GREEN SALAD WITH EGGPLANT

Unless you're feeding a mob, don't go out and buy a whole eggplant for this. If you happen to have some left over, though, try tossing it into a salad. Eggplant can be used raw or cooked in this dish.

MAKES 4 SERVINGS

1 head of Bibb lettuce	Low-Calorie French Dressing
1 cup cubed eggplant,	(p. 279), made with ½ cup
raw or cooked	minced chives

Clean lettuce and chill. Break into pieces. Add the eggplant cubes to the lettuce. Pour dressing over, toss lightly, and serve immediately.

FRESH MUSHROOM SALAD

For a striking effect try to get very large, very brown mushrooms and slice stem and cap together. The shape is more interesting than when they have been separated.

MAKES 8 SERVINGS

½ pound fresh brown
  mushrooms
1 head of Boston or bronze-
  leaf lettuce
1 head of romaine lettuce

1 cucumber, peeled and
  sliced thin
½ cup French dressing
½ teaspoon dillweed

Wipe mushrooms, slice, and chill. Wash, drain, and chill lettuce leaves. Soak sliced cucumber in salted ice water. Drain when ready to serve. Combine these four ingredients and toss with dressing and dillweed.

SPINACH, RADISH, AND WATER-CHESTNUT SALAD

MAKES 8 SERVINGS

1 pound fresh spinach
2 small heads of Bibb lettuce
1 cup sliced fresh radishes
1 small can (5 ounces) water
  chestnuts, sliced

¼ cup chopped chives
½ cup Basic French Dressing
  or Roquefort French
  Dressing (p. 279)

Clean spinach, lettuce, and radishes. Chill along with the water chestnuts. Tear lettuce and spinach into bite-sized pieces. Add sliced radishes and water chestnuts and the chives. Toss with dressing.

ROSY VEGETABLE SALAD

These particular vegetables seem to go very well with the rosy dressing. From Eleanor Forester of La Jolla, California.

Chop or grate equal amounts of lettuce, celery, tomatoes, and carrots. Add an equal amount of julienne beets and some minced fresh parsley. Mix equal parts of tomato sauce and low-calorie mayonnaise. Add prepared horseradish and lemon juice to taste. Season with salt and pepper. Pour dressing over salad, mix, and chill for several hours.

Serve in individual wooden bowls lined with lettuce leaves.

CAESAR SALAD

Although people are still arguing about the origin of this salad, it almost certainly was created about thirty years ago by Jack, maître d'hotel of La Avenida Restaurant in Coronado, California. Garlic and olive oil are essential to the flavor, croutons and raw egg to the texture.

MAKES 6 TO 8 SERVINGS

1 garlic clove	1 teaspoon salt
3 tablespoons regular oil	Coarse-ground pepper
2 tablespoons olive oil	2 egg whites, lightly beaten
2 heads of romaine lettuce	1 drop of yellow food coloring
2 slices of bread	1 can (2 ounces) anchovy
2 tablespoons lemon juice	fillets (optional)

Peel and slice the garlic and place in a jar with the oils overnight. (If you forget to do this, mince ½ garlic clove and toss it into the salad; or sauté ½ garlic clove with the croutons; rub the salad bowl with the other half of the garlic clove.) Clean and chill romaine leaves. Brush the bread slices with about 1 tablespoon of the oil and cut into cubes. Sauté croutons until browned, stirring all the time.

Tear the romaine into bite-sized pieces and drop into a chilled salad bowl. Add garlic-flavored oil and toss gently to coat. Add lemon juice, salt, and pepper to taste, and toss a few more times. Beat egg whites with food coloring and pour them over the leaves; again mix gently. Add sautéed croutons and anchovies and give a final toss. Serve immediately on chilled salad plates.

GREEK SALAD WITH DRY-CURD COTTAGE CHEESE

MAKES 6 TO 8 SERVINGS

1 small head of iceberg lettuce
1 cup sliced radishes
½ cup chopped green onions
½ cup French dressing
1 can (2 ounces) anchovy fillets

1 cup dry-curd cottage cheese
Garlic salt
Coarse-ground pepper

Wash lettuce and chill. When ready to serve, chop and put into a large salad bowl. Add radishes and onions. Toss with French dressing. Chop anchovies into bite-sized pieces and add to salad. Sprinkle with cheese. Season with garlic salt and pepper and toss again gently.

GREEN AND GOLD SALAD WITH CHEESE

MAKES 6 SERVINGS

1 cup grated raw carrot
3 cups cooked green peas
3 tablespoons minced chives
¼ cup grated "part-skim-milk" Swiss cheese (pp. 418–19)

1 tablespoon prepared mustard
½ cup French dressing
Watercress
Bibb lettuce

Combine carrot, peas, chives, and cheese. Mix mustard with dressing and pour over vegetables. Toss lightly and chill.
Serve in a bowl lined generously with watercress and Bibb lettuce.

HOOP CHEESE, SPINACH, AND BACON SALAD

An excellent luncheon salad for calorie watchers. French dressing gives hoop cheese the zip it needs.

MAKES 4 SERVINGS

1 pound fresh spinach
1 small head of Bibb lettuce
1 pound hoop cheese

2 tablespoons imitation
　bacon bits (p. 430)
⅓ cup French dressing

Wash spinach and lettuce, trim, and chill. Cut hoop cheese into ½-inch cubes. Break spinach and lettuce into bite-sized pieces. Combine all ingredients, toss gently, and serve.

Toasted sunflower seeds make an interesting substitute for bacon bits.

CREAMY COLESLAW

MAKES 4 SERVINGS

½ head of a large cabbage
1 small onion
½ green pepper
2 tablespoons plain low-fat
　yogurt or buttermilk

2 tablespoons mayonnaise
2 tablespoons vinegar
Salt and pepper

Remove outer leaves and core from cabbage. Shred cabbage into fine pieces. Peel and grate onion. Chop pepper. Combine vegetables in a large bowl and pour ice water over them. Chill for 1 hour or longer. Drain and dry with a towel. Add remaining ingredients with seasonings to taste. Mix well, and chill for a few more hours, or overnight if possible.

COLD POTATO SALAD

MAKES 6 SERVINGS

1 pound new potatoes
1 cup chopped celery
½ cup chopped green pepper
½ cup chopped green onion
2 tablespoons chopped
    pimiento
2 tablespoons sweet pickle
    relish
⅔ cup Low-Calorie
    Mayonnaise (p. 280)
Salt and pepper
Greens

Cook potatoes in their jackets. Peel and dice while still warm; there should be 3 cups diced. Add celery, green pepper, onion, pimiento, and relish and toss with salad dressing. Season to taste. Chill. Serve over crisp greens.

HOT GERMAN POTATO SALAD

MAKES 8 SERVINGS

1½ pounds potatoes
4 tablespoons oil
1 cup chopped onion
1 cup shredded dried beef
½ cup water
¼ cup vinegar
½ teaspoon dry mustard
1 teaspoon sugar
1 teaspoon salt
½ teaspoon black pepper
1 tablespoon cornstarch
½ cup chopped celery
¼ cup chopped dill pickle
½ cup chopped parsley

Cook potatoes in their jackets. Peel and slice while hot; there should be 4 cups sliced. Set aside in a large heatproof bowl. Heat 2 tablespoons of the oil in a skillet. Sauté onion and dried beef until lightly browned. Add remaining oil, the water, vinegar, mustard, sugar, salt, pepper, and cornstarch to the onion and dried beef. Stir and heat to boiling. Pour over the potatoes. Add celery, dill pickle, and parsley. Stir gently. Serve while still warm.

APPLE RAISIN SALAD

MAKES 4 SERVINGS

2 red apples, unpeeled
½ head of iceberg lettuce,
  chopped

½ cup raisins
1 teaspoon celery seed
¼ cup French dressing

Quarter the apples and remove cores. Chop apple pieces. Combine with lettuce and raisins. Chill. Sprinkle with celery seed and toss with dressing.

RED CABBAGE, CARROT, AND APPLE SALAD À LA BIRGIT HOLTSMARK

MAKES 6 TO 8 SERVINGS

4 cups shredded red cabbage
2 cups shredded raw carrots
2 cups shredded apples

¼ cup mayonnaise
¼ cup buttermilk
Salt and pepper

Wash and chill vegetables and apples. Shred into a large salad bowl. Mix mayonnaise and buttermilk and add. Season with salt and pepper, and toss until well mixed.

WALDORF SALAD SUPREME

MAKES 8 SERVINGS

4 cups diced unpeeled
  red apples
2 cups grapes, halved
1 cup diced celery
½ cup broken walnut meats

Lemon juice
1 cup miniature marshmallows
⅔ cup Low-Calorie
  Mayonnaise (p. 280)
Lettuce leaves

Prepare fruits, celery, and walnuts, and sprinkle with lemon juice. Stir in marshmallows. Add mayonnaise and chill. Serve over lettuce leaves.

For a simpler salad omit grapes and marshmallows.

Salads and Salad Dressings 271

BANANA GRAPEFRUIT SALAD

MAKES 6 SERVINGS

1 large pink grapefruit
1 head of iceberg lettuce
2 bananas

½ cup dressing: Low-Calorie
    French Dressing (p. 279), or
    Low-Calorie Mayonnaise
    (p. 280), or a sweet salad
    dressing (p. 282)

Peel grapefruit and cut into bite-sized chunks. Chill grapefruit.
Just before serving, chop lettuce into a large salad bowl, and slice
bananas. Add bananas and grapefruit to lettuce. Toss with dressing.

CITRUS SALAD WITH DATES

MAKES 6 SERVINGS

1 large grapefruit, peeled
2 large oranges, peeled
Romaine lettuce leaves

1 cup chopped pitted dates
Sweet French Dressing
    (p. 279)

Slice grapefruit and oranges. Chill until ready to serve. Arrange
grapefruit and orange slices on crisp chilled lettuce leaves. Sprinkle
with dates. Serve with the dressing, or use one of the Sweet Dressings
for Fruit Salads (p. 282).

MANDARIN SALAD

MAKES 4 SERVINGS

1 small head of Chinese cabbage
1 green pepper
1 can (8 ounces) mandarin oranges

1 teaspoon soy sauce
¼ cup Basic French Dressing (p. 279)

Shred cabbage into very fine pieces. Remove seeds and ribs from green pepper and slice into thin slivers. Combine pepper and cabbage in a salad bowl, cover with ice water, and chill for 30 minutes. Place mandarin oranges in refrigerator to chill.

Drain water from cabbage and pepper. Drain oranges and add to cabbage along with soy sauce. Toss with dressing.

GRAPE, CUCUMBER, AND WATERCRESS SALAD

MAKES 4 SERVINGS

1 bunch of watercress
1 medium-sized cucumber
Salt

½ small head of Boston lettuce
1½ cups seedless grapes
¼ cup French dressing

Wash watercress and remove stems. Place leaves in a plastic bag to chill. Peel and slice cucumber. Sprinkle with salt and chill. Wash Boston lettuce and chill along with grapes. Just before serving, break lettuce into fairly large pieces into a chilled bowl, add other ingredients, and toss with a light French dressing.

MOLDED CRANBERRY, KUMQUAT, AND NUT SALAD

Kumquats are native to China; they lend a sweet-sour flavor to this refreshing salad. If unavailable, use an equal amount of oranges. Serve with turkey dinners instead of the usual cranberry sauce.

MAKES 8 SERVINGS

2 cans (16 ounces each)
  jellied cranberry sauce
2 envelopes unflavored gelatin
½ cup cold water

½ teaspoon salt
⅔ cup chopped kumquats
⅔ cup chopped walnuts
½ cup chopped celery

Crush cranberry sauce and melt in a saucepan. Bring to a low boil. Dissolve gelatin in the cold water and add to sauce. Remove from heat and refrigerate until partly jelled. Fold in remaining ingredients. Spoon into a 6-cup mold and chill until firm.

If you are not serving this as an accompaniment to turkey or other poultry, but as a salad, chill it in individual molds or custard cups and turn them out on beds of chicory or Bibb lettuce. Serve with a mayonnaise dressing for fruit salad (pp. 282–83).

CUCUMBER LIME SALAD

MAKES 6 SERVINGS

1 package (3 ounces) lime-
  flavored gelatin
1 teaspoon salt
1 cup hot water
2 tablespoons vinegar
1 teaspoon onion juice
1 cup plain low-fat yogurt

¼ cup mayonnaise
1 cup minced cucumber,
  drained
Lettuce leaves
Chives
Mayonnaise dressing

Dissolve gelatin and salt in hot water. Add vinegar and onion juice. Chill until slightly thickened. Mix yogurt and mayonnaise and fold into gelatin with cucumbers. Pour into a 4-cup mold and chill until firm.

Unmold on lettuce leaves and garnish with chives. Serve with any mayonnaise dressing for fruit salad (pp. 282–83) or with Low-Calorie Mayonnaise I (p. 280).

BASIC CHICKEN SALAD

MAKES 6 SERVINGS

2 cups cubed cooked chicken
1 tablespoon oil
1 tablespoon vinegar or lemon juice
½ teaspoon salt
¼ teaspoon pepper

¼ teaspoon paprika
1 cup diced celery
¼ cup mayonnaise
2 tablespoons liquid skim milk
Lettuce leaves

Marinate chicken cubes in oil and vinegar mixed with salt, pepper, and paprika. Add diced celery. Blend mayonnaise with skim milk and fold into the chicken. Serve on lettuce leaves.

CHICKEN SALAD ORIENTAL

MAKES 6 SERVINGS

2 cups diced cooked chicken
Salt, pepper, paprika
1 tablespoon lemon juice
1 tablespoon oil
1 cup sliced water chestnuts
¼ cup chopped pimiento

¼ cup chopped green pepper
1 tablespoon minced chives
2 cups shredded lettuce
1 teaspoon soy sauce
⅓ cup mayonnaise
⅓ cup liquid skim milk

Season the chicken; marinate it in lemon juice and oil. Add prepared vegetables to chicken. Blend soy sauce, mayonnaise, and skim milk. Pour over all ingredients and toss. Chill.

Salads and Salad Dressings   275

CHICKEN, WALNUT, AND WHITE-GRAPE SALAD

MAKES 6 SERVINGS

2 cups diced cooked chicken
1 tablespoon oil
1 tablespoon vinegar
Salt, pepper, paprika
1 cup seedless white grapes

¼ cup chopped walnuts
¼ cup mayonnaise
2 to 4 tablespoons liquid skim milk or buttermilk
Lettuce

Marinate chicken in oil and vinegar, seasoned with salt, pepper, and paprika. Add grapes and walnuts. Thin mayonnaise with a little skim milk or buttermilk and blend into salad. Chill. Serve on lettuce leaves or shredded lettuce.

CHICKEN, CUCUMBER, AND CAPER SALAD

MAKES 6 SERVINGS

2 cups diced cooked chicken
1 cup diced cucumber
½ cup fine-chopped celery
2 tablespoons capers
¼ cup mayonnaise

2 to 4 tablespoons caper juice
Pepper and paprika
Bibb lettuce
Watercress

Combine chicken, cucumber, celery, and capers. Thin mayonnaise with caper juice, and season with pepper and paprika. Pour over salad, mix, and chill. Serve on Bibb lettuce or any soft-leaved salad green. Decorate with watercress.

RUSSIAN MACARONI SALAD
WITH SALMON

MAKES 8 TO 10 SERVINGS

3 cups cooked elbow macaroni
1 can (6½ ounces) pink
   salmon
2 cups diced celery
½ cup chopped green pepper
½ cup chopped pimientos
¼ cup chopped parsley
½ cup mayonnaise
1 tablespoon wine vinegar
1 teaspoon salt
½ teaspoon pepper

Cook macaroni a day ahead of time. Chill macaroni, salmon, and vegetables overnight. Toss together in a chilled bowl at the last minute, to keep the vegetables crisp. Add dressing ingredients and seasonings and toss again.

TUNA SALAD

For those who like their tuna salads unadulterated.

MAKES 2 OR 3 SERVINGS

1 can (6½ ounces) water-
   packed tuna
¼ cup chopped celery
1 tablespoon chopped chives
4 or 5 tablespoons Low-Calorie
   Mayonnaise III (p. 281)
Lettuce leaves
Sliced tomatoes

Drain tuna, break into large chunks, and combine with celery and chives. Add dressing; mix. Chill for about 1 hour. Serve on crisp lettuce leaves with sliced tomatoes.

TUNA SALAD WITH
GARDEN VEGETABLES

There are many approaches to tuna salad: small shreds or big chunks; lots of vegetables or none at all; capers, nuts, and so on. Here is a version made with fresh garden vegetables.

Salads and Salad Dressings 277

1 can (13 ounces) water-packed tuna

1 cup Low-Calorie Mayonnaise II (p. 280)

4 celery ribs, minced

1 large tomato, chopped

3 cups shredded lettuce

1 tablespoon chopped chives

¼ cup chopped dill pickle

Break up tuna into small pieces. Add mayonnaise and stir until blended. Add remaining ingredients and toss gently with a fork. Chill for 1 or 2 hours. Serve additional dressing as desired.

SALMON SALAD

Substitute a 1-pound can of pink salmon for the tuna in Tuna Salad with Garden Vegetables (above). Use 1 cup of chopped cucumber instead of the celery and tomato.

Variations: Add or substitute any amount of the following: capers, dilled green beans, dillweed, pickle relish, chopped radishes, sunflower seeds, walnuts, or white grapes.

FRENCH DRESSING WITH VARIATIONS

When dressing a salad, the proportions of oil to vinegar can vary as much as the proportions of gin to vermouth in a Martini. The need to limit calories is a factor also. Those who have no concern with calories insist on a ratio of 4 parts oil to 1 part vinegar. The classic proportion, found in most cookbooks, is 3 to 1. My recommendation is a 2 to 1 dressing but there is nothing to keep you from trying a 1 to 1 combination.

For a salad that is flavorful but without excessive calories use ¼ cup oil for 2 quarts chopped greens. This allows for only 1 tablespoon of oil per serving. The next four dressings make enough for 8 servings of salad, or more if you like.

Basic French Dressing

½ cup oil
¼ cup vinegar or lemon juice

1 teaspoon salt
½ teaspoon pepper

Sweet French Dressing

1 cup Basic French Dressing
1 teaspoon sugar

1 teaspoon catsup

Italian-Flavored French Dressing

1 cup Basic French Dressing
1 teaspoon Worcestershire
    sauce

1 teaspoon dry mustard
1 garlic clove, crushed

Roquefort or Blue Cheese French Dressing

1 cup Basic French Dressing
2 tablespoons blue cheese or
    Roquefort salad dressing
    mix or blue cheese dip mix

LOW-CALORIE FRENCH DRESSING

MAKES ENOUGH FOR 4 SERVINGS OF TOSSED SALAD

2 tablespoons oil
2 tablespoons vinegar or
    lemon juice
3 tablespoons water
1 teaspoon Worcestershire
    sauce

¼ cup minced chives
½ teaspoon garlic salt
Seasoned pepper

Mix all together, with pepper to taste. For a richer dressing omit the water.

NO-EGG-YOLK MAYONNAISE

For those who must be especially careful of their cholesterol count.
The key to success in making any mayonnaise is the slow addition of the oil. Use an electric mixer if you have one; otherwise use a hand beater and a few strong muscles.

MAKES 1¼ CUPS

½ teaspoon sugar (optional)   1 egg white
¼ teaspoon dry mustard   1 cup oil
½ teaspoon salt   1 tablespoon lemon juice
Dash of cayenne pepper   1 tablespoon vinegar

Mix sugar, mustard, salt, and cayenne pepper in a small bowl. Add egg white and beat well. While continuing to beat, add half of the oil, drop by drop. Then add the lemon juice, then remaining oil, and finally the vinegar.

LOW-CALORIE MAYONNAISE

There is very little difference among the following low-calorie dressings. The recipes are flexible and can be adapted to whatever is available in your larder. Each recipe makes about 1 cup.

I.

½ cup mayonnaise   ½ teaspoon salt
½ cup buttermilk   ¼ teaspoon pepper
1 teaspoon lemon juice ¼ teaspoon paprika

II.

⅓ cup mayonnaise   ½ teaspoon salt
⅓ cup plain low-fat yogurt   ¼ teaspoon pepper
⅓ cup liquid skim milk   ¼ teaspoon paprika
1 tablespoon garlic-flavored
  wine vinegar

½ cup mayonnaise
¼ cup Whipped Cottage
   Cheese (p. 287)
2 tablespoons wine vinegar

¼ teaspoon garlic salt
¼ teaspoon pepper
¼ teaspoon paprika

For all three versions, combine all ingredients and mix until well blended.

ROQUEFORT OR BLUE CHEESE MAYONNAISE DRESSING

1 cup Low-Calorie Mayon-
   naise I (p. 280)

2 tablespoons blue cheese or
   Roquefort salad dressing mix
   or blue cheese dip mix

The following dressings are also based on 1 cup of mayonnaise, either low-calorie or no-egg-yolk. For a dressing with even fewer calories use ⅓ cup mayonnaise, ⅓ cup plain low-fat yogurt, and ⅓ cup Whipped Cottage Cheese (p. 287). Skim milk or buttermilk can be substituted for cottage cheese, giving a thinner consistency, fewer calories, and less fat content.

Russian Dressing

1 cup mayonnaise
1 teaspoon Worcestershire
   sauce

1 teaspoon minced onion
¼ cup chili sauce or catsup

Thousand Island Dressing

1 cup mayonnaise
¼ cup chili sauce or catsup
2 tablespoons chopped
   pimiento
2 tablespoons chopped pickle
   or India relish

2 tablespoons chopped chives
2 tablespoons chopped parsley
1 or 2 hard-boiled egg
   whites, chopped

Sauce Louis

1 cup mayonnaise
2 tablespoons lemon juice
¼ cup tomato juice
¼ cup chopped green onion

¼ cup chopped green pepper
¼ cup chopped tomato
¼ cup chopped parsley

SWEET DRESSINGS FOR FRUIT SALADS

To the basic dressings below you can add any of the following for extra flavor and color: minced or grated onion or garlic; dry or prepared mustard, or Dijon-style mustard; minced chives, watercress, or parsley; curry powder, cayenne, or paprika; celery seeds or dill seeds; tarragon, basil, rosemary, or orégano leaves; sesame seeds or poppy seeds.

MAKES ABOUT 1 CUP DRESSING, ENOUGH FOR ABOUT 8 SERVINGS

Mayonnaise and Fruit-Juice Dressing

½ cup mayonnaise

½ cup orange or pineapple juice

Mayonnaise and Whipped-Cheese Dressing

⅓ cup mayonnaise
⅓ cup Whipped Cottage Cheese (p. 287)

⅓ cup fresh or concentrated orange juice, or ⅙ cup concentrated lime or lemon juice

Oil and Grapefruit-Juice Dressing

½ cup oil
½ cup sweetened grapefruit juice

¼ teaspoon salt
Pinch of ground ginger

Mayonnaise and Honey Dressing

½ cup mayonnaise
2 to 3 tablespoons honey

Liquid skim milk to make
1 cup

Lemon, Oil, and Honey Dressing

¼ cup lemon juice
¼ cup oil
¼ cup honey

¼ cup water
¼ teaspoon salt
¼ teaspoon paprika

For any of these, combine all ingredients and mix until well blended. Thin, if desired, with a little more of the liquid in the recipe.

Sauces

CHEESE

vhipped cottage cheese. With vari-
icement for rich table cream, sour
ιe able to find a prepared whipped
:h of course is a great convenience.
ddition, you may want a lower fat
cottage cheese from which most of
red. The 2 or 4 percent cheese may
?se somewhat more moist than the
vish to prepare your own, you will
ιe aid of a blender.

rcent fat-free cottage cheese, the 2
:gular 4 percent. Dry cheese will, of
:ontains no salt so it will need more
place of sweet milk you will have
ιg general proportions of cheese to
stc. For cither recipe mix ingredients

se   ¼ teaspoon salt

II.

1 tablespoon liquid skim milk
or buttermilk

Mock Sour Cream

Beth Kent, R.D.

Nutritional Analysis

	2 Tbsp.	1/4 cup
Calories:	22	44
Fat (gm):	.3	.6
Cholesterol (mg):	1.3	2.6
Sodium (mg):	117	234

1 cup low-fat cottage cheese
2 T. Skim milk
1 T. lemon juice

1. Blend cottage cheese, skim milk and lemon juice together in blender until smooth.
2. Scrape sides of container often with rubber spatula while blending. Makes 1 cup.

May be used to top baked potatoes instead of regular sour cream which contains 5 grams fat, 10 mg cholesterol and 52 calories per 2 Tablespoons.

This will not do
for cooking. Ellie

100% fat free,
Dry cottage cheese
has no salt.

SOUR-CREAM SUBSTITUTE I
(for serving cold only)

Use for dessert toppings and cold dips. Do not try to heat this, or it will separate and become watery. From a good friend, Herbie Miles.

1 cup buttermilk (more or less, depending on type of cheese used)

1 cup cottage cheese (dry-curd, low-fat, or regular)
2 teaspoons lemon juice

Whip ingredients to a smooth consistency. For special flavors and occasions, add a) sugar and grated lemon rind, b) rum or brandy, c) mayonnaise (for salads).

SOUR-CREAM SUBSTITUTE II
(for cooking only)

This sauce works very well for casseroles that must cook a long time.

Make Creamy Buttermilk Sauce (p. 291). Add 1 to 2 teaspoons lemon juice to taste.

SOUR-CREAM SUBSTITUTE III
(for cooking only)

This is especially good added to a hot dish just before serving.

1 cup plain low-fat yogurt
1 tablespoon flour

1 teaspoon oil or mayonnaise (optional)

Blend well. Omit oil or mayonnaise if calories are a problem.

To make SOUR MILK:
Add 2 T vinegar to 1 C milk
Stir well.

SOUR-CREAM SUBSTITUTE IV
(for baking in cakes, pies, etc.)

A reliable sour-cream substitute for cheesecakes and pies, or for any occasion when substance and body are needed.

> 1 cup Whipped Cottage Cheese (p. 287)
> 1 tablespoon lemon juice, or more
>
> Sugar
> Liquid skim milk

Whipped cottage cheese bakes very well and will solidify in a moderately hot oven within 5 to 10 minutes. Mix in lemon juice to taste. Add 1 to 2 teaspoons sugar if desired. If the mixture is too thick for your purpose, use a little skim milk to thin the mixture to the desired consistency.

HOMEMADE YOGURT

Add your choice of crushed or puréed fruits to this completely nonfat yogurt. Or try a sprinkling of mixed cinnamon and sugar and top with a few sliced nuts.

> 4 cups liquid skim milk
> ½ cup dry skim milk
>
> 2 to 3 tablespoons commercial yogurt

Stir liquid and dry milks in a heavy saucepan until dry milk is dissolved; heat slowly to the boiling point. Transfer to a bowl and cool until lukewarm. Add commercial yogurt and mix thoroughly. Cover and set in a warm place until mixture has "set" or become like very heavy cream, 6 to 8 hours. Refrigerate.

JACK SPRAT CREAM

Good for coffee, dessert, cereal, etc., but use only if you're as slim as Jack Sprat is!

1 cup cold water
½ cup dry skim milk

3 tablespoons butter-flavored oil, or regular oil with 3 or 4 drops of butter flavoring added

Combine all ingredients in an electric blender and whirl at top speed for a couple of minutes. Chill thoroughly.

WHITE SAUCE

MAKES ABOUT 1 CUP THIN SAUCE

1 tablespoon flour
1 tablespoon oil
1 cup liquid skim milk
¼ cup dry skim milk

1 drop of yellow food coloring
¼ teaspoon salt
⅛ teaspoon pepper
Seasoning of your choice

Blend flour and oil in a heavy saucepan. Cook gently while stirring for 2 to 3 minutes; the flour should be partially cooked but not too brown. Mix liquid and dry milks and add to the *roux* gradually, stirring until thickened. Add food coloring. Season with salt and pepper and any of the following: paprika, cayenne pepper, celery salt, wine, Worcestershire sauce, curry powder, minced chives or parsley.

For medium-thick sauce, increase flour and oil to 1½ to 2 tablespoons each.

For thick sauce, increase flour and oil to 2½ to 3 tablespoons.

BUTTERMILK CREAM SAUCE

Pleasantly rich and piquant in spite of the low-calorie, low-fat content. A refreshing change from the rather bland white sauce made with skim milk.

MAKES ABOUT 1 CUP MEDIUM-THICK SAUCE

1 tablespoon oil	1¼ cups buttermilk
2 tablespoons flour	⅛ teaspoon white pepper

Heat oil in a small saucepan. Add flour and simmer for 1 or 2 minutes, stirring until bubbly. Add buttermilk gradually and stir until thick and creamy. Season with pepper.

BÉCHAMEL SAUCE

MAKES 1 CUP MEDIUM-THIN SAUCE

¼ teaspoon onion powder	1 tablespoon flour
½ teaspoon chicken bouillon granules	½ cup plain low-fat yogurt
½ cup liquid skim milk	Salt and freshly ground pepper

Use a small saucepan. Dissolve onion powder and bouillon granules in the skim milk over low heat. Mix flour and yogurt thoroughly and add to bouillon. Season with salt and pepper to taste. Stir and simmer gently for 1 or 2 minutes.

For a thicker sauce use 2 tablespoons flour.

Fish or chicken—baked, steamed, poached, sautéed, or barbecued— can be enhanced by an unusual sauce. The next six sauces are based on Béchamel Sauce. Try any of these variations to enhance your main dish.

Onion and Tarragon Sauce (Béarnaise)

1 cup Béchamel Sauce
¼ teaspoon dried tarragon

2 teaspoons minced spring
onions

Orange and Sherry Sauce

1 cup Béchamel Sauce
2 teaspoons grated orange rind
1 teaspoon sweet sherry

½ cup chopped mandarin
oranges

Lemon and Parsley Sauce

1 cup Béchamel Sauce
1 teaspoon grated lemon rind

1 teaspoon lemon juice
1 tablespoon minced parsley

Sour Pickle Sauce

1 cup Béchamel Sauce
¼ cup minced dill pickle

¼ teaspoon dry mustard
1 teaspoon wine vinegar

Caper Sauce

1 cup Béchamel Sauce
2 tablespoons chopped capers

1 tablespoon minced parsley
1 tablespoon white wine

Velouté Sauce

In classic cookery this sauce is made with the cooking liquid of the food it is served with. Make Béchamel Sauce; in place of the skim milk use a stock or broth from cooking the food to be sauced, or choose a stock that will be compatible. Serve hot with meat, fish, and vegetables.

CHEESE SAUCE

MAKES ABOUT 1½ CUPS SAUCE

2 tablespoons mayonnaise
2 tablespoons flour
1¼ cups buttermilk
½ teaspoon paprika
2 teaspoons prepared mustard

¼ teaspoon butter-flavored
salt
3 or 4 slices, ¼ inch thick, of
processed vegetable-oil
cheese (p. 419), diced

Blend mayonnaise and flour in a small saucepan. Stir and cook for 1 or 2 minutes. Add buttermilk gradually and stir until thickened. Season with paprika, mustard, and salt. Add the cheese and cook over low heat until melted.

SAP SAGO SAUCE

MAKES 2 CUPS THICK SAUCE

4 tablespoons flour
2 tablespoons oil
2 cups liquid skim milk
½ cup dry skim milk
2 to 3 tablespoons grated Sap
Sago cheese

2 to 3 drops of yellow food
coloring
Salt and pepper

Blend flour and oil in a heavy saucepan. Cook over low heat, stirring all the time, until the *roux* is foamy and golden in color. Mix liquid and dry milks and gradually add to the *roux*, stirring until thickened. Stir in cheese until it melts. Add food coloring and season to taste.

MORNAY SAUCE

MAKES ABOUT 1½ CUPS SAUCE

2 tablespoons flour
2 tablespoons oil
1¼ cups liquid skim milk
⅓ cup dry skim milk
1 tablespoon Sap Sago cheese

2 tablespoons grated Parmesan
   cheese
¼ teaspoon salt
⅛ teaspoon pepper

Follow the method used for Sap Sago Sauce.

CURRY SAUCE

This sauce can be varied by selecting a liquid to suit the dish being served. Evaporated skim milk is relatively sweet; fortified skim (liquid milk mixed with dry skim milk) and low-fat milk are neutral. Buttermilk gives a sour-cream taste. Bouillon makes a brown sauce.

MAKES ABOUT 1 CUP SAUCE

1 tablespoon oil
½ to 1 teaspoon curry powder
2 tablespoons flour
1 cup liquid (evaporated skim
   milk, fortified skim or low-
   fat milk, buttermilk,
   bouillon)

1 teaspoon dried onion flakes
   (optional)

Heat the oil and stir in the curry powder mixed with the flour. Add liquid and onion flakes and heat and stir until thickened and smooth.

Use 2 tablespoons flour for a medium-thick sauce. For thinner sauce, use only 1 to 1½ tablespoons flour, or increase liquid to about 1¼ cups. For a very thick sauce, increase flour to 2½ to 3 tablespoons.

CREAMY MUSHROOM SAUCE

This simple recipe is intended primarily to substitute for the canned cream of mushroom soup so often called for in baked dishes. When mushroom soup is to be served by itself, use the recipe for Fresh Mushroom Soup (p. 57).

MAKES ABOUT 1½ CUPS SAUCE

2 tablespoons oil
2 tablespoons flour
1¼ cups liquid skim milk
½ cup dry skim milk
¼ teaspoon dried onion flakes

1 tablespoon sherry
Salt and pepper
1 can (4 ounces) mushroom
pieces, drained

Combine oil and flour in a heavy saucepan. Stir and cook over low heat for a minute or two. Add the mixed liquid and dry skim milks gradually, along with onion flakes, sherry, and seasonings to taste. Stir with a wire whisk until bubbly and smooth. Mince mushroom pieces and stir into the sauce.

Evaporated skim milk can be used in place of the fortified milk made of liquid and dry skim milks.

BROWN MUSHROOM SAUCE

This quickly made sauce can help when you are assembling a hasty meal. Heat slices of leftover roast in the hot sauce. Add a small can of peas and onions and serve over toast, rice, or spaghetti.

MAKES ABOUT 1¼ CUPS SAUCE

¼ pound fresh mushrooms,
sliced, or 1 can (3 ounces)
1½ tablespoons butter-flavored
oil
2 tablespoons flour

1 cup stock or bouillon
Salt and pepper
Sherry, Worcestershire sauce,
etc. (optional)

Sauté mushrooms in oil. Add flour and heat until well mixed. Stir in stock and seasonings to taste and cook over low heat until thickened and smooth.

BROWN SAUCE

MAKES 1 CUP SAUCE

1 tablespoon oil
2 tablespoons flour
1 cup beef bouillon, canned or
    made with granules

Seasonings (salt, pepper,
    butter flavoring, sherry,
    Worcestershire sauce, onion
    or garlic flakes, herbs, etc.)

Blend oil and flour in a small saucepan. Stir and cook over low heat for 1 or 2 minutes. Add bouillon gradually, stirring until thickened. Season as desired.

BORDELAISE SAUCE

MAKES 1½ CUPS SAUCE

½ cup dry red wine
½ cup chopped green onions
1 cup Brown Sauce (above)

Pepper
Lemon juice
Parsley

Cook red wine and onions until reduced in volume by about half. Add brown sauce. Season to taste with pepper, lemon juice, and minced parsley. Cook until smooth and thickened.

Use for grilled or barbecued steaks or chops.

MADEIRA SAUCE

Prepare Brown Sauce (above). Add ¼ cup Madeira wine to 1 cup sauce and heat to boiling, but do not let it boil.

CREOLE SAUCE

MAKES ABOUT 2 CUPS SAUCE

¼ cup chopped onion
1 green or red pepper,
  chopped
1 garlic clove, minced
1 tablespoon oil
2 cups stewed tomatoes

2 tablespoons chili sauce
1 tablespoon brown sugar
1 teaspoon Worcestershire
  sauce
Salt and pepper

Sauté onion, green or red pepper, and garlic in oil until tender. Add tomatoes, chili sauce, sugar, and Worcestershire and simmer slowly until thickened, 40 to 50 minutes. Season with salt and pepper to taste.

MOCK HOLLANDAISE SAUCE I

This delectably rich sauce is admittedly high in calories and contains approximately 130 milligrams of cholesterol (from the mayonnaise). Limit the size of your portions or use the second recipe if calories are a problem or if your cholesterol diet is too strict.

MAKES ABOUT 1½ CUPS SAUCE

4 tablespoons hot water
1 cup mayonnaise

2 teaspoons lemon juice
Dash of paprika

Stir hot water into mayonnaise in the top part of a double boiler. Heat thoroughly; add lemon juice and paprika.

MOCK HOLLANDAISE SAUCE II

This delicately flavored sauce is appropriate for many occasions; it is quickly made and very low in calories. Use this recipe if the first mock hollandaise is too rich for your diet.

MAKES ABOUT 1 CUP SAUCE

2 tablespoons mayonnaise
1 tablespoon cornstarch
¾ cup chicken bouillon
1 teaspoon lemon juice

Dash each of cayenne pepper
  and paprika
Pinch of ground turmeric

Combine mayonnaise and cornstarch in a small saucepan. Add remaining ingredients and cook slowly until thickened. Stir the sauce with a wire whisk as it cooks.

MUSTARD-HOLLANDAISE SAUCE

Mustard and horseradish lend an added interest to hollandaise. Serve hot over lean ham, sliced veal, steamed chicken breasts, etc. For a complete lunch, arrange on a slice of toast some warmed asparagus or sliced tomatoes, a slice of lean meat, and some sauce.

MAKES ¾ TO 1 CUP SAUCE

3 tablespoons mayonnaise
½ cup plain low-fat yogurt
1½ tablespoons flour
2 teaspoons prepared mustard
½ teaspoon prepared
  horseradish

½ teaspoon dry mustard
½ teaspoon paprika
Liquid skim milk or buttermilk
Chopped mushrooms or capers
  (optional)

Combine all ingredients except milk and mushrooms or capers in a small saucepan. Heat gradually; add skim milk or buttermilk to thin to desired consistency. Add mushrooms or capers if you wish.

298   **Sauces**

HORSERADISH CREAM SAUCE

This has a distinctive flavor well suited to boiled and roasted meats, or meat sandwiches.

MAKES 1 CUP SAUCE

½ cup plain low-fat yogurt
½ cup Whipped Cottage
   Cheese (p. 287)

2 to 3 tablespoons prepared
   horseradish

Mix and chill.

MUSTARD HORSERADISH SAUCE

Good with all meats, but especially with ham or dried beef.

MAKES 1 CUP SAUCE

1 cup Horseradish Cream
   Sauce (above)
1 tablespoon prepared
   mustard

1 teaspoon dry mustard

Mix and chill.

CUCUMBER AND DILL SAUCE

Use this for fish and salads. The sauce is delicious when made with fresh dill. If using dried dillweed, check to be sure yours has not been sitting on the shelf too long.

MAKES ABOUT 2½ CUPS SAUCE

2 medium-sized cucumbers
½ teaspoon salt
½ cup mayonnaise
½ cup Whipped Cottage
   Cheese (p. 287)

1 teaspoon lemon juice
¼ teaspoon pepper
1½ teaspoons minced fresh
   dill or dried dillweed

Peel cucumbers and remove seeds. Mince cucumbers, sprinkle with the salt, and chill for an hour or two. Blend mayonnaise, whipped cottage cheese, lemon juice, pepper, and dill. Drain the cucumbers thoroughly and fold into mayonnaise mixture. Chill again.

TARTAR SAUCE

MAKES 1¼ CUPS SAUCE

¼ cup dry skim milk
¼ cup liquid skim milk
¾ cup mayonnaise
¼ cup chopped sweet or
   dill pickle, drained

2 tablespoons minced chives
Pinch of dry mustard
1 tablespoon chopped capers,
   drained (optional)
1 teaspoon lemon juice

Dissolve dry milk in liquid. Blend well with mayonnaise. Add other ingredients and chill.

ITALIAN SPAGHETTI SAUCE

Almost everyone has his own approach to spaghetti sauce, but occasionally it's fun to try another. Here is my version, with emphasis on lots of tomatoes and tomato sauce. The other school prefers the flavor of tomato paste. If you're one of these, substitute 6 ounces of tomato paste with an equal amount of water for the tomato sauce. The cardinal rule that applies to all, however, is always to make great quantities of sauce so there will be lots left over. It can be used as the basis for such dishes as Easy Lasagne, Moussaka à la Grecque, Easy Chili Beans, etc. All of these recipes can be found in the index.

MAKES 8 SERVINGS, 5 TO 6 CUPS SAUCE

2 large yellow onions
1 large green pepper, seeded
2 tablespoons oil
1 garlic clove, minced
1½ pounds lean beef round, ground
Salt and pepper
1 can (28 ounces) stewed tomatoes
1 can (13 ounces) tomato sauce

1 tablespoon chili powder
1 teaspoon ground cuminseed
2 or 3 bay leaves
½ teaspoon dried orégano
½ cup red wine
1 to 2 cups mushrooms, whole or sliced
Grated Parmesan or Sap Sago cheese

Chop onions and green pepper and sauté in oil along with the garlic until tender. Transfer to a large saucepan. Brown the meat in the same skillet, seasoning with salt and pepper to taste. Remove fat (p. 124) and add meat to the onions. Add all other ingredients except mushrooms and grated cheese. Simmer, uncovered, for at least 1 hour, or until sauce has been reduced to a good consistency. Add mushrooms for the last 10 minutes of cooking.

Serve over spaghetti, with a small amount of grated cheese. (Use only ½ teaspoon cheese for those on a low-fat diet.)

Barbecued meats are enhanced by the addition of a well-flavored sauce. Simmer the sauces until the ingredients are well blended. Use them to marinate and baste the meats, or serve at the table as a separate accompaniment. Remember to buy lean cuts of meat (pp. 423–24) and to remove all visible fat.

BROWN-SUGAR AND GINGER-ALE SAUCE

For ham or pork.

MAKES 1½ CUPS SAUCE

⅓ cup brown sugar
1 cup ginger ale
1 teaspoon dry mustard

1 rounded tablespoon flour
2 tablespoons vinegar

Mix ingredients and heat in a small saucepan over low heat until well blended.

ORANGE HONEY SAUCE

For chicken, pork, or ham.

MAKES 1½ CUPS SAUCE

¼ cup honey
1 cup orange-juice concentrate

3 tablespoons soy sauce
2 tablespoons sherry

Combine ingredients over low heat and heat until honey is well mixed with everything else.

CUMBERLAND SAUCE

Use for chicken, Rock Cornish game hens, ham, or to reheat slices of cooked veal.

MAKES ABOUT 2 CUPS SAUCE

½ cup currant or guava jelly
½ cup Madeira or port wine
1 teaspoon ground ginger

1 orange, juice and grated rind
1 lemon, juice and grated rind

Simmer over low heat for 5 to 10 minutes.

PINEAPPLE SOY SAUCE

For barbecuing beef and chicken.

MAKES ABOUT 2 CUPS SAUCE

1 cup soy sauce
½ cup brown sugar

½ cup pineapple juice
¼ teaspoon garlic powder

Simmer over low heat until the sugar has melted and everything is well blended.

HOMEMADE CHUTNEY

MAKES ABOUT EIGHT 1-CUP JARS

4 pounds fresh peaches, pears, apples, or mangoes
1 cup chopped crystallized ginger root
1 lemon, sliced
¼ cup cider vinegar
1½ cups granulated sugar
1½ cups brown sugar
1 cup raisins
1 cup apple juice

Remove stems and pits from fruit. Peel mangoes; it is not necessary to peel other fruits unless you wish to; peelings add flavor and texture. Chop up the fruit and combine with other ingredients. Cook in a large kettle until fruit is tender and syrup has thickened. Stir often to keep from sticking. Put in jars and seal.

CHEESE CRUMBS

Make up a large batch of this and store in the refrigerator. It keeps for a long time. Use for sprinkling on casseroles, creamed vegetables, etc. Add more cheese for a stronger flavor.

½ cup fine zwieback crumbs or bread crumbs
1 tablespoon grated Sap Sago cheese
1 tablespoon oil
¼ teaspoon salt

Combine ingredients and blend well with a fork.

SESAME CRUMBS

Substitute toasted sesame seeds for bread crumbs in the recipe for Cheese Crumbs. Or make a combination of half and half. Leave out the oil if using all sesame seeds.

Desserts and Dessert Sauces

ORANGE-HONEY BAKED APPLES

MAKES 4 SERVINGS

4 large tart apples
¼ cup orange juice
¼ cup honey

1 tablespoon grated orange
rind

Core apples and pare to about a quarter of the way down from the top. Arrange in a greased baking dish. Combine other ingredients and pour over apples. Bake in a 400°F. oven until tender, basting from time to time.

QUICK APPLE CRISP

Quick and easy for an informal dessert. Select good tart juicy apples and don't overcook them; they should be just tender, not mushy.

MAKES 6 TO 8 SERVINGS

8 cups sliced baking apples
½ cup sugar
Cinnamon

Lemon juice
Topping (below)

You may peel the apples before slicing, or not. I prefer to leave the skins on. Place the apples in a greased baking pan, 10 by 6 inches or 7 inches square. Sprinkle with sugar, cinnamon, and lemon juice. Spread topping over apples. Bake in a 350°F. oven for 30 to 40 minutes, depending on the apples.

Topping

> 1 cup brown sugar   ¾ cup all-purpose flour
> ⅓ cup oil

> Work these ingredients together lightly with a fork.

CHILLED MELON BALLS WITH YOGURT

Scoop out melon balls from any kind of melon; use cantaloupe, casaba, Crenshaw, honeydew, Persian, or watermelon. Fill individual sherbet glasses with melon balls and chill. Top with a heaping tablespoon of fruit-flavored yogurt such as raspberry, peach, strawberry, orange, lemon, etc.

SUMMER FRUITS IN RUM

Guests respond enthusiastically to a simple fruit dessert made festive with the flavor of rum. Pineapple can be added or used as a substitute for one of the other fruits.

MAKES 8 SERVINGS

> 2 pint baskets of fresh straw-   ½ cup rum
> berries   2 ripe bananas
> 1 small cantaloupe
> 2 to 4 tablespoons superfine
> sugar

Wash and hull the strawberries. Peel cantaloupe and cut into ½-inch cubes. Mix both with sugar and rum and chill for several hours.

Slice bananas 15 to 20 minutes before serving and mix with the other fruits. Serve with a Whipped Milk Topping (pp. 342–43) or Whipped Cheese Topping (p. 344) and a few slivered nuts.

POACHED PEACHES IN RASPBERRY SAUCE

MAKES 6 SERVINGS

6 large yellow peaches	1 tablespoon cornstarch
1 cup sauterne	¼ cup currant jelly
2 tablespoons sugar	1 package (10 ounces) frozen
¼ cup water	raspberries, thawed

Dip peaches into boiling water for 1 minute. Plunge into cold water. Peel off skins, cut into halves, and remove pits. Combine sauterne, sugar, and water in a small saucepan. Simmer peaches in this until just tender. Transfer to a serving bowl, reserving the syrup, and chill.

Dissolve cornstarch in cooled syrup. Add jelly and raspberries and simmer in a small saucepan for a few minutes until thickened. Remove from heat and chill.

Serve syrup separately at the table, or pour over peaches just before serving.

PLUM COMPOTE

Use 2 or 3 varieties of plums to add interest to this cool summer dessert.

MAKES 4 SERVINGS

1 pound mixed plums
2 tablespoons sugar
½ cup water
1 tablespoon grated lemon
   rind

1 tablespoon lemon juice
2 tablespoons kirsch

Wash plums and remove pits. Cut into quarters. Combine sugar, water, lemon rind, and juice in a small heavy saucepan. Heat until sugar is dissolved. Add plums, cover, and simmer for 6 to 8 minutes, until plums are soft. With a slotted spoon set plums aside in a serving dish. Reduce liquid slightly. Pour over plums, and chill. Add kirsch when ready to serve.

Top with a small dab of safflower ice cream, plain yogurt, Whipped Cottage Cheese (p. 287), or Sour-Cream Substitute (pp. 288–89).

STRAWBERRIES ROMANOFF

MAKES 10 TO 12 SERVINGS

4 cups fresh strawberries
½ cup confectioners' sugar
¼ cup Cointreau
¼ cup rum
1 cup Whipped Cottage
   Cheese (p. 287)

1 cup plain or strawberry
   low-fat yogurt
1 tablespoon minced fresh
   mint (optional)

Wash and hull strawberries. Set aside a few for topping and crush the rest. Put them in a large serving bowl and mix in the sugar, Cointreau, and rum. Chill for at least 1 hour.

Combine cheese and yogurt, fold into the strawberries, and chill for another hour.

Serve decorated with the whole berries and minced fresh mint.

An alternative way of serving is to chill the dessert in individual dessert glasses.

Many delicious desserts owe their success to meringues. Start with the basic recipe and take off from there. Here are some ideas, using half of the basic recipe for each.

BAKED MERINGUE

MAKES TWELVE 3-INCH MERINGUE SHELLS OR 24 SMALL KISSES

8 egg whites, at room
   temperature
¼ teaspoon salt

¼ teaspoon cream of tartar
2 cups superfine sugar
2 teaspoons vanilla extract

Beat egg whites with an electric mixer until frothy. Add salt and cream of tartar and continue to beat until they are fluffy. Gradually add sugar, 1 to 2 tablespoons at a time, increasing speed from moderately slow to very fast. Add vanilla and beat for a few more minutes at high speed. Spoon mounds of meringue onto a baking sheet greased and floured or covered with brown paper. Bake in a 225°F. oven for about 60 minutes, or until meringues are dry and loose on the pan. They should be cream colored. Leave in the oven for a few minutes.

CRUNCHY CEREAL AND WALNUT MERINGUES

MAKES 6 SERVINGS

½ recipe Baked Meringue
1 cup fine-chopped walnuts

1½ cups of your favorite dry
   breakfast cereal

Fold walnuts and cereal into meringue batter. Bake. Serve plain as cookies, or fill with safflower ice cream and top with sliced bananas.

CINNAMON APPLE MERINGUES

MAKES 6 SERVINGS

½ recipe Baked Meringue   Cinnamon
1 large apple, pared and sliced   Sugar
    very thin

Make 6 shallow meringues. Press a spoon into the top of each meringue to make a hollow. Divide the apple slices among the meringues and sprinkle lightly with cinnamon and sugar. Bake.

Serve plain, or top with a dab of yogurt, ricotta cheese, or Sour Cream Substitute (p. 288).

RASPBERRY JAM MERINGUES

MAKES 6 SERVINGS

Prepare half of the batter for Baked Meringue and shape and bake 6 meringues. Make a very shallow indentation in each one and gently spread a teaspoon of jam on the surface. Bake.

Serve as cookies, or fill with a little vanilla-flavored safflower ice cream and sprinkle with chopped nuts.

COCOA WALNUT MERINGUES

MAKES 6 SERVINGS

½ recipe Baked Meringue   ¼ cup cocoa powder
2 teaspoons water   ½ cup fine-chopped walnuts

Dribble water into the meringue batter as it is being whipped. Add cocoa powder and mix until well blended. Fold in walnuts. Shape into meringues and bake.

FRESH PEACH MERINGUES

Bake individual 3-inch meringue shells. Peel fresh peaches, slice them, and sweeten. Just before serving, spoon chilled peaches and juice into shells, and top with a sprinkling of confectioners' sugar.

MERINGUES GLACÉES

Bake shallow 2-inch meringues. Place a serving of safflower ice cream between 2 baked shells. Put a dab of ricotta cheese on top and sprinkle a few slivered nuts over the cheese.

STRAWBERRY-TOPPED MERINGUES

Bake individual 3-inch meringue shells. When ready to serve, fill with a heaping tablespoon of low-fat strawberry yogurt and top with chilled sweetened fresh strawberries.

COEUR À LA CRÈME

An enchanting French dessert, giving an air of elegance to any meal! The cheeses are molded into the shape of a heart and served with strawberries. Of course there is no cream in this version.

MAKES 10 SERVINGS

1 cup low-fat ricotta cheese
1½ cups Whipped Cottage
   Cheese (p. 287)
¼ cup superfine sugar
1 teaspoon vanilla extract

1 package (10 ounces) frozen
   sliced strawberries, thawed
1 package (10 ounces) frozen
   whole strawberries, thawed

Beat the cheeses, sugar, and vanilla together until smooth. Line a round or heart-shaped mold with several layers of damp cheesecloth. Fill with cheese mixture, pat gently to smooth surface, and fold edges of cloth over top. Refrigerate overnight.

Combine strawberries and serve either in one large bowl or individual bowls. Unmold cheese onto a colorful plate. Serve with small loaves of French bread or hard-crusted rolls, heated, either plain or lightly spread with margarine.

CHOCOLATE MOUSSE I

There are some brands of dry packaged chocolate mousse made with cocoa and containing no fats or egg yolks; this recipe uses one of these mixes as a base.

MAKES 4 SERVINGS

2 large egg whites
¼ cup sugar
Dash of salt

Chocolate mousse dessert mix
   (2 ounces)
½ cup liquid skim milk

Beat egg whites until foamy. Add sugar and salt and beat until stiff peaks form. Dissolve the chocolate mousse mix in the skim milk and add to the egg-white mixture. Spoon into tall-stemmed dessert glasses and chill overnight.

Serve with brandy-flavored Whipped Cheese Topping (p. 344) or Whipped Meringue Topping (p. 345).

CHOCOLATE MOUSSE II

If a dry packaged mousse mixture is not available to you, try this recipe. It takes a few minutes longer, but perhaps it is even better than the first recipe.

MAKES 4 SERVINGS

2 teaspoons unflavored gelatin	¼ cup cocoa powder
1 tablespoon cold water	¼ cup dry skim milk
¼ cup boiling water	2 large egg whites
½ cup sugar	Pinch of salt

Moisten gelatin in the tablespoon of cold water. Pour the boiling water over this and stir to dissolve. Mix ¼ cup of the sugar, the cocoa powder, and dry skim milk together until well blended, and add to the hot gelatin liquid. Stir until well dissolved. Beat egg whites with an electric mixer, add remaining ¼ cup sugar and the pinch of salt, and continue to beat until stiff. Fold the cocoa mixture into the egg whites. Spoon into dessert glasses and chill until firm.

LEMON SPONGE

2 envelopes unflavored gelatin
½ cup cold water
2 cups boiling water
1 cup sugar

6 tablespoons lemon juice
4 teaspoons grated lemon rind
4 egg whites, beaten stiff

Soften gelatin in cold water. Add boiling water, sugar, lemon juice, and grated rind. Stir until sugar and gelatin are dissolved. Cool until the mixture begins to set. Stir the gelatin mixture and fold in the stiff egg whites. Chill thoroughly.

STRAWBERRY SPONGE

MAKES 6 SERVINGS

1 envelope unflavored gelatin
½ cup cold water
½ cup sugar
2 cups mashed fresh strawberries

2 tablespoons fresh lemon
  juice
2 tablespoons rum
2 egg whites
⅛ teaspoon salt

Soften gelatin in cold water in the top part of a double boiler. Heat until gelatin is dissolved. Add sugar and cool until gelatin begins to set. Stir gelatin mixture and add strawberries, lemon juice, and rum. Beat egg whites until stiff. Add salt and fold into sponge. Spoon into a large serving bowl or individual dessert glasses, and chill thoroughly.

MOCHA SPONGE

MAKES 8 SERVINGS

2 envelopes unflavored gelatin
½ cup cold water
2 cups boiling water
2 tablespoons cocoa powder
2 tablespoons instant coffee
   powder

½ cup sugar
4 egg whites
⅛ teaspoon salt

Soften gelatin in cold water. Add boiling water, cocoa powder, coffee powder, and sugar. Stir until cocoa, coffee, and sugar are dissolved. Cool until the mixture begins to set. Beat egg whites with salt until stiff. Stir the gelatin mixture and fold in the egg whites. Chill thoroughly.

Coffee Sponge

Omit cocoa powder in Mocha Sponge and increase instant coffee powder to 3 tablespoons. Add 1 tablespoon brandy.

Chocolate Sponge

Omit instant coffee powder in Mocha Sponge and increase cocoa powder to 3 tablespoons. Add 1 teaspoon orange extract.

STRAWBERRY SOUFFLÉ

MAKES 8 SERVINGS

2 envelopes unflavored gelatin
¾ cup cold water
1 cup sugar
1 quart fresh strawberries, crushed
2 tablespoons lemon juice

3 tablespoons kirsch
1 cup Whipped Cottage Cheese (p. 287)
4 large egg whites (½ cup), at room temperature

Soften the gelatin in the cold water in a small saucepan. Put ½ cup of the sugar in the same saucepan and bring slowly to a boil. Stir to dissolve gelatin and sugar. Remove from heat and combine with crushed strawberries, lemon juice, kirsch, and cheese. Chill until almost set.

Beat egg whites until stiff. Add remaining ½ cup sugar gradually, continuing to beat until the meringue is glossy. Fold the meringue into the strawberries. Pour into a moistened 2-quart soufflé dish, using aluminum foil as a collar to hold the soufflé high. Chill thoroughly.

CHOCOLATE PUDDING

MAKES 4 SERVINGS

⅓ cup sugar
3 tablespoons cornstarch
¼ teaspoon salt
½ cup dry skim milk

3 tablespoons cocoa powder
2 cups liquid skim milk
¼ teaspoon orange extract
1 teaspoon vanilla extract

Mix dry ingredients together in a heavy saucepan or the top part of a double boiler. Add liquid skim milk gradually and cook over low heat or over simmering water, stirring constantly, until thick and smooth. Add orange extract and vanilla. Pour into individual dessert glasses and chill thoroughly.

Serve with plain milk, Jack Sprat Cream (p. 290), an acceptable dairy substitute cream, a little plain low-fat yogurt, or sweetened Whipped Cheese Topping (p. 344).

STEAMED CHOCOLATE PUDDING

MAKES 12 TO 14 SERVINGS

5 tablespoons oil
¾ cup sugar
4 egg whites
2¼ cups all-purpose flour
½ cup cocoa powder

1 tablespoon baking powder
½ teaspoon salt
½ cup dry skim milk
1½ cups liquid skim milk
1½ teaspoons vanilla extract

Combine oil, sugar, and egg whites and beat until light. Sift flour, cocoa powder, baking powder, and salt together. Dissolve the dry milk in the liquid milk. Add dry ingredients to oil-sugar mixture alternately with fortified milk. Stir in vanilla. Pour mixture into a greased and floured 1½-quart mold (a 2-pound coffee can will do) and cover with a tight-fitting lid. Place on a rack in a large pot; bring water up to the halfway mark of the mold. Cover the pot and steam gently for 2 hours, adding more *hot* water to the pot if it steams away.

Remove the pudding from the mold as soon as it is done. Slice the steaming pudding at the table, and accompany with one of the following: Fluffy Hard Sauce (p. 346), Whipped Cheese Topping (p. 344), safflower ice cream (p. 417).

STEAMED PUMPKIN PUDDING

During the winter months, nothing is quite so special for dessert as a piping hot steamed pudding! Unmold it on a handsome platter and serve with a sauce. This makes a welcome substitute for the usual Thanksgiving pumpkin pie.

MAKES 8 TO 12 SERVINGS

1½ cups all-purpose flour
1 teaspoon baking powder
1 teaspoon baking soda
½ teaspoon salt
½ teaspoon each of ground
  cinnamon, ginger, and cloves
½ cup toasted wheat germ

1 cup firmly packed dark
  brown sugar
⅓ cup oil
⅔ cup pumpkin purée
¼ cup buttermilk
3 egg whites, beaten until
  frothy

Desserts and Dessert Sauces 319

Sift together into a large bowl the flour, baking powder, baking soda, salt, and spices. Add wheat germ. Combine sugar, oil, pumpkin purée, and buttermilk, and add gradually to dry ingredients. Blend well. Fold in egg whites. Oil a 1½-quart mold or a 2-pound coffee can and dust with flour. Pour in the batter, and cover with a tight-fitting lid or aluminum foil, securely tied. Place the mold on a rack in a large pot and fill with water to the halfway mark. Steam for 1¾ hours, or until a straw comes out clean.

Loosen from the sides of the mold with a knife and ease onto a heated serving platter. Serve with one of the following: Vanilla Sauce (p. 349), Whipped Milk Topping IV (p. 343) flavored with rum, Whipped Cheese Topping I (p. 344), Fluffy Hard Sauce (p. 346), or Sour-Cream Substitute I (p. 288).

FREEZER DESSERTS

These refreshing desserts are quick to make and at the same time low in calories and saturated fats, some with no saturated fat at all. They are ideal for family as well as company desserts, especially after a large meal. For company serve in elegant long-stemmed glassware. Chopped walnuts or almonds can be sprinkled on top or a teaspoon of liqueur dribbled on at the last minute.

The recipes are presented in order of increasing richness, starting with almost an ice and tending towards a cream. But even the richest has half the calories of the same quantity of whipped cream, sour cream, or ice cream.

Freeze these desserts for 2 or 3 hours only, then remove to regular refrigerator for an hour or two to soften slightly before serving. Stir occasionally. A blender, electric mixer, or rotary beater can be used to make these.

LOW-CALORIE PEACH FREEZE

MAKES 4 TO 6 SERVINGS

3 cups fresh peaches
5 to 6 tablespoons sugar
1 cup dry skim milk

1 cup ice water
2 tablespoons lemon juice

Chill bowl and beaters. Peel peaches, slice them, and sprinkle with sugar. Beat dry milk with ice water until soft peaks form. Add lemon juice and beat a little longer. Crush peaches and fold into milk mixture. Serve immediately, or freeze for 2 hours, stirring occasionally.

BLUEBERRY YOGURT FREEZE

MAKES 4 TO 6 SERVINGS

1½ cups fresh blueberries
4 tablespoons sugar
1 cup liquid skim milk

1 cup plain low-fat yogurt
½ teaspoon lemon extract

Sweeten blueberries with sugar and set aside. Mix skim milk, yogurt, and lemon extract; fold in blueberries. Freeze for 2 to 3 hours, stirring once or twice. Remove from freezer for a short while before serving to soften a little.

BANANA CREAM

MAKES 4 TO 6 SERVINGS

1 cup dry skim milk
1 cup ice water
¼ cup butter-flavored oil
2 tablespoons lemon juice

2 tablespoons vanilla extract
6 tablespoons sugar
3 bananas

Whip dry milk and ice water in a chilled bowl until soft peaks form. Continue to beat and slowly add oil, lemon juice, vanilla, and 4 tablespoons of the sugar. Mash bananas with remaining 2 tablespoons sugar just before folding into cream mixture. Place in freezer and stir from time to time.

RUM-FLAVORED APRICOT YOGURT

MAKES 4 TO 6 SERVINGS

2 cups fresh apricots
¼ cup superfine sugar

2 cups plain low-fat yogurt
¼ cup rum

Purée apricots in an electric blender along with the sugar. Combine with yogurt and rum. Chill in serving glasses.

PEACH CREAM WITH ALMONDS

MAKES 4 TO 6 SERVINGS

2 cups fresh peaches
1 cup plain low-fat yogurt
1 cup Whipped Cottage
   Cheese (p. 287)

6 tablespoons sugar
½ teaspoon almond extract
¼ cup toasted slivered
   almonds

Peel, slice, and crush peaches. Combine with all other ingredients and freeze or chill for 1 to 2 hours.

WHIPPED STRAWBERRY CREAM

MAKES 4 TO 6 SERVINGS

2 cups fresh strawberries
½ cup sugar
1 cup plain low-fat yogurt
1 cup Whipped Cottage
  Cheese (p. 287)

1 teaspoon orange extract
1 tablespoon grated orange
  rind

Crush 1½ cups of the strawberries and sweeten with the sugar. Combine with yogurt, cheese, orange extract, and grated rind. Chill thoroughly. Decorate with remaining strawberries.

SHERBETS

Sherbets are generally less sweet than ices; usually they contain an ingredient such as milk, gelatin, or egg white to help break up the ice crystals. Stirring the sherbet from time to time as it freezes also helps to give a smooth texture.

APRICOT ORANGE SHERBET

MAKES 4 TO 6 SERVINGS

1 can (16 ounces) apricots,
  drained
3 ounces frozen orange-juice
  concentrate

½ cup water
¼ cup dry skim milk

Place all ingredients in an electric blender and whip at high speed until puréed. Turn into a freezer tray and freeze for several hours, stirring and turning over every hour.

LEMON SHERBET

MAKES 4 TO 6 SERVINGS

¾ cup sugar
½ cup water
½ cup lemon juice
1 tablespoon grated lemon
    rind

2 cups liquid skim milk
2 egg whites, at room
    temperature

Simmer ½ cup sugar and the water for 3 to 4 minutes. Cool. Add lemon juice, grated rind, and skim milk. Whip egg whites with remaining ¼ cup sugar until stiff. Fold into lemon-sugar mixture. Freeze in trays, stirring from time to time.

PINK GRAPEFRUIT SHERBET

MAKES 4 TO 6 SERVINGS

2 teaspoons unflavored gelatin
1¼ cups water
¾ cup sugar
½ cup dry skim milk
¼ cup lemon juice

2½ cups freshly squeezed
    grapefruit juice
Salt
Grated rind of 1 grapefruit
2 egg whites

Soak the gelatin in ¼ cup water. Boil the sugar and 1 cup water gently for 5 minutes. Remove from heat and stir in the gelatin until dissolved. Add the dry milk and again stir until dissolved. Chill.

Add the lemon and grapefruit juices, ¼ teaspoon salt, and the grapefruit rind. Freeze for 45 minutes. Remove from refrigerator, transfer to a large bowl, and whip with a wire whisk until mushy. Beat egg whites with ⅛ teaspoon salt until stiff. Fold into the mushy sherbet and freeze again for 3 to 4 hours, stirring at least once an hour. Beat again before serving.

LIME SHERBET

MAKES 4 SERVINGS

2 envelopes unflavored gelatin
2½ cups water
½ cup sugar

1 can (16 ounces) frozen
concentrated limeade

Moisten gelatin in ½ cup cold water. Add sugar and simmer for 3 to 4 minutes to dissolve. Cool. Add frozen limeade and remaining 2 cups water. Pour into a freezer tray and freeze for 3 to 4 hours, stirring every hour or so.

FRESH ORANGE SHERBET

From a friend, Ann Thompson. A simple and delightfully flavored dessert.

MAKES 6 SERVINGS

2 cups freshly squeezed
orange juice
1 cup sugar
3 cups liquid skim milk

½ cup dry skim milk
1 tablespoon grated orange
rind
4 tablespoons lemon juice

Combine ingredients and mix well. Freeze in freezer trays, stirring from time to time to break up ice crystals.

BUTTERMILK PLUM SHERBET

1 cup canned plums with juice
1 cup buttermilk
⅓ cup superfine sugar
3 tablespoons lemon juice

1 teaspoon grated lemon rind
2 egg whites
¼ teaspoon salt

Cut plums into very small pieces and combine with plum juice, buttermilk, sugar, lemon juice, and grated rind. Mix well. Place in a refrigerator tray and freeze until mushy.

Remove from refrigerator and place in a chilled large bowl. Beat egg whites and salt until stiff. Fold into plum mixture. Return to refrigerator tray and freeze again. Stir every hour or so to break up ice crystals.

MEXICAN MARGARITA SHERBET

For a light fillip and a cool ending to a heavy meal, try this dessert-cocktail combination.

MAKES 4 TO 6 SERVINGS

2 teaspoons unflavored gelatin
2½ cups water
½ cup sugar
1 cup dry skim milk
½ cup fresh lemon or
   lime juice

2 teaspoons grated lemon rind
2 egg whites
⅛ teaspoon salt
6 tablespoons tequila
2 tablespoons Triple Sec

Soften gelatin in ¼ cup of the water. Dissolve sugar in remaining 2¼ cups water, and boil for 10 minutes. Dissolve the gelatin in the hot sugar syrup. Add the dry milk and stir to dissolve. Set aside to cool.

Add the lemon juice and grated rind. Beat the egg whites and salt until stiff and fold gently into the gelatin mixture. Place the sherbet in refrigerator trays and freeze for at least 4 hours.

Stir every 30 minutes from back to front to break up ice crystals. Just before serving add the tequila and Triple Sec and beat with a wire whisk or electric beater.

APRICOT RICOTTA WHIP

MAKES 6 SERVINGS

1 cup firmly packed dried
   apricots
1 cup water
⅓ cup superfine sugar

1 cup low-fat ricotta cheese
2 tablespoons rum
2 egg whites, beaten stiff
¼ cup fine-ground walnuts

Soak apricots in the water overnight. Next day purée the apricots, juice, and sugar in an electric blender. Transfer to a bowl and stir in the ricotta and rum. Fold in the egg whites. Spoon into stemmed tall dessert glasses. Chill until firm. Serve sprinkled with ground walnuts.

APPLESAUCE PARFAIT

MAKES 6 SERVINGS

1 can (16 ounces) applesauce
¼ cup chopped walnuts
¼ cup apple butter, or
   1 teaspoon ground cinnamon
   and 2 tablespoons sugar

1 teaspoon vanilla extract
2 tablespoons sugar
1 cup Whipped Cottage
   Cheese (p. 287) or ricotta

Combine applesauce, walnuts, and apple butter. Blend vanilla and sugar into cheese. Make layers of applesauce and cheese in tall parfait glasses, ending with a dollop of cheese. Chill thoroughly.

RICOTTA PARFAIT AU CAFÉ

This Italian cheese lends itself beautifully to a French parfait. Here are two variations on an intriguing Sicilian recipe, found in Simon and How's Dictionary of Gastronomy.

MAKES 6 SERVINGS

1 pound ricotta cheese	¼ cup dark rum
½ cup superfine sugar	4 egg whites
2 tablespoons fine-ground coffee	¼ teaspoon salt

Whip ricotta, sugar, ground coffee, and rum until smooth. Beat egg whites and salt until stiff. Fold into cheese mixture and spoon into individual glasses. Chill for several hours.

Serve plain or with a dab of plain yogurt, slivered walnuts or almonds.

Ricotta Parfait au Chocolat

Substitute 2 tablespoons unsweetened cocoa powder for the coffee. *Variations:* Alternate layers of parfait with Plain Chiffon Cake (p. 366) or Angel Food Cake (p. 354).

Use 1 tablespoon ground coffee and 1 tablespoon cocoa powder for a mocha flavor.

Substitute ¼ cup crème de cacao for the rum.

PEACH SUNDAE

MAKES 4 SERVINGS

2 large fresh peaches	4 tablespoons orange honey
4 scoops of vanilla-flavored safflower ice cream	2 tablespoons kirsch

Peel and slice peaches and chill. Place scoops of ice cream in tall sherbet glasses. Top with peach slices. Spoon 1 tablespoon honey over each serving and sprinkle with kirsch.

FRUIT SHORTCAKE

Make Baking-Powder Biscuits (p. 198) or Buttermilk Biscuits (p. 199), adding 2 tablespoons of sugar to the dry ingredients. Split biscuits after baking and, while still hot, spread with a little margarine. Spoon sweetened fresh or frozen fruit over lower half of biscuit, cap with top half, and spoon more fruit on top. Sprinkle with sifted confectioners' sugar.

HURRY-UP FRUIT COBBLER

A cobbler is very much like a deep-dish pie, but the fruit is topped with an enriched biscuit dough instead of with piecrust. The fruit should be hot when topped with uncooked biscuits so prepare fruit first: while it is heating, make biscuit dough.

MAKES 8 SERVINGS

Apple or Other Fresh Fruit Cobbler

1 tablespoon cornstarch	3 to 4 cups cut-up fruit
⅔ cup sugar	1 tablespoon margarine
1½ teaspoons ground cinnamon	Biscuit dough
½ to 1 cup water (depending on juiciness of fruit)	

Preheat oven to 400°F. Grease a 10-inch baking pan or 2-quart casserole. Mix cornstarch, sugar, and cinnamon together in a large saucepan. Add water and heat slowly until thickened, stirring with a wire whisk. Add cut-up fruit and simmer until hot. Pour into the prepared pan. Dot with margarine. Drop dough by tablespoon onto hot fruit. Or pat dough out to ½-inch thickness and cut into rounds with a biscuit cutter. Dough can also be cut into triangular wedges. Arrange dough pieces on fruit. Bake in the preheated oven for 25 to 30 minutes. Serve warm.

Frozen or Canned Fruit Cobbler

Measure juice to make ½ to 1 cup and use in place of water. Omit sugar if fruit and juice are sweetened. Follow same steps as with fresh fruit, heating fruit before topping with biscuit dough.

For either recipe use ½ recipe for Baking Powder Biscuits (p. 198) or Buttermilk Biscuits (p. 199). Add 1 tablespoon sugar and 1 tablespoon oil.

CREAM PUFFS

Make the dough for Popovers (p. 207). Fill muffin cups only one quarter full. Cook puffs to a crusty brown. Cool and split into halves. Fill with ricotta cheese or Whipped Cheese Topping (p. 344) and dust with confectioners' sugar.

FLAKY PASTRY

Anyone who says it's easy to make this type of pastry is either a wizard, prevaricating, or hasn't tried it yet! Nevertheless it can be done, and it is delicious, tender, and flaky. Along the way, though, it will crumble and crack, need patching here and there, and never get quite as thin as you think it should. Don't give up! After a few exasperating experiences, you'll be able to whip up this tender pastry in very little time. The baking soda is the magical touch that makes the pastry especially tender.

MAKES ENOUGH FOR ONE 2-CRUST PIE, OR TWO 1-CRUST PIES

2 cups all-purpose flour	½ cup oil
1 tablespoon sugar (optional)	4 to 6 tablespoons liquid
1 teaspoon salt	skim milk, cold
½ teaspoon baking soda	

Sift flour, sugar, salt, and baking soda together, mixing ingredients well. Combine oil and milk in a small bowl and whip until frothy. Pour all at once over flour mixture and stir lightly with a fork until well blended. Add another tablespoon of oil and/or milk if needed to hold dough together. Divide the dough into halves and form each half into a ball. Wipe working surface with a damp cloth to keep wax paper from slipping. Roll out one ball of dough between 2 pieces of wax paper (12 by 14 inches) to a circle 11 inches in diameter. Grease a pie pan.

Now get ready for the challenging part. Remove the top piece of wax paper; place the pie plate upside down on top of the pastry with the bottom paper still underneath. With both hands grasp the sides of the pan together with the paper holding the crust, lift up a few inches, and *flip over quickly!* It probably won't be well centered but at least you've got most of it in the pan. Peel off the remaining wax paper. Now patch and trim until it looks presentable.

Proceed with pie filling, then roll out top crust as you did the bottom. Remove top paper, spread out one hand over crust, the other under bottom paper. Flip over gently and ease onto pie. Pinch edges together. Make a few slits for steam to escape. That's all! After a few tries, you'll have no trouble at all.

CRUMB CRUSTS

Crumb crusts can be used unbaked but in that case they should be thoroughly chilled before filling to prevent sticking and breaking apart. If baked, use a slow oven (315°F.) for about 15 minutes. Cool before filling.

WALNUT CRUMB CRUST

1 cup crushed graham-cracker or zwieback crumbs	¼ cup sugar
	¼ cup oil
1 cup ground walnuts	

CEREAL CRUMB CRUST

1½ cups crushed dry cereal
¼ cup sugar

3 tablespoons oil

ZWIEBACK OR BREAD-CRUMB CRUST

1½ cups zwieback or bread
    crumbs
¼ cup sugar

3 tablespoons oil
1 teaspoon ground cinnamon

GRAHAM-CRACKER CRUST I

1½ cups graham-cracker
    crumbs

2 tablespoons oil
4 tablespoons honey

GRAHAM-CRACKER CRUST II

1 cup graham-cracker crumbs
2 tablespoons sugar
3 tablespoons oil

1½ teaspoons ground
    cinnamon (optional)

APPLE PIE WITH STREUSEL TOPPING

MAKES 10 SERVINGS

Pastry for 1-crust 10-inch pie
    (p. 330)
1 cup plain low-fat yogurt
3½ tablespoons flour
2 egg whites
⅛ teaspoon salt

½ teaspoon vanilla extract
⅓ cup sugar
3 cups chopped firm green
    apples
Topping (below)

Preheat oven to 450°F. Prepare pastry; roll out, and line a 10-inch pie plate. Put yogurt in a large bowl and stir in flour until well mixed. Beat egg whites with a fork until frothy. Add to yogurt with salt, vanilla, and sugar. Blend well. Add apples and pour into pastry-lined pan. Bake in the preheated oven for 10 minutes; reduce heat to 350°F. and bake for 30 minutes longer. Remove from oven and sprinkle on topping. Reduce heat once again, to 325°F., and bake for 20 minutes more.

Topping

⅓ cup sugar   1 teaspoon ground cinnamon
⅓ cup flour   ¼ cup oil

Stir ingredients together with a fork until well blended.

BANANA CREAM PIE

MAKES 6 TO 8 SERVINGS

1 pie shell, 8 or 9 inches,   1 egg white
  baked and cooled   2 tablespoons oil
1½ cups liquid skim milk   2 drops of yellow food
½ cup dry skim milk   coloring
¼ cup sugar   ½ teaspoon vanilla extract
3 tablespoons flour   4 or 5 bananas, sliced
¼ teaspoon salt

Bake and cool the pie shell. Scald 1 cup skim milk over boiling water. Mix remaining liquid milk, dry milk, sugar, flour, and salt together. Stir into hot milk and cook slowly until thickened, stirring constantly. Beat the egg white lightly with a fork. Add to the milk mixture and cook for 1 minute longer, continuing to stir. Add oil, food coloring, vanilla, and sliced bananas. Pour into baked pie shell and chill.

Just before serving, spread with chilled Whipped Cheese Topping I (p. 344).

BLUEBERRY BAKE

This simple little dish is the inspiration of my daughter Katy. For less effort and calories, omit piecrust.

MAKES 4 OR 5 SERVINGS

3 to 3½ cups fresh blue-
    berries
½ cup sugar

2½ tablespoons cornstarch
Juice of ½ lemon
Pastry (p. 330)

Preheat oven to 450°F. Grease individual shallow heatproof glass dishes. Wash, hull, and pick over blueberries. Combine sugar and cornstarch. Add to blueberries along with lemon juice. Stir well. Put in the prepared dishes. Cover with strips of pastry arranged in lattice fashion. Bake in the preheated oven for 10 to 15 minutes. Lower heat to 350°F. and bake for 10 minutes more, or until berries are bubbling and piecrust brown.

Serve with Sour Cream Substitute I (p. 288) to which you have added a little grated lemon rind.

BLUEBERRY FLAN

MAKES 10 TO 12 SERVINGS

2 cups sifted all-purpose flour
¾ cup sugar
¼ teaspoon salt
¼ cup oil

5 tablespoons margarine
2 egg whites
3 to 4 cups blueberries

Preheat oven to 450°F. Grease and flour a large flan ring. Combine flour, ¼ cup sugar, and the salt. Add oil and 4 tablespoons of the margarine, cutting in until well mixed. Whip egg whites lightly with a fork and stir in. Roll the dough into a circle on a floured board and use to line the prepared pan. Fill with washed berries. Dot remaining margarine over top and sprinkle remaining ½ cup sugar over all. Bake in the preheated oven for 15 to 20 minutes. Reduce heat to 375°F. and bake for 15 to 20 minutes longer, until berries are cooked and the crust browned.

Apples, peaches, or apricots can be substituted for the berries.

COTTAGE CHEESE PIE WITH CRUMB TOPPING

Thanks to the Cleveland Clinic for suggesting the idea of such a simple cheese pie.

MAKES 6 TO 8 SERVINGS

Graham-Cracker Crust I
  (p. 332)
1 pound cottage cheese
½ cup sugar
3 large egg whites

1½ teaspoons lemon juice
4 drops of yellow food
  coloring
1 teaspoon vanilla extract
1 teaspoon ground cinnamon

Preheat oven to 350°F. Prepare crust mixture and reserve ⅓ cup for the top. Line a pie plate with remaining graham-cracker crust. Place cottage cheese in a colander and run water through it to rinse out the cream. Shake thoroughly to get rid of all water. Combine rinsed cheese and sugar and beat until smooth. Add egg whites, lemon juice, food coloring, and vanilla. Beat until all ingredients are well blended. Pour into the prepared crust. Mix cinnamon with reserved crumbs and sprinkle over pie. Bake in the preheated oven for 25 to 35 minutes, or until a knife inserted in the middle comes out clean.

For variations top with a fruit glaze: cherry, apricot, strawberry, raspberry, etc.

QUICK CHERRY PIE

MAKES 6 SERVINGS

Pastry for 1-crust pie (p. 330)
½ cup sugar
2 tablespoons cornstarch
⅛ teaspoon salt

1 can (16 ounces) water-packed pitted red sour cherries
2 drops of almond extract
1 teaspoon grated orange rind

Prepare pastry, line an 8-inch pie pan, and bake. Cool. Mix sugar, cornstarch, and salt in a saucepan. Add juice drained from cherries, almond extract, and orange rind. Blend and cook over low heat, stirring with a wire whisk, until thickened. Syrup should come to a boil. Spread cherries over the cooked pie shell, cover with the sauce, and chill.

Serve with Brown-Sugar and Rum Sauce (p. 347).

DEEP-DISH CHERRY PIE

MAKES ABOUT 8 SERVINGS

2 cans (16 ounces each) water-packed pitted red sour cherries
1 cup raw sugar

¼ cup cornstarch
1 tablespoon lemon juice
Pastry for large 1-crust pie (p. 330)

Preheat oven to 425°F. Grease a 1½-quart round ovenproof baking dish. Drain cherries, reserving juice. Place cherries in the bottom of the baking dish. Make a thickened sauce with juice, sugar, cornstarch, and lemon juice. Pour over cherries. Cover with pastry, fluting and sealing the edges to the top rim of the baking dish. Make a few small slits toward the center of the crust to allow steam to escape. Bake in the preheated oven for 10 minutes, then reduce heat to 350°F. and continue baking for another 30 minutes, or until crust is golden brown. Serve with Tuma cheese (p. 419), if allowed, or processed vegetable-oil cheese (p. 419).

PEACH PIE IN A SKILLET

MAKES 8 SMALL SERVINGS

1 cup all-purpose flour
1 tablespoon sugar
1½ teaspoons baking powder
2 tablespoons oil
⅓ to ½ cup liquid skim milk

1 to 2 tablespoons dry skim
  milk
6 fresh yellow peaches,
  washed, pitted, and sliced
Topping (below)

Preheat oven to 400°F. Grease an 8-inch skillet. Sift the dry ingredients together. Add oil and mixed liquid and dry milk to make a light dough. Knead lightly and pat out on a floured board to ¼-inch thickness. Place dough in the prepared skillet, letting some of the dough hang over the edges to the outside. Add peaches and sprinkle with topping. Fold extra dough toward the center. Bake in the preheated oven for 25 to 30 minutes.

Topping

⅓ cup sugar
¼ teaspoon salt

¼ teaspoon ground cinnamon
1 tablespoon oil

Combine and mix well.

PUMPKIN PIE

MAKES 8 SERVINGS

Pastry for 1-crust 9-inch pie
  (p. 330)
5 large egg whites, lightly
  beaten
1½ cups pumpkin purée
¾ cup sugar
2 tablespoons molasses
2 tablespoons oil

½ teaspoon salt
½ teaspoon ground ginger
1 teaspoon ground cinnamon
¼ teaspoon ground cloves
1 teaspoon vanilla or rum
  extract
1⅔ cups evaporated skim
  milk

Desserts and Dessert Sauces   337

Preheat oven to 425°F. Make pastry and use it to line a 9-inch pie plate. (Or use Graham-Cracker Crust I, p. 332.)

Mix egg whites, pumpkin purée, sugar, molasses, oil, salt, and spices together until well blended. Add vanilla and milk gradually, continuing to stir into a smooth batter. Pour into the pastry-lined pan and bake in the preheated oven for 15 minutes; then reduce heat to 350°F. and bake for 45 minutes longer, or until a knife inserted into the center comes out clean.

PUMPKIN CHIFFON PIE

MAKES 8 SERVINGS

Graham-Cracker Crust I
  (p. 332)
¾ teaspoon ground ginger
1 envelope unflavored gelatin
¼ cup cold water
½ cup light brown sugar
1¼ cups pumpkin purée

½ teaspoon salt
½ teaspoon ground allspice
1 teaspoon ground cinnamon
½ cup liquid skim milk
3 large egg whites
½ cup granulated sugar

Mix the graham-cracker crust with ¼ teaspoon of the ginger. Press crust into a 9-inch pie plate. Bake the crust in a 315°F. oven for 15 minutes, and cool it.

Soften gelatin in cold water. Combine brown sugar, pumpkin purée, salt, remaining ½ teaspoon ginger, the allspice, cinnamon, and skim milk in a saucepan. Stir and cook until mixture comes to a boil. Continue to cook for 1 more minute. Add gelatin to the hot mixture and mix thoroughly. Cool. When partially set, whip until smooth.

Beat egg whites until soft peaks form, add granulated sugar gradually, and beat until stiff. Fold into pumpkin mixture and pour into prepared crust. Chill thoroughly.

FRESH STRAWBERRY PIE

The juices of this pie are thickened with flour. For a clear glaze, substitute 1 tablespoon cornstarch for the flour.

MAKES 6 TO 8 SERVINGS

9-inch pie shell, baked
  (p. 330)
2 pints fresh strawberries
2 tablespoons flour

¾ cup sugar
Juice of ½ lemon
1 tablespoon margarine

Clean and hull berries. Place half of them in the baked pie shell. Mash remainder well and place in a heavy saucepan. Combine flour and sugar and add to berries in the saucepan along with lemon juice and margarine. Cook slowly until the syrup is very thick, stirring all the while. Spoon over the whole berries. Chill for 1 hour or more.

WINTERTIME STRAWBERRY PIE

MAKES 6 TO 8 SERVINGS

2 packages (10 ounces each)
  sliced frozen strawberries
1 package (3 ounces)
  strawberry-flavored gelatin

9-inch pie shell, baked
  (p. 330)

Thaw strawberries. Drain off juice and add enough water to make 2 cups. Bring this to a boil. Remove from heat, add gelatin, and stir to dissolve. Fold in the strawberries. Pour the mixture into the baked pie shell, and chill.

Serve with Sour-Cream Substitute (p. 288–89) or a whipped topping (pp. 342–45).

STRAWBERRY CREAM PIE

MAKES 6 TO 8 SERVINGS

Strawberry filling
Pastry for 1-crust 9-inch
  pie (p. 330)
1 cup Whipped Cottage
  Cheese (p. 287)

1 tablespoon sugar
1 tablespoon cornstarch
1 tablespoon liquid skim
  milk
1 teaspoon vanilla extract

Prepare the filling for Fresh Strawberry Pie (p. 339) or Winter-time Strawberry Pie (p. 339); chill. Prepare pastry and line the pie pan. Bake the pastry in a preheated 425°F. oven. About 5 minutes before the pastry is baked, remove it from the oven.

Mix remaining ingredients except the strawberry filling. Spread cheese mixture over the inside of the partly baked pastry. Return pie pan to the oven and bake for 5 minutes longer. Remove from oven and cool.

Spread strawberry filling over the cheese layer. Chill.

RUM CHIFFON PIE

This light and delicate dessert makes a perfect finishing touch to a heavy meal. For something slightly more substantial and heady, try Jamaica Rum Pie (p. 341).

MAKES 8 SERVINGS

Zwieback Crust (p. 332)
1 envelope unflavored gelatin
¼ cup cold water
8 egg whites, at room
  temperature
¾ cup sugar
2 tablespoons oil

¼ teaspoon salt
2 drops of yellow food
  coloring
¼ teaspoon cream of tartar
⅓ cup light rum, or 1
  tablespoon rum extract

Line a 9-inch heatproof glass pie plate with two thirds of the crumb mixture, leaving one third for topping. Bake the crust in a preheated 350°F. oven for 5 to 7 minutes. Cool.

Soak gelatin in cold water. Combine 4 egg whites, ½ cup of the sugar, the oil, salt, and food coloring in the top part of a double boiler. Cook over boiling water while beating with a rotary or electric hand beater until fluffed up. Continue to cook, using a rubber scraper to loosen the mixture from sides of the pan, until mixture is fairly firm, usually 7 to 8 minutes. Add gelatin mixture, stirring until well mixed. Set aside to cool.

Beat the other 4 egg whites until foamy, add cream of tartar, and continue to beat until stiff. Add remaining ¼ cup sugar and beat until meringue is glossy. Fold rum into custard mixture, then fold in the meringue. Pour into the crumb-lined pie shell, spreading out evenly. Sprinkle with remaining crumbs and chill thoroughly.

JAMAICA RUM PIE

MAKES 8 SERVINGS

1½ cups Walnut Crumb
   Crust (p. 331)
1 envelope unflavored gelatin
½ cup cold water
¾ cup sugar
1½ tablespoons cornstarch
2 tablespoons butter-flavored
   oil
½ cup dry skim milk

½ cup liquid skim milk
¼ teaspoon salt
2 drops of yellow food
   coloring
4 egg whites, at room
   temperature
¼ teaspoon cream of tartar
½ cup dark rum

Line a 9-inch pie plate with crumb crust, reserving ½ cup for the top. Bake the crust in a preheated 350°F. oven for 10 minutes. Cool.

Soften gelatin in the cold water. Mix ½ cup of the sugar with the cornstarch in the top part of a double boiler. Add oil. Dissolve dry milk in liquid milk, stirring until completely blended. Add to sugar in the double boiler, along with salt and food coloring. Stir and cook over low heat until hot. Add gelatin to mixture and continue to cook for a minute or two. Set aside to cool.

Beat egg whites until frothy. Add cream of tartar and continue to beat until stiff. Add remaining ¼ cup sugar gradually, and beat until meringue is glossy. Fold meringue into cooled cornstarch custard, being sure to scrape the bottom of the bowl so that all gelatin is blended with egg whites. Add rum. Pour filling into the prepared crust. Sprinkle top with reserved crumbs. Chill for several hours.

WHIPPED CREAM SUBSTITUTES

Nothing really substitutes for whipped cream, but a few concoctions come close and are even quite delicious. There are two approaches to the problem. One uses whipped cottage cheese and egg whites; the other, dry milk and ice water. In addition, there are stabilizers, sweeteners, flavorings, and fillers to vary the taste and consistency.

WHIPPED MILK TOPPING I

This is the simplest to prepare, but it must be used immediately or it disintegrates and becomes watery.

½ cup ice water	1 tablespoon lemon juice
½ cup dry skim milk	2 to 4 tablespoons sugar

Chill a small mixing bowl and beaters. Mix ice water and dry milk in the bowl. Whip until soft peaks form, 3 to 4 minutes. Add lemon juice and beat until stiff, 3 to 4 minutes more. Add sugar and beat for another minute. Serve at once.

WHIPPED MILK TOPPING II

½ cup ice water

½ cup dry skim milk

1 teaspoon unflavored gelatin

2 to 4 tablespoons sugar

Chill bowl and beaters. Put ice water in the bowl and sprinkle gelatin over it. When gelatin is softened add dry milk and whip until stiff. Add sugar to taste and beat for another minute. This will keep in the refrigerator for a short while.

WHIPPED MILK TOPPING III

Make Topping I, and gently fold in a little Whipped Cottage Cheese (p. 287). This gives more body and a slightly different taste.

WHIPPED MILK TOPPING IV

For a very stable topping, still based on dry milk, dissolve the gelatin in hot water.

1 teaspoon unflavored gelatin

½ cup dry skim milk

1 tablespoon cold water

½ cup ice water

3 tablespoons boiling water

2 to 4 tablespoons sugar

Moisten gelatin with the tablespoon of cold water. Add the boiling water and stir until dissolved. Cool. Whip dry milk and ice water until stiff peaks form. Add sugar and dissolved gelatin. Place in regular part of refrigerator until ready to use.

Flavor Variations: To above recipes, add any of the following: ½ teaspoon vanilla extract; 1 or 2 tablespoons brandy, rum, or Curaçao; ¼ teaspoon almond, orange, or lemon extract.

If you like, 1 to 3 tablespoons oil can also be added to give body and richness to the topping, but the oil will add calories too.

Whipped cheese toppings come closer to whipped cream in my opinion than any other. Both cottage cheese and ricotta make fine toppings. Whipped cottage cheese has less fat content and a smoother consistency but the flavor of ricotta is sweeter. Try both to see which suits you best.

These toppings can stand up in the refrigerator overnight.

WHIPPED CHEESE TOPPING I

Sugar content is a matter of taste.

2 egg whites
¼ teaspoon cream of tartar
3 to 4 tablespoons sugar

½ cup Whipped Cottage Cheese (p. 287)

Whip egg whites with cream of tartar until stiff but not dry. Add sugar and continue to beat until you have a glossy texture like a meringue. Very gently fold in the cheese. Chill.

WHIPPED CHEESE TOPPING II

2 egg whites
¼ teaspoon cream of tartar

2 to 3 tablespoons sugar
½ cup ricotta cheese

Prepare this like Topping I, but use ricotta instead of cottage cheese.

WHIPPED MERINGUE TOPPING

The proportion of egg whites to sugar makes this a fluffy substitute for whipped cream. This can also be used to frost cakes.

2 egg whites
¼ cup granulated sugar
⅛ teaspoon salt

2 tablespoons cold water
1 teaspoon vanilla extract

Combine egg whites, sugar, salt, and cold water and beat over hot water until stiff. Add vanilla.

For a sweeter taste, use ½ cup sugar.

WHIPPED HONEY TOPPING

One of the best substitutes for whipped cream. Use a mild honey unless you want to accentuate a particular flavor.

1 egg white
½ cup granulated sugar
½ cup honey

Pinch of salt
½ cup Whipped Cottage
Cheese (p. 287)

Beat egg white, sugar, honey, and salt with an electric mixer for 5 to 8 minutes. Fold in cottage cheese.

For a slightly tart flavor, substitute plain low-fat yogurt for the cottage cheese.

HARD SAUCE

MAKES ABOUT 1 CUP

2 tablespoons soft
margarine
1 tablespoon liquid skim
milk

Pinch of salt
1 teaspoon vanilla extract
2 to 2½ cups sifted
confectioners' sugar

Mix everything together and beat until smooth.

Variations: Omit vanilla and add other flavorings.

Lemon: Use 1 teaspoon lemon juice and 1 tablespoon grated lemon rind.

Orange: Omit skim milk, and use 2 tablespoons orange juice and 2 tablespoons grated orange rind.

Brandy: Use 1 tablespoon brandy.

FLUFFY HARD SAUCE

MAKES ABOUT 1½ CUPS

For a very smooth sauce, not quite so sweet, mix regular Hard Sauce with ½ cup Whipped Cottage Cheese (p. 287).

VERY FLUFFY HARD SAUCE

A good substitute for whipped cream.

MAKES ABOUT 1 CUP

1 cup sugar
1 tablespoon soft margarine
1 tablespoon liquid skim
milk, or brandy, rum, etc.

1 teaspoon vanilla extract
2 egg whites
1 teaspoon cold water
⅛ teaspoon salt

Blend ¾ cup of the sugar, the margarine, skim milk, and vanilla together until smooth. Beat the egg whites until foamy. Add remaining ¼ cup sugar, the water, and salt and continue beating until stiff. Fold this meringue into the sugar-margarine mixture and chill for 1 to 2 hours.

BROWN-SUGAR AND RUM SAUCE

MAKES ABOUT 1 CUP

¾ cup Whipped Cottage
  Cheese (p. 287)
¼ cup rum
¼ teaspoon salt

1½ teaspoons lemon juice
2 tablespoons dark brown
  sugar

Whip all ingredients together, and chill.

BUTTERSCOTCH SAUCE

MAKES ABOUT 1½ CUPS

¼ cup dark corn syrup
½ cup light brown sugar
1 tablespoon cornstarch
1 cup evaporated skim milk

1 teaspoon vanilla extract
1 teaspoon butter-flavored oil
⅛ teaspoon salt

Combine all ingredients in a heavy saucepan and heat very slowly, stirring constantly, until thickened and smooth.

For a very strong flavor of butterscotch (and a great many more calories per cup), cut milk to ½ cup and cornstarch to 1½ teaspoons.

CHOCOLATE SAUCE

Many variations are possible when preparing a chocolate sauce. Brown sugar can be substituted for white, coffee for water, orange extract for vanilla, etc. For a thick sauce use the smaller amount of liquid.

MAKES ABOUT 1¼ CUPS

¼ cup cocoa powder
½ cup granulated or light
   brown sugar
1 tablespoon cornstarch
1 tablespoon oil

½ to 1 cup water or
   prepared coffee
1 teaspoon vanilla extract,
   or ½ teaspoon orange
   extract

Mix cocoa powder, sugar, and cornstarch in a small heavy sauce-pan or in the top part of a double boiler. Add remaining ingredients and heat over hot water, stirring, until hot, creamy, and smooth.

COFFEE SAUCE

MAKES ABOUT 1¼ CUPS

1 tablespoon instant coffee
   powder
1 tablespoon cornstarch
¼ cup sugar
1 tablespoon oil

1 teaspoon vanilla extract
1 cup liquid skim milk
¼ cup dry skim milk
⅛ teaspoon salt

Follow directions for Chocolate Sauce, but be sure to use a double boiler so that the fortified skim milk will not stick and burn.

VANILLA SAUCE

MAKES ABOUT 1½ CUPS

⅓ cup sugar
1 tablespoon cornstarch
1 cup boiling water or orange
  juice

2 tablespoons margarine
1½ teaspoons vanilla extract

Combine sugar, cornstarch, and boiling liquid in a saucepan and bring to a boil. Continue to cook, stirring gently, until thickened. Remove from heat and add the margarine and vanilla.

LEMON SAUCE

Substitute 1½ tablespoons lemon juice plus 1 teaspoon grated lemon rind for the vanilla in Vanilla Sauce.

ORANGE SAUCE

MAKES ABOUT 1½ CUPS

¼ cup sugar
1 tablespoon cornstarch
½ cup water
2 tablespoons oil

1 tablespoon grated orange
  rind
1 teaspoon grated lemon rind
½ cup orange juice
⅛ teaspoon salt

Combine sugar, cornstarch, and water in the top part of a double boiler. Stir over hot water until thickened. Remove from heat and add remaining ingredients.

Cakes, Frostings, and Icings

HOW MANY SERVINGS?

It isn't easy to estimate the number of servings to be made from a cake recipe, because any cake can be cut into very small or very large pieces, and people who love cake might want to eat more than one piece. Nevertheless, you will want to have some guide for planning. Follow this guide for average servings.

8-inch round layer cake	about 8 servings
9-inch round layer cake	8 to 10 servings
9-inch tube pan or springform pan	10 to 12 servings
10-inch tube pan or springform pan	12 to 16 servings
9-inch-square pan	9 servings
rectangular pan 9 by 12 inches	at least 12 servings
rectangular pan 9 by 13 inches	12 or more servings

If you are concerned about calories, then serve smaller pieces. In that case, each cake can make more servings.

ANGEL-FOOD CAKE

Angel-food cakes are fun to make even if you can buy them without worrying about the ingredients. Besides they'll taste better if you do make your own.

1¼ cups sifted cake flour	½ teaspoon salt
1½ cups sugar	1 teaspoon cream of tartar
1½ cups egg whites (about 12 eggs)	1 teaspoon vanilla extract
	½ teaspoon almond extract

Preheat oven to 375°F. Sift flour three times with ¾ cup of the sugar. Beat egg whites with the salt until foamy. Add cream of tartar and beat until stiff but not dry. Add remaining sugar, 1 tablespoon at a time, and continue to beat with an electric mixer at slow speed. Gently mix in the vanilla and almond extracts. Fold the flour-sugar mixture into the egg whites, a little at a time, scraping bottom and sides of the bowl with a rubber scraper to mix well. Pour the batter into an ungreased 10-inch tube pan. Bake in the preheated oven for 30 to 35 minutes.

Cocoa Angel-Food Cake

Follow recipe for Angel-Food Cake but substitute ¼ cup cocoa powder for the same amount of flour. Omit almond extract and add ½ teaspoon orange extract.

CARROT ANGEL-FOOD CAKE

A cup of sherry, some grated carrots, and a few sesame seeds add a lot to a package of angel-food cake mix.

1 package (14 ounces) angel-food cake mix	1 tablespoon lemon juice
1 cup sherry	¼ teaspoon ground cinnamon
½ cup oil	1 cup firmly packed fine-grated carrots
½ cup toasted sesame seeds	Thin Orange Glaze (p. 378)

Preheat oven to 350°F. Grease and flour a 9-inch tube pan. Beat cake mix and sherry with an electric mixer at medium speed for 5 minutes. Add oil and sesame seeds and beat for another minute or two, until well mixed. Scrape sides and bottom of the bowl with a rubber scraper. Add lemon juice and cinnamon. Fold in the carrots. Pour batter into prepared pan. Bake in the preheated oven for 45 minutes.

Remove from oven, invert pan, and cool for 15 minutes. Loosen cake by running a knife around the sides. Place on a rack to finish cooling. When cool, pour the glaze over the top.

APPLESAUCE CAKE

Applesauce keeps this tempting cake moist for a long time.

1¾ cups sifted cake flour	2 egg whites
¼ teaspoon baking powder	⅛ teaspoon cream of tartar
1 teaspoon baking soda	½ cup granulated sugar
1 teaspoon salt	1 cup applesauce
½ teaspoon ground cinnamon	⅓ cup oil
½ teaspoon ground cloves	⅓ cup water
½ cup firmly packed dark brown sugar	

All ingredients should be at room temperature. Preheat oven to 350°F. Grease and dust with flour one 9-inch-square cake pan. Sift flour, baking powder, baking soda, salt, and spices into a large bowl. Break up lumps in brown sugar by hand or put through a strainer. Add to flour and stir. Beat egg whites in the small bowl of an electric mixer until foamy. Add cream of tartar and beat until stiff but not dry. Add granulated sugar and continue to beat until glossy, another minute or two. Set aside briefly.

Mix applesauce, oil, and water, beating with a hand rotary beater until well blended. Pour this mixture into the dry ingredients and beat at medium speed until well blended. Fold egg whites lightly into the batter with a slotted spoon. Pour into the prepared pan and bake in the preheated oven for 45 to 50 minutes.

Cool on a rack for 5 minutes. Remove from the pan and cool completely before frosting. Frost with Seafoam Frosting (p. 384) or Caramel Cream Frosting (p. 384).

BANANA NUT CAKE

2 cups sifted cake flour
1 teaspoon baking powder
1 teaspoon baking soda
1 teaspoon salt
1⅓ cups sugar
4 egg whites
¼ teaspoon cream of tartar

1 teaspoon vanilla extract
1 cup mashed banana
⅔ cup buttermilk
½ cup butter-flavored oil
½ cup fine-chopped walnuts
Caramel Cream Frosting
  (p. 384)

Preheat oven to 350°F. Grease and flour two 8- or 9-inch pans, or a rectangular pan 13 by 9 inches and 2 inches deep. Sift flour, baking powder, baking soda, salt, and 1 cup of the sugar together. Beat egg whites in a separate bowl until foamy, add cream of tartar, and beat until stiff. Add remaining ⅓ cup sugar to the egg whites gradually, continuing to beat for another minute. Set aside briefly. Combine vanilla, banana, buttermilk, and oil. Add all at once to dry ingredients and beat to a smooth batter. Fold egg whites and walnuts into the batter and pour into prepared pans. Bake in the preheated oven for 25 to 35 minutes, or until light brown on the top and pulling away slightly from sides.

Frost the cake when cool.

CARROT NUT CAKE

2 cups sifted cake flour
1 tablespoon baking powder
½ teaspoon baking soda
½ teaspoon salt
¾ cup light brown sugar
4 large egg whites
¼ teaspoon cream of tartar

½ cup granulated sugar
½ cup butter-flavored oil
¼ cup apricot nectar
1¼ cups fine-grated raw
  carrots
½ cup chopped walnut meats

Preheat oven to 350°F. Grease and flour a 10-inch tube pan. Sift the flour, baking powder, baking soda, and salt together. Add the brown sugar. Beat the egg whites in a separate bowl until foamy. Add cream of tartar and beat until stiff but not dry. Add granulated sugar gradually, continuing to beat until glossy. Set aside briefly. Combine the oil, apricot nectar, and grated carrots. Add all at once to the dry ingredients. Beat until smooth. Fold the egg whites into the batter, scraping sides and bottom of the mixing bowl with a rubber scraper. Add the nuts and pour into the prepared pan. Bake in the preheated oven for 45 to 50 minutes.

Cool. Frost with a lemon or orange frosting.

BLACK DEVIL'S-FOOD CAKE

This cake is rich, so watch out for the calories.

2 cups sifted cake flour	4 large egg whites (½ cup)
2 teaspoons baking soda	¼ teaspoon cream of tartar
½ teaspoon salt	⅔ cup oil
½ cup cocoa powder	1½ cups buttermilk
2 cups sugar	1 teaspoon vanilla extract

Preheat oven to 350°F. Grease and flour two 10-inch cake pans. Sift flour, baking soda, salt, cocoa powder, and 1½ cups of the sugar together into a large bowl. Beat egg whites until frothy, add cream of tartar, and continue to beat until stiff but not dry. Add remaining ½ cup sugar to the egg whites gradually, and beat until the meringue is glossy. Set aside for a minute. Combine oil, buttermilk, and vanilla in a small bowl. Pour oil-buttermilk mixture into dry ingredients all at once and beat until smooth, 2 to 3 minutes with an electric mixer, 150 to 200 strokes by hand. Fold meringue into the batter and pour into prepared pans. Bake in the preheated oven for 30 to 35 minutes, or until cake springs back when touched lightly with a finger.

Frost with Fluffy Cocoa Frosting (p. 380), Never-Fail Seven-Minute White Icing (p. 388), or Creamy Confectioners'-Sugar Frosting (p. 379).

BLACK POPPY-SEED CAKE

Poppy seeds are mostly grown in Holland; they are used widely in Continental and Asian cooking. The texture and color of black poppy-seed cakes make them completely unlike any others. Remember to soak the poppy seeds for at least 3 hours before starting. The rest takes but a few minutes. This recipe came originally from a friend, Paula Rotenberg. I have made a few alterations and given it a slight lemony flavor.

¾ cup poppy seeds
1 cup buttermilk
⅔ cup oil
1¼ cups brown sugar
2 cups sifted cake flour
¼ teaspoon salt

2 teaspoons baking powder
½ teaspoon baking soda
4 egg whites, beaten stiff
1½ teaspoons grated lemon
  rind

Ingredients should be at room temperature. Stir the poppy seeds into the buttermilk and let stand for 3 to 6 hours.

Preheat oven to 350°F. Oil a 9-inch springform tube pan. Combine oil, brown sugar, and the buttermilk and poppy-seed mixture. Sift together the flour, salt, baking powder, and baking soda. Add to the moist mixture and stir until blended. Fold in egg whites and lemon rind. Pour batter into prepared pan, and bake in the preheated oven for 35 to 40 minutes. The cake should be slightly brown on top and pulling away from sides.

This is good served with cottage cheese as well as with a whipped topping (pp. 342–45). Or just dust with powdered sugar.

EASY CHOCOLATE CAKE

1½ cups sifted cake flour
½ cup cocoa powder
1 tablespoon baking powder
½ teaspoon salt
2 egg whites
¼ teaspoon cream of tartar

1¼ cups sugar
½ cup oil
⅞ cup liquid skim milk
1 teaspoon vanilla extract
1 teaspoon each of butter
  flavoring and orange extract

Preheat oven to 350°F. Grease and dust with flour two 8- or 9-inch layer pans. Sift together flour, cocoa powder, baking powder, and salt. Beat egg whites in a large mixing bowl until foamy. Add cream of tartar and ½ cup of the sugar and beat until soft peaks form. Add remaining sugar and the oil and mix until light and fluffy. Add milk and sifted dry ingredients alternately. Beat with the electric mixer at low speed until well mixed. Add flavorings. Pour into the prepared pans and bake in the preheated oven for 25 to 30 minutes.

BROWN-SUGAR CHOCOLATE LAYER CAKE

A light, moist, buttermilk cake. Follow instructions carefully in order to achieve maximum leavening from ingredients.

⅓ cup cocoa powder
1⅔ cups sifted cake flour
1 teaspoon baking powder
1 teaspoon baking soda
½ teaspoon salt
1 cup firmly packed light
   brown sugar

3 egg whites
¼ teaspoon cream of tartar
½ cup granulated sugar
1 cup buttermilk
½ cup oil

Preheat oven to 375°F. Grease and dust with flour two 8- or 9-inch cake pans. Sift dry ingredients, including the brown sugar, into a large bowl. Beat egg whites until foamy, add cream of tartar, and continue to beat until stiff but not dry. Add granulated sugar to the egg whites gradually, beating for another minute or two. Set aside briefly.

Whip buttermilk and oil together in a small bowl with a hand beater. Pour this into the dry ingredients all at once and beat into a smooth batter. Fold the egg whites gently into the batter with a slotted spoon. Fill both prepared pans and bake in the preheated oven for 30 to 35 minutes.

Cool in the pans on racks for 5 minutes. Remove from pans, invert, and cool completely.

ECONOMY WHITE BUTTERMILK CAKE

2 cups sifted cake flour
2 teaspoons baking powder
½ teaspoon baking soda
1 teaspoon salt
1 cup sugar
2 egg whites

¼ teaspoon cream of tartar
1 cup buttermilk
¼ cup oil
1 teaspoon vanilla extract
4 drops of yellow food
   coloring

Preheat oven to 350°F. Grease and flour two 8- or 9-inch cake pans. Sift together flour, baking powder, baking soda, salt, and ½ cup of the sugar. Beat egg whites with cream of tartar until stiff. Add remaining ½ cup sugar to the egg whites gradually, continuing to beat until meringue is glossy. Set aside for a moment. Combine buttermilk, oil, vanilla, and food coloring in a small bowl. Stir liquids into dry ingredients and beat to a smooth batter. Fold in the meringue. Pour into the prepared pans and bake in the preheated oven for 30 to 35 minutes.

SNOWY WHITE LAYER CAKE

This smooth-textured cake is exceptionally tender and light. If a heavier cake is desired, and it may be for some purposes, omit the cream of tartar, and follow Mixing Method II. All ingredients should be at room temperature.

2¼ cups sifted cake flour
1 tablespoon baking powder
¾ teaspoon salt
½ cup oil
1 cup liquid skim milk
1 teaspoon vanilla extract

¼ teaspoon almond extract
1 teaspoon grated lemon rind
4 egg whites
¼ teaspoon cream of tartar
1¼ cups superfine sugar

Mixing Method I

Preheat oven to 375°F. Grease and flour two 8- or 9-inch layer-cake pans. Sift flour, baking powder, and salt into a large bowl. Make a well in the center. Pour in the oil and half of the skim milk. Beat with an electric mixer for 1 minute, or 100 strokes by hand. Add remaining milk, the vanilla and almond extracts, and lemon rind, and beat again for the same amount of time, scraping the sides and bottom of the bowl with a rubber scraper.

Whip the egg whites in a separate bowl until foamy. Add the cream of tartar and then the superfine sugar, about 2 tablespoons at a time. Continue to beat until the egg whites are stiff but not dry. Fold them gently into the batter and pour into the prepared pans. Bake in the preheated oven for 25 to 30 minutes.

Mixing Method II (no cream of tartar)

Sift dry ingredients, including all the sugar, into a large mixing bowl. Add oil and ½ cup milk. Mix as in Method I. Add remaining milk, extracts, lemon rind, and unbeaten egg whites. Mix to a smooth batter. Pour into prepared pans and bake as in Method I.

Almost any frosting or icing can be used to decorate this cake.

DELUXE WHITE OR YELLOW CAKE

A tender fine-grained cake that goes well with almost any frosting. In addition, this can be used as a basis for many fancy desserts (see next recipes). A few drops of yellow food coloring make the only difference between the white and yellow cakes. (Ordinarily, added egg yolks give yellow cake its color.)

2¼ cups sifted cake flour	½ teaspoon cream of tartar
1½ cups sugar	⅔ cup butter-flavored oil
1½ teaspoons baking powder	1¼ cups buttermilk
1 teaspoon baking soda	1½ teaspoons vanilla extract
¾ teaspoon salt	3 drops of yellow food
4 egg whites	coloring (for yellow cake)

Preheat oven to 350°F. Grease and flour two 9-inch cake pans. Sift flour, 1 cup of the sugar, the baking powder, baking soda, and salt into a large bowl. Beat egg whites until foamy, add cream of tartar, and beat until stiff but not dry. Add remaining ½ cup sugar to egg whites gradually, beating until meringue is glossy. Set aside for a minute or two.

Combine oil, buttermilk, vanilla, and food coloring (for yellow cake). Stir until well mixed. Pour this mixture into the dry ingredients all at once and beat into a smooth batter. Fold in meringue, using a rubber scraper to clean bottom and sides of bowl. Pour batter into the prepared pans. Bake in the preheated oven for 30 to 35 minutes, or until just firm to the touch and beginning to leave sides of pan. Cool on racks.

BOSTON CREAM PIE

This dessert calls for a single layer of the Deluxe Yellow Cake (p. 361), which is sliced horizontally to make 2 thin layers. To do this, either halve the ingredients or make the full recipe, reserving 1 layer for a later occasion.

½ recipe Deluxe Yellow Cake   Lemon or Orange Filling
   (p. 361)   Thin Chocolate Frosting

Lemon Filling

½ cup sugar   1 tablespoon oil
2 tablespoons cornstarch   ½ cup water or orange juice
2 tablespoons dry skim milk   1 tablespoon grated lemon
⅛ teaspoon salt   rind
4 tablespoons lemon juice

Mix together sugar, cornstarch, dry milk, and salt in the top part of a double boiler. Add liquid ingredients gradually, stirring, until sauce becomes hot and thickened. Add grated rind. Set filling aside to cool.

Orange Filling

¼ cup sugar
2 tablespoons cornstarch
2 tablespoons dry skim milk
⅛ teaspoon salt
½ tablespoon lemon juice

1 tablespoon oil
½ cup orange juice
1 tablespoon grated orange
rind

Follow the same method as for Lemon Filling.

Thin Chocolate Frosting

2 tablespoons oil
6 tablespoons cocoa powder
¼ cup boiling water

2½ cups sifted confectioners'
sugar
1 teaspoon vanilla extract

Combine ingredients and beat until well blended.

To ASSEMBLE THE CAKE: Bake the cake in one 9-inch layer, cool it, then slice horizontally into 2 thin layers. Spread one layer with either filling. Cover with the second layer, and frost with chocolate frosting.

MARMALADE CREAM TORTE

A luscious dessert. If the full recipe for the cake is made, one layer can be saved for another occasion. A packaged angel-food cake can be substituted but the richer cake makes a better dessert.

½ recipe Deluxe White Cake
(p. 361)
½ cup orange marmalade
½ cup Whipped Cottage
Cheese (p. 287)

2 egg whites, at room
temperature
¼ teaspoon cream of tartar
¼ cup sugar

Bake the cake in one 9-inch layer-cake pan. Cool. Slice horizontally into 2 thin layers. Combine marmalade and cottage cheese. Beat egg whites until foamy, add cream of tartar, and beat until stiff but not dry. Add sugar gradually and beat until meringue is glossy. Fold meringue into marmalade-cheese mixture. Use to frost cake layers. Chill thoroughly before serving.

MOCHA MERINGUE TORTE

½ recipe Deluxe White Cake (p. 361)
3 tablespoons cocoa powder
1 tablespoon instant coffee powder
3 tablespoons and ½ cup sugar

2 to 3 tablespoons water
¾ cup Whipped Cottage Cheese (p. 287)
3 egg whites
¼ teaspoon cream of tartar

Bake the cake in one 9-inch layer-cake pan. Cool. Slice horizontally into 2 thin layers. Mix cocoa powder, instant coffee, and 3 tablespoons sugar. Add water gradually, using just enough to dissolve all ingredients. Blend into the whipped cheese. Beat egg whites until foamy, add cream of tartar, and beat until stiff but not dry. Add ½ cup sugar gradually, beating until meringue is glossy. Fold meringue into mocha mixture. Use to frost both layers and sides. Refrigerate the torte until well chilled.

STRAWBERRY WALNUT TORTE

½ recipe Deluxe White Cake (p. 361)
4 cups whole strawberries, fresh or frozen
½ cup Whipped Cottage Cheese (p. 287) or ricotta cheese

2 egg whites
¼ teaspoon cream of tartar
½ cup sugar
¼ teaspoon rum extract
⅓ cup sliced walnuts

Bake the cake in one 9-inch layer-cake pan. Cool. Slice horizontally into 2 thin layers. Pick out 1 cup of the most perfect berries, all the same size if possible. Cut the rest of the strawberries into halves and blend them into the cheese. Beat egg whites until foamy, add cream of tartar, and beat until stiff but not dry. Add sugar gradually and beat until meringue is glossy. Add rum extract. Fold meringue into the strawberry-cheese mixture. Use to frost both layers of cake. Decorate the top with remaining whole strawberries. Chill the cake thoroughly. Just before serving sprinkle top with sliced walnuts.

STRAWBERRY CHEESE TORTE

1 rectangular angel-food cake, about 4 by 8 inches
1 cup strawberry low-fat yogurt
½ cup confectioners' sugar, sifted
2 cups Whipped Cottage Cheese (p. 287)
1 teaspoon vanilla extract
1 package (10 ounces) frozen sliced strawberries, drained

Slice cake horizontally into 3 thin layers. Beat yogurt, sugar, and cheese until well blended. Fold in vanilla and strawberries. Use to frost layers and sides of cake. Chill overnight, or for several hours.

LEMONY LAYER CAKE

1½ cups sifted cake flour
1½ cups sugar
1½ teaspoons baking powder
1 teaspoon baking soda
¾ teaspoon salt
4 egg whites
¼ teaspoon cream of tartar
⅓ cup oil
3 tablespoons lemon juice
1 tablespoon grated lemon rind
¾ cup buttermilk
3 drops of yellow food coloring

Preheat oven to 350°F. Grease two 8-inch layer-cake pans and dust with flour. Sift together flour, 1 cup of the sugar, the baking powder, baking soda, and salt into a large bowl. Beat egg whites until foamy, add cream of tartar, and beat until stiff but not dry. Add remaining ½ cup sugar to the egg whites gradually and continue to beat until meringue is glossy. Do not overbeat. Set aside for a minute or two.

Combine oil, lemon juice, lemon rind, buttermilk, and food coloring. Mix with a rotary beater until well blended. Pour this mixture into the dry ingredients all at once and beat to a smooth batter. Fold the meringue very gently into the batter. Fill prepared pans, and bake in the preheated oven for 30 to 35 minutes, until center is firm to the touch. Cool on racks.

Frost with Lemon Glaze (p. 378), Lemon Butter Frosting (p. 382), or Lemon Cheese Frosting (p. 381).

ORANGE CHIFFON LAYER CAKE

Fresh orange flavor in both cake and icing makes this a particularly refreshing summer dessert.

2 cups sifted cake flour
1¼ cups sugar
2 teaspoons baking powder
¼ teaspoon baking soda
1 teaspoon salt
8 egg whites
½ teaspoon cream of tartar
3 tablespoons grated orange rind

½ cup orange juice
¼ cup liquid skim milk
½ cup butter-flavored oil
4 drops of yellow food coloring
Orange Butter Frosting (p. 382)

Preheat oven to 325°F. Have all ingredients at room temperature. Sift together into a large bowl the flour, sugar, baking powder, baking soda, and salt. Beat egg whites with cream of tartar until stiff but not dry. Set aside. Combine orange rind and juice, skim milk, oil, and food coloring. Pour liquids into dry ingredients and beat until smooth. Fold egg whites into batter, scraping bottom and sides of the bowl with a rubber scraper and folding the batter toward the center. Pour into an ungreased 10-inch tube pan. Bake in the preheated oven for 55 minutes, then at 350°F. for 10 to 15 minutes.

Invert pan and cool. Remove the cake from the pan, turn onto a cake plate, and frost.

Plain Chiffon Cake

Follow recipe for Orange Chiffon Layer Cake (above), substituting for the orange juice and rind 2 teaspoons vanilla extract, 1 teaspoon grated lemon rind, and ½ cup liquid skim milk (making ¾ cup milk in all).

Banana Chiffon Cake

Follow recipe for Orange Chiffon Layer Cake (above), substituting for the orange juice and rind 1 cup mashed bananas and 2 teaspoons vanilla extract.

RASPBERRY JAM MARBLE CAKE

A simple but decorative cake. For variety try a different jam from time to time.

2½ cups sifted cake flour
1 teaspoon baking powder
1 teaspoon baking soda
1 teaspoon salt
½ teaspoon ground cinnamon
4 egg whites

¾ cup sugar
½ cup oil
⅔ cup buttermilk
1 tablespoon lemon juice
1 cup seedless red raspberry
jam

Preheat oven to 350°F. Grease and flour two 9-inch layer-cake pans. Sift flour, baking powder, baking soda, salt, and cinnamon into a large bowl. Beat egg whites until foamy. Add sugar to egg whites gradually, continuing to beat until meringue holds firm peaks. Set aside for a few minutes. Add oil, buttermilk, and lemon juice all at once to flour mixture. Beat until smooth. Fold in the meringue, scraping sides and bottom of the bowl with a rubber scraper. Stir in the jam with a fork; use a few quick strokes, leaving a streaked effect. Do not mix completely or the cake will be lavender! Pour into the prepared pans, and bake in the preheated oven for 30 to 35 minutes.

Cool and ice as desired.

PUMPKIN CAKE

2¼ cups sifted cake flour
1 teaspoon baking soda
1 teaspoon salt
1½ teaspoons baking powder
1 teaspoon ground cinnamon
¼ teaspoon ground cloves
½ cup firmly packed light
   brown sugar
4 egg whites

¼ teaspoon cream of tartar
¾ cup granulated sugar
⅔ cup oil
½ cup buttermilk
1¼ cups pumpkin purée
1 cup each of golden raisins
   and chopped walnuts
Banana Icing (p. 385)

Preheat oven to 350°F. Grease and flour two 9-inch pans. Sift the dry ingredients together. Add brown sugar. Beat egg whites until foamy, add cream of tartar, and beat until stiff but not dry. Add granulated sugar to the egg whites gradually, and beat until meringue is glossy. Set aside for a minute. Combine oil, buttermilk, and pumpkin purée and add all at once to the dry ingredients. Beat until well blended. Fold the meringue into the cake batter. Add raisins and chopped walnuts. Pour batter into prepared pans. Bake in the preheated oven for 30 to 35 minutes.

Cool the cake. Frost the layers and put together.

Dark raisins and unsalted sunflower seeds can be substituted for golden raisins and walnuts.

SOUR MILK SPICE CAKE

2½ cups sifted cake flour	4 egg whites
1 teaspoon baking powder	¼ teaspoon cream of tartar
1 teaspoon baking soda	¾ cup granulated sugar
1 teaspoon salt	⅔ cup oil
2 teaspoons ground cinnamon	1½ cups buttermilk
1 teaspoon ground cloves	1 teaspoon vanilla extract
¼ teaspoon grated nutmeg	⅔ cup each of raisins and
1 cup light brown sugar	walnut meats

Preheat oven to 350°F. Grease and flour a baking pan 9 by 12 inches and 2 inches deep. Sift first seven ingredients together into a large bowl. Add brown sugar. Whip egg whites in a small bowl until foamy, add cream of tartar, and whip until stiff. Add granulated sugar to the egg whites gradually, continuing to beat until meringue is glossy. Set aside. Combine oil, buttermilk, and vanilla. Pour liquids into dry ingredients and beat until smooth. Fold in the meringue, scraping bottom and sides of the bowl with a rubber scraper and folding the batter toward the center. Add raisins and walnuts. Pour into the prepared pan. Bake in the preheated oven for 40 to 45 minutes.

Cool in the pan. Remove from pan and spread top and sides with Banana Icing (p. 385) or a lemon or orange frosting.

PINEAPPLE UPSIDE-DOWN CAKE

A handsome dessert with an especially good cake batter made with honey and pineapple juice. The recipe is intentionally large as this cake will keep fresh and moist for a long time. For half of the recipe, use an 8-inch-square pan or 8-inch skillet rather than the larger size.

MAKES 14 TO 16 SERVINGS

8 canned pineapple slices
1¼ cups pineapple juice
¾ cup oil
1 cup brown sugar
8 maraschino cherries (optional)
3 cups all-purpose flour

1½ teaspoons baking soda
¾ teaspoon salt
1 cup honey
2 drops of yellow food coloring
2 teaspoons vanilla extract
4 egg whites, lightly beaten

Preheat oven to 350°F. Drain pineapple and add enough extra juice to make 1¼ cups. Combine ¼ cup of the oil and ¼ cup of the juice in a 10-inch skillet, 9-inch-square pan, or baking pan 8 by 10 inches. Sides should be 1½ to 2 inches deep. Sprinkle with the brown sugar and arrange drained pineapple slices over the sugar. Place a maraschino cherry in the center of each pineapple slice if desired.

Sift flour, baking soda, and salt into a large bowl. Mix honey, remaining 1 cup pineapple juice, remaining ½ cup oil, the food coloring, vanilla, and egg whites together. Pour all at once into the dry ingredients. Beat until smooth. Pour batter over pineapple slices in the prepared pan. Bake in the preheated oven for 45 to 50 minutes, or until a straw comes out clean and the center is firm to the touch. Immediately turn upside down onto a serving plate to let sugar mixture run down over the cake.

Serve warm, with or without sauce; use a whipped topping (pp. 342–45) or sour-cream substitute (pp. 288–89).

PRUNE PUDDING SPICE CAKE

A rich, heavy, cakelike pudding. Almost any frosting is suitable, including chocolate, which will give a particularly interesting contrast in flavors.

1 cup dried prunes
1½ cups sifted cake flour
1 teaspoon baking soda
½ teaspoon salt
2 teaspoons ground cinnamon
½ teaspoon each of ground
   allspice and cloves
1 cup firmly packed light
   brown or raw sugar

2 egg whites
⅓ cup buttermilk
½ cup oil
2 tablespoons lemon juice
1 tablespoon grated lemon
   rind
½ cup chopped walnut meats
   (optional)

Preheat oven to 350°F. Grease and flour a 9-inch-square pan 2 inches deep. Cook prunes according to directions, reserving ⅓ cup of the juice. Pit them and chop them into small pieces.

Sift together flour, baking soda, salt, and spices. Add sugar and mix well. Beat egg whites lightly with a rotary beater. Add reserved ⅓ cup prune juice, the buttermilk, oil, lemon juice and rind, and beat a little more until well blended. Pour liquid ingredients into dry ingredients and stir until smooth, 150 to 200 strokes by hand or for 2 to 3 minutes with the electric mixer at medium speed. Fold in chopped prunes and walnuts. Pour into the prepared pan. Bake in the preheated oven for 50 minutes, or until firm and pulling away slightly from the sides of the pan. Cool.

Frost with Orange or Lemon Glaze (p. 378), Chocolate Frosting (p. 380), or other frosting. Or serve the cake topped with a glob of Whipped Cheese Topping (p. 344) for a scrumptious dessert.

OLD-TIME MOLASSES GINGERBREAD

This dark luscious gingerbread really needs no accompaniment and should be eaten straight from the oven while still hot and steaming.

2¼ cups all-purpose flour
1½ teaspoons baking soda
½ teaspoon salt
1½ teaspoons ground ginger
1 teaspoon ground cinnamon
½ teaspoon ground cloves

¼ cup sugar
½ cup oil
1 cup boiling water
1 cup molasses
2 egg whites, beaten stiff

Preheat oven to 325°F. Grease and flour a 9-inch-square pan. Sift dry ingredients including sugar together into a large bowl. Combine oil, boiling water, and molasses in a small bowl. Pour all at once into the dry ingredients. Beat until smooth. Fold in the egg whites. Pour into the prepared pan, and bake in the preheated oven for 45 to 50 minutes.

Cut into squares while still hot. For a special treat serve with ricotta cheese or one of the whipped toppings (pp. 342–45).

YORKSHIRE PARKIN

An ancient recipe from the northern part of England. It is much like gingerbread, but the oats give it a heavier texture. Traditionally parkin is kept for a week or two before being eaten, but that is easier said than done!

MAKES 9 TO 12 SERVINGS

1 cup all-purpose flour
½ teaspoon ground ginger
¼ teaspoon ground cloves
½ teaspoon salt
¾ teaspoon baking soda

½ cup sugar
2 cups rolled oats
⅔ cup molasses
½ cup oil
⅓ cup buttermilk

Preheat oven to 350°F. Grease and flour an 8-inch-square pan 2 inches deep. Sift flour, ginger, cloves, salt, and baking soda into a large bowl. Add sugar and rolled oats. Combine molasses, oil, and butter-milk, and add all at once to the dry ingredients; stir quickly. Pour into the prepared pan. Bake in the preheated oven for 30 minutes.

Serve with a whipped topping (pp. 342–45), or spread with soft margarine and eat like a bread while still warm.

COTTAGE PUDDING

This dessert is really a cake in spite of its name, but it is traditionally served with a sauce and not frosted. Serve hot with one of the dessert sauces listed in the index, or with stewed or puréed fruit.

2 cups sifted all-purpose flour	1¼ cups buttermilk
2 teaspoons baking powder	⅓ cup oil
½ teaspoon baking soda	1 teaspoon each of vanilla
⅔ cup sugar	extract and butter flavoring
¼ teaspoon salt	2 drops of yellow food
2 egg whites, lightly beaten	coloring

Preheat oven to 350°F. Grease and flour an 8-inch-square pan. Sift the dry ingredients together. Combine remaining ingredients in a small bowl. Add all at once to dry ingredients and beat to form a smooth batter. Spoon into the prepared pan. Bake in the preheated oven for 20 to 25 minutes. Serve warm.

APPLE, PEACH, OR PLUM KUCHEN

1 cup sifted all-purpose flour	2 tablespoons liquid skim milk
1½ teaspoons baking powder	4 to 5 cups peeled and sliced
¼ teaspoon salt	apples, plums, or peaches
6 tablespoons sugar	½ teaspoon ground cinnamon
2 tablespoons oil	1 tablespoon margarine
2 egg whites, lightly beaten	¼ cup currant jelly, melted
½ teaspoon vanilla extract	
2 drops of yellow food coloring	

Preheat oven to 425°F. Grease a 9-inch-square pan. Sift together flour, baking powder, salt, and 2 tablespoons of the sugar. Add the oil and mix well with a fork. Combine egg whites, vanilla, food coloring, and skim milk. Add all at once to dry ingredients. Stir quickly until blended, adding another tablespoon or two of milk if necessary. Dough should be just soft enough to handle. Pat out dough with hands or a rolling pin to fit the prepared pan and have edges come up ½ inch on the sides. Lay fruit slices snugly together in uniform rows, pressing them lightly into the dough. Sprinkle with remaining 4 tablespoons sugar combined with the cinnamon. Dot with the margarine. Bake in the preheated oven for 25 minutes, or in a 375°F. oven for 35 minutes.

Remove from oven. Spread with melted jelly. Cool.

For an even more striking effect make 3 rows of fruit, each one a different kind. Serve with safflower ice cream (p. 417), a sour-cream substitute (p. 288), or Whipped Cheese Topping (p. 344).

GREEN APPLE CAKE FOR PICNICS

The apple pieces remain intact and distinguishable in this dark, moist, rough-textured cake. Ideal for picnics. Serve directly from the pan.

4 cups diced unpeeled green apples	1 teaspoon vanilla extract
2 egg whites, beaten until frothy	2 cups sifted all-purpose flour
	2 teaspoons baking soda
2 cups raw sugar	2 teaspoons ground cinnamon
½ cup oil	¾ teaspoon salt
	1 cup chopped walnuts

Preheat oven to 325°F. Grease and flour a cake pan 11 by 7 inches, or one 9 by 13 inches. Mix apples and egg whites in a large mixing bowl. Add sugar, oil, and vanilla. Sift together flour, baking soda, cinnamon, and salt. Mix well with apple-sugar mixture. Stir in the walnuts. Pour into the prepared pan. Bake in the preheated oven for 50 to 60 minutes.

BLUEBERRY TEACAKE

A smashing success at office parties or morning coffee klatches. Substitute 2 cups drained canned blueberries for frozen berries if you prefer.

2 cups sifted all-purpose flour	1 teaspoon grated lemon
2½ teaspoons baking powder	rind
½ teaspoon salt	1 package (10 ounces) frozen
⅔ cup sugar	blueberries, thawed and
2 egg whites	drained
⅓ cup oil	Topping (below)
½ cup liquid skim milk	

Preheat oven to 375°F. Grease and flour a 9-inch-square pan. Sift together the flour, baking powder, salt, and sugar into a large bowl. Beat egg whites lightly in a small bowl; stir in oil, skim milk, and lemon rind. Add liquid ingredients to dry all at once and stir vigorously for a few minutes. Fold in blueberries and pour into the prepared pan. Sprinkle on topping. Bake in the preheated oven for 45 to 55 minutes. Serve warm.

Topping

2 tablespoons oil	⅓ cup all-purpose flour
⅓ cup light brown or raw	1 teaspoon ground cinnamon
sugar	

OLD-FASHIONED HOOP CHEESECAKE

In grandmother's day cheesecakes were not the rich and creamy con-coctions they are today. Instead of cream cheese they were made with cottage cheese, farmer's cheese, pot cheese, and sometimes hoop cheese, a dry pressed cottage cheese. The somewhat coarse, quite dry texture of this cake does not appeal to everyone. To others, the subtle cheese-almond flour has a distinct charm.

1 cup sugar	1 teaspoon salt
1 cup evaporated skim milk	¼ cup flour
4 egg whites	1 pound hoop cheese or other
½ cup oil	dry-curd cottage cheese
1 teaspoon vanilla extract	4 egg whites, beaten stiff
½ teaspoon almond extract	Zwieback Crust (p. 332)
3 tablespoons lemon juice	Slivered almonds (optional)
1 tablespoon grated lemon	
rind	

Combine sugar and milk in an electric blender. Add egg whites, oil, vanilla and almond extracts, lemon juice and rind, and salt. Whirl for a few seconds to blend. Add flour and whirl again. Break hoop cheese into small pieces and add gradually to the mixture in the blender. It is usually easier to do this in two parts; pour half of the liquid into a separate container and combine the rest in the blender with half of the cheese. Set this aside in a large bowl and repeat with remaining cheese and liquid. When all is blended, combine both parts in a large bowl. Fold in the stiff egg whites.

Make the crust mixture with Holland rusk crumbs; use only 3 table-spoons sugar. Line a 9-inch springform pan with two thirds of the crumb mixture. Pour in the cheesecake batter. Sprinkle remaining crumbs over top, adding a few slivered almonds if desired.

Bake the cake in a 350°F. oven for 10 minutes. Lower heat to 325°F. and bake for about 1 hour longer. Turn oven off; open door and let cake cool to room temperature in open oven. Chill for several hours.

APRICOT ICEBOX CHEESECAKE

Walnut Crumb Crust
 (p. 331)
2 envelopes unflavored gelatin
1 cup liquid skim milk
¼ cup dry skim milk
8 egg whites
4 tablespoons oil
1 cup sugar
1 tablespoon lemon juice

2 tablespoons fine-grated
 lemon rind
1 teaspoon vanilla extract
4 cups Whipped Cottage
 Cheese (p. 287)
⅛ teaspoon salt
1 can (16 ounces) apricots,
 drained and chopped

Line an 8- or 9-inch springform pan with walnut crumb crust, reserving one third of the crust mixture for the top of the cake. Soak gelatin in ½ cup of the liquid skim milk. Set aside. Dissolve dry milk in remaining liquid milk. Combine with 4 egg whites and the oil in the top part of a double boiler. Before placing over heat, beat with a rotary beater until well mixed. Add sugar and place over hot water. Cook, stirring, until thickened. Add gelatin mixture and stir until blended. Remove from heat. Add lemon juice and rind, vanilla, and cheese. Cool.

Beat remaining 4 egg whites until frothy, add the salt, and beat until stiff. Fold them into the cheese mixture. Add the chopped apricots. Pour the mixture into the prepared pan. Sprinkle with reserved crust mixture. Chill thoroughly.

PINEAPPLE CHEESECAKE

MAKES 8 TO 10 SERVINGS

Graham-Cracker Crust II
 (p. 332)
2 cups canned crushed
 pineapple
2 envelopes unflavored
 gelatin
1 pound hoop or dry-curd
 cottage cheese

¼ teaspoon salt
½ cup fine granulated sugar
¼ cup oil
1 cup plain low-fat yogurt
2 egg whites, beaten stiff

Prepare graham-cracker crust; reserve ½ cup of the mixture and use the rest to line a 10-inch pie plate. Drain pineapple, saving ¾ cup syrup. Soak gelatin in pineapple syrup in a small saucepan until gelatin has softened. Heat slowly until gelatin dissolves. Place half of the cheese in an electric blender and add half of the gelatin-syrup mixture. Blend until smooth, then pour into a large bowl. Repeat with remaining cheese and syrup. Add salt, sugar, oil, and yogurt and mix well. Fold in the crushed pineapple and egg whites. Pour into the crumb-lined pie plate, and sprinkle reserved ½ cup crumbs over the top. Chill for 2 to 3 hours.

MILK GLAZE

MAKES ABOUT ¾ CUP

1 cup sifted confectioners'
   sugar

4 teaspoons hot skim milk
½ teaspoon vanilla extract

Mix to desired consistency.

CHOCOLATE GLAZE

MAKES ABOUT ¾ CUP

1 cup sifted confectioners'
   sugar
2 tablespoons cocoa powder

1 to 2 tablespoons boiling
   water

Combine sugar and cocoa. Add enough water to bring to desired consistency.

SIMPLE CITRUS GLAZE

MAKES ABOUT ¾ CUP

Mix 1 cup sifted confectioners' sugar with 3 to 4 teaspoons fresh or concentrated citrus juice. Beat until smooth.

LEMON GLAZE

MAKES ABOUT ¾ CUP

1 cup sifted confectioners' sugar

1 tablespoon lemon juice

1 teaspoon grated lemon rind

Blend together until smooth.

ORANGE GLAZE

MAKES ABOUT 1½ CUPS

2½ cups sifted confectioners' sugar

1 tablespoon grated orange rind

2½ tablespoons orange juice

Blend together until smooth.

THIN ORANGE GLAZE

MAKES ABOUT ¼ CUP

⅓ cup sifted confectioners' sugar

2 teaspoons orange juice

1 teaspoon grated orange rind

Beat ingredients to a smooth consistency.

APRICOT GLAZE

MAKES ABOUT 2 CUPS

⅔ cup apricot pulp (Baby food works well.)

1 teaspoon lemon juice

1½ to 2 cups sifted confectioners' sugar

Blend ingredients well; bring to desired consistency with added sugar or a little skim milk for thinning.

VANILLA FROSTING

MAKES ABOUT 2 CUPS

3 cups sifted confectioners' sugar

2 teaspoons vanilla extract

¼ teaspoon salt

3 to 4 tablespoons boiling water

3 tablespoons butter-flavored oil

Beat ingredients together until smooth.

CREAMY CONFECTIONERS'-SUGAR FROSTING

The large amount of oil makes this a rich high-calorie icing.

MAKES 1½ CUPS

2 cups sifted confectioners' sugar

½ cup butter-flavored oil, or 1 teaspoon butter flavoring mixed with regular oil

Pinch of salt

1 teaspoon vanilla extract

Combine sugar, salt, and vanilla. Beat in enough oil for right spreading consistency.

Variations: Add chopped nuts, grated orange, lemon, or grapefruit rind, almond instead of vanilla extract.

Peppermint Frosting

Add ⅓ cup crushed peppermint candy and 2 or 3 drops of red food coloring to Creamy Confectioners'-Sugar Frosting.

CHOCOLATE FROSTING

MAKES ABOUT 2 CUPS

2½ cups sifted confectioners' sugar
¼ teaspoon salt
⅓ cup cocoa powder

2 tablespoons oil
¼ to ⅓ cup boiling water

Sift dry ingredients together. Add oil and enough water to give the desired consistency. Beat until smooth.

FLUFFY COCOA FROSTING

Hershey's fine recipe with some alterations—fewer calories and no saturated fats.

MAKES ABOUT 3 CUPS, ENOUGH FOR TWO 9-INCH LAYERS

¾ cup cocoa powder
4 cups confectioners' sugar
⅓ cup oil

1 teaspoon vanilla extract
½ cup buttermilk or evaporated skim milk

Sift cocoa and confectioners' sugar together. Add remaining ingredients and beat to desired consistency, adding more liquid if necessary.

ROYAL HONEY FROSTING

1 egg white	½ cup granulated sugar
Pinch of salt	½ cup honey

Beat egg white and salt with an electric mixer until foamy. Gradually add sugar and continue to beat until soft peaks form. Add the honey. Beat at medium speed for about 4 minutes longer.

MAPLE FROSTING

MAKES 1½ TO 2 CUPS

Sift 2 to 3 cups confectioners' sugar. Add enough maple syrup to bring to desired consistency.

LEMON CHEESE FROSTING

MAKES ABOUT 1 CUP

1 cup sifted confectioners' sugar	¼ cup ricotta cheese or Whipped Cottage
1½ tablespoons lemon juice	Cheese (p. 287)
½ tablespoon grated lemon rind	

Combine sugar, lemon juice, and rind, and beat until well blended. Fold in the cheese, adding more sugar if necessary for a good consistency.

Orange Cheese Frosting

Substitute orange juice and orange rind for the lemon juice and rind in Lemon Cheese Frosting. Add more sugar or more orange juice if necessary for a good consistency.

Cakes, Frostings, and Icings   381

LEMON BUTTER FROSTING

MAKES ABOUT ½ CUP

1 cup sifted confectioners'
sugar
2 teaspoons lemon juice

1 tablespoon margarine or
butter-flavored oil

Blend together until smooth.

ORANGE BUTTER FROSTING

MAKES ABOUT 1½ CUPS

2 tablespoons oil
1 tablespoon soft margarine
2 cups sifted confectioners'
sugar

2 to 3 tablespoons orange
juice
1 teaspoon lemon juice

Mix all ingredients together and beat to a smooth consistency.

RUM BUTTER FROSTING

MAKES ABOUT 2½ CUPS, ENOUGH FOR A LARGE 2-LAYER CAKE

3½ cups sifted confectioners'
sugar
¼ cup liquid skim milk

¼ cup soft tub margarine
1½ teaspoons rum
flavoring

Add sugar and milk to margarine alternately. Beat well until
creamy and smooth. Add flavoring.

If you prefer the real thing, substitute rum for the milk and omit
rum flavoring.

WEDDING CAKE FROSTING

MAKES ABOUT 1½ CUPS

1 large egg white, or 2
small egg whites
2 cups sifted confectioners'
sugar

¼ teaspoon cream of tartar
⅛ teaspoon almond extract

Beat egg white with an electric mixer. Gradually add sugar and cream of tartar, and continue to beat until soft peaks form. Add almond extract. Beat until of right consistency to spread.

NO-COOK MARSHMALLOW FROSTING

This recipe with variations comes from Creative Cooking with Corn Syrup, *a publication of Best Foods, and is used by permission.*

MAKES ABOUT 1½ CUPS, ENOUGH FOR TWO 9-INCH LAYERS

¼ teaspoon salt
2 egg whites
¼ cup sugar

¾ cup Karo light or dark
corn syrup
1¼ teaspoons vanilla extract

Beat salt and egg whites with an electric mixer or rotary beater until soft peaks form. Gradually add sugar and beat until smooth and glossy. Add corn syrup slowly as you continue to beat. Fold in vanilla.

Coffee Frosting

Omit vanilla extract in No Cook Marshmallow Frosting and add 1 tablespoon instant coffee powder with the corn syrup.

Spice Frosting

Omit vanilla extract in No Cook Marshmallow Frosting and add ½ teaspoon ground ginger, ¼ teaspoon ground cinnamon, and a dash of ground cloves with the dark corn syrup.

Cakes, Frostings, and Icings   383

SEAFOAM FROSTING

MAKES ABOUT 2 CUPS

2 egg whites
1½ cups firmly packed
  brown sugar

Pinch of salt
⅓ cup water
1½ teaspoons vanilla extract

Combine all ingredients except vanilla in the top part of a double boiler. Place over boiling water. Beat with an electric hand mixer at high speed for about 7 minutes, or until stiff peaks form. Remove from heat, add vanilla, and beat until stiff enough to spread.

CARAMEL CREAM FROSTING

This frosting can be made without heat. However, the color and texture seem slightly improved if it is brought just to a boil.

MAKES ABOUT 3 CUPS, ENOUGH FOR TWO 9-INCH LAYERS

6 tablespoons oil
⅓ cup dark corn syrup
¼ teaspoon salt
1 teaspoon vanilla extract

1 to 2 tablespoons liquid
  skim milk
4½ cups sifted confectioners'
  sugar

Combine all ingredients and beat until smooth. Or heat ingredients in a small heavy saucepan until the mixture begins to bubble, stirring to a smooth consistency. Remove from heat and let cool. Add more milk or confectioners' sugar as needed to reach the right spreading consistency. Spread on cake layers.

DARK CARAMEL FROSTING

MAKES ABOUT 3 CUPS, ENOUGH FOR TWO 9-INCH LAYERS

6 tablespoons oil
½ teaspoon salt
2 tablespoons liquid skim
   milk or buttermilk

1 cup firmly packed dark
   brown sugar
3 to 3½ cups sifted
   confectioners' sugar

Combine oil, salt, milk, brown sugar, and 3 cups confectioners' sugar. Heat over low heat until bubbly. Remove from heat immediately and beat until creamy. Add remaining sugar or more milk as needed for the right consistency.

BANANA ICING

MAKES ABOUT 2½ CUPS

½ cup dark brown sugar
2 tablespoons cornstarch
1 tablespoon oil
⅛ teaspoon salt
⅓ cup evaporated skim milk

1 teaspoon vanilla extract
½ cup mashed banana (about
   1 medium-sized banana)
4 cups sifted confectioners'
   sugar

Combine brown sugar, cornstarch, oil, salt, and skim milk. Stir and heat slowly until syrup comes to a boil and has thickened. Remove from heat and cool to lukewarm. Add vanilla and banana and enough confectioners' sugar to bring to right spreading consistency.

BUTTERSCOTCH ICING

MAKES 1¼ CUPS

¼ cup dark corn syrup
½ cup light brown sugar
2 tablespoons cornstarch
1 tablespoon oil

⅛ teaspoon salt
⅓ cup evaporated skim milk
2 cups sifted confectioners'
sugar

Combine all ingredients except confectioners' sugar and heat slowly until syrup comes to a boil. Stir constantly. Remove from heat and cool. Add enough confectioners' sugar to bring to right spreading consistency.

BROWN-SUGAR ICING

MAKES ABOUT 2 CUPS

2 tablespoons margarine
2 tablespoons oil
⅓ cup liquid skim milk
1 cup firmly packed dark
brown sugar

1½ cups sifted
confectioners' sugar

Combine margarine, oil, skim milk, and brown sugar in a heavy saucepan or the top part of a double boiler. Slowly bring to a boil, stirring all the while to keep the mixture from sticking. Remove from heat and beat in the confectioners' sugar until of right consistency.

QUICK JELLY ICING

MAKES ABOUT 1 CUP

½ cup any kind of jelly
1 egg white

Pinch of salt

Place ingredients in the top part of a double boiler over hot water. Beat with an electric hand mixer for about 5 minutes. Remove from heat and continue to beat until icing holds up in peaks.

MOCHA CREAM ICING

MAKES ABOUT 2 CUPS, ENOUGH FOR TWO 8-INCH LAYERS

2 tablespoons oil
2 tablespoons margarine
3 tablespoons liquid skim milk
1 tablespoon freeze-dried
  coffee granules

½ cup cocoa powder
2 to 2½ cups confectioners'
  sugar

Combine all ingredients except sugar in a heavy saucepan or in the top part of a double boiler. Heat very slowly, stirring with spoon or wire whisk until well blended. Remove from heat and beat in enough sugar to bring to right spreading consistency.

ORANGE MARSHMALLOW ICING

MAKES ABOUT 3 CUPS, ENOUGH FOR TWO 9-INCH LAYERS

2 unbeaten egg whites
¾ cup sugar
3 tablespoons orange juice
¼ teaspoon cream of tartar

⅛ teaspoon salt
8 large marshmallows, diced,
  or 32 miniatures
2 teaspoons grated orange rind

Combine egg whites, sugar, orange juice, cream of tartar, and salt in the top part of a double boiler. Place over boiling water and beat with a rotary beater for 7 minutes. Add marshmallows and orange rind. Stir gently to mix. Leave over boiling water until the marshmallows are partly dissolved, then beat until smooth.

NEVER-FAIL SEVEN-MINUTE WHITE ICING

MAKES ABOUT 3 CUPS, ENOUGH FOR TWO 9-INCH LAYERS

2 unbeaten egg whites
3 tablespoons cold water
1 cup sugar

¼ teaspoon cream of tartar
⅛ teaspoon salt
1 teaspoon vanilla extract

Combine all ingredients except vanilla in the top part of a double boiler. Place over boiling water and beat with a rotary egg beater for 7 minutes, or with an electric hand mixer for about 3 minutes. Icing should be fluffy and reasonably stiff. Add vanilla and stir in.

Cookies and Small Cakes

APRICOT-FILLED NUT BARS

MAKES ABOUT 30 BARS

1 cup diced dried apricots
1 cup water
1 cup all-purpose flour
1 teaspoon baking powder
½ teaspoon baking soda
1 teaspoon salt
2 cups rolled oats

1 cup brown sugar
½ cup oil
¼ cup orange or other
    fruit juice
½ cup chopped walnuts
Confectioners' sugar

Preheat oven to 350°F. Grease and flour a baking pan 9 by 11 inches. Simmer apricots and water until liquid is almost absorbed, about 10 minutes. Cool and set aside for the filling.

Sift flour, baking powder, baking soda, and salt into a bowl. Mix in oats and brown sugar. Combine oil and fruit juice and stir in. If necessary, add another tablespoon or so of juice to hold batter together. Stir in the walnuts. Spread half of this mixture in the prepared pan. Cover with the filling, spreading it out evenly. Spread remaining cookie dough over the filling. Bake in the preheated oven for 25 to 30 minutes, until lightly browned.

Cut into bars (roughly 1½ by 2 inches) while warm, and roll in confectioners' sugar.

DATE AND NUT HONEY BARS

MAKES ABOUT 40 BARS

1 cup all-purpose flour
1 teaspoon baking powder
¼ teaspoon baking soda
⅛ teaspoon salt
4 egg whites
½ cup honey

2 tablespoons oil
½ cup orange or grapefruit
juice
2 cups chopped dates
1 cup chopped walnuts
Confectioners' sugar

Preheat oven to 350°F. Grease and flour a baking pan 9 by 13 inches. Sift dry ingredients together into a large bowl. Beat egg whites until foamy. Combine with honey, oil, and fruit juice. Pour liquids into dry ingredients and stir rapidly until mixed. Fold in dates and walnuts. Pour into the prepared pan. Bake in the preheated oven for 20 to 25 minutes, or until center is firm to the touch.

Cut into bars (roughly 1½ by 2 inches) when cool, and roll in confectioners' sugar.

MOLASSES RAISIN AND NUT BARS

MAKES ABOUT 40 BARS

2 cups all-purpose flour
¼ teaspoon salt
½ teaspoon baking soda
1 teaspoon ground cinnamon
¼ teaspoon ground cloves
½ cup dark brown sugar
½ cup buttermilk

¼ cup oil
½ cup molasses
2 egg whites, lightly beaten
1 cup chopped walnuts
1 cup raisins
Lemon Butter Frosting
(p. 382)

Preheat oven to 350°F. Grease and flour a baking pan 9 by 13 inches. Sift flour, salt, baking soda, cinnamon, and cloves together. Add brown sugar. Combine buttermilk, oil, molasses, and egg whites. Pour into the dry ingredients and stir until well mixed. Add walnuts and raisins. Spread evenly in the prepared pan and bake in the preheated oven for 25 minutes, or until a straw comes out clean.

When cool, spread with frosting. Cut into bars about 1½ by 2 inches.

CHOCOLATE BROWNIES

MAKES ABOUT SIXTEEN 2-INCH SQUARES

¾ cup all-purpose flour
1 cup sugar
¼ cup cocoa powder
1 teaspoon baking powder
½ teaspoon salt

2 egg whites
⅓ cup oil
1 teaspoon vanilla extract
½ cup chopped walnuts

Preheat oven to 350°F., and grease a 9-inch-square cake pan. Sift all dry ingredients together. Beat egg whites with an electric mixer at medium speed, then add oil and vanilla. Add dry ingredients to liquids and mix well. Fold in the walnuts. Spread evenly in the prepared pan and bake in the preheated oven for 30 to 40 minutes.

Cool and cut into squares.

BUTTERSCOTCH BROWNIES

MAKES ABOUT SIXTEEN 2-INCH SQUARES

1 cup all-purpose flour
1 teaspoon baking powder
½ teaspoon salt
1 cup light brown sugar

2 egg whites
⅓ cup oil
1 teaspoon vanilla extract
½ cup chopped walnuts

Follow the same procedure as for Chocolate Brownies.

CHOCOLATE BROWN-SUGAR BROWNIES

MAKES TWENTY-FIVE 2-INCH SQUARES

¾ cup cake flour
¼ cup cocoa powder
1 teaspoon baking powder
½ teaspoon salt
1¼ cups brown sugar

2 egg whites
½ cup oil
1 teaspoon vanilla extract
½ cup chopped walnuts

Preheat oven to 350°F. Oil a 10-inch-square cake pan. Sift together all dry ingredients including brown sugar. Beat egg whites with an electric mixer at medium speed, then add oil and vanilla. Add dry ingredients to liquids and beat until light and fluffy. Fold in the walnuts. Pour the batter into the prepared pan and bake in the preheated oven for 30 to 40 minutes.

Cool and cut into squares.

CHOCOLATE-CHIP COOKIES

MAKES ABOUT 4 DOZEN 2-INCH COOKIES

2 cups all-purpose flour
1 teaspoon baking powder
1 teaspoon baking soda
1 teaspoon salt
1 cup dark brown sugar
½ cup granulated sugar

4 egg whites
⅔ cup oil
2 teaspoons vanilla extract
1 cup chopped walnuts
1 cup homemade Cocoa
  Chips (p. 407)

Preheat oven to 375°F. Sift together flour, baking powder, baking soda, salt, and sugars. Beat egg whites until stiff. Combine with oil and vanilla. Mix into dry ingredients. Add walnuts and cocoa chips. Drop batter by teaspoons onto greased cookie sheets. Bake in the preheated oven for 10 to 12 minutes, until a delicate brown.

SOFT MOLASSES DROPS

MAKES ABOUT 2 DOZEN 2-INCH COOKIES

1½ cups all-purpose flour
¾ teaspoon baking soda
¼ teaspoon salt
½ teaspoon each of ground
   ginger and cinnamon
⅓ cup sugar

¼ cup oil
½ cup molasses
¼ cup buttermilk or
   prepared coffee
½ teaspoon vanilla extract
½ cup raisins or chopped nuts

Sift dry ingredients together. Combine oil, molasses, buttermilk or coffee, and vanilla. Add liquids all at once to dry ingredients and mix well. Fold in the raisins or nuts. Chill the dough for 1 hour.

Preheat oven to 400°F. Drop batter by teaspoons onto greased baking sheets. Bake in the preheated oven for 8 to 10 minutes.

OATMEAL COOKIES

MAKES 3 DOZEN COOKIES

1 cup all-purpose flour
½ cup brown sugar
½ cup granulated sugar
½ teaspoon baking powder
¼ teaspoon baking soda
½ teaspoon salt
1 teaspoon ground cinnamon

1 teaspoon grated nutmeg
½ cup oil
2 egg whites, lightly beaten
¼ cup liquid skim milk
1½ cups rolled oats
1 cup raisins

Preheat oven to 400°F. Sift together flour, sugars, baking powder, baking soda, salt, and spices into a large bowl. Combine in a separate bowl the oil, egg whites, and skim milk. Add liquids all at once to dry ingredients and stir until well mixed with a few swift strokes. Add the rolled oats and raisins. Drop batter by teaspoons onto greased baking sheets. Bake in the preheated oven for 10 to 12 minutes, until brown at the edges.

Oatmeal Chocolate-Chip Cookies

Substitute ½ cup homemade Cocoa Chips (p. 407) for the raisins in Oatmeal Cookies.

OATMEAL MACAROONS

MAKES ABOUT 4 DOZEN 2-INCH COOKIES

½ teaspoon salt	1 teaspoon vanilla extract
2 egg whites	½ teaspoon almond extract
1 cup sugar	2 cups rolled oats

Preheat oven to 350°F. Beat salt and egg whites until almost stiff. Add sugar gradually, continuing to beat to make a stiff meringue. Add vanilla and almond extracts. Fold in rolled oats. Drop batter by teaspoons onto greased baking sheets. Bake in the preheated oven for about 12 minutes, or until light tan.

SHREDDED-WHEAT CURRANT COOKIES

MAKES 2 DOZEN 2-INCH COOKIES

1 cup all-purpose flour	2 egg whites
1 teaspoon baking powder	⅓ cup oil
½ teaspoon baking soda	½ cup applesauce
½ teaspoon salt	2 cups bite-sized shredded
1 teaspoon ground cinnamon	wheat
¼ teaspoon ground cloves	1 cup dried currants
1 cup firmly packed brown sugar	

Preheat oven to 350°F. Sift together flour, baking powder, baking soda, salt, and spices into a large mixing bowl. Stir in brown sugar. Whip egg whites lightly in a small bowl. Add oil and applesauce. Pour liquids into dry ingredients all at once and stir until well mixed. Crush shredded wheat with hands or rolling pin. Add to batter. Fold in currants. Drop batter by teaspoons onto greased baking sheets. Bake in the preheated oven for 15 to 20 minutes.

HERMITS

1½ cups all-purpose flour
½ teaspoon each of baking
  soda and salt
1 teaspoon each of ground
  cinnamon and grated
  nutmeg

1 cup brown sugar
2 egg whites, lightly beaten
⅓ cup oil
¼ cup strong prepared coffee
1 cup raisins
½ cup chopped walnuts

Sift dry ingredients together. Add brown sugar. Combine egg whites, oil, and coffee. Add liquids to dry ingredients and mix well. Fold in raisins and walnuts. Chill for 1 hour.

Preheat oven to 375°F. Drop batter by teaspoons onto greased baking sheets. Bake in the preheated oven for 12 to 14 minutes, or until lightly browned on top.

SNOWY WALNUT COOKIE BALLS

MAKES ABOUT 18 COOKIES

1 cup sifted all-purpose flour
⅛ teaspoon salt
1 teaspoon baking powder
2 tablespoons granulated sugar
½ cup fine chopped walnuts

⅓ cup oil
1 teaspoon vanilla extract
3 tablespoons buttermilk
Confectioners' sugar

Preheat oven to 325°F. Sift flour, salt, baking powder, and granulated sugar together into a large bowl. Stir in the walnuts. Combine oil, vanilla, and buttermilk, whipping together with a fork. Pour liquids into dry ingredients and stir until well mixed. Chill. Shape into 1½-inch balls and place on greased baking sheets. Bake in the preheated oven for 20 to 25 minutes, or until lightly browned. Roll in sifted confectioners' sugar.

LACY SESAME COOKIES

1 cup granulated sugar
1½ cups sifted all-purpose
  flour
1 teaspoon baking powder
½ teaspoon baking soda
¼ teaspoon salt

½ cup plus ⅓ cup sesame
  seeds
¼ cup oil
¼ cup honey
2 egg whites, lightly beaten
⅓ cup light brown sugar

Preheat oven to 350°F. Sift dry ingredients together. Add ½ cup sesame seeds. Combine oil, honey, and egg whites and add all at once to dry ingredients. Mix well. Form into 1-inch balls, mixing in more flour if dough is too sticky to handle. Mix remaining ⅓ cup sesame seeds and the brown sugar. Roll balls in seed and sugar mixture. Place balls on greased baking sheets at least 3 inches apart. Bake in the preheated oven for 10 to 15 minutes, until quite brown. Cool before removing from baking sheet.

PEANUT-BUTTER COOKIES

1 cup all-purpose flour
1 teaspoon baking powder
¼ teaspoon salt
½ cup brown sugar
2 rounded tablespoons peanut
  butter

2 egg whites
¼ cup oil
½ cup fine-chopped walnuts

Preheat oven to 375°F. Sift together flour, baking powder, and salt. Blend brown sugar and peanut butter in a large mixing bowl. Beat egg whites lightly and combine with oil. Add to brown sugar and peanut butter. Mix well. Stir dry ingredients into sugar-oil mixture. Add chopped walnuts. Roll into balls the size of walnuts, or drop by teaspoons onto greased baking sheets. Flatten with a fork dipped into flour. Bake in the preheated oven for 12 to 15 minutes, or until the color is a delicate tan.

CRISP SUGAR COOKIES

MAKES ABOUT 5 DOZEN 3-INCH COOKIES

3½ cups sifted all-purpose
   flour
1 teaspoon salt
½ cup oil
½ cup margarine
1 cup granulated sugar

4 egg whites
1 teaspoon vanilla extract
4 drops of yellow food
   coloring
Granulated sugar

Preheat oven to 375°F. Sift flour and salt together. Cream oil, margarine, and sugar. Whip egg whites with a fork and add to sugar mixture; beat well. Add vanilla and coloring. Stir flour into the shortening-sugar mixture and beat until well mixed. Roll out to ⅛-inch thickness. Cut with a round cookie cutter. Dust with granulated sugar. Place on greased baking sheets and bake in the preheated oven for 9 or 10 minutes, or until edges are lightly browned.

COCOA SNAPS

MAKES ABOUT 3 DOZEN COOKIES

½ cup corn syrup
½ cup oil
½ cup sugar
½ cup cocoa powder

1½ cups sifted all-purpose
   flour
½ teaspoon baking soda
½ teaspoon salt

Preheat oven to 350°F. Combine corn syrup and oil. Sift together sugar, cocoa powder, flour, baking soda, and salt. Mix liquid with dry ingredients and stir until well blended. Roll out dough on a floured board until very thin, about ⅛ inch thick, and cut into rounds. Place on greased baking sheets and bake in the preheated oven for 10 minutes.

GINGER SNAPS

MAKES ABOUT 3 DOZEN COOKIES

6 tablespoons oil
½ cup dark molasses
2 cups sifted all-purpose flour
½ cup firmly packed brown
  sugar

½ teaspoon baking soda
½ teaspoon salt
2 teaspoons ground ginger
Pinch each of ground
  cinnamon and cloves

Preheat oven to 350°F. Combine oil and molasses. Sift together flour, brown sugar, baking soda, salt, and spices. Stir liquids into dry ingredients. Mix until well blended. Roll out dough to ⅛-inch thickness and cut into small rounds. Place on greased baking sheets and bake in the preheated oven for 15 to 18 minutes. They should be very crisp.

LEMON SNAPS

MAKES ABOUT 3 DOZEN COOKIES

½ cup corn syrup
4 tablespoons oil
2 tablespoons fine-grated
  lemon rind
2 tablespoons lemon juice, or
  2 teaspoons lemon extract

1½ cups sifted all-purpose
  flour
½ teaspoon baking soda
½ teaspoon salt

Preheat oven to 350°F. Combine corn syrup, oil, lemon rind, and lemon juice or extract, and beat until smooth. Sift together flour, baking soda, and salt. Stir liquids into dry ingredients and mix until well blended. Roll out dough to ⅛-inch thickness and cut into small rounds. Place on greased baking sheets and bake in the preheated oven for 10 minutes, or until delicately browned.

ZINNERSTERNE

MAKES ABOUT 2 DOZEN COOKIES

1 cup sugar
3 egg whites
1 tablespoon grated lemon rind

2 tablespoons oil
8 ounces walnuts, ground fine
½ teaspoon ground cinnamon
½ cup flour

Preheat oven to 300°F. Beat sugar and egg whites with an electric mixer at medium speed for 5 minutes. Mix in lemon rind, oil, ground walnuts, cinnamon, and flour. Stir with a wooden spoon until well blended. Roll out to ⅛- to ¼-inch thickness, and cut into stars or crescents. Arrange on greased baking sheets and bake in the preheated oven for 30 minutes, or until cookies have turned a delicate golden brown.

LEBKUCHEN

A German Christmas honey cake.

MAKES ABOUT 2 DOZEN CAKES

¼ cup honey
¼ cup molasses
⅜ cup brown sugar
1 egg white, lightly beaten
½ tablespoon lemon juice
½ teaspoon grated lemon rind
1 tablespoon oil
1½ cups sifted all-purpose flour

¼ teaspoon baking soda
½ teaspoon each of ground cloves and allspice
¼ cup fine-chopped walnuts
½ cup citron (optional; increase nuts to ½ cup if not using citron)

Bring honey and molasses to a boil in a small saucepan. Cool. Add brown sugar, egg white, lemon juice and rind, and oil. Sift dry ingredients together and stir into honey mixture. Blend well. Add walnuts and citron. Chill dough overnight.

Preheat oven to 375°F. Take dough from refrigerator and roll out as quickly as possible to ¼-inch thickness. Or keep half chilled while rolling out the other half. Cut the dough into rectangles 1½ by 2½ inches. Place on greased baking sheets and bake in the preheated oven for 10 to 12 minutes.

RAISIN GRIDDLE COOKIES

MAKES ABOUT 2 DOZEN COOKIES

1¼ cups sifted all-purpose
flour
⅓ cup sugar
½ teaspoon baking powder
¼ teaspoon baking soda
½ teaspoon salt

2 egg whites, lightly beaten
¼ cup oil
¼ cup liquid skim milk
2 drops of yellow food coloring
Flavoring
⅔ cup raisins

Vanilla flavoring: Add 1 teaspoon vanilla extract and ½ teaspoon grated cinnamon.

Orange flavoring: Add 2 tablespoons orange juice and 1 tablespoon grated orange rind; use only 2 tablespoons milk.

Lemon flavoring: Add 1 tablespoon lemon juice and 2 teaspoons grated lemon rind; use only 3 tablespoons milk.

Sift dry ingredients together. Combine egg whites, oil, skim milk, food coloring, and flavorings in another bowl. Pour liquids into dry ingredients. Mix well. Add raisins. Roll out on a floured board to ¼-inch thickness. If dough is too sticky, work in a little more flour. Cut into circles with a 2- or 3-inch cookie cutter. Bake on a hot greased griddle, turning once, until brown on both sides. Watch carefully to avoid burning them. It may be necessary to reduce heat a little.

These are delicious eaten hot straight from the pan. Spread them with a little margarine. Store what's left in a stone cookie jar.

RAISIN CAKES

MAKES 2 DOZEN 2-INCH CUPCAKES

2 cups sifted all-purpose flour
1 cup firmly packed dark
   brown sugar
2 teaspoons baking powder
½ teaspoon salt

2 egg whites
½ cup oil
½ cup liquid skim milk
1 teaspoon vanilla extract
2 cups raisins

Preheat oven to 375°F. Grease and flour 24 muffin cups. Sift together flour, sugar, baking powder, and salt. Whip egg whites lightly and combine in a small bowl with oil, milk, and vanilla. Add liquids all at once to dry ingredients and mix until batter is smooth. Fold in raisins. Fill prepared muffin cups two thirds full. Bake in the preheated oven for 20 minutes, or until golden brown and firm when pressed with a finger.

ROLLED OAT CUPCAKES

MAKES 15 SMALL CUPCAKES

1 cup all-purpose flour
1 teaspoon baking soda
½ teaspoon salt
1½ teaspoons ground
   cinnamon
⅓ cup light brown sugar

2 egg whites
¼ cup oil
¾ cup buttermilk
1 cup rolled oats
⅓ cup raisins

Preheat oven to 375°F. Grease 15 small muffin cups. Sift together flour, baking soda, salt, cinnamon, and sugar into a large bowl. Beat egg whites lightly in a separate bowl. Add oil and buttermilk. Pour liquids into dry ingredients all at once and stir briskly until batter is smooth. Fold in oats and raisins. Fill muffin cups half full. Bake in the preheated oven for 12 to 15 minutes.

DOUGHNUT BALLS

2 cups all-purpose flour
⅓ cup sugar
1 tablespoon baking powder
½ teaspoon salt
½ teaspoon grated nutmeg
   or mace
½ teaspoon grated lemon rind

2 egg whites, lightly beaten
¾ cup liquid skim milk
3 tablespoons dry skim milk
4 tablespoons oil
Additional oil for frying
Cinnamon sugar

Sift together flour, sugar, baking powder, salt, and nutmeg or mace. Combine lemon rind, egg whites, mixed liquid and dry milk, and 4 tablespoons oil. Stir into dry ingredients until smooth. Pour oil into a deep heavy pan to reach a depth of 1 inch. Heat oil to 365°F. on a frying thermometer. Drop dough by teaspoons into the hot oil. Turn puffs after a few seconds, then brown on both sides, turning again. Lift out with a slotted spoon and drain on paper towels. Roll in cinnamon sugar. Serve warm.

Candy

COCOA CHIPS AND CURLS

These take only a short time to prepare, and they can be stored indefinitely. Use for chocolate-chip cookies, cakes, etc.

MAKES ABOUT 1 CUP

1 cup granulated sugar
⅓ cup cocoa powder
1 tablespoon cornstarch

½ cup liquid skim milk
1 tablespoon oil
1 teaspoon vanilla extract

Mix sugar, cocoa powder, and cornstarch in a small saucepan. Add milk gradually, and bring mixture to a boil. Boil at medium heat, without stirring, until the soft-ball stage is almost reached at about 234°F. Remove from heat. Add oil and vanilla and let cool to lukewarm. Beat until creamy. Pour into a greased pan immediately while still warm.

When cool, turn candy out onto a breadboard. To make *cocoa chips*, break into small chips by pounding with a mallet or a rolling pin. Store in an airtight container.

To make *cocoa curls*, grate cooled candy with a coarse grater, or shred with a paring knife.

CANDIED GRAPEFRUIT PEEL

1 large grapefruit   ½ cup granulated sugar
¼ cup water

Wash grapefruit, remove peel, and cut peel into strips. (Use the fruit for something else.) Place strips in cold water and bring to a boil. Drain. Add more water and boil for 20 minutes. Drain again.

Make syrup from ¼ cup water and the sugar; bring to a boil in a small saucepan. Add grapefruit peel to the syrup and boil slowly, uncovered, until syrup is all absorbed.

Remove grapefruit peel and dry on a rack. Roll in extra granulated sugar. Dry again. Store in a covered container.

DIVINITY

2 cups granulated sugar   Pinch of salt
½ cup water   1 teaspoon vanilla extract
½ cup corn syrup   ¾ cup walnut meats
2 egg whites

Cook sugar, water, and corn syrup over low heat, stirring, until sugar is dissolved. Continue to cook without stirring until the hard-ball stage has been reached, 252° to 254°F. Meanwhile, beat the egg whites and salt with an electric mixer until stiff. Pour the hot syrup over the egg whites gradually, continuing to beat. Beat at medium speed until mixture begins to thicken. Add vanilla and walnuts and pour into a greased pan. Cut into squares when cool.

PENUCHE

1 cup evaporated skim milk	⅛ teaspoon salt
1 cup granulated sugar	1 tablespoon oil
1 cup brown sugar	1 cup chopped walnuts

Mix skim milk, both sugars, and salt in a heavy saucepan. Bring to a boil, stirring constantly. Cook to the soft-ball stage, 234° to 238°F. Remove from heat and add the oil. Cool the mixture by placing the saucepan in cold water. When the bottom is cool beat the candy until smooth and creamy. Do not let it harden completely. Add the walnuts. Spread in a greased 8-inch-square pan or drop by spoonfuls onto wax paper.

PLAIN FUDGE

2 cups granulated sugar	1 tablespoon margarine
3 tablespoons cocoa powder	1 tablespoon oil
⅛ teaspoon salt	1 teaspoon vanilla extract
¾ cup liquid skim milk	

Combine sugar, cocoa powder, salt, and skim milk in a saucepan. Heat slowly, stirring constantly, until sugar is dissolved. Cook to the soft-ball stage, 234° to 238°F. Stir in margarine and oil and cool to lukewarm. Add vanilla and beat with a spoon until mixture is almost stiff. Pour into an oiled pan. Cool, and cut into squares.

COCOA NUT FUDGE

2 cups granulated sugar
5 tablespoons cocoa powder
¾ cup liquid skim milk

2 tablespoons margarine
1 teaspoon vanilla extract
1 cup chopped walnuts

Combine sugar, cocoa powder, and skim milk in a saucepan. Cook, stirring, until sugar is dissolved. Continue to cook over very, very low heat until the soft-ball stage has been reached, 238°F. Do not stir. Add margarine and set aside. When almost cool (lukewarm), add vanilla and beat until creamy. Stir in the walnuts. Pour into an oiled pan. When quite cool, cut into squares.

SNOW-WHITE FUDGE

2 cups granulated sugar
½ cup buttermilk
⅓ cup white corn syrup
2 tablespoons oil
¼ teaspoon cream of tartar

¼ teaspoon salt
1 teaspoon vanilla extract, or
 ¼ teaspoon almond extract
1 cup chopped walnuts

Combine first six ingredients in a saucepan. Slowly bring to a boil, stirring constantly until sugar dissolves. Boil without stirring to the soft-ball stage, 234° to 238°F. Remove from heat and let stand for 10 to 15 minutes, until cooled. Add vanilla and beat until milky. Fold in walnuts. Pour into a greased pan. Cut into squares when completely cooled.

FONDANT

2 cups granulated sugar
⅔ cup water
⅛ teaspoon cream of tartar

Coloring (optional)
Flavoring extracts, almond,
peppermint, etc. (optional)

Stir sugar, water, and cream of tartar over low heat until sugar is dissolved. Remove sugar from sides with a spatula. Cook without stirring to the soft-ball stage, 238°F. Add a little coloring or flavoring if desired. Pour into a large platter or metal bowl and cool.

When cold, beat the fondant until smooth. Fondant can be kept in an airtight container for a long time.

SALTWATER TAFFY

2 cups granulated sugar
1 cup light corn syrup
1½ cups water
1½ teaspoons salt

1 teaspoon vanilla extract, or
¼ teaspoon peppermint
extract
2 tablespoons margarine

Combine all ingredients except margarine and cook over low heat, stirring, until sugar is dissolved. Continue to cook to the hard-ball stage, 252° to 254°F., without stirring. Remove from heat and stir in the margarine. Pour into a greased shallow pan.

When cool enough to handle, pull taffy with greased hands until it becomes lighter in color. Pull taffy into long strands and cut into 1 inch pieces. Wrap each piece in wax paper.

GUM DROPS OR TURKISH DELIGHT

2 envelopes unflavored gelatin
½ cup water
½ cup jelly (raspberry, currant, etc.)
1 cup granulated sugar
1 tablespoon lemon juice

1 tablespoon cinnamon candies
½ cup chopped walnuts
Food coloring (optional)
Confectioners' sugar

Soften gelatin in ½ cup water in a heavy saucepan. Add jelly, sugar, lemon juice, and cinnamon candies. Stir over low heat until syrup comes to a boil. Continue to boil for 3 minutes. Remove from heat. Add walnuts and a little food coloring if coloring is not right. Pour into a greased shallow 8-inch-square pan. Chill overnight.

Cut into squares and dust with confectioners' sugar.

ORANGE BUTTERSCOTCH CANDY

2 cups granulated sugar
½ cup light corn syrup
½ cup orange juice

1½ tablespoons butter-flavored oil

Cook sugar, corn syrup, and orange juice in a greased heavy saucepan to the hard-crack stage, 280° to 300°F., stirring after the temperature has reached 260°F. Remove from heat and quickly beat in the oil. Pour into a greased shallow pan. Cut into squares when almost cool.

RICE KRISPIES CRUNCH

40 marshmallows
½ cup butter-flavored oil

5 cups Rice Krispies

In a large pot combine marshmallows and oil over low heat, and stir until marshmallows have melted. Remove from heat and stir in the cereal. Spread out in a greased pan while still warm, pressing flat with wax paper. Cut into squares when cool.

CHOCOLATE RAISIN OR NUT CLUSTERS

2 tablespoons oil
1¼ cups water
2 cups sugar
½ cup dry cocoa
1 teaspoon dry citric acid

¼ cup dry skim milk
(optional)
1 or more cups raisins or
chopped walnuts

Heat oil and water in a small Teflon or heavy saucepan. Sift sugar, cocoa, and dry citric acid together and add to the water. Stir until dissolved. Boil at a very low temperature until medium to hard stage has been reached. Remove from fire and cool slightly. Beat in the dry skim milk. Add the raisins or nuts and drop by teaspoon onto wax paper or pour into pan and cut into squares when cool.

BOURBON BALLS

3 cups crushed zwieback or
Holland rusk crumbs
1 cup fine-ground walnuts
2 cups sifted confectioners'
sugar
½ cup light corn syrup
¼ cup bourbon

1 teaspoon vanilla extract
2 tablespoons cocoa powder
(optional)
½ cup liquid skim milk, more
or less
Confectioners' sugar

Combine all measured ingredients, adding just enough milk to moisten the mixture and hold it together. Form into 1-inch balls and roll in confectioners' sugar.

Stocking the Larder

OR BRINGING HOME THE RIGHT GROCERIES

My three-year struggle with a modified-fat diet has made one thing very clear. It is this: by far the most important step toward becoming an expert is bringing home the right groceries. A properly stocked larder is half the battle.

This chapter tells you how to do just that. There are no miracles, but there are bits of information that I think you'll find useful—hints on buying food in general, what to stock your larder with and why, pointers on buying meat, basic cooking techniques, how to evaluate the "information" on package labels, and so on.

All this I have divided into six primary food groups, with recommendations on certain foods to stock and others to avoid. These are headed *Recommended* and *To be avoided*. Major emphasis is given to the first three groups: milk products, fats and oils, and meats.

A surprising amount of information was supplied by food companies to which I sent inquiries. I say surprising because it was *lack* of clear information on their package labels which prompted me to write in the first place. However, the most important sources of information have been the American Heart Association, the National Institutes of Health, the University of Iowa College of Medicine, the American Medical Association, and the School of Medicine at the University of California, San Diego. There are many secondary sources too numerous to list here.

One more thing—all of this information will be more meaningful if you know a little about cholesterol and fats—not very difficult and explained by Dr. Steinberg in Appendix I (p. 433).

I. MILK PRODUCTS, INCLUDING CHEESES

Recognizing acceptable dairy products is not too difficult. To be acceptable, the fat content should be 4 percent or lower. However, I have included in the recommended group a few borderline cases for special occasions and uses; use these only if your dietary restrictions allow it.

Following the two classifications are comments pertaining to certain of these foods.

RECOMMENDED

(The approximate percentage of saturated fats is shown in parentheses.)

Nonfat or skim liquid milk (0)

Nonfat or skim dry milk (0)

Low-fat milk (2)

Cultured buttermilk (0 to 2)

Low-fat yogurt (2)

Evaporated skim milk (0)

Safflower ice cream (0)
   (12 percent polyunsaturated fat content)

Dry-curd cottage cheese (0)

Hoop cheese (baker's, farmer's, pot) (0)

Low-fat cottage cheese (2)

Low-fat ricotta cheese (5 to 9) *

Whipped cottage cheese (4)

Special cheeses made from part-skim milk (0 to 30) †

TO BE AVOIDED

Whole milk—fresh, dried condensed, or evaporated (4)

Imitation milk (4)

Whipping or heavy cream (36)

Half-and-half (12)

Nondairy dry cream substitutes (36)

Commercial whipped toppings (20 to 30)

Ice cream (16 to 20)

Imitation ice cream (10)

Ice milk (5)

Whole-milk yogurt (4)

Creamed cottage cheese (4)

Cheeses made from whole milk (35 to 45)

Sour cream (20)

Sour-cream substitutes (20)

Churned buttermilk (4)

Imitation and substitute dairy products often contain coconut or palm oil, both highly saturated; therefore do not use them unless their

* Use only for special occasions.
† Use only for *very* special occasions.

labels indicate otherwise. Commercial products that contain cream, whole milk, or cheeses should also be avoided.

Nonfat or skim milk may take a bit of getting used to if you're accustomed to homogenized milk. A good system is to start with low-fat milk and substitute more skim milk each time. If you cannot buy fortified skim milk, a great deal more palatable and nourishing than regular, add a little dry skim milk to the liquid skim milk. In recipes calling for fortified skim milk, add ¼ cup dry to 1 cup liquid nonfat milk. Recipes in this book using fortified skim milk specify how much of the dry to use in each case.

Nonfat dry or powdered milk is invaluable in cooking cream-type sauces, soups, baked goods, pancakes, and as a substitute for the powdered cream often used in coffee. Powdered milk can sour, however, so unless you are using it in fairly large quantities, it is best to buy it in small amounts. If used as a cream substitute, keep it in a covered container.

Buttermilk—The only two cautions on this old favorite are (1) select *cultured* buttermilk made from skim milk, not *churned* made from whole milk, and (2) remove visible butter floating on top, or make your own from dry skim milk. Buttermilk's piquant flavor is useful for many things.

Yogurt—Delicious in itself, with so many available flavors, it is also a mainstay in cooking as a replacement for sweet cream and sour cream. The low-fat yogurt is a little more watery than the regular but doesn't present insurmountable problems.

Evaporated skim milk is used to replace regular evaporated milk in all recipes that use this ingredient. Evaporated skim milk is available in most markets but few people are aware of it.

Safflower ice cream is also available in many markets. Safeway stores carry a brand on the West Coast, called Hi-Saff, which is quite delicious. The difference between Hi-Saff vanilla and regular vanilla ice milk is hard to detect, but Hi-Saff is a little richer. The safflower oil content is approximately 12 percent so it is not without calories. Hi-Saff is undoubtedly not the only brand available but you may have to check around before finding some, or ask the manager of your market to investigate it for you. Having an ice cream that can be used safely is an invaluable help on a low-cholesterol diet. Here are a few suggestions: use as a substitute for whipped cream on any dessert; as a filling for cream puffs or meringues; in angel-food refrigerator desserts, sauces for steamed puddings, and parfaits; with chocolate (made from cocoa), strawberry, and other fruit sundaes, etc.

Hoop cheese and dry-curd cottage cheese are made from skim milk as all cottage cheese is but there is no cream added. (Other names for hoop cheese are baker's, pot, or farmer's, depending primarily on which part of the country you live in. In this book this type of cheese will be called hoop, but any of the others may be substituted. Hoop cheese consists of large curds, like those of large-curd cottage cheese, pressed together with no salt or cream added.) They are therefore dry and unpalatable by themselves, but they can be easily used in your cooking. They provide a valuable protein contribution. Dress them up with liquids (milk, yogurt, oils, mayonnaise, stewed tomatoes, etc.), which you add according to use and recipe. You will see them often in this book. Most markets have these cheeses but they may be difficult to find because of the small quantities displayed. If you have trouble spotting them, see your old friend, the store manager. Another approach is to rinse the cream out of regular cottage cheese by putting it in a strainer and running cold water through it.

To initiate you in the use of these dry cheeses, here is a first suggestion: take ½ cup cubed hoop or dry-curd cottage cheese and toss it into your romaine salad. French dressing will give it all the flavor it needs, the salad will look interesting, and you'll be getting some protein besides. It tastes great, too!

Ricotta cheese is an Italian cottage cheese; it has a most delicious sweet flavor especially suitable for desserts. Get the low-fat variety; use for special occasions or as recipes direct.

Whipped cottage cheese is regular cottage cheese finely blended, with a consistency similar to that of sour cream. The commercial kind usually has a 4 percent fat content and should not be used to replace low-fat cottage cheese for normal use but only for special recipes such as cheesecakes, dips, etc. It is not as commonly available as the regular cottage cheese, so it may require a little shopping around before you find it. If you use it often, you should learn to make your own. This can be done fairly satisfactorily with a strainer, and with an electric blender it is simple (see p. 287). You can keep the saturated fat content down to almost nothing by using the low-fat or nonfat dry-curd cottage cheese.

Other low-fat cheeses—There are some cheeses, both domestic and foreign, which have a lower fat content than the standard cheeses made from whole milk. For you these are worth getting acquainted with. They are usually found in delicatessens, or more likely, in specialty cheese stores. Labeled "part skim-milk cheese," these cheeses are derived from 40 percent skim milk.

In California a cheese company makes a fresh solid white cheese, called *Tuma*, which is 9 percent fat; this can be used in many ways. Although it is not shipped out of the state of California, there may be similar products in other states.

Sap Sago, a Swiss "green cheese" made since the Roman Empire, is 100 percent fat-free and can be used as a replacement for grated Parmesan cheese. The flavor is very concentrated and for this reason the cheese is used only when grated, replacing Parmesan in about a 1 to 4 ratio. It can be combined with dry-curd cottage cheese, bread crumbs, sesame seeds, toasted wheat germ, etc., and used to sprinkle on baked dishes (see p. 304). It is used as a flavoring agent for soups, pasta, and sauces. Other possibilities include flavorings for salads, spreads, dips, and casseroles.

Gouda, Edam, and mozzarella are three more cheeses with a slightly lower fat content than Cheddar or club but their fat content is still pretty high, around 25 percent.

Processed cheese foods and especially imitation cheese foods have lower fat contents than real cheeses. The Fisher Cheese Company (P.O. Box 12, Wapakoneta, Ohio 45895) manufactures two kinds of special cheeses used by patients at the National Institutes of Health. One called Cheez-ola is high in polyunsaturated fats; the other, called Count Down, is 99 percent fat-free. These can be ordered, or perhaps found in specialty cheese stores, in 2-pound loaves at reasonable prices and are excellent substitutes for processed American cheese. Use the Fisher cheeses whenever recipes call for *processed vegetable-oil cheese*. Watch for similar brands which may appear on the market or keep in touch with the National Institutes of Health, U.S. Department of Health, Education, and Welfare for information on the latest products available.

Stocking the Larder, or Bringing Home the Right Groceries 419

Other cheeses worth mentioning, even though rare, are Gammelost, pot cheese, and Primost. These cheeses contain 5 percent or less fat.

II. FATS AND OILS

RECOMMENDED

Corn oil	Sunflower oil
Cottonseed oil	"Special" margarines (see below)
✗ Safflower oil	Mayonnaise
Sesame oil	Nut butters
Soybean oil	* Olive
* Canola oil	Peanut

TO BE AVOIDED

Butter	~~Peanut oil~~
Animal fats	Coconut oil
Shortenings made from	Palm oil
animal fats	Cocoa butter
~~Olive oil~~	Regular margarines

All of the recommended oils have a high proportion of polyunsaturated to saturated fats. Remember that unsaturated can mean *mono-* or *poly-*unsaturated and that a high proportion of polyunsaturated fatty acids over saturated is what you're after. Polyunsaturates tend to offset saturates. Monounsaturates are neutral in their action and do not offset the saturated fats. For complete percentage figures on fats and oils see the reference tables (p. 465). For a discussion of saturated and unsaturated fats see Appendix I (p. 433).

wrong

p. 467

If you're not acquainted with butter-flavored oils, try to find them in your market. They open up a whole new dimension of cooking and add a lovely savor to foods both fried and baked. In case your market does not stock this item, here's a do-it-yourself method. Buy your own oil and butter flavoring and mix them in approximately the following proportions.

2 or 3 drops to 1 teaspoon oil
8 drops to 1 tablespoon oil
1 teaspoon to ½ cup oil

Other new butter-flavored products are now obtainable—salt and maple syrup. Probably many more are on the way.

Butter, processed animal fats (lard, etc.), and fats on meat cuts should be avoided at all times because they have a very high saturated fat content.

Olive oil and peanut oil have a higher monounsaturated fat content than the recommended oils. Therefore use these only occasionally for flavoring.

Now seen as good for you!

Coconut oil and palm oil are the exceptions to the rule that liquid oils are unsaturated. These are highly saturated. Because of their low cost, they are found frequently in commercial products. Packaged products that are likely to contain either of these two oils, especially coconut oil, are substitute dairy products, packaged cakes, cookies, muffins, pancake mix, potato chips, corn chips, and so on. Usually this ingredient is listed simply as "vegetable oil." Do not buy such products unless you know which oil is being used.

Cocoa butter is one of the products of the cacao bean, from which chocolate is made. This yellowish fat is highly saturated and therefore products containing chocolate should be avoided. Cocoa powder, on the other hand, is made by removing most of this fat and pulverizing the remainder into a powder. It makes an excellent substitute for chocolate and can be used to make chocolate cakes, pies, cookies, etc. Be sure to check the ingredients of chocolate cake mixes, frostings, etc. Only buy those made with cocoa powder.

"Special" margarines—There are important criteria in judging the safest margarines to buy. As the first ingredient named on a label is the predominant one, margarines that list a "liquid oil" first are the ones to buy. This oil, of course, must be an acceptable one. The second ingredient may be partially hardened or hydrogenated. Soft tub margarines are often the best because they are the least hydrogenated, but check the first ingredient on the label. Never buy unspecified shortenings or products containing these. This type of labeling will often be found on packages of cake mixes, muffins, biscuits, etc. Some safe bets: angel-food cake mixes, some frosting mixes, and some buttermilk pancake mixes. These usually contain no shortenings at all.

Stocking the Larder, or Bringing Home the Right Groceries   421

Mayonnaise contains some egg yolk but not enough to worry about unless you are on a very strict low-cholesterol diet. One tablespoon of mayonnaise contains about 8 milligrams of cholesterol; 1 egg yolk contains 250 milligrams. A recipe for mayonnaise without egg yolks can be found on page 280 for those who need it. It is quite simple to prepare.

Peanut, walnut, almond, and other nut butters can be used but not excessively. Watch out, though, for butters made from nuts high in fat content (p. 465).

III. MEAT AND VEGETABLE PROTEIN FOODS

For the majority of people, controlling meat fats seems to be the most difficult problem of all to solve and yet it is of prime importance. Eating too much of the wrong kind of meat presents a great physiological hazard. Not eating these same meats can cause great psychological disturbances. If you set about depriving the "red-blooded American male" of his daily portion of protein, it frustrates and angers him and makes him feel far less red-blooded. It does no good to tell him it's all in his mind. Red meat has been for too long the symbol of virility. If I speak of "he" rather than "she," it is because that's the way it usually is. Heart attacks strike women on the average about 20 years later than men, primarily because female hormones seem to play an active part in keeping the arteries soft and atherosclerosis under control.

Getting back to red meat, however, if you want to lure your husband away from eating too much of it, you might casually mention that one stalwart American, Thomas Jefferson, was essentially a vegetarian. He considered meat to be a condiment rather than the main part of a meal! I am afraid that it will take more than this story, though, to start you permanently on a happy reduced-meat course for the future. So what are the possibilities of lessening the difficulties of this problem?

To start with, you are two jumps ahead if your family is naturally inclined toward gourmet cooking. If they are, you can enjoy dabbling in exotic and fanciful dishes. A change from one kind of meat to another can then be disguised quite easily behind a delectable sauce or two. Barring the subterfuge of the high-cuisine approach, we are left with the alternative of simply facing up to the problem and proceeding from there. This usually works out best in the long run. Certain conditions are required for optimum results—an honest appraisal of the problem that exists; an understanding of the dietary changes that need to be made in order to solve the problem; and finally, a creative, imaginative, and flexible approach in the kitchen. Assessment of your specific problem naturally relates to your own individual circumstances. Have you had a heart attack? Do you have a very high lipid count and is it mostly cholesterol or triglyceride? Has your doctor set limitations? Or are you in perfect health and feel that a low-cholesterol diet is going to keep you that way?

Appraising the problem and setting rigid dietary restrictions is up to you.

Explaining something about the chemistry of fats and the fat content of foods is done briefly in this section and in Appendix I. (Also consult the reference tables in Appendix IV.)

Mainly, though, this book is concerned with helping you become creative and imaginative in the kitchen under your new restrictions, and doing so as easily and pleasantly as possible.

Meats

RECOMMENDED

Beef

Beef round	Rump roast
Round roast	Sirloin tip
Ground round	Tenderloin
Corned beef round	Dried or chipped beef
Smoked beef	

Veal

Arm steak	Loin chop
Sirloin roast and steak	Rump roast

Pork

Sirloin roast	Canadian bacon
Center-cut loin chop	Tenderloin
Center-cut ham steak	Lean ham

Lamb

Roast leg   Loin chop

Fatty meats   Wieners and sausages
Organ meats (heart, liver,   Spareribs
    brains, kidney)   Pork butt
Meats canned or frozen   Picnic shoulder
    in gravy   Pork steak
Fried meats   Bacon
Canned meat products   Lamb blade chops
Luncheon meats or   Corned beef brisket
    cold cuts   Pork and beans
Hamburger already ground   Frozen or package dinners
    or packaged   Frozen convenience foods

Although certain cuts of beef, lamb, and pork—especially the lean cuts—are on the recommended list, it should be remembered that poultry, veal, and fish are much more desirable because of their lower saturated-fat content. Check the reference tables (p. 465). Here is a good set of rules to follow:

1. When buying, always choose the leanest-looking meat, and avoid expensive marbled cuts.

2. Concentrate on veal more than on the other meats, or use fish or poultry. Avoid eating excessive amounts at one meal. A good target to aim at is 3 to 4 ounces per meal.

3. Trim all visible fat before cooking. This applies to the person on a strict diet, not necessarily to other members of the family, although it wouldn't hurt them a bit either.

4. Concentrate on cooking techniques that do not cause the absorption in the muscle of the invisible fat still remaining in the grain of the meat after trimming. In other words, use your oven for baking, broiling, and roasting as often as possible. Or use the barbecue. Learn to remove fat from stews and other dishes cooked on top of the stove as well as all gravies (p. 117). Avoid deep-frying.

5. Do not buy packaged ground meat, especially hamburger. Select your own piece of lean round steak and ask the butcher to grind it for you after removing *all* the fat.

424   Stocking the Larder, or Bringing Home the Right Groceries

Veal

Not enough people eat veal nowadays, except with a bottle of Chianti at a favorite Italian restaurant. So if you should decide to try home-cooked *scaloppine* or to make this highly recommended meat a major item in your family's diet, you may be in for a surprise when you try to buy some. By knowing this ahead of time, you'll be less frustrated. You *can* get it, of course, but there are obstacles between you and enjoyment of this healthy, tasty variety of meat.

First of all there's the definition—what *is* veal, anyway? And why is it so desirable? The standard definition runs something like this: "Flesh of the calf from six weeks to three months old. The meat should be white, not even pink, with little or no fat." So, veal is very young beef, with less fat than its elders have. For its leanness, then, it is recommended over beef, lamb, or pork. While this leanness makes veal a better food, it also—according to an old butchers' tale—makes it less profitable to sell. This may account for its scarcity; it is hard to find in the market. Therefore be prepared to canvass more than one store before finding any at all. One approach is to become friendly with your butcher; tell him your problems and ask him to save veal for you when he has it.

Your next surprise, also an unhappy one, will be the price of veal. Not only is it higher than beef for comparable cuts, but psychologically, it seems even higher because veal is usually sliced much thinner than steak and so it *looks* as if you're getting less for your money. The butcher packages it under a variety of names such as veal cutlet, veal chops, veal steak, veal *scaloppine*, and so on.

Still another and unhappy surprise is veal's appearance. Seldom is it as white and, therefore, as young—as our definition says it should be. Some of it is pretty pink, as a matter of fact, and looks as if it might be approaching middle age. There is nothing much you can do about this.

There is something you can do about circumventing the exorbitant cost of precut veal. My solution is to buy one large, lean veal roast per week and do my own carving with a large heavy butcher's knife. Although veal roasts usually disappear from the meat counter in a hurry, you can generally reserve one in advance to be sure you'll get one. This could be a rump, round, or sirloin roast of 5 or 6 pounds. It should net you two or three dinners for the next week and an equal number of lunches. If you roast the whole thing the first night, use the leftover meat for hash, casseroles, stew, sandwiches, etc. If you slice off half of it before cooking you can make many dishes that you will find in this book, and still have half a roast the first night with a little left over for a sandwich or two. As you can see, there are lots of pleasing solutions provided by this weekly roast approach to meal planning.

One last point of difference between veal and the more standard meats. Except when sliced very thin for quick sautéing, veal requires longer, slower cooking if it is to be juicy and tender when served. Given enough time at low heat, even a veal roast can be served rare —and delicious.

Poultry

Chicken	Rock Cornish game hen
Turkey	Game birds

All poultry skin	Duck
Deep-fried chicken	Goose

Dark meat has more iron

If you've always been partial to dark meat it's too bad, because you're going to have to change your ways. That juiciness comes from extra fat stored up in the muscle. From now on ask for white meat and no skin or stuffing either, unless perhaps in a small fryer or Cornish hen that is small enough not to have stored up much fat. Here are a few rules for poultry:

1. Eat the white meat of chicken and turkey most of the time. Chicken breasts may seem expensive but in actuality are a great buy.
2. Don't eat the skin, it contains far too much fat. If you need convincing that there is fat in poultry skin, take a look at an uncooked cut-up fryer just home from the market. What do you see if you lift up the skin? Great gobs of fat—probably a cupful per chicken. So either trim off skin entirely, or, if you want to keep the skin on while cooking, at least cut off as much fat as you can see. Again, chicken

breasts are a great buy! The skin peels off with no trouble. And if you're worried about the expense, remember, you're cutting down to 3 to 4 ounces of meat per meal, which is just about what half of a double chicken breast weighs. Compared to the amount of chicken you used to eat, you're probably saving money.

3. Skip the stuffing—especially from turkeys and large roasters. The larger the bird, the more fat accumulated, the longer it takes to cook, and the more time for the fat to drip down on what's inside, namely the stuffing.

4. Cook turkeys and roasting chickens on racks. The fat drips down away from the bird.

5. Eat gravy only when made in one of the acceptable ways (p. 117).

Fish and Shellfish

RECOMMENDED

All fish except those that are specifically excluded. No shellfish are recommended.   *no longer true*

TO BE AVOIDED

Deep-fried fish	Oysters
Abalone	Shrimps — ok in mod.
Caviar	Scallops
Clams	Lobster — ok "
Crabs	

Except for the forbidden shellfish, eat all you want. The more the merrier—and the healthier. If you're not a fish enthusiast, concentrate on that old standby, tuna, which continues decade after decade to be loved by just about everybody. Keep a stock of it on hand in the largest cans you can find. It is better to buy your tuna packed in water rather than in oil. In this way you can more easily add your own healthful oils or mayonnaise. There are many recipes in this book to add to the ones you undoubtedly already have. Be sure to check your recipes for unacceptable ingredients such as canned cream soups, potato chips, etc.

Don't forget canned salmon, too! It has a lower fat content than tuna and offers just as many possibilities.

Dried Beans and Peas

Kidney beans, lima beans, baked beans, lentils, soybeans—all contain vegetable protein. Use them often as substitutes, fillers, and alternatives to large helpings of meat. You'll have more healthful meals if you do. You just may have tastier meals, too. Take baked beans for example. You may not think it possible to make Boston baked beans without salt pork. If so, you are in for a pleasant surprise. You'll find the recipe on page 145.

Above all, get acquainted with soybeans if you have missed them so far. They can be bought at health-food stores in all forms including cooked and uncooked. Uncooked soybeans can be baked in almost the same manner as navy beans (p. 145). There is even a toasted variety; these resemble partially defatted peanuts except for having a lighter, crisper texture. They come in various kinds of packages, either salted or unsalted, and it takes only a few to stave off that hungry feeling. Soybeans are extremely rich in protein, more so than other beans.

Nuts and Seeds

Nuts and seeds should be eaten sparingly; there are a few that should be avoided altogether: *coconuts, cashews,* and *macadamias.* An examination of the fat content of nuts (p. 465) will show you that English walnuts, because of the high polyunsaturated count, are more acceptable by far than any other kind. Filberts, almonds, pecans, hickory nuts, and black walnuts at first glance seem as acceptable as the English walnuts because of their relatively low saturated-fat content. Unfortunately, the unsaturated-fat content is high in mono- rather than poly-unsaturates. So concentrate on the English walnuts most of the time.

Seeds provide another way to add fun, flourish, and nutrition to your diet. In moderation, they are reasonably harmless. For cooking, poppy and sesame seeds are a pleasure; for just plain nibbling, try sunflower seeds.

Eggs

Eggs can create quite a problem if you let them. The amount of cholesterol in the yolks is almost prohibitively high. And three egg yolks a week is all you should have, the experts say. If it's all that bad, then my feeling is, why have even those if you don't have to?

On the other hand the whites are essential to cooking. Combined with oil they take the place of a whole egg and help to bind things together, aerate them, and so forth. Besides, they are full of protein and very good for you. The whites are useful, the yolks are not; but since they both arrive in the same container, this poses a question: What are you going to do with all those yolks?

Except for an occasional shampoo, egg yolks are best dumped in the garbage or fed to the dog, who seems better able to handle cholesterol. But unless you're used to feeding egg yolks to the garbage or dog, either course of action is apt to give you a guilty conscience. The first because of thrift, the second because it's a dirty trick to treat your dog that way. The best approach is to start conditioning yourself to throwing them away without worrying about it. After all, a few cents is hardly worth the fuss when you consider the alternative—consuming the most concentrated single source of cholesterol except for brains. Really, throwing out egg yolks is quite painless. Just try it a few times. I'll guarantee you'll soon be doing it regularly, just as I do—with no qualms at all!

IV. VEGETABLES, FRUITS, AND CONDIMENTS

Vegetables and Fruits

RECOMMENDED

All fresh, canned, frozen, or dried fruits and vegetables barring only the two exceptions mentioned below.

To Be Avoided

Olives   Avocados

Now and then a tablespoon or two of chopped olives or a slice of avocado will be an absolute must to ensure the success of a dish. Except for those rare occasions, do not use them. Both are high in fat calories, avocados especially, and not the best kind of fat at that (monounsaturated).

On the other hand I would like to pay special homage to the onion and the mushroom, all shapes, sizes, and varieties. Their texture and flavor make their contribution to the diet especially important. Keep plenty on hand and use lavishly. Remember, the method of preparing mushrooms has changed a great deal since Grandma's day, when the prescribed technique was to peel the caps, throw out the stems, and sauté them in a sea of butter.

Herbs, Spices, Condiments, and Other Cooking Helps

The role of these seasoning and flavoring ingredients is an important one. Apply your creative talents and use these to add a bit of flair to your cooking. Keep plenty of your favorites on the shelf and let your imagination go! Here are the ones I'm never without:

Herbs—basil, dried dillweed (recently packed for better flavor), dill seeds, marjoram, orégano, tarragon, thyme; celery salt; dehydrated onion, garlic, parsley, and green-pepper flakes; capers, pimientos

Spices—cinnamon, cloves, cuminseeds, ginger, nutmeg, paprika; prepared and dry mustard; coarse-ground pepper flavored with lemon (Lemon Pepper); curry powder

Seeds—poppy seeds, sesame seeds, toasted sunflower seeds

Condiments—good wine vinegars, chili sauce, catsup, soy sauce, barbecue sauce, teriyaki sauce, tomato sauce, Mexican hot sauce

Dried fruits and nuts—dried currants and raisins; soybeans; walnuts

Cheese for flavoring—grated Sap Sago and Parmesan; blue cheese seasoning (use sparingly)

Other cooking helps—beef and chicken bouillon granules or canned bouillon; canned consommé; cooking wines; almond, lemon, orange, and vanilla extracts; imitation bacon and sausage bits made from soy protein

A special word about imitation bacon and sausage bits, which can be found in the spice section of your market: Read the label to verify that soy protein, rather than dried bacon, is the main ingredient. These useful flavorings can add much variety and interest to your diet. Many of the old favorite recipes which probably have been shelved because they began with the familiar phrase, "Fry a piece or two of bacon," can now be reinstated in the family recipe box. To give you some idea of the possibilities, here are a few suggestions.

1. Add 1 or 2 tablespoons to a tossed green salad.
2. Sprinkle 1 tablespoon on a lettuce and tomato, peanut-butter, or cold turkey sandwich.
3. Add 1 tablespoon to an omelet for two.
4. Add 2 tablespoons to a recipe making 10 pancakes.
5. Add to any dips or spreads, 1 tablespoon for ½ cup.
6. Combine with 1 tablespoon of plain yogurt and 1 tablespoon minced chives for a baked potato.
7. Add to hot or cold potato salad, ¼ cup to a 4-serving recipe.
8. Mix 2 tablespoons with 1 pound of ground beef round before barbecuing.
9. Sauté with onion in a little oil before quick-frying vegetables.
10. Incorporate in cheese sauces, fondues, casseroles, and baked beans.

V. BREADS, CEREALS, CRACKERS

The important thing to remember about breads is to avoid those made with butter, eggs, and whole milk, whether bought from a store or made at home. With this in mind, the following have been classified as either good or bad.

RECOMMENDED

White enriched	Rye	All pasta except egg noodles
Raisin	Indian	Melba toast, matzo, pretzels, rye
Whole-wheat	Gluten	crisp, saltines, bread sticks,
English muffins	Soya	flat breads
Italian	Sourdough	All homemade biscuits, muffins,
French	Wheat-germ	rolls, etc., with acceptable
Oatmeal	Millet	ingredients
Pumpernickel	All cereals, hot	
Boston brown	and cold	

All products containing butter, egg yolks (fresh or dried), whole milk, including:

Butter rolls	Commercial biscuits, muffins,
Egg bread	corn breads, griddle cakes,
Cheese bread	waffles, crackers, potato or
Croissant or brioche	other chips
	Mixes for any of the above

Some people live to eat; others eat to live. It is especially gratifying when you can eat to live—and enjoy it at the same time. You may want to cut down on your meat consumption. If so, bread can become a significant part of your diet. All enriched and whole-grain breads provide a great deal of nourishment, including vegetable protein. If you find time to bake your own bread, you will discover it is an exciting and rewarding experience to say the very least. However, if you don't have time for bread making, and most people don't, there are still many interesting varieties to be found on the market. You will find a few ideas in the sandwich recipes (beginning on p. 219).

More important, start making your own muffins, pancakes, waffles, cakes, cookies, and the like. These items contain a higher proportion of fat than bread does. Do not buy them ready-made or in package form, unless labeling clearly indicates that the shortening used is an acceptable type of oil.

Begin to construct some of your meals—notably breakfast and lunch —around breads, and also use many of the cold and hot cereals that are now so plentiful. Combine them with fruits, cottage cheese, skim milk, or yogurt for breakfast; serve with soup or salad for lunch, or with cocoa for an afternoon or evening snack.

One way or another, if you haven't already done so, acquaint yourself with these various versions of the staff of life.

VI. DESSERTS

RECOMMENDED

Fresh and canned fruits, nuts, jams and jellies, pure sugar candy; desserts that do *not* contain cream or whole milk, saturated fats, egg yolks, chocolate, or coconut. Cocoa is all right.

All homemade and commercial cakes, pies, cookies, mixes, puddings, ice creams, etc., that contain saturated or hydrogenated fats, egg yolks, whole milk or cream, coconut or coconut oil, and chocolate.

Read labels and stick to these recommendations and from then on let your conscience be your guide. I'm speaking of calories, of course, and possible sugar restrictions. Here are some suggestions for desserts that are light and won't add too many pounds: sherbets, angel-food cakes, gelatin dishes, puddings made with skim milk, freezer desserts, fresh fruit combinations, and so on. Some enticing suggestions can also be found among the recipes in the dessert chapter of this book. If calories are no problem, then you can choose one of the fancier cakes or desserts, all made with polyunsaturated oils.

Appendix I

A PRIMER ON DIET AND HEART DISEASE

by Daniel Steinberg, M.D., Ph.D., Professor of Medicine, Head of the Division of Metabolic Disease, University of California, San Diego, School of Medicine; Past-Chairman, Council on Arteriosclerosis, American Heart Association

This Appendix is designed to answer the questions most frequently put to me by patients advised to go on a diet designed to lower their blood lipid levels (cholesterol and/or triglycerides). As such, it may be useful not only to the patient but also to the practicing physician who may choose to refer his patient to this source as a "primer." In the course of answering these questions we present the basic information on what blood lipids are, the nature of the evidence that relates elevated blood lipid levels to heart disease, what arteriosclerotic or coronary heart disease is, the scientific basis for the use of diet treatment in lowering blood lipid levels, and the evidence for the effectiveness of such diet treatment. We stress again the need for considering the *total* diet as opposed to making limited, token deletions or substitutions. Some of the more sophisticated medical aspects are covered for the sake of completeness, but these fine-print sections are not integral to the major thrust of the chapter. I hope the core material is sufficiently straightforward and interesting. The finer points include an explanation of lipoproteins and lipoprotein classes, some simple lipid chemistry, an outline of the different types of hyper-lipoproteinemia with comments on the dietary approaches to each, mention of drug treatment to supplement diet, and some remarks on hereditary factors.

Finally, there is a short discussion of other risk factors in coronary heart disease (hypertension, smoking, obesity, diabetes) and the importance of having medical advice with regard to them. Proper medical management of the patient with established coronary heart disease or at high risk of developing it may call for the most serious consideration of a number of factors beyond diet. Even if diet is all that is indicated,

Appendix I: A Primer on Diet and Heart Disease   435

that diet should be followed *under a physician's guidance*. Periodic follow-up visits with blood lipid measurements are obviously necessary to see if the diet is really doing what it is supposed to do. If not, it needs to be changed. Furthermore, a person at increased risk because of high blood lipid levels should be checked at regular intervals and advised of other steps he should take. In short, self-treatment makes no more sense here than it does in other areas of medicine. True, the patient must be a senior partner and assume a large measure of responsibility when it comes to dietary treatment or prophylaxis, but he should not be in business for himself. This section may help him to be an informed and responsible partner.

I. What is meant by a heart attack?

All body tissues depend for their survival on a steady, continuing supply of oxygen. That vital supply of oxygen, picked up by the blood in its passage through the lungs, is continuously delivered to all the organs of the body via a complex, branching network of blood vessels (*arteries*). If the oxygen supply is suddenly cut off (for example, by a blood clot obstructing the artery), the oxygen-starved cells will die. Death of tissue in this way is termed an *infarction*.

Tissues vary widely in their ability to withstand interruption of oxygen supply. The brain is the most sensitive, irreversible damage occurring within 5 to 10 minutes. In contrast, the tissues in the arm or leg can withstand even 30 minutes or more of oxygen starvation without harm. The brain and other tissues may be damaged severely even with partial rather than total interruption of blood supply. The balance between oxygen requirement and oxygen supply appears to be the central issue. Thus, infarction may not occur when the blood supply is reduced if the tissue requirements for oxygen remain low; the same degree of impairment of blood supply may lead to infarction if the tissue requirements are or become increased. Mention should be made also of the function of the blood circulation in removal of waste products from the tissues. When circulation is interrupted the substances resulting from breakdown of cell constituents start to accumulate. Many of these are acidic in nature and their accumulation contributes to cell damage and death.

The heart, whose pumping action circulates blood through all of the organs of the body, also depends on a steady flow of oxygen-containing blood for its own survival. This it takes care of in a self-service manner by way of two major vessels called the *coronary arteries*.

These arch out to the left and right over the surface of the heart and branch down into its muscular walls, the *myocardium*. If the flow of blood through a coronary artery is interrupted (coronary occlusion), the portion of myocardium supplied by that artery will be irreversibly damaged, i.e., undergo what we have called infarction. In short, "heart attack" refers to the death of a piece of heart muscle due to impairment of blood supply to it; *myocardial infarction* is the technical term for the same thing.

II. What are the consequences of a heart attack?

The outcome depends on how much of the heart muscle has been damaged, on whether or not the rhythmic properties of the heart are seriously affected, and especially on how soon the patient comes under proper medical management. The sobering fact is that about one quarter of first heart attacks are fatal. The sooner the patient can be brought to a modern, appropriately equipped coronary care unit the better his chances of survival. However, many patients die during the first hour or two. It should be clear that *prevention* must be our goal.

Turning things around, we can also state that a heart attack is by no means necessarily a death sentence nor is it necessarily the end to a meaningful and long life. President Eisenhower suffered his first heart attack in office in 1955 but went on to win a second term in the Presidency; Lyndon Johnson also suffered a heart attack in 1955 while serving in the Senate, but he went on to succeed President Kennedy and to get elected to the Presidency in his own right, and he continues an active full life.

The patient who has had his first heart attack is more likely to have a subsequent one and there is no blinking the fact that, on the average, his life span is going to be shortened. The patient who has had a heart attack may develop heart failure and he may have to restrict his activities. While a great deal of progress has been made in treating the heart attack after it occurs, saving lives and restoring patients to more or less full activity, and while clever surgical corrective measures are under active exploration, it seems unlikely that any really satisfactory solution to the problem will be found except in prevention, as discussed in the following pages.

Appendix I: A Primer on Diet and Heart Disease   437

III. How common are heart attacks?

Heart attacks account for more deaths in the United States than any other single cause (about 600,000 each year). One fourth of these occur before age 65. In this younger age group, the attack rate in men is three times that in women; after age 65 (and probably beginning at the time of menopause) the risk for women increases and becomes similar to the risk for men. To put it more graphically, men in this country have one chance in three of dying, sooner or later, of a heart attack.

There is no way of knowing with certainty beforehand that any particular individual is going to have a heart attack at any particular time. Even the most complete physical examination backed up by the most sophisticated laboratory tests may reveal no abnormalities in a patient who may, nevertheless, suffer a heart attack the very next day. On the other hand, another patient may have clear evidence of disease of the coronary arteries (characteristic symptoms or electrocardiographic changes) and yet that patient may never have a heart attack. However, we *can* say a great deal about the probabilities involved on the basis of our experience in studying large numbers of patients over the years. Let's take 100 men at age 40 who have no evidence of heart disease. Our experience tells us that over the next decade ten of them will have a heart attack, although we can't say *which ones*. All we can say is that *on the average* 10 percent of men age 40 will have a heart attack before they are 50. In other words, we can only speak about odds—the statistics rather than the specifics.

IV. What is the nature of the disease that causes a heart attack?

The inner lining of the arteries is normally smooth, white, and glistening. The blood flows smoothly through these tubular conduits. However, beginning very early in childhood and continuing relentlessly throughout life, there is in essentially every individual a gradual deterioration of that smooth arterial lining. It begins with deposits of fatty substances just beneath the surface (fatty streaks). Later a process analogous to scar formation sets in and causes a progressive thickening and toughening of the lining so that it protrudes into the channel, tending to reduce the flow of blood. Still later, the inner lining breaks down with development of ulcerations. Deposits of calcium are found in the muscular wall of the artery and there may be seepage of blood into the damaged area. It is this progression of changes in the artery wall that we call *atherosclerosis* or "hardening of the arteries," and it is this disease that causes heart attacks.

Two points are worth emphasis here. First, this is not a disease limited to or peculiar to certain individuals, although the speed with which it develops and its severity may vary widely. Everybody past age 30 or 40 has some degree of atherosclerosis. Second, the disease begins very early in life. Not uncommonly children have fatty streaks in their arteries and by age 21 most individuals have significant degrees of atherosclerosis. Seldom, however, does this early stage of the disease announce itself in any way nor does it cause signs or symptoms. It is "clinically silent" and only becomes a threat after it has developed further. The progressive thickening of the artery lining narrows the channel for blood flow and ultimately may reduce blood flow to the point where oxygen supply becomes inadequate. The roughening and deterioration of the artery lining favors the formation of a blood clot within the artery and this may lead to a very sudden stoppage of blood flow. This, then, is the way in which atherosclerosis leads to myocardial infarction (see question I).

V. What causes atherosclerosis?

Nobody can answer this question in a fully satisfactory way. Very likely the answer is that there is no one single cause but rather a number of contributing causes that act together. There is little doubt that somehow the deposition of fatty substances (lipids; see question VI) just beneath the artery lining plays an essential role in initiating the disease process. The most widely accepted theory as to how the disease begins, based on a great deal of experimentation in animals and careful study of the disease in man at autopsy, holds that fatty substances penetrate through the inner lining of the artery, become trapped there, and start the chain of events that we have discussed above (the infiltration theory).

While we are going to concern ourselves here primarily with the importance of cholesterol and other lipids in the blood, *we cannot overemphasize the fact that a number of other factors may be of the greatest importance and must not be forgotten or ignored*. For example, we know that people with high blood pressure (hypertension) are more likely to develop serious atherosclerosis, but not all of them do. We know that cigarette smokers are more likely to develop serious athero-sclerosis, but not all of them do. People with high concentrations of cholesterol in the blood are more susceptible, but by no means do all of them succumb. Finally, people who have high blood pressure, who smoke cigarettes *and* have high blood cholesterol levels are much more likely to have a heart attack than are nonsmokers with normal blood pressure and normal cholesterol levels. In fact, the risk of a heart attack may be as much as ten times greater in people with all three of these so-called *risk factors*.

VI. *What do we mean by lipids?*

Lipid is the name given to any of a large group of different sub-stances that share the common property of dissolving readily in alcohol, ether, or other such solvents, but dissolving very poorly in water. You remove a grease spot with rubbing alcohol, carbon tetrachloride, or gas-oline, but not with water. Chemists who work with lipids are some-times banteringly referred to by their colleagues as "grease monkeys." So the term *lipid* is a very broad, general term embracing a wide variety of substances with special solubility properties.

Familiar examples of lipids include butter and lard. These are made up primarily of molecules called *triglycerides* (see question VIII). However, mixed with the large bulk of triglycerides is a much smaller amount of another type of lipid, namely, *cholesterol*. Also present in small amounts are lipids of still a third type—the *phospholipids*, so named because of the presence of the element phosphorus in their structure. These are the three major lipid constituents in our diet and in our blood. The phospholipids are quantitatively less important in the diet and rarely relevant clinically. Thus we need concern ourselves here only with *triglycerides* and *cholesterol*.

VII. *What are fatty acids? What is a polyunsaturated fatty acid?*

Fatty acids make up the bulk of the fats and oils we eat. They are not present as such but in chemical combinations with glycerol (triglycerides; see question VIII).

Fatty acids are molecules that have a "backbone" consisting of a long string of carbon atoms (usually 16 to 20) tightly hooked to one another. Each carbon atom in a molecule is able to make, and does make, exactly four connections. This property of being able to make exactly four connections or *bonds* with other atoms is a fundamental characteristic of carbon atoms. They are not able to make any more. If every carbon atom along the chain in a fatty acid is connected to the 2 carbon atoms on either side of it and to 2 hydrogen atoms, then it is not possible to add any more hydrogen atoms to the chain. We say that such a fatty acid is *saturated*—all the positions available for hydrogen atoms are taken up. Palmitic acid is an example of a saturated fatty acid.

Now let's consider another common kind of fatty-acid molecule, palmitoleic acid. This fatty acid differs from palmitic acid in only one small feature—two adjacent carbon atoms in the middle of the chain each carry only *one* hydrogen atom instead of two. These carbon atoms are connected to each other by two linkages—a *double bond*. They are *not* saturated with all the hydrogen they could carry. We say that this is an *unsaturated* fatty acid. With the proper chemical procedure we can add a pair of hydrogen atoms at the double bond positions. That chemical procedure is called *hydrogenation* and it is used extensively in the food industry. A hydrogenated fat is one that has been treated in such a way as to reduce the number of double bonds—to make the fat more saturated—and that process tends to make the fat solid at room temperature.

Some fatty acids contain more than one double bond. For example, linoleic acid has a backbone of 18 carbons and 3 double bonds. These are the *poly*unsaturated fatty acids—containing more than one double bond. For your reference the common names of the major fatty acids in foods and their number of double bonds are given below:

FATTY ACIDS COMMONLY FOUND IN FOODSTUFFS

Name of fatty acid	Number of carbon atoms	Number of double bonds	Type	
Palmitic acid	16	0	Saturated	
Stearic acid	18	0	Saturated	
Palmitoleic acid	16	1	Monounsaturated	
Oleic acid	18	1	Monounsaturated	
Linoleic acid	18	2	Polyunsaturated	*safflower*
Linolenic acid	18	3	Polyunsaturated	*soy*
Arachidonic acid	20	4	Polyunsaturated	*peanut*

Appendix I: A Primer on Diet and Heart Disease   441

VIII. What is a triglyceride?

A triglyceride is a molecule made up of three fatty acids (see question VII) connected to one glycerol molecule. The three fatty acids may all be the same (e.g., all palmitic acid) or, more commonly, a mixture (e.g., one palmitic acid, one palmitoleic acid, one linoleic acid).

Food fats like bacon fat or corn oil consist primarily of mixtures of triglycerides. The glycerol anchor to which the fatty acids are bound is a constant feature; the differences lie in the fatty acid makeup and the fatty acids account for 90 percent of the material in food fats. Therefore when we talk about the differences among food fats we are dealing mainly with the composition of the fatty acid mixture going into them.

IX. What is the difference between a saturated fat and a polyunsaturated fat?

A saturated fat is one in which *most* of the fatty acids are of the *saturated* type, i.e., all available positions for attachment of hydrogen atoms are filled (see question VII). A polyunsaturated fat is one in which *most* of the fatty acids are of the polyunsaturated type, i.e., they have two or more positions that can accept additional hydrogen atoms. All natural fats actually contain *both* some saturated and some polyunsaturated fatty acids, not exclusively one or the other. They also contain monounsaturated fatty acids with just one double-bond position available to accept hydrogen atoms (e.g., oleic acid). These appear to be "neutral" in terms of effects on blood lipid concentration and we do not need to concern ourselves with them here. Consequently we should more properly refer to a *relatively* saturated or a *relatively* polyunsaturated fat. For example, butterfat is a *highly* saturated fat; fully 70 percent of the fatty acids in it are of the saturated type. In contrast, corn oil is a highly unsaturated fat; over 50 percent of the fatty acids in it are of the polyunsaturated type.

X. How does one evaluate a food fat in terms of its polyunsaturation?

The most generally used measure is the relative amounts of polyunsaturated and saturated fatty acids, expressed as the P/S ("P to S") ratio. For example, if a fat contains 50 percent polyunsaturated fatty acids and 25 percent saturated fatty acids, it has a P/S ratio of 2. If it contains equal weights of polyunsaturated and saturated fatty acids, the P/S ratio is 1. If it contains only half as much polyunsaturated fatty acid as saturated fatty acid, the P/S ratio is one half or 0.5.

Another way of expressing the degree of unsaturation of a fat is the *iodine number*. A fatty acid molecule can combine at each point where it is unsaturated (has a double bond; see question VII) with iodine under the proper chemical conditions. Thus a *poly*unsaturated fatty acid can combine with an amount of iodine proportional to the number of double bonds in it. The *iodine number* is a measure of the amount of iodine that combines with a standard amount of a fat. The higher the iodine number the more unsaturated the fat. Thus corn oil, containing a lot of polyunsaturated fatty acids, has an iodine number of about 120; butterfat, containing mostly saturated fatty acids, has an iodine number of about 35.

The P/S ratio omits from consideration the *mono*unsaturated fatty acids. These do not appear to influence blood cholesterol values one way or the other. Because they are "neutral" in this sense they need not be included in evaluation of a fat in the present context. The iodine number, on the other hand, measures all unsaturated fatty acids including the *mono*unsaturated. For this reason the P/S ratio may be a somewhat better index than the iodine number for our purposes, but in general the two parallel each other rather closely.

XI. What is cholesterol?

Cholesterol is a lipid, like triglycerides, but very different in chemical structure. It contains 27 carbon atoms arranged rather intricately so as to form 4 rings. In pure form it is a white powder at room temperature but it never occurs in nature that way.

Cholesterol is present in all animal tissues but is never found in the plant kingdom. Highest concentrations of cholesterol are found in eggs, brains, liver, and other internal organs, but there are significant amounts in all tissues, including muscle (i.e., meat). Cholesterol is one of the major lipids in blood, and the following questions deal with the nature of blood cholesterol and the effects of different diets on blood cholesterol level or concentration.

XII. Which lipids are present in blood and in what amounts?

Let's start by pointing out that blood consists of two major parts—*cells* and *plasma*. If you prevent clotting of blood and let blood stand in a test tube (or better, put the test tube in a centrifuge to increase the force of gravity on it), the blood cells can be separated from the blood plasma. Normal plasma is a clear, transparent yellow fluid and the lipids we are concerned with are contained in it. (Blood cells also contain lipids but these are not relevant, at least in a direct way, to the subject at hand.) If the blood is allowed to clot, the cells are trapped in the clot, leaving a clear yellow fluid above it which we call *serum*. The serum has much the same composition as *plasma* and in particular the same lipid content. Note that measurements of lipids are made either on plasma or serum, not on whole blood. Because everyone is familiar with it, we tend to speak loosely of "blood cholesterol" or "blood triglyceride" concentrations. Technically this is incorrect and we should speak of "plasma cholesterol" or "plasma triglycerides" (same values as "serum cholesterol" or "serum triglycerides").

Before we can talk about "normal values" for cholesterol we have to recognize that this depends on age and sex. For example, newborn babies have much lower cholesterol levels than adults. During the first year of life the level rises considerably and then it rises more slowly during childhood and continues to rise at a slow rate to about age 60 or 70. Adult women, up to the time of menopause, have somewhat lower cholesterol levels than men of the same age. Consequently we should not ask "What is the normal cholesterol level?" but rather "What is the normal cholesterol level for women (or men) at this particular age?"

A second important point is that even for individuals of a given age and sex there is no one single normal value but rather a range of normal values. For example, suppose we determined the plasma cholesterol level in 100 men at age 40. We would find that two thirds of them would have values between 175 (mg/100 ml) and 285 (mg/100 ml); the other third would have values above or below these extremes. We might find that only 5 percent of the men have values above 300. Now that handful of men with values above 300 might be considered to be "abnormal" and in fact usually are so considered. But what about the men with values of 299? Are they really that different from those with a value of 300? Probably not. The point is that we are not dealing with an all-or-none, black-and-white situation. There is no sound logical or scientific basis for picking any particular cutoff point and calling anything above that value "abnormal" and anything below it "normal." The selection of such a cutoff point is arbitrary. The important decision, however, is not whether to call a certain value "normal" or "abnormal" but whether to do something about it or not. As discussed under question XV, the risk of developing a heart attack increases as the cholesterol level increases without any sharp cutoff point in this relationship. For this reason some physicians take the position that their patients should not be satisfied to bring their cholesterol levels down into the middle range but to get it as low as possible—to aim not for a "normal" value but an "ideal" value.

In view of the foregoing discussion you can see that a hard and fast answer cannot be given to the question of "What are normal values?" However, a good rule of thumb accepted by most physicians is that at any age and for either sex a cholesterol level above 300 milligrams per 100 milliliters and/or a triglyceride value above 200 should be considered "abnormal."

now 200 to 150

One last point—the triglyceride level in blood plasma increases for several hours after a meal containing fat and the increase is related to the amount of fat eaten. This is perfectly normal. The physician wants to know the triglyceride level *independent* of these meal-induced changes. Therefore, blood must be drawn after an overnight fast and before breakfast. Cholesterol levels are only influenced to a small degree by meals and it is less critical that blood be drawn in the fasting state. Usually both measurements are made at the same time so that a fasting sample is generally used for both.

XIII. What are lipoproteins?

Lipids are not readily soluble in watery solutions (see question VI) and plasma consists mostly of water. In fact, the amount of lipid present in 100 milliliters of plasma is much more than would dissolve in 100 milliliters of water if the lipid were present in simple, uncombined form. The only reason it can be present at the concentrations found is that the lipid is intimately attached to certain large protein molecules. These proteins *are* readily dissolved in watery solutions and the lipids in a sense piggyback on the proteins. Only in that way can they manage to stay in the solution. *Lipoprotein* simply refers to any large molecule made up of such a combination of lipid and protein.

There are several different kinds of lipoproteins in blood plasma, differing in size and shape, and differing in the relative amounts of lipid and protein they contain.

Each of the different kinds of lipoproteins in the blood plasma contains both cholesterol and triglycerides (and also phospholipids) but in different proportions. One can think of the lipoproteins as little packages made up of proteins bearing different total loads of lipid with the makeup of the lipid load being different for each kind of lipoprotein. For example, one kind of lipoprotein carries a large load of triglyceride and very little cholesterol; another kind carries a large load of cholesterol and very little triglyceride. If, in a given individual, there is a marked increase in the concentration of the kind of lipoprotein carrying primarily cholesterol, his cholesterol level will be very high but his triglyceride level may be only slightly high or even normal. Conversely, a patient in whose plasma there is mainly an increased concentration of lipoproteins rich in triglycerides will show a markedly elevated triglyceride level and only a minimally elevated cholesterol level. It is now apparent that the levels of cholesterol and triglyceride in plasma reflect the concentrations of the different lipoproteins in plasma. If the concentration of any one of several classes of plasma lipoproteins is elevated, the patient is said to have hyperlipoproteinemia (hi-purr-lip-oh-pro-teen-ee′-mee-uh); hyper- (high); -lipoprotein- (lipid-protein packages); -emia (in the blood). You can see at once that it might be more informative actually to measure the different kinds of lipoproteins in a more direct and specific way. And that is just what is done when more sophisticated information is wanted—the so-called *lipoprotein pattern* is determined by special laboratory methods.

XIV. *What is meant by lipoprotein pattern? Lipoprotein typing?*

The blood plasma contains four major kinds of lipoproteins. A patient may have an increased level of any one of them, or of two or more in combination. A *lipoprotein pattern* is simply a description of which class or classes of lipoprotein are present at elevated concentrations. Experience with many patients having elevated lipoprotein levels shows that they can be conveniently classified into six groups or *types*, each having a characteristic lipoprotein pattern and characteristic clinical features. Some diseases (e.g., liver disease, thyroid disease, some forms of kidney disease) can cause lipoprotein levels to increase in different patterns. In these cases, the blood lipids are abnormal *secondary* to the underlying disease. In other cases, there is no such identified underlying disease and the condition is designated *primary*. In the latter case, the condition may be found in close relatives, reflecting a strong genetic element not yet fully understood. The most commonly used classification system for *lipoprotein typing* is that introduced by Drs. Donald S. Fredrickson, Robert I. Levy, and Robert S. Lees at the National Heart and Lung Institute and recently adopted in slightly modified form by the World Health Organization.

XV. What is the evidence that having high blood lipid concentrations is associated with an increased risk of having a heart attack? (See also Chapter I, Diet and Health.)

First, one of the earliest signs of atherosclerosis and one of the most characteristic is deposition of lipids in the artery wall.

Second, by feeding animals (rabbits, rats, dogs, pigs, monkeys) special diets and, if necessary, treating them in other ways that cause their plasma lipid concentrations to rise, it is possible to induce atherosclerosis in their arteries very much like human atherosclerosis. It has been shown that most of the cholesterol depositing in the damaged areas of the arteries in these animals comes from the plasma cholesterol.

Third, individual patients with high blood cholesterol (and/or triglyceride) levels are much more likely over the years to develop a heart attack than normal individuals. This is especially striking in some families in which both parents have markedly elevated cholesterol levels and in which the children, also having high cholesterol levels, may have heart attacks even before age 20! Less striking but of more general relevance are the several studies carried out on large numbers of people initially free of apparent heart disease and followed over a number of years. Uniformly these studies show that persons having a high cholesterol level at the beginning of the study are several times more likely to have a heart attack than persons whose cholesterol levels were low. For example, in the widely quoted study carried out by the National Heart and Lung Institute in Framingham, Massachusetts, men having cholesterol levels above 260 were three times more likely to develop a heart attack than men with cholesterol levels below 200. Even men with low cholesterol levels suffer heart attacks. There is no assurance of immunity. However, the risk is closely related to the cholesterol level, increasing steadily as that level rises.

Fourth, in countries where cholesterol levels are generally much lower than they are in the United States (e.g., Japan), the heart attack rate is considerably lower than it is here. This is probably not on a genetic basis because when the Japanese migrate to San Francisco and start living and eating like Americans, their blood cholesterol levels are found to be higher and their risk of heart attack approaches that of the American population.

XVI. If I do have a high lipid level, will lowering it actually reduce my risk of having a heart attack? (See also Chapter I, Diet and Health.)

This is, of course, the *key* question. A high plasma cholesterol level might indicate increased susceptibility (as discussed under question XV), but might not in and of itself be the *cause* of atherosclerosis and thus of the heart attack. Or even if a high blood lipid level is indeed one of the causes, maybe it is too late to do any good by lowering it after a certain age. However, the answer to the question is a slightly qualified "yes!"

Direct evidence has been presented from a number of experimental studies in which diets *have* been used to lower blood lipid levels and in which favorable effects *have* been reported. These are discussed in Chapter I, Diet and Health. More such research is needed. However, on balance, the evidence is sufficiently compelling to make it current best medical practice to treat at least those individuals with definitely elevated blood lipid levels.

XVII. What changes should I make in my diet to lower my cholesterol or my triglyceride level?

First of all, you should know that a high cholesterol or a high triglyceride level may be the signal that there is an underlying disease of some kind that requires treatment. For example, patients with abnormally low thyroid activity almost always have an elevation of cholesterol level in the blood. Obviously the treatment here is not diet but the proper thyroid medication. There are several other disorders that affect plasma lipid levels so you should see a physician before plunging ahead.

Second, even if the elevated lipid level is not secondary to some other disease it can be any one of a number of different types. The diet called for is different according to the type of lipid elevation one is dealing with. For these reasons it should be clear that a physician's advice and guidance are needed, to be sure there are not complicating factors and to be sure that the diet selected is appropriate to your case. However, matters are not as complicated as they may seem because for the majority of patients with elevated plasma lipid levels there are common factors in dietary management. It is for that reason that the recipes in this book will be usable and useful for most patients who are advised to go on a special diet. The two critically important elements are: 1) The *amount* and the *kind* of fat in the diet; and 2) the amount of cholesterol in the diet. Diets containing large amounts of saturated fats (see question IX) and/or large amounts of cholesterol (see question XI) tend to increase the concentrations of lipoproteins in the plasma (see question XIII). This is true for normal individuals as well as for individuals with abnormally high plasma lipid levels, but the effects in the latter are greater. The basic goal is to reduce the amounts of saturated fat and cholesterol in the diet as much as possible. Now a diet that is totally free of fat is just not acceptable to most people. Fortunately the polyunsaturated fats do not share with saturated fats the property of increasing cholesterol and/or triglyceride levels in the blood. Therefore the usual practice is to *substitute* polyunsaturated fats for saturated fats while at the same time reducing somewhat the total amount of fat in the diet.

The second important step is to reduce the amount of cholesterol in the diet. To be effective the diet must contain no more than 300 milligrams of cholesterol in a daily ration. Better effects can be had by lowering it still further, but that poses more difficult problems for the cook.

Information about saturated and polyunsaturated fat and cholesterol content of some common foods will be found in the reference tables (Appendix IV).

One last, but terribly important, point relates to *total* food intake. People who are gaining weight will almost invariably have an increase in the blood lipid levels. Conversely, many people who have elevated levels, especially of triglycerides, can normalize them simply by reducing. If you are overweight or if you are in the process of getting there, your physician will undoubtedly advise you that steps to prevent or correct overweight may be as important as anything else you can do to correct your plasma lipid picture.

Finally, let me repeat with great emphasis that only a physician with the proper laboratory tests in hand is in a position to advise you definitively with regard to the correct diet for your particular problem. After he has ruled out some of the less common conditions that require special management and if he recommends a low-cholesterol, polyunsaturated fat diet, then Polly Zane's recipes are here to help you and to help him get the desired results.

XVIII. Do I need to know what lipoprotein type I am before I know what diet to follow?

Strictly speaking, yes. In some unusual types it is essential to reduce the *total* fat content of the diet, the degree of restriction depending upon how severe the condition is. In some cases reduction of calorie intake and reaching ideal body weight is extremely important. So there are some differences in the dietary approaches to different types. For this reason, you can see the importance of having a physician's advice before you hit the kitchen. However, in most cases the decision will be for a low-cholesterol, polyunsaturated-fat diet—the diet for which this book is your guide.

Of course the final decision on whether a diet is the right diet or not is its effectiveness in bringing down plasma cholesterol and/or triglyceride levels. You and your physician will want to know whether the diet is working. Therefore it is important to have levels of cholesterol or triglyceride checked periodically, preferably every six months or so. Just as you would not go on a reducing diet without checking your weight periodically to see how you are doing, you should not embark on a diet of this kind without checking to see if the cholesterol or triglyceride level is coming down.

XIX. Aren't there just a few simple changes I can make—like avoiding cream and butter—without concerning myself further?

No. The *overall* diet needs to be modified. Token deletions or spotty substitutions will accomplish little or nothing. However, as Polly Zane will show you, you don't have to go strictly vegetarian, wear a hair shirt, or lose the real pleasures of the table. As she shows, by changing certain items in your basic larder and by learning a few new tricks in the kitchen, you can keep interest at the table up and cholesterol in the blood down.

XX. Suppose my cholesterol and triglyceride levels are normal on my present diet—is there any point in changing it?

The key word is "normal." We have discussed this rather tricky question earlier (question XII) and pointed out the difficulty of defining an absolute normal. The evidence that lowering lipid levels is beneficial comes mostly from studies of people who had high levels to begin with. In those experimental studies the people with the highest levels initially seem to be the people who have benefited the most. At the present time there is no firm scientific basis for urging people with normal levels to seek treatment. However, some physicians argue, with at least theoretical justification, that the lower the levels are the greater the chance of postponing the onset of heart disease. As you can see, the question cannot be answered in a dogmatic way; it is a matter of judgment and decision by you and your physician. (See also Chapter I, Diet and Health.)

XXI. Aren't there some drugs I can take so that I don't have to change my diet?

No. Drugs are not available that will *substitute* for diet. There are drugs that are useful and even necessary as a *supplement* to dietary treatment but they are not fully effective if diet is ignored. There are no drugs completely free of adverse side effects and so diet treatment is always preferable. If conscientious adherence to diet does not give a satisfactory result, your physician may advise you to add drug treatment but not to substitute it for diet treatment.

XXII. Is heredity important?

Yes, in some but not all cases. When both parents have high blood lipid levels, we find a greater frequency of high blood lipid levels in their children, although this may not be apparent when they are very young. So when one member of a family has been found to be abnormal it's probably a good idea to have all the close relatives tested. When only one parent is abnormal the frequency of abnormality in the children is less but still above average. While there is thus clearly a genetic component in some cases, there are others (so-called sporadic cases) where no inherited tendency is apparent.

Appendix I: A Primer on Diet and Heart Disease   451

XXIII. Doctor, can you summarize all this in a nutshell?

Stated simply:

1. People with high concentrations of lipids (cholesterol and/or triglycerides) in their blood plasma run a higher risk of having a heart attack.

2. There is evidence strongly suggesting that when a person with high lipid levels follows a corrective diet his risk of having a heart attack is reduced.

3. The precisely correct diets for persons with different types of blood lipid elevation may be somewhat different. However, for most patients the essential elements in an effective diet are:

    a. a very low intake of foods rich in saturated fats (mainly animal fats), and

    b. a very low intake of cholesterol-rich foods.

4. The recipes in this book are designed to help you follow a diet low in saturated fat and low in cholesterol—and they taste good!

Appendix II

CONVERTING RECIPES FOR THE LOW-CHOLESTEROL DIET

Many of your favorite recipes may seem doomed to oblivion because they are too high in the wrong kinds of fat, but this need not be the case. With a little knowledge and a bit of perseverance you can convert these favorites into acceptable and still delicious mealtime regulars.

This section offers suggestions and ideas on how to go about this conversion. For more information study the chapter "Stocking the Larder" beginning on page 415, which contains many facts about basic ingredients and their fat contents. It should help you in understanding the substitutions listed below.

Following the table of substitutions (and a few notes) is a discussion of special problems involved in baking cakes, cookies, fruit and nut breads, muffins, and so on. In spite of the difficulties, it is still possible to convert most recipes. The exceptions are those recipes which depend *primarily* on an unacceptable ingredient, such as chiffon cakes with 6 or more whole eggs or high-butter cakes and cookies; these are too difficult or impossible to transform. Usually most recipes will work out better than you expect.

The following ingredients have a fat content equal to that of the ingredient for which they are substituting. In many instances, however, it is advisable to cut down substantially on this amount because of the calories. Quite often the use of a smaller amount of oil is hardly noticed in the finished product.

Original Ingredient	Substitution
1 ounce (1 square) chocolate	3 tablespoons cocoa powder plus 1 tablespoon oil
1 cup butter or margarine	⅞ cup oil
1 whole egg	1 egg white plus 1 tablespoon oil *or* 2 tablespoons water plus 1 tablespoon oil
1 cup liquid skim milk	⅞ cup water plus 4 tablespoons dry skim milk *or* ½ cup evaporated skim milk plus ½ cup water
1 cup low-fat milk	1 cup skim milk plus 1 teaspoon oil
1 cup whole milk	1 cup skim milk plus 2 teaspoons oil
1 cup light or coffee cream	⅞ cup skim milk plus 3 tablespoons oil
1 cup heavy or whipping cream	⅓ cup oil plus ⅔ cup skim milk (See p. 342 for whipped cream substitutes with a much lower fat content.)
1 cup cultured sour cream	⅔ cup buttermilk plus ⅓ cup oil (See p. 288 for sour-cream substitutes with lower fat content.)

Fortified skim milk

Liquid skim milk, fortified with added dry skim milk, is excellent for soups, sauces, batters, breads, cookies, etc. Dissolve the dry milk in the liquid before adding milk to other ingredients. Beware of burning when cooking over high heat.

Sour cream

Substitutes for sour cream, such as buttermilk and low-fat yogurt, tend to become watery when cooked. To correct this, blend in flour beforehand. Yogurt is more stable than buttermilk, especially for long oven cooking. Buttermilk is very adaptable for top-of-the-stove sauces.

Oil and food coloring

When oil is used to replace egg yolks and butter, add a few drops of yellow food coloring. Food that looks the same is more apt to taste the same.

Butter-flavored oil

Butter flavoring and butter-flavored oils lend taste appeal. These oils are good for sautéing, frying, and baking.

BAKING—A SPECIAL CASE

Cakes, cookies, and other baked products, when made without eggs, butter, or whole milk, tend to be tough, heavy, dry, and often flavorless. But this sorry situation can all be changed if you know your ingredients and a few tricks of the trade! Here are some pointers to get you off to a good start.

1. Increase leavening by 20 to 25 percent to compensate for the natural air bubbles that solid shortenings produce when baking. (Oils do not produce such air bubbles.)
2. Increase the amount of egg whites over the number of eggs called for by 50 to 100 percent. This will make up for the binding effect which is lost when you omit egg yolks.
3. Maximum leavening from egg whites can be achieved by beating them separately and folding them in at the last moment. Great care should be taken in the beating, however, as overbeating causes toughness. This is generally the best procedure:
   a. Beat egg whites until frothy.
   b. Add a small amount of cream of tartar, about ¼ teaspoon. This gives stability to the egg foam.
   c. Continue to beat until *stiff but not dry.*
   d. Add ¼ to ½ cup granulated sugar (subtracted from total amount of sugar in the recipe) and continue to beat until glossy. Do not beat after this, as the mixture will lose its glossiness and shrink in size.
   e. Fold this meringue into the batter immediately before putting it into a preheated oven.

4. Do not grease the sides of a cake pan. Cakes rise more easily with something to cling to.
5. The method of mixing oil cakes is very important. Generally, the following procedure is the best to follow:
   a. Sift dry ingredients together into a large bowl.
   b. Beat egg whites as described under point 3 and set aside for a few minutes, but no longer than the time necessary to complete the following step.
   c. Quickly combine oil and liquid in a small bowl and add all at once to the dry ingredients. Beat rapidly to a smooth batter.
   d. Fold in the egg whites and bake as instructed.
   Note: Sometimes a heavier cake is desired, in which case the egg whites may not be beaten separately.
6. The moistness of a cake is increased when brown or raw sugar is used in place of granulated. A combination is often satisfactory. Molasses and honey have a similar effect. Reduce sugar by ¾ cup and liquid by ⅓ cup for each cup of honey or molasses. Molasses also calls for baking soda. For each cup of molasses, add ½ teaspoon baking soda to the recipe and subtract that amount of baking powder.

   In addition to moistness, these sweeteners enhance the flavor a great deal more than regular granulated sugar.
7. Baking soda tends to tenderize. It also neutralizes acids. Sour milk, buttermilk, citrus juices, and molasses are all acidic. Combined with baking soda, they produce a more tender and moist cake than one made with skim milk and baking powder. To substitute 1 cup buttermilk for 1 cup sweet milk, change leavening ingredients by adding ½ teaspoon baking soda and subtracting 1 teaspoon baking powder.
8. A small amount of baking soda, ¼ to ½ teaspoon, can be added to cookies, sweet breads, cakes, etc., as a tenderizer, even if an acid is not present.
9. Fresh and canned fruit, chopped or puréed, can be used in conjunction with baking soda for the same tenderizing effect. Generally, for 1 cup of puréed fruit reduce liquid by ½ cup; for 1 cup chopped fresh fruit reduce liquid by ⅓ cup.
10. A fairly high proportion of oil and sugar to flour is necessary in oil cakes to ensure a light cake with good texture. Be careful,

therefore, not to cut down too severely on these ingredients merely for the sake of lowering calories, unless, of course, you prefer low calories to high quality! Use 1 cup of sugar or more to 2 cups flour for the correct proportion in a high sugar cake. Use ¼ cup oil to 1 cup flour for an equally good proportion for the oil content. However, do not feel bound by these proportions. There are exceptions to any rule.

11. With cakes using cocoa powder, reduce flour by the amount of the cocoa and sift the cocoa in with the flour.
12. When butter is to be replaced by oil and where egg yolks are eliminated, take the following two things into account for any given recipe:
    a. Butter is approximately 80 percent fat; oil is 100 percent fat; therefore you need less oil to replace the butter.
    b. Egg yolks are equal to about 1 tablespoon oil, therefore you need to add 1 tablespoon of oil for each egg yolk eliminated. All this often adds up to an even exchange of oil for butter.
13. Don't forget the possibility of using butter-flavored oils. These are optional of course, but they may add just the right flavor to suit your family.
14. Above all, don't forget the yellow food coloring. Add at least 1 drop for each egg yolk you have eliminated, and another 1 or 2 drops for the butter not used. Don't bother, naturally, if your cake is dark in color.

Appendix III

MEAL PLANNING FOR THE
LOW-CHOLESTEROL DIETER

OVERALL DIET RECOMMENDATIONS

General

1. Daily intake of cholesterol should be reduced to less than 300 milligrams.
2. Fats of any kind should compose no more than 35 percent of total calories.
3. Less than 10 percent of total calories should come from saturated fats.
4. At least 10 percent of total calories should come from polyunsaturated oils.

Specific

1. Avoid fat cuts of meat, large portions of meat, and processed meats high in saturated fats.
2. Use low-fat dairy products and avoid dairy products high in saturated fat.
3. Avoid egg yolks, bacon, butter, lard, suet, and margarines and shortenings high in saturated fat.
4. Use cooking oils, shortenings, salad oils, and margarines that are low in saturated fat.
5. Correct obesity by lowering caloric intake.

DAILY AND WEEKLY MEAL PLANNING

Weekly—General (taken from American Heart Association material)

1. *Goals:*
    a. Meeting nutritional needs for protein, vitamins, minerals, etc.
    b. Maintaining a desirable weight by control of calories.
    c. Limiting intake of saturated fat and cholesterol.
    d. Eating more polyunsaturated fats and fewer saturated fats.
2. *Controls for cholesterol-rich foods:*
    a. No more than 3 eggs a week (including hidden ones).
    b. Limit shellfish and organ meats.
3. *Controls for amount and type of fat:*
    a. Concentrate on fish, chicken, turkey, and veal. Eat only 5 moderate-sized portions of other meats.
    b. Select lean cuts of meat, cut off any extra fat, and discard any that cooks out of the meat.
    c. Use cooking methods to remove fat—baking, boiling, broiling, roasting, stewing. No deep-frying.
    d. Use no processed meats.
    e. Switch from butter and other fats that are solid or hydrogenated to liquid oils and margarines.
    f. Switch from whole milk and cheeses made from whole milk and cream to skim milk and cheeses made from skim milk.

DAILY MEAL PLAN—SPECIFIC

1. *Meats, Poultry, Fish:* a total of 6 to 8 ounces daily, cooked, not including bone or fat.
    RECOMMENDED: Chicken, turkey, veal, fish, for most meals.
    Beef, lamb, pork, ham, no more than 5 times a week.
    Shellfish, 4-ounce serving as substitute for meat twice a week.
    Nuts, beans, and peas can be used.
    Egg whites, eat all you want.

Avoid fatty meats, organ meats, processed meats.

Limit yourself to 3 egg yolks per week.

Use no bakery products made with eggs.

2. *Vegetables and fruits:* at least 4 servings a day of ½ cup each.

RECOMMENDED: 1 serving from foods rich in vitamin C.

1 serving from foods rich in vitamin A.

USE SPARINGLY: olives and avocados (high in fats), and starchy vegetables if loss of weight is desired.

3. *Breads and Cereals:* 4 servings daily—1 slice of bread or ½ cup cooked cereal or 1 cup cold cereal.

RECOMMENDED: Whole-grain, enriched, or restored breads, made with a minimum of saturated fat.

Avoid bakery products high in fats or egg yolks.

4. *Milk Products:* skim milk fortified with vitamins A and D; differing amounts depending on age.

5. *Fats and Oils:* polyunsaturated—about 2 to 4 tablespoons daily, depending on weight.

6. *Desserts:* moderation in desserts rich in sucrose. Avoid coconut and coconut oil, chocolate products, all commercial products with unacceptable ingredients.

HOW TO ORDER IN RESTAURANTS
(taken from American Heart Association material)

AVOID: cream soups, fried foods, casseroles and other mixed dishes, gravies, cheeses, ice creams, puddings, etc.

CHOOSE: first course: clear soup, tomato juice, fruit cup.

main course: baked or broiled fish or chicken (remove skin), sliced turkey, veal, London broil (flank steak), vegetables without butter.

dessert: fruit, sherbet, gelatin, angel-food cake without frosting.

Appendix IV

REFERENCE TABLES

Liquid Measures

Dash	less than ⅛ teaspoon
60 drops	1 teaspoon
3 teaspoons	1 tablespoon
2 tablespoons	⅛ cup
4 tablespoons	¼ cup
5⅓ tablespoons	⅓ cup
8 tablespoons	½ cup
10⅔ tablespoons	⅔ cup
12 tablespoons	¾ cup
14 tablespoons	⅞ cup
16 tablespoons	1 cup
1 cup	8 fluid ounces
2 cups	1 pint
2 pints	1 quart
4 quarts	1 gallon

Dry Measures

1 gram	0.035 ounces
1 ounce	28.35 grams
16 ounces	1 pound (453.59 grams)

Package Sizes of Canned, Frozen, and Dried Foods

Canned foods are packed in cans of every size from 1 ounce (for truffles) to 104 ounces (for institutional sizes of vegetables). Mushrooms, for instance, are packed in at least ten different sizes. Only the most usual sizes are listed here with the can size, ounces, and cup contents.

Can size	Weight in ounces	Cup contents
4 oz.	4	½
8 oz.	8	1
Picnic	10½ to 12	1¼ to 1½
No. 300	14	1¾
No. 303	16 to 17	2
No. 1 tall	16	2
No. 2	20	2½
No. 2½	29	3½
No. 3	32	4
No. 3 special	46	5¾
No. 10	96 to 104	12 to 13

Frozen foods are packed most usually in rectangular cartons holding about 10 ounces; most vegetables and fruits will be found in this size. However, some unusual vegetables like Chinese pea pods can be found in smaller packages of 7 ounces, and other foods are packed in 8-, 9-, and 12-ounce cartons. Favorite vegetables like green beans, peas, and corn kernels are sometimes packed in large film bags (loose pack) of 20, 24, and 32 ounces. Some fruits such as whole strawberries, cherries, and blackberries are also available in such packages. Round cartons of 16 ounces with snap-in lids are used for fruits usually, but sometimes for other foods.

Dried foods such as grains (rice, barley, oatmeal, cracked wheat) come in 8-ounce or 1-pound packages usually, but such an expensive grain as wild rice can be found only in smaller packages in most markets. Dried legumes (peas, beans, lentils, garbanzos) are usually packed in 1-pound packages, either cardboard cartons with see-through windows in the front, or in plastic film bags.

Oven Temperatures

250° to 275°F.	very slow
300° to 325°F.	slow
350° to 375°F.	moderate
400° to 425°F.	hot
450° to 475°F.	very hot
500° to 525°F.	extremely hot

If your broiler is in your oven, you may have a further setting of 550°F. and then a setting for Broil (or B). Some ovens have a lower setting than 250°F. and that may be marked Low.

General Cooking Equivalents

Apples	1 pound, unpared	3 cups chopped
Baking powder	1 teaspoon	¼ teaspoon baking soda plus ½ teaspoon cream of tartar
	1 teaspoon	¼ teaspoon baking soda plus ½ cup sour milk or buttermilk
	1 teaspoon	¼ teaspoon baking soda plus 1½ teaspoons vinegar or lemon juice with sweet milk to make ½ cup
	1 teaspoon	¼ teaspoon baking soda plus ¼ to ½ cup molasses
Bananas	3 to 4 medium-sized bananas	2 cups mashed
Beans, dry	1 pound, 2⅓ cups	6 cups cooked
Buttermilk	1 cup	1 cup sweet milk and 1 tablespoon lemon juice or vinegar
Cornstarch	1 tablespoon	2 tablespoons flour, for thickening
Cottage cheese	½ pound	1 cup
Cream, sour	1 cup	3 tablespoons fat plus 1 cup buttermilk
Dates, figs, prunes	1 pound	2½ cups pitted
Egg whites	4 large	½ cup
	8 to 9 large	1 cup
Flour	1 pound	4 cups sifted
Lemon juice	1 medium-sized lemon	2 to 3 tablespoons juice
Lemon rind	1 medium-sized lemon	2 to 3 teaspoons grated rind
Macaroni	1 cup uncooked	2 to 2½ cups cooked
Mushrooms	3 ounces dried	1 pound fresh
	6 ounces canned	1 pound fresh
	½ pound raw, sliced	2½ cups raw

Onion	1 medium-sized onion	⅔ to 1 cup chopped
Orange juice	1 medium-sized orange	6 to 8 tablespoons juice
Orange rind	1 medium-sized orange	2 tablespoons grated rind
Parsley	1 tablespoon dried	2 tablespoons fresh
Rice	1 cup uncooked	3 cups cooked
Spaghetti	1 cup uncooked	2 to 2½ cups cooked
Sugar, brown	1 pound	2¼ cups firmly packed
Sugar, confectioners'	1 pound	3½ cups sifted
Sugar, granulated	1 pound	2¼ cups
Walnuts, in the shell	1 pound	1½ to 2 cups walnut meats
Walnuts, pieces	5 ounces	1 cup chopped

Fat and Cholesterol Content of Basic Foods

The following tables are included to acquaint the reader with approximate fat and cholesterol content of basic foods. Both should be taken into account in the low-cholesterol diet, as explained in Appendix I. P/S ratios are also noted, where significant, because of growing evidence of their importance in controlling blood serum cholesterol.

Only foods with a significant fat content have been included, with a few exceptions. Thus, large groups of foods having at most a negligible fat content, such as fruits, vegetables, and grains, have been omitted. Ready-to-eat prepared products such as biscuits, cakes, pies, etc., are also not included as the customary fat content differs so greatly from items bearing similar names in this cookbook.

The data for these tables have come from primarily two sources: *Composition of Foods*, Agriculture Handbook No. 8, Agricultural Research Service, United States Department of Agriculture, 1963; and *Cholesterol Content of Foods*, by Ruth M. Feeley, Patricia E. Criner, and Bernice K. Watt, Consumer and Food Economics Research Division, Agricultural Research Service, United States Department of Agriculture, published in the *Journal of the American Dietetic Association*, 1972.

A blank in the tables indicates that no information was available; a dash shows insignificant fat content.

Approximate Fatty Acid Composition of Certain Foods
Per 100 Grams Edible Portion*

(The weight of 100 grams is roughly equal to 3½ ounces.)

	Total Fat Grams	Saturated Grams	Mono-unsaturated Grams	Poly-unsaturated Grams	P/S* Ratio	M+P/S Ratio *(handwritten)*
					Ideal is 1.5 – 3.0 (handwritten)	
Fats						
Butter	81	46	27	2	.05	.6
Lard	100	38	46	10	.3	1.5
Margarine: regular	81	18	47	14	.8	3.4
special	81	19	31	29	1.5	3.2
Mayonnaise	80	14	17	40	3.0 ✓	4.0
Peanut butter	51	9	25	14	1.5	4.3
Nuts						
Almonds	54	4	36	11	2.7	11.8
Brazil	67	13	32	17	1.3	
Cashew	46	8	32	3	.4	4.4
Coconut	35	30	2	—	—	
Hickory	69	6	47	12	2.0	
Peanuts	49	11	21	14	1.3	3.2
Pecans	71	5	45	14	3.0	11.8
Pistachio	54	5	35	10	2.0	9.0
Walnuts: Black	59	4	21	28	7.0	
English	64	4	10	40	10.0	15.0
Oils						
Cottonseed	100	25	21	50	2.0	
Coconut	100	86	7	—	—	
Corn	100	10	28	53	5.3	8.1
Olive	100	11	76	7	.6	7.6

* Figures have been taken from *Composition of Foods*, Agriculture Handbook No. 8, Agricultural Research Service, United States Department of Agriculture, 1963.

Appendix IV: Reference Tables   467

(handwritten) * higher is better

	Total Fat Grams	Sat- urated Grams	Mono- unsat- urated Grams	Poly- unsat- urated Grams	P/S Ratio	m + P/s ratio
Oils (*cont'd*)						
Palm	100	45	40	8	.2	1.1
Peanut	100	18	47	29	1.6	4.2
Safflower	100	8	15	72	9.0 ✓	10.9
Sesame	100	14	38	42	3.0	5.7
Soybean	100	15	20	52	3.5	4.8
Sunflower	100	12	20	63	5.3	6.9
Seeds						
Safflower	60	5	9	43	8.6	10.4
Sesame	49	7	19	21	3.0	5.7
Sunflower	47	6	9	30	5.0	6.5

Meat,* Poultry

	Total Fat Grams	Sat- urated Grams	Mono- unsat- urated Grams	Poly- unsat- urated Grams	
Beef					
Carcass, trimmed, raw:					
choice grade	25	12	11	1	1.0
good grade	20	10	9	—	
standard grade	16	8	7	—	
Retail Cuts					
entire chuck, choice grade					
total, edible, raw	20	9	9	—	
lean, edible, raw	7	4	3	—	
porterhouse, choice grade					

* All meat is raw, without skin or bone, except as specified.

	Total Fat Grams	Sat- urated Grams	Mono- unsat- urated Grams	Poly- unsat- urated Grams
Meat, Poultry (*cont'd*)				
total, edible, raw	36	17	16	1
sirloin, double-bone				
choice grade	29	14	13	1
rib, choice grade				
total, edible, raw	37	18	16	1
lean, edible, raw	12	6	5	—
round, choice grade				
total, edible, raw	12	6	5	—
lean, raw	5	2	2	—
rump, choice grade				
total, edible, raw	25	12	11	1
Hamburger (ground beef)				
lean, raw	10	5	4	Trace
regular ground, raw	21	10	9	Trace
Corned, medium-fat				
uncooked	25	12	11	Trace
cooked	30	15	13	1
canned	12	6	5	Trace
Dried, chipped	6	3	3	Trace
Chicken				
Broilers, flesh only	4			
Roosters, flesh only	5			
Fryers, flesh only	3			
flesh and skin	5			
light meat without skin	2			
light meat with skin	4			
dark meat without skin	4	1	1	1
dark meat with skin	6	2 *	2	1

* = 33 % of total fat

	Total Fat Grams	Saturated Grams	Mono-unsaturated Grams	Poly-unsaturated Grams
Meat, Poultry (*cont'd*)				
Pork				
Picnic, total	25	9	10	2
Picnic, lean	7	3	3	1
Loin roast, total	25	9	10	2
Loin roast, lean (incl. chops)	11	4	5	1
Ham				
Roast, total	23	8	10	2
Roast, lean	9	3	4	1
Boston butt, total	24	9	10	2
Boston butt, lean	12	4	5	1
Picnic, total	24	8	10	2
Picnic, lean	8	3	4	1
Lamb				
Shoulder, total	24	13	9	1
Shoulder, lean	8	4	3	Trace
Leg, total	16	9 *	6	Trace
Leg, lean	5	3	2	Trace
Loin, total	25			
Loin, lean	6			
Rib, total	30	17	11	1
Rib, lean	8	5	3	Trace
Veal				
Roast (rump, raw) medium fat	10	5 **	4	—
Roast, lean	6			

470   Appendix IV: Reference Tables

* = 56 % of total fat
* * = 50 % " " "

	Total Fat Grams	Sat- urated Grams	Mono- unsat- urated Grams	Poly- unsat- urated Grams

Meat, Poultry (cont'd)

Sausages, Cold Cuts, etc.

Braunschweiger	27	10	12	2
Bologna	28			
Country-style sausage	31	11	13	3
Deviled ham	32	12	14	3
Frankfurters	13			
Liver sausage	27			
Lunch meat	25	9	11	2
Pork sausage	51	18	21	5
Salami	38			
Scrapple	14			
Thuringer	25			
Vienna sausage	20			

Fish

Abalone	1			
Albacore	8	3	1	Trace
Anchovy	10			
Bass: black sea	1			
striped	3			
white	2			
Bluefish	3			
Bonito	7			
Catfish	3			
Caviar	16			
Clams: soft	2			
hard	1			
canned	3			
Cod	.3			

	Total Fat Grams	Sat- urated Grams	Mono- unsat- urated Grams	Poly- unsat- urated Grams
Fish (*cont'd*)				
Crab: fresh	2			
canned	3			
Flatfish (flounder, sole, sanddabs)	1			
Haddock	.1			
Halibut	1			
Herring: Atlantic, raw	11	2		2
Pacific, raw	3	Trace		Trace
canned	14			
smoked, kippered	13			
Lobster	2			
Mackerel: Atlantic	12			
Pacific	7			
salt	25			
Mussels	1			
Ocean perch: Atlantic	1			
Pacific	2			
Oysters	2			
Pike	1			
Pompano	10			
Red and Gray Snapper	1			
Rockfish	2			
Roe	2			
Salmon: Atlantic	13			
Chinook	16	5	5	Trace
Pink	4	1	1	Trace
Smoked	9			
Sardines, Atlantic, canned in oil, drained	11			
Shad	10			
Shrimps	1			

	Total Fat Grams	Saturated Grams	Mono-unsaturated Grams	Poly-unsaturated Grams
Fish (*cont'd*)				
Swordfish	4			
Trout: lake	10			
brook	2			
rainbow	11	3	2	Trace
Tuna: fresh	4	1	1	Trace
canned in oil	21	5	4	8
canned in oil, drained	8	3	2	2
canned in water	1			
Whitefish	8			
Dairy Products				
Milk				
Fluid: whole	4	2	1	Trace
low fat (%)	2	1	—	—
skim	.1	—	—	—
Canned: evaporated, regular	8	4	3	Trace
evaporated, skim	.1	—	—	—
condensed, sweet	9	5	3	Trace
Dry: whole	28	15	9	1
skim	1	—	—	—
Buttermilk	.1	—	—	—
Cream: half-and-half	12	6	4	Trace
light, coffee	21	11	7	1
light, whipping	31	17	10	1
heavy, whipping	38	21 *	12	1
cream substitute	27	15 *	9	1
Cheese: Cheddar	32	18	11	1
Cottage, whole milk	4	2	1	Trace
Cottage, low-fat milk	2	1	—	—
Cottage, dry curd (also hoop, baker's,				

* = 55% of total fat

	Total Fat Grams	Saturated Grams	Mono-unsaturated Grams	Poly-unsaturated Grams
Dairy Products (*cont'd*)				
pot, farmer's)	.1	—	—	—
Cream cheese	38	21 *	12	1
Sap Sago	—	—	—	—
Swiss	28	15	9	1
Yogurt: whole milk	4	2	1	Trace
low-fat milk	2	1	—	Trace
Ice cream	13	7 **	4	Trace
Ice milk	5	3 **	2	Trace
Miscellaneous				
Avocado	17	3	8	2
Candy: Butterscotch	3	2	1	
caramel	11	7	4	—
chocolate, milk	35	20	13	1
fudge	16	6	8	1
peanut brittle	10	2	4	3
Chocolate, bitter, for baking	53	30	20	1
Cocoa, dry, unsweetened	2	1	1	
Coconut: fresh	35	30	2	—
dried, unsweetened	65	56	5	—
dried, sweetened	39	34	3	—
Coconut milk	25	22	2	—
Olives: ripe, black	14	2	10	1
ripe (Mission)	20	2	15	1
green	10	1	7	1
Greek, in oil	36	4	27	3

* = 55% of total fat
** = 54% " " "

Approximate Amounts of Cholesterol per 100 Grams (3½ ounces) Edible Portion*

	Milligrams
Beef, raw	65
Brains	2000
Butter	250
Buttermilk	2
Caviar	300
Cheese:	
Blue	(87)
Camembert	(90)
Cheddar	99
Cottage: creamed, 4% fat	19
creamed, 1% fat	9
uncreamed	7
Cream	111
Edam	(102)
Mozzarella, part skim	66
Neufchâtel	(76)
Parmesan, grated (1 cup not packed)	(95)
Ricotta, regular	(51)
Ricotta, part skim	(32)
Swiss	100
Pasteurized process cheese	(90 to 93)
Pasteurized process cheese food	(72)
Pasteurized process cheese spread	(64)
Chicken, raw:	
white meat	67
dark meat	87
Clams (total sterols, 125[a])	50

(handwritten annotations: "but high in sodium" beside cottage cheese values; "✓" beside Ricotta, part skim; "> beef" beside white meat 67; "> ''" beside dark meat 87)

* Figures have been taken from *Cholesterol Content of Foods*, by Ruth M. Feeley, Patricia E. Criner, and Bernice K. Watt, Consumer and Food Economics Research Division, Agricultural Research Service, United States Department of Agriculture, published in the *Journal of the American Dietetic Association*, 1972. Figures in parentheses were imputed from closely related products.

[a] Total sterol figures have been extrapolated by the author from cholesterol figure and based on the following statement of the Feeley, Criner, and Watt report: "Recent published and unpublished data have shown that in clams, cholesterol accounts for only 40 percent of the total sterol. Several studies have shown that in oysters only 40 percent of the total sterol was cholesterol and, in scallop muscle,

Cod	50
Crab	100
Cream:	
half-and-half	43
light table	66
sour	66 = beef
whipping	133
Eggs, whole (approximately 2 large)	3 × 504 = 1512
Egg whites, fresh	0
Egg yolks, fresh (approximately 6 large)	1480
Flounder	50
Gizzards	145
Haddock	60
Halibut	50
Heart, raw	150 to 170
Herring	85
Ice cream (regular to very rich)	180 to 260
Ice milk	20
Kidneys	375
Lamb	70
Lard	95
Liver:	
beef	300
chicken	555
Lobster	85[b]
Mackerel	95
Margarine:	
all vegetable fat	0
two thirds animal fat, one third vegetable fat	50
Milk:	
whole	14
low fat, 1%	6
low fat, 2%	9
skim	2

only 30 percent of the total was cholesterol." Further nutritional study will be needed to determine harmful effects of these other sterols.

[b] This represents a drop of 120 milligrams from previously published material.

Noodles:	
dry	94
cooked	31
Oysters (total sterols 125[a])	50
Pork	62 < beef
Roe, salmon	11
Salmon	(35)
Sardines	(120)
Sausage, frankfurters	65
Scallops (total sterols, 116[a])	35
Shrimps	150 > beef
Sweetbreads	250
Trout	55
Turkey:	
light meat	60 < beef
dark meat	75 > "
Tuna (canned in water)	(63)

Appendix V

A GLOSSARY OF MEDICAL AND TECHNICAL TERMS

by Daniel Steinberg, M.D., Ph.D.

These brief definitions may be helpful when reading Appendix I and in using the reference tables on Fat and Cholesterol Content of Basic Foods in Appendix IV. Most of the terms are explained in more detail in Appendix I in the answers to the questions in italics.

ARTERIOSCLEROSIS: a general term for a *group* of diseases affecting arteries. Atherosclerosis is one particular form of arteriosclerosis.

ATHEROSCLEROSIS: a disease affecting the larger arteries ("hardening of the arteries") and leading to heart attacks and strokes (see question IV).

CEREBRAL ARTERIES: the arteries supplying blood to the brain.

CHOLESTEROL: a lipid (fatty substance) found in animal tissues and as a normal constituent in blood; present in high concentration in arteries affected by atherosclerosis (see question XI).

"CHOLESTEROL COUNT": a layman's term for the concentration of cholesterol in blood. This usage arises from mistaken analogy with "blood count," which refers to the actual number of cells in a measured volume of blood. Cholesterol concentration (or level) is expressed as the number of milligrams of cholesterol in 100 milliliters of blood plasma or serum (see question XII).

CORONARY ARTERIES: the arteries supplying blood to the heart musculature (see question I).

FATTY ACIDS: lipids that make up the largest bulk of common fats and oils (see question VII).

HYDROGENATION: a process for converting unsaturated fats to partially or completely saturated forms (see question VII).

HYPERLIPIDEMIA: elevation of either blood cholesterol or blood triglycerides or both.

Appendix V: A Glossary of Medical and Technical Terms   479

HYPERLIPOPROTEINEMIA: elevation of the concentration of any one or more of the four major classes of lipoproteins in the blood plasma.

HYPERTENSION: high blood pressure, one of the factors predisposing to heart attacks (see question V).

INFARCTION: death of a part of an organ or tissue due to inadequate supplies of oxygen to it (see question I).

IODINE NUMBER: a measure of the amount of unsaturated fatty acids relative to saturated fatty acids in a fat or oil (see question X).

LIPIDS: substances with very limited solubility in water but dissolving readily in ether, alcohol, or other organic solvents (see question VI).

LIPOPROTEINS: combinations of lipids with protein. All lipids in blood occur in such combined form.

LIPOPROTEIN TYPING: a system for characterizing patients with high cholesterol and/or triglyceride levels in terms of the particular lipid-protein complexes present at abnormally high concentrations.

MONOUNSATURATED FAT: a fat or oil relatively rich in fatty acids, containing just one double bond (see questions VII and X). It is capable of absorbing additional hydrogen but not as much hydrogen as a polyunsaturated fat. These fats in the diet have little effect on the amount of cholesterol in the blood. One example is olive oil. (See Polyunsaturated fat.)

1991
Now that to
lower →
LDL
but not HDL

MYOCARDIAL INFARCTION: death of a portion of the heart muscle due to inadequate supply of oxygen (see question I).

MYOCARDIUM: the muscular wall of the heart.

PERIPHERAL ARTERIES: arteries supplying blood to the arms and legs.

PERIPHERAL VASCULAR DISEASE: disease (usually atherosclerosis) affecting the peripheral arteries.

PHOSPHOLIPIDS: a class of lipids containing phosphorus atoms; not usually measured or relevant in evaluating risk of atherosclerosis (see question VI).

PLASMA: the clear yellow part of blood after removal of the cells.

POLYUNSATURATED FAT: a fat or oil relatively rich in fatty acids, containing more than one double bond (see questions VII and X). Generally liquid at room temperature (oil). However, the food industry has devised processes for hardening oils while still retaining much of their polyunsaturated character. Vegetables oils are usually of the polyunsaturated type; coconut oil is an exception.

P/S RATIO: the number obtained by dividing the amount of polyunsaturated fatty acids by the amount of saturated fatty acids (see question X).

RISK FACTORS: conditions that are believed to increase susceptibility to a disease. Risk factors for heart attacks include: 1) high cholesterol level; 2) high triglyceride level; 3) high blood pressure; 4) cigarette smoking; 5) increasing age; 6) being male.

SATURATED FAT: a fat relatively rich in fatty acids containing no double bonds (see questions VII and X). Generally solid at room temperature. Animal fats (especially beef, sheep, and pork fat) are of the saturated type.

SERUM: the clear, yellowish liquid part of blood, not containing any blood cells, that remains after blood has clotted.

STROKE: brain damage due to inadequate oxygen supply as when a cerebral artery is blocked (cerebral infarction).

TRIGLYCERIDES: fatty substances made up of three fatty acids combined with one glycerol molecule (see question VIII).

INDEX

Index   483

488 Index

Index   489

Index   491

496   Index

Sour Milk, 288

75 76 77 10 9 8 7 6 5 4 3 2